WHAT WORKS FOR WORKERS?

Public Policies and
Innovative Strategies for
Low-Wage Workers

Stephanie Luce,
Jennifer Luff,
Joseph A. McCartin,
and Ruth Milkman,
Editors

Russell Sage Foundation
New York

The Russell Sage Foundation

The Russell Sage Foundation, one of the oldest of America's general purpose foundations, was established in 1907 by Mrs. Margaret Olivia Sage for "the improvement of social and living conditions in the United States." The Foundation seeks to fulfill this mandate by fostering the development and dissemination of knowledge about the country's political, social, and economic problems. While the Foundation endeavors to assure the accuracy and objectivity of each book it publishes, the conclusions and interpretations in Russell Sage Foundation publications are those of the authors and not of the Foundation, its Trustees, or its staff. Publication by Russell Sage, therefore, does not imply Foundation endorsement.

Library of Congress Cataloging-in-Publication Data

What works for workers? : public policies and innovative strategies for low-wage workers / Stephanie Luce, Jennifer Luff, Joseph A. McCartin, Ruth Milkman, editors.
    pages cm
    Includes bibliographical references and index.
    ISBN 978-0-87154-571-8 (alk. paper)
    1. Unskilled labor—United States. 2. Working poor—United States. 3. Minimum wage—United States. 4. Labor policy—United States. I. Luce, Stephanie.
    HD8072.5.W465 2013
    331.12'0424—dc23

                                                                                    2013030555

Text design by Genna Patacsil.

RUSSELL SAGE FOUNDATION
112 East 64th Street, New York, New York 10065
10   9   8   7   6   5   4   3   2   1

Contents

Tables and Figures

Contributors

STEPHANIE LUCE is associate professor of labor studies at the Murphy Institute, School of Professional Studies, CUNY.

JENNIFER LUFF is lecturer in the Department of History at Durham University in the United Kingdom.

JOSEPH A. McCARTIN is professor of history and director of the Kalmanovitz Initiative for Labor and the Working Poor at Georgetown University.

RUTH MILKMAN is professor of sociology at the City University of New York Graduate Center and academic director of labor studies at CUNY's Murphy Institute.

EILEEN APPELBAUM is senior economist at the Center for Economic and Policy Research and former director of the Center for Women and Work at Rutgers University.

PETER B. EDELMAN is professor of law at the Georgetown University Law Center and faculty director of the Georgetown Center on Poverty, Inequality, and Public Policy.

RICHARD B. FREEMAN is the Ascherman Chair in Economics at Harvard University and faculty codirector of the Labor and Worklife Program at the Harvard Law School, as well as senior research fellow in labour markets at the London School of Economics' Centre for Economic Performance and fellow of the American Academy of Arts and Science.

JENNIFER GORDON is professor of law at Fordham University School of Law.

SARAH HAMERSMA is assistant professor of public administration and international affairs in the Maxwell School at Syracuse University.

HARRY J. HOLZER is professor of public policy at the Georgetown Public Policy Institute and is institute fellow at the American Institutes for Research.

ALICE O'CONNOR is professor of history at the University of California, Santa Barbara.

JOHN SCHMITT is senior economist at the Center for Economic and Policy Research in Washington, D.C.

PAUL OSTERMAN is NTU Professor of Human Resources and Management at the MIT Sloan School.

DAVID WEIL is professor of markets, public policy and law and Everett W. Lord Distinguished Faculty Scholar at Boston University School of Management, as well as codirector of the Transparency Policy Project at Harvard's Kennedy School of Government.

JEFFREY B. WENGER is assistant professor of public policy analysis at the University of Georgia and NIH/NIA research fellow in the study of aging at the RAND Corporation in Santa Monica, California.

Introduction |

Stephanie Luce, Jennifer Luff,
Joseph A. McCartin, and Ruth Milkman

The other America, the America of poverty, is hidden today in a way that it never was before. Its millions are socially invisible to the rest of us.

—Michael Harrington, 1962

HALF A CENTURY ago, in his best-selling book *The Other America*, Michael Harrington awakened the nation to the persistence of grinding poverty alongside its unprecedented postwar affluence. Harrington revealed an "economic underworld" in urban tenements and remote Appalachian towns, populated largely by the aged, the unemployed, and racial minorities. Chronic unemployment, inadequate housing, racial discrimination, a thin social safety net, and a culture of hopelessness were characteristic features of this "other America." Harrington's book helped persuade the federal government to launch the War on Poverty by creating new federal programs like Medicaid, Medicare, and Head Start, institutionalizing what was then a pilot food stamp program, and launching a massive expansion of housing assistance and job training programs.

In Harrington's America, poverty was strongly associated with unemployment, apart from workers in occupations excluded from federal minimum wage laws and collective bargaining protections, such as farmworkers and domestic workers, or in a few other industries with dirty and dangerous poorly paid jobs, such as mining. African American workers were highly concentrated in these fields. But in 1962, when *The Other America* appeared, unemployment accounted for a far more significant share of poverty. Harrington (1962/1993, 37) highlighted the plight of "old and obsolete workers who are over forty, the married and family men at the wrong place in the economy, the ones with no skill or the wrong skill," who had been shut out of the labor market entirely. The primary problem for them was not low pay or bad working conditions, but not working at all.

1

Two decades later, however, Harrington noticed a change. In the original edition of *The Other America*, Harrington never used the phrase "working poor." But in his afterword to the 1981 edition, entitled "Poverty and the Eighties," he pointed out that nearly half of all families below the poverty line in 1976 had an employed head of household. "Obviously, these are people with low-paying jobs," Harrington (1962/1993, 219) wrote, "perched just above the poverty line." The War on Poverty had made progress—albeit halting and inadequate—toward improving the situation of the "other America." But by the early 1980s, Harrington hinted, a new problem was growing: the problem of employment that did not eradicate poverty but rather perpetuated it.

Since then, the ranks of the "working poor" have continued to expand. While poverty persists among the populations that Harrington identified fifty years ago—the aged, rural dwellers, and the chronically unemployed—employed workers account for a large and growing share of those living below the official poverty line. Since the mid-1970s, a dramatic polarization of the U.S. labor market has generated many jobs in high-wage, high-skill occupations, but far more in low-wage, low-skill fields (Kalleberg 2011). In the same period, wages, working conditions, benefits, and social supports have steadily deteriorated at the bottom of the labor market, well before the Great Recession of 2007 to 2009 added double-digit unemployment to the increasingly dismal picture. By 2011, as the economy struggled to recover from that crisis, more than one-fourth (28 percent) of the U.S. labor force earned poverty-level wages (Mishel et al. 2012).

The proliferation of the twenty-first-century "working poor" is the result of developments that had already begun when Harrington's book appeared in 1962, including deindustrialization and technological change, de-unionization, and deregulation. The relentless offshoring of manufacturing, which dates back to the 1950s but accelerated in the late 1970s and 1980s, has eliminated most of the high-wage factory jobs that were the bulwark of midcentury American prosperity. In addition, the proliferation of computer-based technology has automated many of the data management and record-keeping functions that once provided reasonably paid employment for secretaries, bookkeepers, and other office workers and has also mechanized many jobs in those factories that remain inside the United States (Autor 2010).

Today's working poor are heavily concentrated in the service sector. A worker would need to earn $23,492 a year, or $12 an hour, to meet the 2012 poverty threshold for a family of four.[1] The U.S. Bureau of Labor Statistics (BLS) Occupational Employment Statistics (OES) show ninety-five occupations with a median hourly wage below $12, accounting for 38 million workers, or nearly 30 percent of total employment. Table I.1 shows the ten

Table I.1   Top Ten U.S. Occupations with a Median Hourly Wage
Below $12, 2012

Occupational Title	Total Employment
Retail salespersons	4,340,000
Cashiers	3,314,010
Combined food preparation and serving workers, including fast food	2,943,810
Waiters and waitresses	2,332,020
Laborers and freight, stock, and material movers, hand	2,143,940
Janitors and cleaners, except maids and housekeepers	2,097,380
Stock clerks and order fillers	1,806,310
Nursing assistants	1,420,020
Security guards	1,046,420
Cooks, restaurant	1,000,710
Total	22,444,620
All occupations	130,287,780
Percent of Total	17.2%

Source: Authors' calculations based on data from the U.S. Department of Labor, U.S. Bureau of Labor Statistics (2012a).

largest low wage occupations, which account for over 22 million workers, or 17.2 percent of the total. These occupations are primarily in the retail and restaurant industries. (Of course, not all workers in these occupations earn less than $12 per hour; exactly half of them do).[2]

Data on new job growth are fairly similar, as table I.2 shows. Twelve of the thirty occupations that the U.S. Bureau of Labor Statistics expects to grow most through 2020 have a median wage below $12 per hour, accounting for about 4.4 million jobs. Taken together, the data in these two tables suggest that certain occupations must be targeted by policies aiming to improve the circumstances of a significant number of low-wage workers. Those key occupations include retail sales, food preparation, waitstaff, home health aides, personal care aides, and cashiers.

The decline of U.S. labor unions, which reached their membership peak in the 1950s, when they covered about one-third of the private-sector labor force, also contributed greatly to the erosion of pay and working conditions, especially for non-college-educated workers. In the midtwentieth century, strong unions set wage floors and enforced labor standards for their members and indirectly helped improve pay and conditions for non-union workers as well. The systematic erosion of federal protections for

Table I.2   Occupations with the Largest Projected Job Growth with a Median Hourly Wage Below $12, 2010 to 2020

Occupation	Employment (In Thousands)		Job Growth (In Thousands)	Median Wage
	2010	2020		
Retail salespersons	4,262	4,968	707	$10.15
Home health aides	1,018	1,724	706	10.01
Personal and home care aides	861	1,468	607	9.57
Combined food preparation and serving workers, including fast food	2,682	3,080	398	8.78
Laborers and freight, stock, and material movers, hand	2,068	2,387	319	11.49
Nursing aides, orderlies, and attendants	1,505	1,807	302	11.74
Child care workers	1,282	1,544	262	9.38
Cashiers	3,363	3,613	250	9.12
Janitors and cleaners, except maids and housekeeping cleaners	2,310	2,557	246	10.73
Landscaping and grounds-keeping workers	1,152	1,392	241	11.33
Waiters and waitresses	2,260	2,456	196	8.92
Security guards	1,036	1,231	195	11.52

Source: Authors' calculations based on data from U.S. Department of Labor, U.S. Bureau of Labor Statistics (2012b, 2012c).

collective bargaining and sustained resistance to unionization by employers throughout the private sector have contributed to a steep secular decline in wages and fringe benefits across the economy. Loss of the union wage premium—on average, approximately 13 percent—directly reduced the incomes of workers who had previously enjoyed union contracts; simultaneously, union decline removed the indirect boost to non-union workers' compensation. Defined-benefit pensions and employer-sponsored health insurance, once standard features of unionized jobs, declined in tandem with wages as deunionization swept across the economy. Whereas in the past, unionization disproportionately benefited workers without college degrees, the deunionization of recent years has disproportionately harmed them, turning many formerly sustainable jobs into precarious ones (Mishel and Walters 2003).

Deregulation and the erosion of laws buttressing workplace standards also contributed to the deterioration of working-class jobs. The federal minimum wage is a case in point. Beginning in the late 1970s, Congress failed to pass regular increases, and the legal minimum wage soon began to lag behind increases in the cost of living. By 2012, the federal minimum wage was $7.25 an hour, but had it kept pace with the Consumer Price Index (CPI) since 1968 it would have been $10.52. Furthermore, if it had increased at the same pace as worker productivity in the same period, the minimum wage would have been $21.72 in 2012 (Schmitt 2012).

Whereas the War on Poverty, inspired in part by Harrington's book, included expanding the coverage of the Fair Labor Standards Act (FLSA), which sets maximum working hours and overtime rules (as well as minimum wages), in recent years the coverage and effectiveness of FLSA has declined. In part this reflects the growing shift toward the employment of "independent contractors," including many workers who are improperly classified as contractors. At the same time, the steady erosion of federal enforcement capacity permitted the spread of outright violation of wage and hour laws, with many employers simply not paying workers the wages legally due to them. "Wage theft" is rampant in a variety of industries, from manufacturing and residential construction to retail, restaurants, and personal services (Bernhardt et al. 2009). In the past half-century, the gap separating workers in the "affluent society" from Harrington's immiserated poor has widened dramatically.

Demographic shifts have intersected in a complex way with the rise of the working poor. In the early 1960s, African American workers earned on average less than 60 percent of what their white counterparts earned, as Harrington (1993, 62) noted. By 2011, the gap had narrowed somewhat: African American men's median hourly wage was 74 percent of that of their white counterparts, while for African Americans overall the figure was 83 percent (Mishel et al. 2012). Yet these aggregate figures obscure an internal polarization among African Americans: the growth of the black middle class has widened earnings inequality between low-wage and college-educated black workers, as in the U.S. labor force as a whole. Moreover, deunionization disproportionately affected African Americans, particularly females, who were overrepresented among private-sector union members relative to their share of the labor force and thus suffered disproportionate earnings losses as union density declined (Rosenfeld and Kleykamp 2012).

Today African Americans continue to make up a large share of the working poor, but race is no longer as strong a proxy for poverty as it was in Harrington's time. He had remarkably little to say about the situation of women workers or female poverty in 1962, but the changes that have taken place for women workers in the past half-century have been even more dramatic than for African Americans. Owing in part to the growth of female labor force participation and the reduction in job segregation by gender that began in the 1970s, the overall gender gap in pay has been reduced over the past fifty years, although, at 7.6 percent, a slightly greater proportion of female than male workers were in the ranks of the working poor in 2010 (U.S. Department of Labor 2012a). Yet pay disparities between female college graduates and their less-educated counterparts have grown as well, even as female college graduation rates have overtaken those of males. And within many dual-earner households, the economic gains of female workers over the past fifty years have been offset by the economic losses of male workers (Autor 2010, 10–11).

The growth of the immigrant workforce complicates the story still further. Harrington made little mention of foreign-born workers, apart from a brief discussion of California farmworkers, because he was writing during a period of sharp restriction of immigration to the United States. That changed in 1965 when the passage of the Immigration and Nationality Act (the Hart-Cellar Act) led to a massive increase in immigration to the United States from Latin America, Asia, and Africa. Undocumented immigration also surged, especially after the passage of the Immigration Reform and Control Act (IRCA) in 1986. These changes in immigration policy helped stimulate the growth of a vast new low-wage labor force, not only in agriculture (where undocumented immigrants were initially concentrated after the end of the bracero program in 1964) but increasingly in low-wage jobs throughout the economy. As U.S.-born workers abandoned once-desirable jobs that had deteriorated as a result of deunionization and other types of restructuring, many employers began hiring immigrants, both those with legal status and the undocumented, who were even more susceptible to minimum wage and other FLSA violations than other workers. Although Latino immigrant workers often proved more willing than many native-born workers to engage in labor protest and union organizing, the scale of such activity was limited (Milkman 2006). By 2010, Latinos (including U.S.-born Latinos, immigrants with legal status and the undocumented) were more likely than African Americans, whites, or Asians to be among the working poor (U.S. Department of Labor 2012a). At the same time, inequalities between Latinos with college degrees and those with more limited education expanded, paralleling the situation of African Americans.

For the U.S. population as a whole, income inequality has spiked dramatically since Harrington's day. In 1968 the bottom 40 percent of U.S. households took home 15.3 percent of the nation's total income; by 2010 their share had fallen to only 11.8 percent. In sharp contrast, over the same period the income share of the top 5 percent rose from 17.2 to 21.3 percent.[3] The nation's poverty rate has soared to a level higher than that in any other OECD country (Mishel et al. 2012). The "other America" of the twenty-first century is different in some respects from what Harrington described half a century ago, and the modest progress that followed the reception of his book has been sharply reversed in recent decades.

Although there is extensive documentation of the ways in which the economic playing field has tilted to increasingly disadvantage low-wage workers, their plight has received limited attention from elected officials. If their rhetoric is any indication, Democrats and Republicans alike believe that the creation of "jobs, jobs, jobs" must be the top priority of national economic policy, with little or no attention to job quality. Each major political party touts its job-creating credentials while blaming the other party for destroying jobs. Republicans assert that the only legitimate way to create new jobs is via the market and regularly deride public policy interventions, from the Patient Protection and Affordable Care Act of 2010 to the minimum wage, as "job killers."

Democrats all too often fail to challenge the logic of this approach or to promote a theoretically coherent program of their own. As a result, their policies are often haphazard in relation to job creation and job quality. For example, during the Clinton administration, millions of jobs were generated in what was then labeled "the great American jobs machine" — in contrast to Europe. However, the new jobs were disproportionately low-wage jobs, to a much greater extent than in an otherwise comparable period of job growth in the 1960s (Wright and Dwyer 2003). In addition, both the Clinton and Obama administrations have promoted free trade agreements as a solution to job creation, despite research that shows the deleterious impact of free trade on jobs, and in particular on the non-college-educated workers who are increasingly overrepresented among the working poor. Economist Laurie Kletzer (2004) found that 21 percent of workers displaced from manufacturing jobs in the 1990s were high school dropouts and that they were more likely than other displaced workers to be from racial minority groups.

Instead of promoting a comprehensive jobs program, Democrats have more often sought to gain short-term political advantages over their opponents on the jobs issue. They have directed their energies toward criticizing the policy failures of Republicans, accusing them of aiding and abetting the corporations and private equity firms that profit by laying off workers and shipping jobs overseas, while portraying the Democratic Party as the champion of the middle class. As a result, neither side has focused public attention on the quality of the jobs created in the U.S. economy or fought for a comprehensive set of policies addressing the needs of low-wage workers.

If the working poor have been ignored by mainstream politicians, the Great Recession, the Occupy Wall Street movement, and a wave of grassroots labor protests have increasingly attracted public and media attention to the issues of poverty and low-wage work, creating new opportunities for those who are concerned about the fate of the working poor. However, the substantial research literature that has recently documented the experiences of low-wage workers has also all too often ignored the arena of public policy interventions. Nor have recent political debates shed much light on the ways in which public policies interface with or help to shape the situation of low-wage workers. This is unfortunate, for just as previous public policies helped to create and reproduce the nation's burgeoning low-wage job market, a new set of policy interventions could improve the lot of the nation's most exploited and insecure wage-earners. Thus, the time is ripe for a renewed discussion of the policy options—and specifically about policies that can work for low-wage workers.

By contrast, on the ground there has been a burst of experimentation in recent years with innovative interventions and strategies that address the rapid growth of low-wage work. They range from traditional approaches like raising the minimum wage and fostering unionization, to investments in primary and secondary education and job training, to more innovative "living wage" laws and efforts to leverage and secure effective enforcement of labor and employment standards in existing law. Yet systematic empirical analysis of the efficacy of these various efforts has been limited.

Which policy approaches are most effective, and under what conditions have they succeeded? What is the impact of each approach on the most vulnerable populations, such as low-wage immigrants and African Americans? What elements of these efforts might contribute most to a reformulated national approach to the problems facing the working poor? Developing answers to questions like these is essential if we are ever to get beyond the current political polarization and renew the nation's commitment to ensuring that work provides social and economic security.

The Murphy Institute for Worker Education and Labor Studies of the City University of New York and the Kalmanovitz Initiative for Labor and the Working Poor of Georgetown University collaborated on a conference, organized by this volume's editors and held at Georgetown in February 2012, to examine public policy interventions and their impact on low-wage workers. Designed with the goal of "bringing the state back in," the conference featured leading academic researchers in a range of fields, including economics, sociology, history, and law, and put them in a sustained dialogue with practitioners, including government officials, advocates, and organizers, who brought their own experiences and observations to the table. The essays in this volume reflect the dialogue that took place at the conference.

The conference participants—scholars and practitioners alike—were all aligned with one of Harrington's essential insights: public policy is consequential, and a crucial resource in the fight against poverty. Each chapter in this volume has a different angle, but they all start from that perspective. Part I, "Low-Wage Work in Historical Perspective," describes the origins of public policy for low-wage workers and the recent transformations that underlie current conditions. Alice O'Connor's chapter, "An Economy That Works for Workers," opens the volume with an analysis that historicizes the assumptions and politics behind today's social policies. She embeds her analysis in the context of the broader political economy, illuminating just how narrow contemporary debates about low-wage work have become. O'Connor examines key developments in social provision for low-income workers in relation to broader shifts in economic policy and reform politics since the late 1960s, showing how New Deal norms of economic citizenship were eroded by a radically altered public policy atmosphere in which the assumptions of free-market individualism increasingly predominated. Through this approach, she highlights the historical transformations in politics and political economy that have undermined both the material living standards and the longer-range social and political prospects of low-wage workers and the U.S. working class. O'Connor argues that any efforts to advance the interests of low-wage workers are inextricably tied to the pursuit of "fairness, freedom, and political as well as economic democracy" and must therefore begin not with menus of specific policy options but rather with a staking out of the "moral high ground of American democracy."

The next chapter, "What Can Labor Organizations Do for U.S. Workers When Unions Can't Do What Unions Used to Do?" by Richard Freeman, explores in detail one of the primary causes of increased working poverty: the decline of unions. Reframing a question that he and James Medoff (1984) famously asked three decades ago in their classic study *What Do Unions Do?* Freeman begins by acknowledging that most experts no longer believe that unions can do much for low-wage workers at this historical juncture. However, he then goes on to contest this conventional wisdom, arguing that the surprisingly energetic mobilization of public-sector unions against legislative efforts to eliminate the right to bargain collectively and the emergence of new opportunities for dissidents to use the Internet and social media to galvanize citizens for change have created an opening for a possible union resurgence. Nevertheless, he suggests, any such resurgence will require unions to move beyond traditional collective bargaining and collaborate with other community actors, while using the new social media to obtain and disseminate information. In this way, organized labor could help organize workers and citizens on a broader basis and break out of the narrow channels to which it has recently been confined.

Part II, "Workers on the Edge: Marginalized and Disadvantaged," exposes the challenges faced by workers who are especially disadvantaged in the twenty-first-century U.S. labor market: young workers, especially those of color; immigrants; and employees whose labor is subcontracted. These chapters point to the disparities between the existing policy regime and the current structure of the workplace and workforce. Chapter 3, Peter Edelman and Harry Holzer's essay "Connecting the Disconnected: Improving Education and Employment Outcomes Among Disadvantaged Youth," examines a key population that has chronically suffered over the last three decades and was hit hardest by the Great Recession. Edelman and Holzer survey a range of efforts to improve education and employment outcomes among disadvantaged youth, especially young black men, and they argue that programs that offer a combination of skill development and paid work experience, those that incentivize employment by "making work pay," and those that target the most troubled groups, such as ex-offenders, have often shown strong results at improving employment outcomes for these youth.

In chapter 4, "Mending the Fissured Workplace," David Weil argues that the nation's increasingly anachronistic workplace policies are in urgent need of revision. Since the New Deal era, he points out, U.S. workplace policies have been primarily designed around an employment model that presumes a relationship between stable, long-term workers who labor for large firms in markets where competition is limited. That model no longer corresponds to labor market realities: employment has increasingly shifted to smaller business units that seek a more flexible relationship with their workers. These new units typically operate in far more competitive markets than the large-scale firms of the past, and the quality of the jobs they offer tends to be poorer. Employers in this sector have often failed to comply with existing labor regulations, and Weil suggests several ways to address that problem. Drawing on recent innovations in labor standards and health and safety enforcement, he explores policies that can harness existing enforcement tools in new ways, focusing regulatory pressure at higher levels of subcontracting chains to tackle the structures that often drive noncompliance in low-wage jobs.

In chapter 5, "Holding the Line on Workplace Standards: What Works for Immigrant Workers (and What Doesn't)?," Jennifer Gordon focuses on the impact of immigration law and highlights the situation of low-wage immigrant workers. She points out that U.S. immigration law and policy are often very different in theory and in practice. Although in theory immigrants have the same rights as other workers, she explains, actual immigration enforcement has had largely negative effects on foreign-born workers.

Gordon sketches the evolution of current policy since the passage of IRCA in 1986, focusing on the failure of employer sanctions and later of efforts to achieve comprehensive immigration reform. She documents the ways in which immigrant workers have organized effectively nonetheless, with the help of worker centers and community-based organizations as well as unions. Comparing the U.S. experience to that of the United Kingdom and the European Union, she argues that ensuring the free mobility of immigrants across borders, though a necessary policy goal, would be insufficient by itself to address the problem facing low-wage immigrant workers. She calls instead for innovative government enforcement of labor standards as well as fuller collaboration among unions, community groups, worker centers, and government agencies to transform low-wage immigrants' theoretical rights into reality on the ground.

What about existing labor market policy interventions? In part III, the volume turns to assessments of the efficacy of three key programs. In the chapter entitled "Career Ladders in the Low-Wage Labor Market," Paul Osterman examines the role of job training and career ladders in improving the quality of work in low-wage settings. Drawing on his own fieldwork as well as previously published accounts, he assesses the effectiveness of training programs administered by unions, business associations, nonprofits, and community groups. In addition, he examines the crucial and in some respects untapped role of community colleges in helping workers move up career ladders. Osterman argues that the available evidence demonstrates the effectiveness of career ladder programs in reducing the extent of low-wage employment, suggesting that this is one key tool to help workers climb out of low-wage employment. What is lacking, he suggests, is an adequate level of commitment to such training programs from employers, political leaders, and policymakers.

In chapter 7, "Employment Subsidies to Firms and Workers," Sarah Hamersma compares the differential impact on labor markets of two types of tax subsidies, one aimed at employers (the Work Opportunity Tax Credit) and the other at workers (the Earned Income Tax Credit). Both programs have low administrative costs and offer the promise of increased employment and income for low-wage workers, but as Hamersma points out, they operate in fundamentally different ways, producing vastly different participation patterns and employment outcomes. The WOTC firm subsidy operates at lower costs, but also furnishes far fewer credits and has a minimal impact on employment; by contrast, the more expensive EITC delivers a far greater impact. Hamersma's findings highlight the effectiveness of the EITC, in spite of its increasing costs, in protecting low-wage workers.

In her chapter "Living Wages, Minimum Wages, and Low-Wage Workers," Stephanie Luce offers a review of the literature on minimum wage policy, showing how economists have slowly improved their research techniques and changed their assessment. Whereas the dominant view a few decades ago was that raising minimum wages leads to job loss, more recent research finds that this negative prediction does not hold in practice. Raising the minimum wage can help large numbers of low-wage workers, although the raises are mostly small and do not lift a worker above poverty. In that context, Luce offers a candid assessment of one of the most prominent forms of worker-oriented public policy activism to have emerged in recent decades. Living wage ordinances have been enacted in over 125 cities and counties around the country since Baltimore passed the first one in 1994. The goals of living wage campaigns have included forging coalitions that build political power, influencing public debate on wages and economic development, laying the groundwork for new union organizing, and strengthening unions' bargaining power. The impact of living wage laws on directly raising the incomes of low-wage workers has been difficult to measure, however, because, as Luce points out, enforcement is often lax. Nonetheless, her research dispels the myth that living wage laws primarily cover teenagers as well as the myth that their enactment has a negative impact on workers at the bottom of the labor market by encouraging employers to replace them with more skilled workers. In documenting the ways in which living wage ordinances have helped workers, Luce points out that, unlike minimum wage laws, they cover only a tiny portion of the nation's low-wage workforce.

Finally, part IV looks at "Social Insurance Programs and Low-Wage Work." Jeffrey B. Wenger's chapter, "Improving Low-Income Workers' Access to Unemployment Insurance," examines the U.S. unemployment insurance (UI) system in the context of changes in work organization, the increased presence of women in the workplace, and growing concern regarding caregiving and the issues associated with sick leave and family leave. Over time, he argues, the UI system has become less effective in meeting the needs of workers. Fewer than half of the nation's unemployed have applied for benefits in recent years, and denied claims are on the rise. Wenger explores states' efforts to raise earnings requirements and erect other barriers to UI eligibility while simultaneously reducing benefits, linking those shifts to the decline in the use of UI by low-wage workers. He calls on the federal government to require that states maintain adequate UI reserves and raise the taxable base of income that funds the program, and also to set limits on the mechanisms that states use to disqualify workers from receiving benefits.

Chapter 10, "Can the Affordable Care Act Reverse Three Decades of Declining Health Insurance Coverage for Low-Wage Workers?" looks closely at the crucial and contentious area of health insurance. Using Current Population Survey (CPS) data, John Schmitt reviews trends in health-insurance coverage rates for low-wage workers over time, highlighting the dramatic increase in the proportion of low-wage workers who lack coverage, a figure that had reached 38 percent by 2010, primarily owing to the steady decline of employer-provided health insurance. Although public insurance coverage for low-wage workers has expanded, the increase has been insufficient to offset the decline in private insurance. The evidence suggests that the Affordable Care Act could have a substantial positive effect on health insurance coverage rates for low-wage workers, although it does not offer a comprehensive solution to the nation's health care crisis.

Ruth Milkman and Eileen Appelbaum conclude the volume with their chapter on California's pioneering paid family leave program, which began operating in 2004. It was designed especially to benefit low-wage workers, who seldom have access to employer-provided wage replacement when they need to take time off to care for a new child or a seriously ill family member. California was the first state to develop a paid leave program, and Milkman and Appelbaum collected data on its effectiveness through original surveys of employers and workers. Their chapter analyzes the gap between the promise and the reality of this innovative program, focusing particularly on the needs of low-wage workers.

The chapters collected in this volume address a broad range of specific topics, but taken together they highlight some themes that merit further attention. First, the fluidity of labor markets and "flexible" work can pose methodological challenges; policymakers and scholars, for instance, do not have a consensus definition of what counts as "low-wage work" or agreement on what the primary target of public policy should be. None of the policies discussed here operate in isolation from the others, and low-wage workers may move through different types of policies over time—moving, for example, from job training and gaining access to jobs at one point, to surviving periods of unemployment and underemployment at another.

Second, much of this research shows that public policy is effective only if it is properly enforced. The policy examples analyzed in this volume are often complex and may even require multiple agencies to implement. Workers are not always educated about their rights or about the existence of programs that could benefit them. Policy guidelines are often revised and rewritten in the course of the legislative process. Advocates must not abandon their efforts when a law is passed but must continue to monitor its implementation to ensure the best outcomes for meeting the initial policy goal.

Third, none of the policies analyzed here offers a panacea. Each benefits some group of workers, but each has limitations. To be effective, a new "war on poverty" would have to develop a comprehensive framework defining how each of these policies can best be used and how each intersects with other interventions such as unionization, education, and civic and political engagement.

Taken together, these contributions echo the central point that Michael Harrington advanced so eloquently decades ago. Although these authors show how complex and deeply entrenched the structures of poverty are for low-wage workers today, their analyses also remind us that these structures are not immutable. To the contrary, the structural developments that have worsened the plight of low-wage workers in recent years reflect the policy choices of men and women. It follows that different policy choices could meet Harrington's challenge and build a different kind of political economy that genuinely works for its workers.

NOTES

1. This assumes that an individual is working forty hours a week for fifty weeks a year (with two weeks of unpaid leave).
2. In twelve occupations in the 2012 OES—including "combined food preparation" and "cashiers"—the seventy-fifty percentile wage is less than $10.64 an hour. Those earning this wage make up about 7 percent of all workers.
3. For census data on household income, see U.S. Census Bureau, "Table H-2: Share of Aggregate Income Received by Each Fifth and Top 5 Percent of Households, All Races, 1967 to 2010," *Current Population Survey, Annual Social and Economic Supplements*, available at: http://www.census.gov/hhes/www/income/data/historical/household/2010/H02AR_2010.xls.

REFERENCES

Autor, David. 2010. "The Polarization of Job Opportunities in the U.S. Labor Market: Implications for Employment and Earnings." Washington, D.C.: Center for American Progress (April).

Bernhardt, Annette, Ruth Milkman, Nik Theodore, Douglas Heckathorn, Mirabai Auer, James DeFilippis, Ana Luz Gonzalez, Victor Narro, Jason Perelshteyn, Diana Polson, and Michael Spiller. 2009. *Broken Laws, Unprotected Workers: Violations of Employment and Labor Laws in America's Cities*. Available at: http://www.nelp.org/page/-/brokenlaws/BrokenLawsReport2009.pdf?nocdn=1 (accessed September 2013).

Freeman, Richard B., and James L. Medoff. 1984. *What Do Unions Do?* New York: Basic Books.

Harrington, Michael. 1993. *The Other America*. New York: Simon & Schuster. (Originally published in 1962.)

Kalleberg, Arne. 2011. *Good Jobs, Bad Jobs: The Rise of Polarized and Precarious Employment Systems in the United States, 1970s to 2000s*. New York: Russell Sage Foundation.

Kletzer, Laurie. 2004. "Trade-Related Job Loss and Wage Insurance: A Synthetic Review." *Review of International Economics* 12(5): 724–48.

Milkman, Ruth. 2006. *L.A. Story: Immigrant Workers and the Future of the U.S. Labor Movement*. New York: Russell Sage Foundation.

Mishel, Lawrence, Josh Bivens, Elise Gould, and Heidi Shierholz. 2012. *The State of Working America*, 12th ed. Ithaca, N.Y.: Cornell University Press.

Mishel, Lawrence, and Matthew Walters. 2003. "How Unions Help All Workers." Briefing paper no. 143. Washington, D.C.: Economic Policy Institute. Available at: http://www.epi.org/publication/briefingpapers_bp143 (accessed September 2013).

Rosenfeld, Jake, and Meredith Kleykamp. 2012. "Organized Labor and Racial Wage Inequality in the United States." *American Journal of Sociology* 117 (5, March): 1460–1502.

Schmitt, John. 2012. "The Minimum Wage Is Too Damn Low." Issue brief. Washington, D.C.: Center for Economic and Policy Research (March).

U.S. Department of Labor. U.S. Bureau of Labor Statistics. 2012a. "A Profile of the Working Poor, 2010." Report 1035. Washington: U.S. Department of Labor (March).

———. 2012b. "May 2012 National Occupational Employment and Wage Estimates." Washington: U.S. Department of Labor. Available at: http://www.bls.gov/oes/ (accessed July 2013).

———. 2012c. "Employment Projections: 2010–2020 Summary." Washington: U.S. Department of Labor. Available at: http://www.bls.gov/news.release/ecopro.nr0.htm (accessed September 13, 2013).

Wright, Erik Olin, and Rachel Dwyer. 2003. "The Patterns of Job Expansions in the USA: A Comparison of the 1960s and 1990s." *Socio-Economic Review* 1(3): 289–325.

Part I | Low-Wage Work in Historical Perspective

Chapter 1 | An Economy That Works for Workers

Alice O'Connor

For the past three decades, the problem of low-wage work has become a central preoccupation among poverty analysts and advocates. While it would be an exaggeration to say they have coalesced around a unified policy agenda, collectively they have produced an impressive body of knowledge about the deteriorating prospects for low-wage workers in our New Gilded Age economy (see, for example, Danziger and Gottschalk 1995; Ehrenreich 2001; Freeman 2007; Greenhouse 2008; Handler and White 1999; Holzer and Nightingale 2007; Munger 2002). As subsequent chapters in this volume show, they also point us to a variety of strategies to empower low-wage workers or otherwise "make work pay" through tax subsidies and other targeted policy interventions, unionization and living wage campaigns, education and training programs, and employee profit-sharing plans.

As most people involved in this work would acknowledge, however, such strategies can only do so much in the face of the seemingly relentless long-range trends—rising income and wealth inequality, declining unionization rates, the global outsourcing of once-better-paying jobs, and now the vastly unequal fallout from the Great Recession—that keep workers from getting a stable foothold in the economy, let alone getting ahead. What workers really need is an economy that is not so steeply stacked against them—one that certainly would look very different from the deeply inequitable and otherwise undemocratic version of capitalism that prevails in the United States today. A discussion about what works for workers, then, must situate strategies to improve the conditions of low-wage workers within a broader strategy of political economic and social policy reform.

19

In this chapter, I provide some historical grounding for that discussion by examining trends in social policy since the late 1960s, when federal policy-makers first began to focus on the needs of a group that would only later be commonly referred to as the "working poor." At the time that group consisted largely of workers who had been left out of the rights and pro-tections of the New Deal social contract, through racially stratified occupa-tional exemptions among other means; the task of social policy, as liberal and progressive advocates saw it, was to break down or otherwise reform restrictive provisions to make a New Deal for all. Since then, the "working poor" has come to include growing numbers of workers in covered occu-pations who are nevertheless experiencing deteriorating wage and labor standards, alongside increasingly diminished sources of social support. These trends signal the erosion of the New Deal social contract itself.

My discussion focuses on income support and housing, tracing policy measures that have figured prominently in efforts to improve low-wage workers' living conditions and that are historically significant for other rea-sons as well. One reason is that these measures reflect the more general— and growing—tendency in social policy to target individuals and families for compensatory assistance rather than intervening directly to improve, regulate, or prevent the deterioration of market standards and conditions: they deal with the problem of low-wage work by providing relief rather than structural reform, as a problem of inadequate income and assets rather than of labor and employment more broadly conceived. The other is that viewing income and housing policies in tandem underscores the critical importance of a whole host of non-employment social welfare provisions— including subsidies for homeownership—to the well-being of the compara-tively privileged segments of the postwar working class and to the relative disadvantage of racially disenfranchised middle- and working-class minor-ities. Such provisions, and the disparities they generated, would only grow in importance amid post-1970s wage declines. The juxtaposition of income and housing policies also underscores the critical importance of more recent ideological shifts in social politics as social policy has come over the past three decades to focus more heavily on individual ownership rather than on wage-earning as the gateway to economic citizenship. Taken together, then, historical developments in income and housing policy offer insights into the much diminished policy environment facing low-wage workers—past, present, and future—as a consequence of the late-twentieth-century shift in economic policy and reform politics from its moorings in New Deal norms of full employment, wage-earner rights, and collective social provision to a regime built around debt-financed growth, private property ownership, and a public philosophy of free market individualism. In drawing atten-tion to the impact of this broader shift, I aim to expand the focus of policy agenda-setting for low-wage workers to include the political and economic transformations that have been undermining both the immediate material living standards and the longer-range social and political prospects of the American working class.

Foremost among these transformations has been the global restructuring of capitalism through government and corporate strategies of globalization, deregulation, financialization, and deunionization that have left American workers more exposed to wage-lowering competition from global labor markets as well as to the labor-reducing logic of maximum shareholder value. The fortunes of workers have similarly been undermined by a fundamental shift in American political economy away from its Keynesian commitment to high (if not full) employment, fiscally managed growth, mass purchasing power, and a moderately redistributive welfare state and toward variants of the neoliberal or "free market" economics popularized by economist Milton Friedman (among others), with its emphasis on deregulation, limited government, low taxation, monetarist inflation-fighting, and the "trickle-down" benefits of privately accumulated wealth. Changes in the tax code have only reinforced the shift in priorities from wage-earning to wealth, while contributing to a shocking degree of income and wealth concentration at the very top. As reported in a recent Congressional Research Service (CRS) study, reductions in capital gains and dividend income tax rates since 2001 have only exacerbated the already steepening rise in inequality, while the overall tax code has continued to grow less progressive in its impact, as well as in its design.[1] The bottom fifth have actually paid more of their income in taxes since the "end of welfare" in 1996, principally reflecting the impact of the admittedly regressive payroll tax (Hungerford 2011, 4; see also Mishel, Bernstein, and Shierholz 2009). More recently, wages have reached historic lows as a share of national income as corporate profits have reached record highs (Aron-Dine and Shapiro 2006).

U.S. social policy has also been significantly transformed since the 1970s as a restructuring and repurposing has left most Americans more insecure and vulnerable to risk and a substantial proportion of the low-wage workforce subject to the discipline of the carceral state as well as to the harsh rules of a deregulated labor market. In the name of promoting marriage and "personal responsibility," discouraging "dependence," and ending the "era of big government," public assistance has been cut back, time-limited, devolved to the state and local levels, and, for working-age people, made contingent on participation in the paid labor force and compliance with a host of behavioral rules (Katz 2001). Wage-earning, though a necessity for more and more people, has actually been devalued in social policy as institutional supports such as the minimum wage, job training, employer-provided health and pension benefits, and fair labor standards have given way to a reliance on more targeted, individualized, and "hidden" subsidies provided to low-wage workers—and indirectly to low-wage employers—through the tax code. While insisting that more and more people should become "self-sufficient" and provide for their own needs through savings, investment, and participation in the paid labor force, social policy has actually undermined their capacity to do so by accommodating the transition to an economy in which lower wages, fewer benefits, and generally degraded working conditions are accepted as the "new normal." As other sources of income support have declined, the Earned Income Tax Credit has become the single most important source of public assistance for low-income working-class families and, at significant points, has increased in value. At the same time, as a benefit that has been used as an alternative to higher wages, its growth and its bipartisan popularity signal a structural shift in social policy toward heavier reliance on tax expenditures of all sorts that works far more to the advantage of the affluent than the poor (Katz 2001, 294–98; see also Howard 1997; Mettler 2011).

Meantime, buoyed by the irrational exuberance that fueled credit market expansion, social provision became increasingly financialized in the 1990s and 2000s. There was growing emphasis in both official and nongovernmental organization policy circles on a variety of "ownership" and "asset-building" initiatives that hinged on access to deregulated and highly speculative credit markets—turning the wages, the savings, and especially the debt of the lowest wage-earners into risk capital for the profits of giant mortgage originators and Wall Street banks. Low and moderate earners were, in turn, that much more vulnerable to the housing market and global financial collapse of 2008 (Bricker et al. 2012; Kearns 2012). Thus, in the shift to a more market-based social policy, deregulated and globalized labor markets served as instruments of discipline and reform, while deregulated and globalized financial markets became powerful—and regressive—instruments of upward redistribution. The "market turn" in social policy did not, however, translate uniformly into the retreat of the state. The past three decades have witnessed what amounts to a vast reallocation of public resources, especially at the state and local levels, from education, social services, youth employment and training, and a host of other opportunity-building programs to the carceral state. Indeed, it is not an exaggeration to say that, for the growing segment of the population—disproportionately young, minority males—who have been jailed or otherwise caught up in it, the system of mass incarceration has replaced the functions of social welfare in what the Children's Defense Fund (2007) has dubbed the "cradle to prison pipeline." The consequences for the low-wage workforce have been devastating and far-reaching, as measured in the lifetime loss of earnings for inmates and their families; the long-term impact of parent incarceration on children's economic fortunes and social-psychological well-being; the drain and spillover effects of high rates of incarceration on low-income communities of color; and the basic erosion of civil rights and liberties associated with what criminal law scholar Jonathan Simon (2009) calls "governing through crime" (see also Alexander 2010; Gottschalk 2006, Raphael and Stoll 2009; Thompson 2010; Western 2006; Western and Pettit 2010).

American workers have been considerably disempowered by transformations in American politics since the 1970s as well, and most visibly by the triumph of what scholars have come to refer to as "winner-take-all" politics—the outcome of the growing influence of big money on both major political parties and of well-organized economic elites in governance and national affairs (Bartels 2010; Gilens 2012; Hacker and Pierson 2010; Lessig 2011). Organized corporate interests have grown especially aggressive in their efforts to undermine organized labor through anti-union campaigns, weakened labor laws, and political pressure to leave existing regulations unenforced (Greenhouse 2008; Lichtenstein 2002). But equally consequential for the political fortunes of workers has been the reconfiguration of social movement and associational politics—the politics of expertise, advocacy, and interest group influence—along more sharply polarized ideological lines. For the past three decades, such politics has been dominated by the powerfully if uneasily combined forces of the anti-statist, pro-corporate, free-market, and morally "traditional" right. Joined in mutual animosity to New Deal and Great Society liberalism, this alliance has proved especially effective at commandeering a language of political economy that, in contrast to that of its more technocratic liberal counterparts, frames policy issues in terms of stark moral choices: between free-market capitalism and big government collectivism; between individual responsibility and welfare dependency; between the right to work and "enforced" unionism (Friedman 1962; Friedman and Friedman 1979). Similarly, when movement Republicans swept into the U.S. House of Representatives in the 1994 midterm elections, they came heralding nothing short of a new social contract based on the principles of individual liberty, personal responsibility, and limited government (Republican National Committee 1994, 4).

As a number of recent historical studies have recognized, the structural transformations in American capitalism, social policy, and politics do not represent the unfolding of somehow inexorable historical or economic forces. Nor did they happen overnight. They are rooted in decades of hard-fought political battles and in policy decisions that were not so much necessitated as made possible by the storied "end" of postwar American affluence in the 1970s and the extended bouts of economic crisis and decline, high unemployment mixed with inflation, and slow growth that the decade ushered in (Cowie 2010; Rodgers 2011; Schulman 2001; Schulman and Zelizer 2008; Stein 2010).

Organized labor, challenged and energized by insurgent leadership and worker activism alike, stood as a countervailing force. Though never fully or adequately implemented, the labor-backed Humphrey-Hawkins Act of 1978 reasserted full employment as an economic policy goal at a moment when Keynesian economic management was under fire. Despite declining membership overall, sectors within the labor movement made significant inroads in the drive to unionize service and other groups of workers outside the more traditional industrial union mold, and they have played an important part in the community-based living wage campaigns that began to gain momentum in the 1990s (Boris and Klein 2012; Luce 2004; Milkman 2006; Pollin and Luce 2000). Antipoverty advocates worked with some success to leverage resources from the shrinking welfare state, often in collaboration with private nonprofits, and actively resisted the shredding of the federal social safety net, including the now-ended welfare entitlement for families with children. But even the most successful advocates recognize that they are operating within a federal policy environment that has been hollowed out by the initially gradual, constantly escalating, and unsuccessfully contested erosion of the New Deal commitment to making an economy in which wage-earning is the basis of economic security, opportunity, civic standing, and, more generally, the entitlements associated with full social and political citizenship.

Still, in order to understand the genesis of social policy for low-wage workers, it is also important to recognize that the problems of low-wage work did not start in the 1970s. These problems stem from deeper and more long-standing inequities—experienced along the overlapping lines of class, race, gender, and occupation—that the New Deal order had been ill equipped to address and in some instances had helped to advance. Those inequities came sharply into view in the 1960s in social movement demands for economic justice and in President Lyndon B. Johnson's declaration of the War on Poverty. And they were at the heart of ambitious policy initiatives that promised to respond to the neglected needs of low-wage workers in particular: on the one hand, by eliminating outdated and stigmatizing restrictions to extend federal income support relief to the near-poverty- and below-poverty-earning working class, and on the other, by extending the reach of the federal subsidy for homeownership to employed but low-earning households. Thus, the basic elements of policies for low-wage workers first took shape within an atmosphere of expansive public purpose and political possibility that has all but disappeared but that nevertheless remains relevant for its basic understanding that social policies, in order to "work" for low-wage workers, must first and foremost be embedded in an economy that produces adequate employment, wages, and opportunities for advancement. In the context of slowed economic growth and structural change, the failure to address those inequities through expansive liberal programs would contribute as much as organized opposition from the right to the erosion of popular support not only for New Deal and Great Society programs but for their ideas about shared prosperity and the role of government in achieving it.

A NEW DEAL FOR LOW-WAGE WORKERS

"It Can Be Done!" So reads the headline of an essay published in *The New Republic* by the Yale University economist James Tobin in 1967. As a former member of the Kennedy-Johnson administration Council of Economic Advisers (CEA), Tobin was recognized as one of the leading practitioners of the liberal Keynesian "new economics" that, at least for the moment, was credited for the country's impressive run of economic growth and prosperity. Exuding the blend of confidence, high expectations, and pragmatism shared by much of the Keynesian policy establishment at the time, Tobin laid out a six-point plan for "conquering poverty in the U.S. by 1976" that called for federal government commitments to continued economic growth, full employment, and an end to racial discrimination along with increased investments in public services and education and training. Tobin also endorsed an idea that was rapidly gaining support from across the ideological spectrum, albeit in widely varying forms: a basic guarantee of "adequate income" for "everyone in need" to replace what analysts and activists considered to be the scandalously ungenerous and unequal system of categorical public assistance (Tobin 1967). Spectacularly ambitious though these proposals may seem in retrospect, what marks Tobin's essay as part of a bygone era are the core assumptions that inform it—about shared social aspirations, about the role of government in achieving them, and about wage-earning and economic citizenship—as much as the particulars of the plan.

Thus, the plan Tobin outlined begins from the basic legitimacy of the idea of ending poverty, not merely as an achievable goal but as a statement of public purpose—a purpose that, in the world's most affluent democracy, he assumed would or at least should be widely shared. This had, of course, been the central premise of Lyndon B. Johnson's official declaration of the War on Poverty three years before as the centerpiece of an extraordinarily ambitious domestic policy agenda that by the end of 1965 had succeeded in passing landmark federal civil rights legislation as well as major expansions of federal aid to education, housing and urban development, and Medicare and Medicaid. In these and other ways, the policies and programs collectively known as the Great Society had extended significantly beyond the parameters of New Deal social provision. Now, in the far more divided political environment of the late 1960s, Tobin was joining with Office of Economic Opportunity (OEO) director Sargent Shriver to urge Congress to finish the job, specifically by adopting the agency's "Ten-Year Anti-Poverty Budget," which projected an end to poverty by 1976. That the federal government would play a central role in ensuring a decent standard of living for its citizens was not the issue; nor was the idea, established decades earlier in the New Deal, that the federal government would intervene in the economy to achieve domestic policy goals. The issue, at least for Tobin and poverty warriors at the OEO, was not whether but how much further to extend and otherwise revise New Deal provisions to meet the needs of those left behind.

At the same time, it is important to recall that Tobin's plan for ending poverty also hinged on the original New Deal commitment to wage-earning work as the cornerstone of its economic recovery and growth policies as well as of the social contract between citizens and the state. Fully employed workers would provide the mass purchasing power to fuel economic growth, as well as the tax revenues to fund the social security system. Wage-earning work would in turn be an entrée to the entitlements of economic citizenship required of modern industrial democracy, as enumerated by Franklin D. Roosevelt, in language deliberately evocative of the U.S. Constitution, in his "Economic Bill of Rights": the rights to jobs at decent wages; to health, homes, and education; and to a fair playing field free of racial discrimination, economic privilege, and monopoly. Together, these "self-evident" rights represented the New Deal's commitment to making what FDR had famously called "Freedom from Want" a reality for every American (Roosevelt 1941, 1944; see also Donohue 2003).[2] For postwar Keynesians like Tobin, delivering on this commitment meant building on the edifice of the fair labor standards, minimum wage, and collective bargaining rights established in New Deal labor legislation. More than anything, however, it meant maintaining high economic growth and generously defined levels of "full" employment—the two most effective "weapons," as CEA economists never tired of repeating, in the Great Society's War on Poverty (O'Connor 2001). Ending poverty, they argued, was not only compatible with but integral to sustaining high growth, high wages, and equitably distributed income. Tobin even called for raising "our concept of full employment" from 4 percent unemployment to 3 percent. Ending poverty, then, was about creating an economy in which the interests of the poor, and of all disadvantaged workers, could be tied to the interests of everyone else.

Still, as even the most committed Keynesians were prepared to admit, there were limits to what growth and full employment could accomplish. Even with the combination of New Deal labor and social welfare protections and equitably distributed economic growth, full employment would leave millions of working-age wage-earners in poverty and below socially acceptable standards of living, according to Tobin's and official OEO projections. Ending poverty would thus also require a more expansive concept of what in Progressive Era and New Deal parlance had been known as the "social economy"—the health, welfare, educational, and other quality-of-life goods that were essential to overall social well-being and that the market could not or would not provide (Brick 2006; U.S. Department of Health, Education, and Welfare 1969). By the late 1960s, that concept of social economy had in many ways expanded to include rising health, educational, and environmental standards even as, in the eyes of widely read critics such as economist John Kenneth Galbraith and environmentalist Rachel Carson, the gap between private affluence and public goods had increased as well. For Tobin and a growing number of liberal economists, shoring up and reforming the woefully inadequate system of public assistance was a way of closing that gap and of institutionalizing a universal, if admittedly basic, social minimum of economic security for all. With official poverty rates for families still at 17 percent, Tobin's critique of New Deal public assistance focused on the low benefits, gaps in coverage, "petty surveillance," and work punishments that kept millions of poor people—the vast majority in fact—either still in poverty or off the rolls. Especially troubling were the categorical restrictions that confined welfare eligibility to single-parent (mostly female) non-wage-earning families while denying benefits to families headed by (mostly male) wage-earners. That such restrictions had been partially removed in some states had only added to the inequities within the system. Freedom from want meant eliminating those and other categorical restrictions and extending welfare benefits to previously excluded workers who met the income criteria—breaking down, at least for policy purposes, invidious distinctions between the "welfare poor" and the "working poor." More broadly, it meant transforming the New Deal's unfair, scattershot, and frequently punitive system of public assistance into a system of guaranteed minimum income support (O'Connor 1998; Steensland 2008).

The real impetus for a more expansive and inclusive system of social provision in the late 1960s, however, came from the movement politics of the liberal left—that is, from the widening array of locally and nationally organized movements that drew their demands (for guaranteed jobs and income, a more equitable distribution of wealth and opportunity, universalized health and housing benefits, and an end to the war in Vietnam) from a longer history of struggle for economic justice. These movements also pressed for an end to the distinctions between welfare poor and working poor, but their reform agenda was considerably more far-reaching than that. Even as they staked their claims in New Deal concepts of economic citizenship and civil rights, women's and labor movement activists had come to these expansive demands through decades of organizing to overcome the wider array of structural inequities built into the New Deal welfare state. Most glaring were the categorical restrictions that had shut minority working-class people and white working-class women out of the benefits and labor protections of New Deal economic citizenship by excluding agricultural, domestic, and certain categories of service work from access to old-age pensions, unemployment insurance, collective bargaining rights, and minimum wage protections under the terms of the Social Security Act of 1935, the National Labor Relations Act of 1935 (the Wagner Act), and the Fair Labor Standards Act (1937). The economic impact of those original exclusions would reverberate for decades, even after they had gradually been eliminated by the 1970s. Still, the achievement of inclusion within the basic New Deal framework was a significant advance for millions of workers who could now claim entitlements to social security and other employment-related protections, as well as the right to organize and to demand a decent wage (Boris and Klein 2012; Gordon 1994; Hamilton and Hamilton 1997; Katznelson 2005; Poole 2006).

The New Deal also provided a framework for postwar struggles against discriminatory employment practices. Building on the model that FDR had established under pressure from A. Philip Randolph and other civil rights activists during World War II, women's and civil rights activists pushed for more robust, permanent, and far-reaching fair employment practices legislation throughout the postwar decades. Those decades of organizing had brought millions to the civil rights movement's March on Washington for "jobs and freedom" in August 1963 and found partial realization in the employment provisions of the Civil Rights Act of 1964 (Chen 2009; McLean 2006).

But movement activists also drew attention to the need to challenge some of the basic premises of New Deal social provision—especially as implemented in postwar liberal policy—in their drive for economic justice and freedom from want. These challenges spoke directly to the millions of people employed in low-paying jobs and in what welfare rights advocates argued was the uncompensated labor of caregiving for family members. One set of concerns had to do with the problem of jobs, which by the 1960s was looming as *the* central issue for civil rights and labor activists in the deindustrializing cities and more generally among groups of workers and communities who stood to suffer from the impact of jobs-displacing technology (A. Philip Randolph Institute 1966; Countryman 2006; McGee 2008; Sugrue 1996). Although marginalized in establishment policy circles, labor economists writing about these and other forms of structural unemployment voiced an influential critique of postwar Keynesianism, which relied heavily on fiscally stimulated growth and military industrial spending as the road to full employment. Joined by civil rights organizations, they called for a return to the direct job creation strategies of the New Deal era as a way to meet the needs of structurally disadvantaged workers in particular. The A. Philip Randolph Institute, for example, called for a "structural" approach to reaching full employment in its own ten-year plan for ending poverty, pointing explicitly to the need for a large and permanent store of meaningful and socially useful low-skilled jobs.

While endorsing guaranteed jobs and income, National Welfare Rights Organization (NWRO) activists also challenged a whole set of cultural and economic biases embedded in New Deal social policy in their efforts to establish a right to welfare and abolish the invidious distinctions between the working and welfare poor. These biases—about single mothers, about what constituted legitimate "work," about who could and should be the household breadwinner, and about the degrading influence of welfare "dependency"—stood at the very core of the New Deal's preference for wage-earning as the gateway to the full benefits of social and economic security. Among other things, challenging these biases would require taking on the institutional structure as well as the categorical restrictions of what feminist scholars would later refer to as the "two-channel" welfare state by shifting the administration of means-tested public assistance from often racially biased state and local authorities to the federal government and treating such assistance as an entitlement on par with social insurance (Gordon 1994; Kessler-Harris 2001; Kornbluh 2007; Lieberman 1998; Nelson 1994). More controversially, challenging these biases required transgressing age-old proscriptions against cash relief for able-bodied men in particular—a taboo, as welfare rights activists were quick to point out, that rested on largely fictional distinctions. Large numbers of poor women, whether categorically eligible for public assistance or not, were expected to work in the low-wage labor force, an expectation enforced by low benefits and arbitrary welfare rules keyed to the needs of local low-wage labor markets, among other things. An adequate welfare system would empower them to avoid exploitative labor and to raise their children in dignity. At the same time, what these women in the unorganized low-wage labor force needed was what their feminist counterparts in the labor movement had long been pushing for: equal pay, employment and training for better jobs, and, especially, access to affordable child care (Cobble 2004). This challenge in turn pointed to yet another set of inequities created by the public-private or "divided" structure of the New Deal welfare state, which made access to health coverage, child care, fuller pensions, and other benefits that many considered to be public goods dependent on privately negotiated employee or union contracts—leaving millions of lower-wage workers out in the cold (Hacker 2002; Klein 2003; Michel 2000).

But what would prove to be the most divisive and fiercely resisted set of challenges to the inequities and exclusions of the New Deal order had to do with the largely hidden subsidies it provided for the nation's burgeoning postwar middle class in housing policy, which throughout the postwar decades had been the largely unrecognized battleground of white racial and class privilege. Here, too, the challenge mounted by civil rights and housing reform advocates had important implications for a substantial proportion of the low-wage working class.

As a system officially dedicated to providing "a decent home and a suitable living environment for every American family," New Deal housing policy had all the problems of income support—and then some.[3] It was structurally bifurcated into deliberately ungenerous, locally controlled public housing and a far more generous, if hidden, system of subsidies for working- and middle-class homeowners. By the mid-1940s, that hidden infrastructure had come to include a sizable public-private mortgage market anchored by the Federal National Mortgage Association (the New Deal–era government agency, subsequently privatized, colloquially known as Fannie Mae), federally insured mortgages, targeted benefits for veterans through the GI Bill of Rights, and a wide variety of tax incentives and subsidies for real estate developers and homeowners alike, including the federal income tax deduction for mortgage interest costs. The system both relied on and helped to institutionalize an also unacknowledged structure and geography of racial, class, and gender exclusions, upheld by the rules and underwriting practices that regulated access to mortgage credit, judicially sanctioned zoning laws, local land use planning, and widespread (if officially unconstitutional in the wake of the *Shelley v. Kraemer* decision of 1948) use of racial covenants. Segregationist policies and practices, in the meantime, were justified in the neutralized language of scientifically determined credit risk and property values (Freund 2007; Morgan 2003).

Housing policy was also beholden to a wide array of well-organized private interests—from the real estate, mortgage banking, savings and loan, and insurance industries to the building and construction trade unions. Despite significant differences among them, private housing industry interests were unified in their opposition to anything that hinted of "socialist" housing, in their deepening investment in private single-family homeownership, and in their interest in maintaining a steady stream of subsidies for the private housing market. In the late 1940s, during the extended debates leading up to the passage of the landmark Housing Act of 1949, private interests had aligned with conservatives in Congress to restrict the reach and otherwise to contain the growth of public housing by confining eligibility to the very poor. They had also organized to block legislative support for the construction of cooperative housing—an idea favored by generations of progressive housing advocates as a way to build affordable housing for the low-paid working classes (Biles 2011, 25–40; O'Connor 1999; Radford 1996). The result was a federal housing system that was notoriously inadequate in its provisions for the bottom "one-third of a nation" targeted by the New Deal housers in their initial plans. Public housing was chronically underfunded, regularly fell short of its legislatively mandated production goals, and was subject to the widely divergent standards and biases of local authorities. Thanks to legislatively imposed income ceilings and racial bias, it was also inaccessible to most of the low-wage working class. The system was chronically inattentive and basically without institutional mechanisms for maintaining affordable rental housing for the millions of working-class families who for reasons of income, race, or gender were basically shut out of the national drive to promote affordable homeownership and the comparatively generous, destigmatized public subsidies that it provided.

These gaps and inequities in provision were only compounded by the postwar veneration of homeownership—ideological as well as material—as a badge of solid citizenship and a source of at least modest wealth accumulation for the nation's working and middle classes. As homeownership rates began to rise in the postwar decades—from 44 percent in 1940 to 65 percent in 1970 overall, with highs of 80 percent among affluent white households and substantial racial gaps at all income levels—home equity became the most important source of accumulated assets for these households. Policymakers had also come to recognize homeownership as a hedge against inflation—a consideration that would only grow in importance amid rapidly rising inflation rates in the late 1960s and 1970s—though of course this was the case only for homeowners with access to fixed, insured mortgages and reliably appreciating housing markets. But even more important than its association with wealth accumulation and financial stability was the pride of place that homeownership quickly assumed within postwar social policy as a gateway to the amenities of upward mobility—middle-class status, civic standing, access to credit and to favored educational opportunities, and, especially in the face of civil rights movement demands, a privileged political identity (Nicolaides 2002; Self 2003). Indeed, the push for federal fair housing provisions was the most stubbornly resisted plank in the civil rights movement's legislative agenda; such provisions were finally passed in 1968, more than two decades after President Harry Truman's Committee on Civil Rights had called for an end to discrimination in housing in its report *To Secure These Rights* (President's Committee on Civil Rights 1947).

As a major, hard-fought breakthrough for the postwar civil rights movement, the 1968 Fair Housing Act was part of a more ambitious reform agenda that defined its goals in terms of the expansive promises of the 1949 Housing Act while aiming to redress the many gaps and inequities that had been created in its wake. Passed amid intensified pressure to invest in the nation's cities in the wake of mass urban uprisings and the release of the *Kerner Report* (National Advisory Commission on Civil Disorders 1968), the Johnson administration's massive Housing and Urban Development Act of 1968 garnered approval for a huge expansion in the production of low- and moderate-income units. It also created an expansive new program, known as Section 235, to subsidize homeownership for white and minority low-wage earners, especially but not exclusively in inner-city neighborhoods. Homeownership, LBJ said in a message tying the initiative to the "crisis of the cities," would give low-income Americans access to a "cherished dream" as well as the psychological boost of "something to be proud of" within their communities (Johnson 1968).

The Section 235 program was very much built into the existing system of public subsidy for public-private interest—which goes a long way toward explaining its popularity in the private real estate, banking, and home-building industries, as well as its bipartisan appeal. It operated much like the increasingly generous homeownership benefit for veterans under the auspices of the GI Bill, which by the mid-1950s was subsidizing growing numbers of working- as well as middle-class soldiers and veterans, with assistance for down payments, deeply subsidized mortgages, and federally guaranteed insurance (Frydl 2009, 263–302). Under the Section 235 program, first-time low-earning buyers—households traditionally too poor to make down payments and keep up a mortgage—paid steeply reduced interest rates (as low as 1 percent) on mortgages issued in the private market. Low-income homeowners were expected to pay 20 percent of their monthly income toward mortgage and insurance costs; the Federal Housing Administration (FHA), by then absorbed within the Department of Housing and Urban Development (HUD), subsidized the rest through direct payments to private providers. Administration officials also pushed the program as a way to stabilize ghetto neighborhoods and to close the gap between minority and white homeownership rates. Embarrassed by revelations of rampant and officially sanctioned redlining practices, federal officials and private industry providers also promised to promote homeownership in minority and mixed-race neighborhoods where they had not been willing to lend before, by stopping past discriminatory practices.

For all its expansive promise, however, the 1968 Housing Act left critical structural imbalances intact. Keyed to private industry interests, the Section 235 program had few mechanisms for guarding first-time buyers against the hazards of deceptive lending practices, shoddy construction, or the very real risks of declining housing values, especially in low-income and segregated minority neighborhoods (Bratt 2007, 45–50). Nor, promises of change to the contrary, did it do much to change the segregated structure of private housing markets (Civil Rights Commission 1971). Despite the legislation's emphasis on producing moderate-income rental housing, low-wage workers remained at least partly shut out from its benefits after conservatives insisted on maintaining restrictive income ceilings on eligibility for subsidized housing of any kind (Biles 2011).

Like left-liberal proposals to establish an encompassing guaranteed income, then, the Johnson administration's expansive housing initiatives underscored the ambitions and limitations of Great Society efforts to extend and revise the terms of the New Deal social contract to include low-wage workers. Despite important differences among them, what Great Society liberals like James Tobin and movement activists of the liberal left had in common was a basic recognition that informed their efforts to achieve fuller guarantees of jobs, income, housing, and economic rights: even at the height of postwar affluence, and despite all it had done to create a genuinely prosperous working and middle class, the New Deal order was failing a substantial proportion of the non-unionized working class—those who, for reasons of race, gender, geography, or class, had been unequally treated or excluded altogether. The struggle to redress these inequities had been central to progressive working-class and civil rights politics for decades, and it realized important successes.

And yet, in structuring their efforts around the needs of low-wage workers as low-income or "working poor" families, liberal policymakers in particular tended to minimize the need for more direct interventions to deal with the tangle of structural inequities embedded in labor and housing markets. Nor would the idea of expanding the reach of social welfare policy prove nearly as straightforward as it once might have seemed—raising, as it did, all sorts of questions about deservingness and un-deservingness and about work versus welfare "dependency" that were deeply ingrained in American political culture as well as in the existing structure of the welfare state. The very features that made the existing system inequitable, fragmented, and incomplete also "channeled" its social politics in ways that made it difficult to sustain broad-based coalitions for even the more modest versions of the universalizing reforms envisioned in their various plans to end poverty, achieve at least a minimum level of economic security for all, stabilize minority working-class neighborhoods, and extend housing and homeownership subsidies to the low-wage working class. This would be even more the case in the face of growing division within the Vietnam War–torn Democratic Party and increasingly well-organized opposition from the political right. Equally significant, the viability of such plans rested on the ability to sustain New Deal liberalism—reformed and re-envisioned as the Great Society—as both an economic and a political proposition by sustaining full employment, rising wages, and economic growth. In the absence of these conditions, the quest for some version of a New Deal for low-wage workers would prove increasingly difficult to sustain.

THE END OF AFFLUENCE AND THE CHANGING POLITICS OF SOCIAL PROVISION

Whatever their limitations, by the early 1970s the most ambitious Great Society antipoverty and housing efforts were largely stalled. The guaranteed income did become a centerpiece of President Richard M. Nixon's domestic policy agenda in 1969, in the comparatively limited form of the Family Assistance Plan (FAP), which, among other things, included work requirements and reduced benefits for large segments of those already on welfare. Various versions of Nixon's FAP were subject to intense debate in Congress (and within the administration) before its final demise in 1972 in the face of opposition from congressional conservatives and welfare rights advocates and waning support from Nixon himself (Steensland 2008, chs. 3–4). From the start, however, FAP had been tuned much more to the politics of welfare reform than to efforts to end poverty, a politics Nixon sought to play to his own electoral advantage by stoking resentments among the "working" poor families who stood to gain benefits from his program and the "nonworking" welfare poor who would be eligible for less (O'Connor 1998).[4]

The Section 235 homeownership program similarly experienced early momentum followed by major roadblocks. Early assessments treated it as a major success story, based on measurable increases in low-income homeownership. But the program was soon tainted by an enormous scandal when new home-buyers in ghettoized neighborhoods in Detroit, Philadelphia, and other major cities found themselves subject to rampant fraud, shoddy construction, fast-declining property values, and draconian foreclosure proceedings—leading to widely publicized 1971 investigations and congressional hearings that found evidence of collusion between FHA officials and unscrupulous, unregulated mortgage lenders.[5] By then, housing had also become the front line of the politics of backlash against both civil rights and the New Deal welfare state in battles that were beginning to spread from city neighborhoods to the hitherto racially exclusive suburbs.

More important than these internal dynamics, however, were two broader developments during the 1970s that undercut the income support and housing reform initiatives first launched in the late 1960s and limited their capacity to meet the needs of the low-wage working class. The first was the onset of a series of destabilizing economic "shocks"—including two recessions, major oil shortages, sustained "stagflation" in the latter years of the decade, and industrial stagnation—that marked the end of proverbial postwar affluence and the beginning of an era of wage declines and rising inequality. These and related developments in turn undercut the political-economic basis of New Deal and Great Society social provision and undermined Keynesian confidence in the capacity to sustain full employment while keeping inflation in check.

Second, and related, was an accompanying shift in electoral and movement politics in which the allegiances of the "silent" or "forgotten" white working- and middle-class majority would figure prominently (Cowie 2010; Lassiter 2007). Although the full contours of political change—and the role of an ideologically charged conservative movement in bringing it about—were still far from view, Nixon's intense determination to dismantle the liberal "excesses" of the Great Society, starting with the War on Poverty, was an indicator of important shifts in the politics of social provision to come. Nixon announced his Family Assistance Plan as part of a broader "New Federalism," a strategy to rechannel if not necessarily to stem government growth through a combination of block grants, decentralization, privatization, and reliance on more individualized, market-based approaches to public assistance. And like the battle over his Family Assistance Plan, the struggle to meet the housing needs of the lower-wage working class—those left out of the New Deal promise of economic security—gave Nixon an opening to exploit the racial fears and economic anxieties that would divide the New Deal electoral base. It also provided an opportunity to make institutional inroads toward a less collectivized, more market-based, and less generous vision of government responsibility for the poor, even as market-based subsidies were growing more important for the stability—as well as the sense of entitlement—of the more affluent working and middle classes.

It was within this context that the Earned Income Tax Credit (EITC) was created as the chief means of providing federal income support for low-wage workers (later supplemented by earned income credit provisions in some states). The EITC is a refundable tax credit that effectively operates as a wage subsidy for low-income workers with dependent children. Many consider it to be the most important and effective social policy for low-wage workers, mostly because of its fairly consistent bipartisan support (at least until the late 1990s, when its rapid growth into the nation's largest antipoverty program drew the ire of the more and more extremist antigovernment factions of the conservative movement), and because it is one of the few antipoverty programs that has expanded substantially since its establishment in 1975, to the point where it now reaches low-wage earning families above as well as below the federal poverty line.[6] And yet, the dynamics of the EITC's evolution and growth have also been shaped by the political and economic trends that have seriously undermined the standing of the low-wage working class, even as they have expanded its ranks.

The origins and early genesis of the EITC point to just how much the politics of social provision had changed by the early 1970s. Where Great Society efforts had centered on increased benefits and expanded eligibility for direct income support, the EITC was framed as a way to provide tax relief for low-wage workers—who at the time were facing social security payroll tax hikes that would only rise further over the course of the next two decades—and to keep them off the welfare rolls. The tax credit was also a product of the extended struggles over Nixon's FAP and welfare reform more generally—and one reason why, from the beginning, EITC benefits have targeted families with children. Among the EITC's lead sponsors in Congress was Senator Russell Long, a conservative Democrat (Louisiana) well known for his animosity toward welfare rights; he proposed the credit as a "work bonus" scheme designed to supplement low-wage workers' incomes while providing an incentive to stay in the workforce rather than turn to welfare. After several failed attempts, the EITC was passed as part of the Tax Reduction Act of 1975. It initially offered modest benefits and remained limited in reach (Howard 1997).

Starting in the 1980s, the EITC would figure more and more prominently in efforts not just to reform welfare and boost the incomes of low-wage workers but to bring the era of "big government" liberalism to an end, through a growing emphasis on wealth-favoring tax cuts, selective spending limits, cutbacks in direct spending for the poor, and tax code changes that made the system less progressive. The first major expansion in EITC coverage and benefits came in the wake of dramatic tax and spending cuts in the first years of the Reagan administration that severely restricted welfare eligibility, ended provisions that had allowed recipients to retain income from work, and raised poverty rates among low-wage workers while lowering taxes for the affluent. EITC expansion was incorporated into the Tax Reform Act of 1986, which effectively eliminated federal income tax (though not payroll tax) liability for families at the very bottom of the income distribution, in part as a way of offsetting the distributional impact of the tax rate reductions at the upper end (Howard 1997, 145–49). These and subsequent EITC expansions (in 1990 and 1993) also took place during a period when federal policymakers showed little inclination to stem the tide of declining wages and had decisively turned away from full employment in favor of inflation-fighting in economic policy. Indeed, the EITC had bipartisan appeal for conservative Democrats and Republicans in part because it was an alternative to a minimum wage hike (Gitterman 2009; Howard 1997, 150–52).

Low-income housing policy showed a similar pattern of escalating retreat from Great Society spending and direct provision commitments accompanied by a shift toward more modest, indirect, and privatized measures delivered as market subsidies and through the tax code. Using the Section 235 scandals and rising inflation fears as justification, the Nixon administration pursued a strategy of massive resistance—most overtly to the civil rights provisions of the 1968 housing acts, but more broadly to their expansive affordable housing production goals. In a public and humiliating standoff, the administration forced a halt to Housing and Urban Development Secretary George Romney's efforts to enforce antidiscrimination legislation and otherwise to back integration in the suburbs (Bonastia 2006). In 1973 Nixon declared a moratorium on public and subsidized housing production and subsequently implemented a major overhaul of the entire system by shifting away from construction altogether to individual (Section 8) vouchers for use in the private rental market. Low-income housing was targeted for even deeper cutbacks during the early years of the Reagan administration. In 1986, as part of the same sweeping tax reform legislation that expanded the EITC, Congress established the Low-Income Housing Tax Credit (LIHTC) to attract private (for-profit and nonprofit) developers into the low- and moderate-income rental market. Although the LIHTC remains a mainstay of affordable rental housing production for low-wage workers, it is minuscule in comparison to the home mortgage deduction subsidy for homeowners, which disproportionately benefits upper-income households and was preserved in the 1986 tax reforms following intensive lobbying from the real estate and banking industries, among others. Nor has the combination of vouchers and tax credits ever come close to bridging the gap between what low-wage workers make and what they need to pay the rent—a gap that continues to grow (Dolbeare and Crowley 2007; National Low Income Housing Coalition 2012).

In the meantime, structural changes in broader housing and labor markets would prove far more consequential for low-wage workers, albeit in ways that would only later become fully apparent. Critical to the postwar housing boom had been a fairly stable combination of high employment, high growth, stable (if necessarily subsidized) credit markets and housing prices, and, especially, wages sufficient for at least the more privileged segment of the white male working class to afford a down payment and fixed monthly mortgage payments. All that was to change starting in the late 1960s and early 1970s, when the combination of falling wages, rising inflation, the fallout from an international credit "crunch" that shook up U.S. mortgage markets, and the ongoing squeeze from the war in Vietnam threatened to send the homeownership industry into decline. That looming threat, which was especially keenly felt by the mortgage banking industry, had led to one of the lesser-noticed provisions of the 1968 Fair Housing Act, the semiprivatization of Fannie Mae and the authorization of mortgage securitization. This began a sequence of interventions that, in the name of saving the "American dream" of homeownership, completely changed the dynamics of mortgage markets.

Over the course of several years, these interventions would lay the political and institutional groundwork for the push to "financialize" homeownership and to promote it as both a form and a source of investment capital, beginning with the extension of Fannie Mae and newly established Freddie Mac benefits to the "conventional" mortgage market in 1970; a spate of judicially sanctioned challenges to state usury laws throughout the 1970s and 1980s that opened the door first to higher interest rates and eventually, along with a much wider array of deregulatory measures, to the exploding market for subprime mortgages; the emergence of a new array of mostly unregulated mortgage origination and lending institutions; and legislation that authorized Wall Street's entry into the market for securitized mortgage debt, along with the ever-more "innovative" financial instruments, such as collateralized debt obligations, designed to raise more and more investment capital—and profit—from other people's debt. In an era of unsteady wages and employment, homeownership—and access to the credit necessary to attain it—would grow in importance as a promise of stability for working- and middle-class families, but it would take an enormous amount of ultimately destabilizing interventions to prop it up (Hyman 2011; Immergluck 2009). As would become all too clear in the wake of the subprime mortgage collapse, this promise was also based on the illusion that housing values could only go up.

THE TRIUMPH OF NEOLIBERAL REFORM

More than any other set of issues, however, reforming the nation's poor laws would be the centerpiece of an ideological reform agenda meant, among other things, as a definitive break from the New Deal social contract and a reorientation of social policy from wage-earning to wealth. Laid out in stark terms by the 1994 Republican "Contract with America," the reform agenda envisioned by avowedly "limited government" conservatives called for measures ranging from balanced budget and tax limitation

constitutional amendments to federal "tough on crime" measures, a unilat-
eralist approach to national security, and congressional term limits. Though
never fully realized, the Contract with America had immense material and
political consequences for low-wage workers, and indeed for all working-
age people facing any degree of economic hardship or insecurity. Nowhere
was this more evident than in the "end of welfare as we know it," signed
into law as the Personal Responsibility and Work Opportunity Reconciliation Act (PRWORA) of 1996 by President Bill Clinton. Framed as an attack
on welfare "dependency," out-of-wedlock birth, the legitimacy of single-
motherhood, and the growth of a permissive "big government," the bill
crystallized many of the resentments that Nixon had been trying to engage
in his efforts to appeal to the "forgotten men" of the white working class.
But considered as a way of responding to what, by the 1990s, was a growing
and more widely recognized crisis of low-wage work, the end of welfare
also fit in with a much older tradition—that of using poor law reform to
unshackle labor markets from the obligations and regulations imposed by
the state and in the process asserting the primacy of the deregulated market
as the ultimate arbiter of the common good. This deregulation linked the
end of welfare to the earlier reform efforts of the 1970s as part of a longer
history in which episodes of economic crisis and change have created openings for reforms that involve a basic rewriting of the social contract (Block
and Somers 2003; Katz 1996; Piven and Cloward 1971; Polanyi 1944/1971).

Thus, as outlined in the Contract with America, the vision of welfare-
ending reform that would eventually become law stood in stark contrast to
the poverty-ending minimum income guarantee plans of the late 1960s. Ending, rather than extending, the entitlement to welfare was the new poor law's
signature goal: no longer would public assistance of any kind be available
as a matter of right to people who met even the most stringent of eligibility
requirements. Nor would the federal government claim responsibility for
ensuring economic security for anyone, let alone for all: funding would be
allocated through block grants to the states and would also be subject to
annually reduced spending caps. Although given added leeway to design
their programs, states would be subject to escalating penalties if they did
not move quickly enough to reduce their rolls. Regardless of need, families
would no longer be eligible for assistance after variable periods of time. (Time
limits vary by state, but are federally capped at five years over the lifetime.)
Wage-earning work, rather than a gateway to the collective entitlements of
economic citizenship, would be an object lesson in the virtues of fending
for oneself: recipients of assistance from what was renamed the Temporary
Assistance for Needy Families (TANF) program would be required to work
in the paid labor force as a condition of receiving aid and to cooperate in
state efforts to establish paternity and collect child support. The role of the

state would be to conform to the demands of the deregulated market, rather than the other way around.

The end of welfare once again set the stage for the expansion of the Earned Income Tax Credit, in this case as one of a wider array of so-called nonwelfare measures to supplement the wages of a low-wage workforce that, by design, would swell with the entry of single mothers—which is to say, the formerly "welfare" poor. Whether supportive of the 1996 reforms or not, advocacy groups and administrators in some localities promised to use the combination of TANF, the EITC, child support, subsidized child care, and education and training as a work support program, and they managed, in the context of initially raised state budgets and high employment rates, to meet with limited success. By 2005, however, in the wake of economic downturn, rising unemployment, federal and local budget cuts, and a new round of hard-line conservative gains in Congress, any initial gains for the newly "working" poor had largely been reversed. Reauthorization legislation in 2005 put even more severe limitations on TANF's education, training, and work support provisions, and even more aggressive pressure was put on local administrators, and their budgets, to put people to work, keep them off the rolls, and further shrink the social safety net (Morgen, Acker, and Weigt 2012; National Poverty Center 2012; Trisi and Pavetti 2012; Zedlewski 2012).

Even more than the social policy particulars, the end of welfare heralded the triumph of an anti–New Deal political economy and economic reform agenda. Wealth, not full employment and high wages, would be the engine of growth. The role of government was to protect the rights and interests of property and otherwise to step out of the market's way. Taxes, especially on capital gains, were to be lowered at all costs. The balanced budget would rein in government spending. None of this could be accomplished without concerted and ongoing government intervention, whether to dismantle or, in the case of welfare, to impose an ever-expanding host of disciplinary rules.

It was in this much-altered political economy, driven by much-altered economic priorities, that policymakers, foundations, nonprofit organizations, and a widening cadre of academics and community-based activists returned to the idea of promoting homeownership as a solution to poverty and a ticket to upward mobility for the low-wage working class, but more tellingly as a personally and socially transformative form of asset accumulation that would give poor people access to the advantages of wealth (Immergluck 2009; Katz 2009). Though it picked up on ideas about promoting tenant ownership in public housing that had been pushed by Margaret Thatcher and the Reagan-era HUD secretary Jack Kemp in the 1980s, something resembling a homeownership and assets-building movement did not come more prominently into view until the early 1990s (McCulloch 2001; Sherradan 1991). By then, the wealth-building approach had an ideologically eclectic but decidedly bipartisan base of support, and it drew on analyses that focused on the material as well as the (allegedly) cultural value of homeownership (Rohe and Watson 2007). By the late 1990s, the most exuberant enthusiasts were touting homeownership as the ultimate postwelfare solution to poverty. In this, they were boosted by two federal initiatives—the first by the Clinton administration and the second by the George W. Bush administration—to expand homeownership to unprecedented levels (which they reached in 2004 at 68 percent overall) by targeting low-income minorities for assistance. As would become all too powerfully clear, these initiatives did little more than paper over the deeper problems of inequality, declining wages, and the growing insecurity of wage-earning itself, all of which made easy access to ownership—and taking on huge amounts of debt—seem like not so much a sure way as the only way to get ahead.

As even this partial survey suggests, recent history has produced a number of ideas about social policies that provide much-needed relief for low-wage workers—with decidedly mixed results. These interventions pale in significance, however, in comparison to the underlying shift from New Deal to neoliberal political and economic priorities that has contributed to the proliferation and declining conditions of low-wage work and the workers it employs. This is especially pronounced in the demise of full employment as a central commitment of economic policy and as the centerpiece of a more encompassing antipoverty agenda, as envisioned by James Tobin and other Great Society liberals more than four decades ago. It is also evident in the political and ideological retreat from a commitment to fair labor standards, economic security, and "freedom from want" as signposts of economic health. In these and other ways, history points us to where the conversation about contemporary policy and politics needs to start and also shows us what it needs to include if we are not to lose sight of the standards of fairness, decency, and economic justice established by earlier generations of organizers and policy advocates for what an economy that works for workers looks like and what wage-earning for *all* workers can and should provide.

Thus, the contemporary policy discussion starts from the recognition that the problem of low-wage work is not about declining income alone. It is about the historically degraded condition of wage-earning as a valued social and economic endeavor and the role of political choices over the past three decades in bringing that condition about. It is about the striking decline in mobility for all American workers since the late 1970s, especially in comparison to their counterparts in advanced industrial democracies

(Russell Sage Foundation and Pew Charitable Trust 2011). It is about the millions of workers who have been left less economically secure, less well represented in politics and in the workplace, and more subject to degrading demands from their employers (Ehrenreich 2001; Greenhouse 2008; Shulman 2005). And it is about the by-now-familiar economic indicators of the New Gilded Age: falling wages at the bottom; rising concentrations of wealth at the very top; and, more recently, the decidedly top-heavy nature of the "recovery" from the Great Recession of 2008 (O'Connor 2011; U.S. Financial Crisis Inquiry Commission 2010).

The policy agenda for low-wage workers likewise extends beyond income and assets to encompass a broader scope, starting with economic policies committed to achieving full employment and better jobs and including the range of interventions considered in subsequent chapters in this volume. Collectively, they call attention to the need for a comprehensive policy and political agenda that reopens channels for effective work- and community-based organizing; establishes effective and effectively enforced labor standards; creates a new version of the deliberately shredded safety net for the poor and unemployed; and reintroduces fair compensation and equitable distribution as baseline principles of political economy.

History also reminds us that creating an economy that works for workers does not mean simply going back to the way we (never) were. Relevant though it remains as a framework for more just and inclusive economic citizenship, the New Deal left many gaps and inequities that made low-wage work an enduring problem throughout the postwar years—and that remain unresolved today. What it does mean is using the New Deal social contract much as movement activists did in the 1960s: as a framework for asking how the economic rights and commitments that the New Deal envisioned can be realized in a much-altered twenty-first-century economic environment, and on more fully inclusive terms. This approach to framing the issues is especially important in light of the key policy challenges ahead: the challenge of creating and sustaining high standards of employment in an ever-more globalized economy; the challenge of making housing affordable in a culture still entrenched in private homeownership; and the challenge of creating a sense of shared need and common fate in a political culture that has grown more skeptical of collectivized social provision.

Finally, history offers a powerful sense of just how much is wrapped up in the questions of work and wages—and why. While it has become something of a cliché to tie well-paid work opportunities and shared prosperity to the pursuit of the American dream of upward mobility, a deeper look at the historical record underscores how central they have been to the pursuit of fairness, freedom, and political as well as economic democracy. To frame a discussion of an economy that works for workers in these terms may not provide an exact blueprint for how to get there, but it establishes the discussion on the moral high ground of American democracy, which, as history reminds us, is both a powerful and an appropriate starting point for reform.

NOTES

1. Binyamin Appelbaum and Robert Gebeloff, "Tax Burden for Most Americans Lower Than in the 1980s," *New York Times*, November 29, 2012; see also Hungerford (2011).

2. FDR first laid out the Economic Bill of Rights in his 1944 State of the Union Address, but it subsequently became a central campaign theme. It represents a distillation of rights he had enumerated in his famous 1941 "Four Freedoms" speech, delivered amid the looming threat of world war, in which he laid out four "essential freedoms" fundamental to the preservation of democracy: freedom of speech, freedom of worship, freedom from want, and freedom from fear (Roosevelt 1941, 1944). For a fuller discussion of the political and ideological traditions FDR was drawing on, see Donohue (2003).

3. This was the language of the Housing Act of 1949, which would frequently be reiterated in subsequent legislation through the 1960s.

4. The Family Assistance Plan would have provided $1,600 for a family of four and was contingent on work requirements; Tobin's plan would have set the minimum at the poverty line, at the time roughly $3,000 for a family of four, while welfare rights activists called for significantly higher levels.

5. See, for example, Donald L. Barlett and James B. Steele, "Speculators Make a Killing on FHA Program," *Philadelphia Inquirer*, August 22, 1971.

6. The maximum EITC for 2012 ranged between $5,200 and $5,800 for families with two or three children and earning up to $45,000, or approximately double the federal poverty line. Recent analysis from the Center on Budget and Policy Priorities indicates that the EITC raised the incomes of 5.7 million families above the federal poverty line (approximately $23,000 for a family of four) (Sherman 2012).

REFERENCES

A. Philip Randolph Institute. 1966. *A "Freedom Budget" for All Americans: Budgeting Our Resources, 1966–1975, to Achieve "Freedom from Want."* New York: A. Philip Randolph Institute.

Alexander, Michelle. 2010. *The New Jim Crow: Mass Incarceration in the Age of Color Blindness*. New York: New Press.

Aron-Dine, Aviva, and Isaac Shapiro. 2006. "Share of National Income Going to Wages and Salaries at Record Low in 2006, Share of Income Going to Corporate Profits at Record High." Washington, D.C.: Center on Budget and Policy Priorities.

Bartels, Larry M. 2010. *Unequal Democracy: The Political Economy of the New Gilded Age.* New York: Russell Sage Foundation.

Biles, Roger. 2011. *The Fate of Cities: Urban America and the Federal Government, 1945–2000.* Lawrence: University Press of Kansas.

Block, Fred, and Margaret Somers. 2003. "In the Shadow of Speenhamland: Social Policy and the Old Poor Law." *Politics and Society* 31(2): 283–323.

Bonastia, Christopher. 2006. *Knocking on the Door: The Federal Government's Attempt to Desegregate the Suburbs.* Princeton, N.J.: Princeton University Press.

Boris, Eileen, and Jennifer Klein. 2012. *Caring for America: Home Health Workers in the Shadow of the Welfare State.* New York: Oxford University Press.

Bratt, Rachel. 2007. "Homeownership for Low-Income Households: A Comparison of the Section 235, Nehemiah, and Habitat for Humanity Programs." In *Chasing the American Dream: New Perspectives on Affordable Homeownership,* ed. William M. Rohe and Harry L. Watson. Ithaca, N.Y.: Cornell University Press.

Brick, Howard. 2006. *Transcending Capitalism: Visions of a New Society in Modern American Thought.* Ithaca, N.Y.: Cornell University Press.

Bricker, Jesse, Arthur B. Kinnickell, Kevin B. Moore, and John Sabelhaus. 2012. "Changes in Family Finance from 2007 to 2010: Evidence from the Survey of Consumer Finances." Washington, D.C.: U.S. Federal Reserve. Available at: http://www.federalreserve.gov/econresdata/scf/scf_2010.htm (accessed January 2013).

Chen, Anthony. 2009. *The Fifth Freedom: Jobs, Politics, and Civil Rights in the United States, 1941–1972.* Princeton, N.J.: Princeton University Press.

Children's Defense Fund. 2007. "Programs and Campaigns: Cradle to Prison Pipeline Campaign." Washington, D.C.: Children's Defense Fund. Available at: http://www.childrensdefense.org/programs-campaigns/cradle-to-prison-pipeline/index.html (accessed January 2013).

Civil Rights Commission. 1971. "Homeownership for Lower Income Families: A Report on the Racial and Ethnic Impact of the Section 235 Program." Washington, D.C.: Civil Rights Commission.

Cobble, Dorothy Sue. 2004. *The Other Women's Movement: Workplace Justice and Social Rights in Modern America.* Princeton, N.J.: Princeton University Press.

Countryman, Matthew. 2006. *Up South: Rights and Black Power in Philadelphia.* Philadelphia: University of Pennsylvania Press.

Cowie, Jefferson. 2010. *Stayin' Alive: The 1970s and the Last Days of the Working Class.* New York: New Press.

Danziger, Sheldon, and Peter Gottschalk. 1995. *America Unequal.* Cambridge, Mass.: Harvard University Press.

Dolbeare, Cushing N., and Sheila Crowley. 2007. *Changing Priorities: The Federal Budget and Housing Assistance, 1976–2007*. Washington, D.C.: National Low Income Housing Coalition.

Donohue, Kathleen G. 2003. *Freedom from Want: American Liberalism and the Idea of the Consumer*. Baltimore: Johns Hopkins University Press.

Ehrenreich, Barbara. 2001. *Nickel and Dimed: On (Not) Getting By in America*. New York: Metropolitan Books.

Freeman, Richard B. 2007. *America Works: The Exceptional U.S. Labor Market*. New York: Russell Sage Foundation.

Freund, David. 2007. *Colored Property: State Policy and White Racial Politics in Suburban America*. Chicago: University of Chicago Press.

Friedman, Milton. 1962. *Capitalism and Freedom*. Chicago: University of Chicago Press.

Friedman, Milton, and Rose Friedman. 1979. *Free to Choose: A Personal Statement*. New York: Harcourt Brace.

Frydl, Kathleen. 2009. *The GI Bill*. New York: Cambridge University Press.

Gilens, Martin. 2012. *Affluence and Influence: Economic Inequality and Political Power in America*. Princeton, N.J.: Princeton University Press.

Gitterman, Daniel. 2009. *Boosting Paychecks: The Politics of Supporting America's Working Poor*. Washington, D.C.: Brookings Institution Press.

Gordon, Linda. 1994. *Pitied but Not Entitled: Single Mothers and the History of Welfare*. Cambridge, Mass.: Harvard University Press.

Gottschalk, Marie. 2006. *The Prison and the Gallows: The Politics of Mass Incarceration in America*. New York: Cambridge University Press.

Greenhouse, Steve. 2008. *The Big Squeeze: Tough Times for the American Worker*. New York: Anchor Books.

Hacker, Jacob. 2002. *The Divided State: The Battle over Public and Private Social Benefits in the United States*. New York: Cambridge University Press.

Hacker, Jacob S., and Paul Pierson. 2010. *Winner Take All Politics: How Washington Made the Rich Richer—and Turned Its Back on the Middle Class*. New York: Simon & Schuster.

Hamilton, Dona, and Charles Hamilton. 1997. *The Dual Agenda: Race and Social Welfare Policies of Civil Rights Organizations*. New York: Columbia University Press.

Handler, Joel F., and Lucie White, eds. 1999. *Hard Labor: Women and Work in the Post-Welfare Era*. Armonk, N.Y.: M. E. Sharpe.

Holzer, Harry J., and Demetra S. Nightingale. 2007. *Reshaping the American Workforce in a Changing Economy*. Washington, D.C.: Urban Institute Press.

Howard, Christopher. 1997. *The Hidden Welfare State: Tax Expenditures and Social Policy in the United States*. Princeton, N.J.: Princeton University Press.

Hungerford, Thomas L. 2011. "Changes in the Distribution of Income Among Tax Filers Between 1996 and 2006: The Role of Labor Income, Capital Income, and Tax Policy." Washington: Congressional Research Service.

Hyman, Louis. 2011. *Debtor Nation: The History of America in Red Ink.* Princeton, N.J.: Princeton University Press.

Immergluck, Dan. 2009. *Foreclosed: High-Risk Lending, Deregulation, and the Undermining of America's Mortgage Market.* Ithaca, N.Y.: Cornell University Press.

Johnson, Lyndon B. 1968. "Special Message to Congress on Urban Problems: 'The Crisis of the Cities.' " Santa Barbara, Calif.: University of California, The American Presidency Project (February 22). Available at: http://www.presidency. ucsb.edu/ws/index.php?pid=29386 (accessed January 2013).

Katz, Alyssa. 2009. *Our Lot: How Real Estate Came to Own Us.* New York: Bloomsbury.

Katz, Michael B. 1996. *In the Shadow of the Poor House: A Social History of Welfare in America.* New York: Basic Books.

———. 2001. *The Price of Citizenship: Redefining the American Welfare State.* New York: Metropolitan Books.

Katznelson, Ira. 2005. *When Affirmative Action Was White: An Untold History of Racial Inequality in America.* New York: W. W. Norton.

Kearns, Jeffrey. 2012. "Fed Says Family Wealth Plunged 38.8% in 2007–2010 on Housing." *Bloomberg,* June 11. Available at: http://www.bloomberg.com/news/ 2012-06-11/fed-says-family-wealth-plunged-38-8-in-2007-2010-on-home-values.html (accessed January 2013).

Kessler-Harris, Alice. 2001. *In Pursuit of Equity: Women, Men, and the Quest for Economic Citizenship in Twentieth-Century America.* New York: Oxford University Press.

Klein, Jennifer. 2003. *For All These Rights: Business, Labor, and the Shaping of America's Public-Private Welfare State.* Princeton, N.J.: Princeton University Press.

Kornbluh, Felicia. 2007. *The Battle for Welfare Rights: Politics and Poverty in Modern America.* Philadelphia: University of Pennsylvania Press.

Lassiter, Matthew. 2007. *The Silent Majority: Suburban Politics in the Sunbelt South.* Princeton, N.J.: Princeton University Press.

Lessig, Lawrence. 2011. *Republic, Lost: How Money Corrupts Congress—and a Plan to Stop It.* New York: Twelve.

Lichtenstein, Nelson. 2002. *State of the Union: A Century of American Labor.* Princeton, N.J., Princeton University Press.

Lieberman, Robert C. 1998. *Shifting the Color Line: Race and the American Welfare State.* Cambridge, Mass.: Harvard University Press.

Luce, Stephanie. 2004. *Fighting for a Living Wage.* Ithaca, N.Y.: Cornell University Press.

McCulloch, Heather. 2001. *Sharing the Wealth: Resident Ownership Mechanisms.* Oakland, Calif.: Policy Link.

McGee, Guian. 2008. *Liberalism and the Problem of Jobs.* Chicago: University of Chicago Press.

McLean, Nancy. 2006. *Freedom Is Not Enough: The Opening of the American Workplace.* Cambridge, Mass.: Harvard University Press.

Mettler, Suzanne. 2011. *The Submerged State: How Invisible Government Policies Undermine American Democracy.* Chicago: University of Chicago Press.

Michel, Sonya. 2000. *Children's Interests, Mother's Rights: The Shaping of America's Child Care Policy.* New Haven, Conn.: Yale University Press.

Milkman, Ruth. 2006. *L.A. Story: Immigrant Workers and the Future of the U.S. Labor Movement.* New York: Russell Sage Foundation.

Mishel, Lawrence R., Jared Bernstein, and Heidi Shierholz. 2009. *The State of Working America, 11th ed.* Ithaca, N.Y.: Cornell University Press.

Morgan, Guy. 2003. *Discriminating Risk: The U.S. Mortgage Lending Industry in the Twentieth Century.* Ithaca, N.Y.: Cornell University Press.

Morgen, Sandra, Joad Acker, and Jill Weigt. 2012. *Stretched Thin: Poor Families, Welfare Work, and Welfare Reform.* Ithaca, N.Y.: Cornell University Press.

Munger, Frank, ed. 2002. *Laboring Below the Line: The New Ethnography of Poverty, Low-Wage Work, and Survival in the Global Economy.* New York: Russell Sage Foundation.

National Advisory Commission on Civil Disorders. 1968. *Report of the National Advisory Commission on Civil Disorders (Kerner Report).* New York: Bantam.

National Low Income Housing Coalition. 2012. *Out of Reach, 2012.* Washington, D.C.: National Low Income Housing Coalition.

National Poverty Center. 2012. "Extreme Poverty in the United States, 1996 to 2011." Ann Arbor: University of Michigan, Gerald R. Ford School of Public Policy.

Nelson, Barbara. 1994. "The Two-Channel Welfare State." In *Pitied but Not Entitled: Single Mothers and the History of Welfare,* edited by Linda Gordon. Cambridge, Mass.: Harvard University Press.

Nicolaides, Becky. 2002. *My Blue Heaven: Life and Politics in the Working-Class Suburbs of Los Angeles, 1920–1965.* Chicago: University of Chicago Press.

O'Connor, Alice. 1998. "The False Dawn of Poor Law Reform." *Journal of Policy History* 10(1): 99–129.

———. 1999. "Swimming Against the Tide: A Brief History of Federal Assistance to Poor Communities." In *The Future of Community Development,* ed. Ronald Ferguson and William Dickens. Washington, D.C.: Brookings Institution Press.

———. 2001. *Poverty Knowledge: Social Science, Social Welfare, and the Poor in Twentieth Century U.S. History.* Princeton, N.J.: Princeton University Press.

———. 2011. "The End of Capitalism as We Know It and the Beginning of Reform." *Labor: Studies in Working Class History of the Americas* 8(4, December 21).

Piven, Frances Fox, and Richard A. Cloward. 1971. *Regulating the Poor: The Functions of Public Welfare.* New York: Vintage Books.

Polanyi, Karl. 1971. *The Great Transformation.* Boston: Beacon Press. (Originally published in 1944.)

Pollin, Robert, and Stephanie Luce. 2000. *The Living Wage: Building a Fair Economy.* New York: New Press.

Poole, Mary. 2006. *The Segregated Origins of Social Security*. Chapel Hill: University of North Carolina Press.

President's Committee on Civil Rights. 1947. *To Secure These Rights*. Available at: Harry S. Truman Library and Museum, http://www.trumanlibrary.org/civilrights/srights1.htm (accessed January 2013).

Radford, Gail. 1996. *Modern Housing for America: Policy Struggles in the New Deal Era*. Chicago: University of Chicago Press.

Raphael, Stephen, and Michael Stoll, eds. 2009. *Do Prisons Make Us Safer? The Benefits and Costs of the Prison Boom*. New York: Russell Sage Foundation.

Republican National Committee. 1994. *Contract with America: The Bold Plan by Newt Gingrich, Rep. Dick Armey, and the House Republicans to Save the Nation*. New York: Times Books.

Rodgers, Daniel. 2011. *Age of Fracture*. Cambridge, Mass.: Harvard University Press.

Rohe, William M., and Harry L. Watson, eds. 2007. *Chasing the American Dream: New Perspectives on Affordable Homeownership*. Ithaca, N.Y.: Cornell University Press.

Roosevelt, Franklin D. 1941. "State of the Union Address: The Four Freedoms." January 6. Available at: http://americanrhetoric.com/speeches/fdrthefourfreedoms.htm (accessed January 2013).

———. 1944. "State of the Union Message to Congress." January 11. Available at: http://www.fdrlibrary.marist.edu/archives/address_text.html (accessed January 2013).

Russell Sage Foundation and Pew Charitable Trust. 2011. "Does America Promote Mobility as Well as Other Nations?" Washington, D.C.: Pew Charitable Trusts.

Schulman, Bruce. 2001. *The Seventies*. New York: Free Press.

Schulman, Bruce, and Julian Zelizer. 2008. *Rightward Bound*. Cambridge, Mass.: Harvard University Press.

Self, Robert. 2003. *American Babylon: Race and the Struggle for Postwar Oakland*. Princeton, N.J.: Princeton University Press.

Sherman, Arloc. 2012. "Off the Charts: SNAP (Food Stamps) and Earned Income Tax Credit Had Big Antipoverty Impact in 2011." Washington, D.C.: Center on Budget and Policy Priorities, September 22. Available at: http://www.offthechartsblog.org/snap-food-stamps-and-earned-income-tax-credit-had-big-antipoverty-impact-in-2011/ (accessed January 2013).

Sherradan, Michael. 1991. *Assets and the Poor*. Armonk, N.Y.: M. E. Sharpe.

Shulman, Beth. 2005. *The Betrayal of Work: How Low-Wage Jobs Fail 30 Million Americans*. New York: New Press.

Simon, Jonathan. 2009. *Governing Through Crime: How the War on Crime Transformed American Democracy and Created a Culture of Fear*. New York: Oxford University Press.

Steensland, Brian. 2008. *The Failed Welfare Revolution: America's Struggle over Guaranteed Income Policy*. Princeton, N.J: Princeton University Press.

Stein, Judith. 2010. *Pivotal Decade: How the United States Traded Factories for Finance in the 1970s*. New Haven, Conn.: Yale University Press.

Sugrue, Thomas J. 1996. *Origins of the Urban Crisis*. Princeton, N.J.: Princeton University Press.

Thompson, Heather. 2010. "Why Mass Incarceration Matters: Rethinking Crisis, Decline, and Transformation in Postwar American History." *Journal of American History* 97(3): 703–34.

Tobin, James. 1967. "It Can Be Done! Conquering Poverty in the U.S. by 1976." *The New Republic* (June 3): 14–18.

Trisi, Danilo, and LaDonna Pavetti. 2012. "TANF Weakening as a Safety Net for Poor Families." Washington, D.C.: Center on Budget and Policy Priorities.

U.S. Department of Health, Education, and Welfare. 1969. *Toward a Social Report*. Washington: U.S. Government Printing Office.

U.S. Financial Crisis Inquiry Commission. 2010. "The Financial Crisis Inquiry Report." Washington: U.S. Government Printing Office.

Western, Bruce. 2006. *Punishment and Inequality in America*. New York: Russell Sage Foundation.

Western, Bruce, and Becky Pettit. 2010. *Collateral Costs: Incarceration's Effect on Economic Mobility*. Washington, D.C.: Pew Charitable Trusts.

Zedlewski, Sheila R. 2012. "Welfare Reform: What Have We Learned in Fifteen Years?" Washington, D.C.: Urban Institute.

Chapter 2 | What Can Labor Organizations Do for U.S. Workers When Unions Can't Do What Unions Used to Do?

Richard B. Freeman

THE STARTING POINT for any realistic assessment of what labor organizations can do for American workers is recognition that the traditional union model of organizing workers through representation elections and bargaining collectively with management has reached a dead end. With private-sector union density in single digits and falling and public-sector collective bargaining under attack, the only sensible answer to this chapter's title question is that unions will not accomplish much unless they find ways to have an impact on economic outcomes outside of collective bargaining.

In some ways the situation of labor in the early twenty-first century resembles that in 1932 when George Barnett, then president of the American Economic Association, declared that "I see no reason to believe that American trade unionism will . . . become in the next decade a more potent social influence . . . trade unionism is likely to be a declining influence in determining conditions of labor."[1] Barnett's analysis was predicated on the continuous fall in union density in the 1920s and Great Depression levels of joblessness that seemed to strengthen employers' ability to defeat any organizing efforts. Today a similar view would follow from the continuous fall in union density from the 1960s through the early 2010s, the weak job market during the Great Recession of 2007 to 2009, and the sluggish jobs recovery.

Barnett's prognostication was invalidated almost immediately after his address—millions of workers turned to unions for economic protection during the Great Depression. But the Great Recession has seen no such response. Indeed, the recent recession has, if anything, produced the opposite reaction: it has emboldened conservative attacks on public-sector

50

bargaining and union security clauses and forced unions into a circle-the-wagons defense of existing practices.

If defending the declining percentage of workers with access to collective bargaining was the entire story of labor in the 2000s, this chapter would end with a short rest in peace epitaph. But in the 2000s, declining union density and the Great Recession notwithstanding, labor activists, social entrepreneurs, and some unionists have developed new ways to mobilize workers and the public to press for improvements in labor conditions outside of collective bargaining. If unions and other labor organizations find ways to bring these successful innovations to scale, the answer to the title question will be "quite a bit" rather than "not much."

This chapter explores what unions and related labor organizations have begun to do for workers outside of collective bargaining. I begin by reviewing the problem posed for labor by the failure of the firm-based collective bargaining model, then examine some promising non–collective bargaining initiatives, and conclude by considering how these initiatives might expand to make labor a more potent influence on economic outcomes than it is today.

THE CONTRACTION OF COLLECTIVE BARGAINING

Union density declined in many advanced countries from the 1990s to the 2010s. The loss of density weakened the ability of unions to represent labor in society more in the United States, however, than in most other countries because many EU countries mandate the extension of collective agreements from signatory unions and employer federations or firms to workers or firms in entire sectors or regions. Mandatory extension maintains collective bargaining as the mode of setting pay and conditions of work despite falling union density. In the United States, by contrast, from the enactment of the National Labor Relations Act (NLRA) in 1935 to the present, private-sector unionism and collective bargaining have been coterminous. U.S. unions view themselves primarily as bargaining agents for workers in firms that recognize unions and as having little or no relation to other workers. When a worker leaves a unionized workplace, most unions make little or no effort to continue to provide services to that worker. Making collective bargaining the core activity of unions worked well when unions bargained for a substantial share of the workforce. But from the 1960s to the present, the collective bargaining model has run aground on the inability of unions to organize private-sector workers in the face of management opposition; economic conditions that reduce union bargaining power with employers; and political conditions that stymie union efforts to get Congress to amend the NLRA to make it easier for workers to form unions and bargain with employers. In the public sector, where union density has remained high,

Great Recession–induced reductions in public-sector revenues sparked a conservative effort to curb public-sector bargaining in the late 2000s by taking advantage of changes in density, concession bargaining, and changes in the use of work stoppages.

Density is fundamental to union strength. In 2012 private-sector density was at 6.6 percent—the lowest it has been since 1900, when total density, then based almost entirely on private-sector workers, was 6.8 percent (Freeman 1998, 291; see also U.S. Department of Labor 2013). In the 2000s, unions initiated National Labor Relations Board (NLRB) representation elections for so few workers that even had unions won all of the elections, the impact on density would have been barely noticeable.[2] Organizing outside the NLRB was too limited to counterbalance the natural drop in density when union plants closed or shrank and new establishments became non-union. Indicative of the decline of unionism, in 2009 more workers viewed company-appointed non-union committees as representing them with employers—presumably illegal under section 8(a)(2) of the NLRA—than reported that elected unions represented them (Godard and Frege 2010).

Within the organized sector, economic conditions forced many unions into *concession bargaining*. Consider the relation between the United Automobile Workers (UAW) and the "Big Three" auto firms. Between 2003 and 2008, plant closings and buyout and early-retirement programs reduced UAW membership at General Motors, Ford, and Chrysler from 350,000 to 139,000 workers.[3] When GM and Chrysler came close to collapse in the Great Recession, federal bailout aid kept them alive and helped Ford survive as well. The UAW took responsibility for retiree health care, accepted lower-pay entry jobs and profit-sharing arrangements in place of fixed pay, and acceded to other cost-saving givebacks.[4] The auto firms survived, and in the ensuing recovery workers gained substantial bonuses.[5] But from 2008 to 2011, employment in motor vehicles and motor vehicle manufacturing dropped 24.2 percent, and even with the rescue package and recovery, employment in mid-2012 was still 15.9 percent below its mid-1998 level.[6]

Work stoppages, which were once synonymous with workers striking for higher pay or better benefits, have increasingly become an employer's weapon to pressure workers to accept wage or benefit cuts or to break unions through lockouts.[7] More lockouts were reported in the early 2010s than ever before, from professional sports to manufacturing firms to the New York City Opera.[8] About 9 percent of work stoppages from 2010 to late 2012 resulted from lockouts, double the 4.6 percent of work stoppages that were lockouts in the 1990s and 2000s (Combs 2012a). Lockouts tend to be longer than strikes and have increased in length as some firms use long lockouts to destroy their existing unions (Combs 2012b). The greater length of lockouts means that the share of persons on a work stoppage due to a lockout at any point in time increased more than the lockout share of stoppages.

To arrest the decline in density unions have tried to convince Congress to enact pro-union labor law reforms whenever the Democrats control the federal government. Their efforts came up short in the 1970s under President Jimmy Carter, in the 1990s under President Bill Clinton, and in the 2000s under President Barack Obama. Efforts to invigorate union organizing by elevating former organizing directors to leadership roles in unions and the 2005 withdrawal of several major unions from the AFL-CIO to form the Change to Win coalition also failed to arrest the drop in density.

The public sector is the only place where unions held their own. Public-sector union density stabilized at around 37 percent in the 2000s.[9] With private-sector density falling and public-sector density rising, public-sector union membership surpassed private-sector membership in 2010. When recession-induced budget crises hit cities and states nationwide, however, opponents of unions launched a massive attack on public-sector bargaining on the grounds that collective bargaining had contributed substantially to the public-sector deficit problem (Freeman and Han 2012).[10] The American Legislative Exchange Council (ALEC), an association of conservative legislators, corporations, and foundations, promulgated bills to restrict public-sector bargaining and limit dues checkoffs, agency fees, and union political activities. The battle in Wisconsin over Republican governor Scott Walker's 2011 budget bill that ended public-sector collective bargaining except for police and fire induced a massive union response (Schneider 2011).[11] State petitions forced Governor Walker into a recall election but the pro–collective bargaining forces were unable to unseat him in the election. In Ohio, unions and their allies were more successful in overturning a bill to end collective bargaining for all public-sector employees in a statewide referendum. But in December 2011, a lame-duck Republican legislature in Michigan enacted a right-to-work law that outlawed agency shops for workers, with the exception of police and firefighters.[12] In these states and others, unions spent considerable resources defending the status quo against well-financed opponents who seemed orc-like in their efforts to accelerate the ongoing decline in collective bargaining.

What explains the continued decline of unions during the Great Recession and recovery compared to the spurt in unionism during the Great Depression?

Opinion polls suggest that the two economic disasters altered public attitudes toward unions differently. When unions had their Great Depression growth spurt between 1934 and 1939, the vast majority of Americans appear to have strongly favored unions (Freeman 1998, 268, table 8.1). The Gallup poll data in figure 2.1 show that in 1936 (the first time Gallup asked

Figure 2.1   Approval of Labor Unions Among Americans,
               1936 to 2011

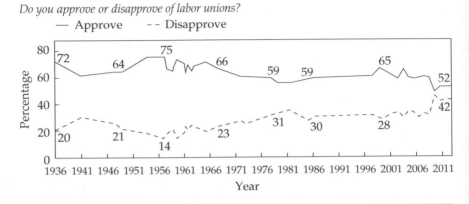

Do you approve or disapprove of labor unions?
— Approve   - - Disapprove

about attitudes toward unions), 72 percent approved of unions compared to 20 percent who disapproved.[13] The Depression had destroyed faith in the established economic order and convinced workers to seek new ways to structure their work lives and the economy. Attitudes toward unions in the Great Recession went the other way. The percentage approving unions fell from 60 percent in 2007 to 48 percent in 2009 and remained low, at 52 percent, through 2012. This fits with a general post–World War II pattern in which public approval of unions rises when unemployment is low and falls when unemployment is high (Silver 2009, data from 1948 to 2008; Madland and Walter 2010, 7).

Figure 2.2 shows a concomitant change in the responses of citizens to whether they want unions to have less, more, or the same influence on society. Between 2007 and 2009, the proportion who wanted unions to have less influence increased from 28 percent to 42 percent, after which it changed little through 2012. One possible explanation for the reduced support for unions in the Great Recession is the concentration of unionism among government employees, whose wages and benefits were obtained from taxes paid by private-sector workers who had little chance of unionizing and gaining higher wages and benefits from their employers. Many respondents may also have viewed the bailout of the auto firms as the UAW using its political power to get the federal government to help unionized auto workers at the expense of the rest of society (Madland and Walter 2010; Meyerson

Figure 2.2   Americans' Attitudes on the Influence of Labor Unions,
2000 to 2012

Would you personally like to see labor unions in the United States have more influence than they have today, or less influence than they have today?
— Same   - - Less   ····· More

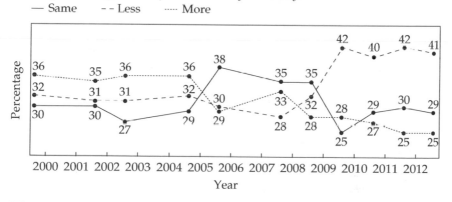

2012). Consistent with this, while before the Great Recession a majority of Americans believed that unions benefit not only their members but other workers as well, after the recession a majority believed that unions mostly harm nonmembers.[14]

But the most telling aspect of the increasingly negative attitudes toward unions is its partisan nature. Figure 2.3 shows that between 1999 and 2011 Republican approval of unions fell from 51 percent to 26 percent. By contrast, Democrats maintained a high approval of unions, while independents' approval of unions fell modestly. The Democratic-Republican gap in approval doubled from twenty-six points in 1999 to fifty-two points in 2011. The 2011 negative Republican attitude toward unionism is a far cry from the Republican attitude in the 1950s, when President Dwight Eisenhower thanked unions for their "unique contribution to the general welfare of the Republic—the development of the American philosophy of labor" (Eisenhower 1955).

Figure 2.4 shows another factor that may help explain union weakness in the current period: the widespread belief that unions will become weaker in the future. Although Gallup did not ask, "Will labor unions become stronger or weaker?" in the 1930s, the burst of strikes in 1933 and 1934, the development of industrial unionism in the mid-1930s, and the

Figure 2.3   Approval of Labor Unions, by Political Party, 1999 to 2011

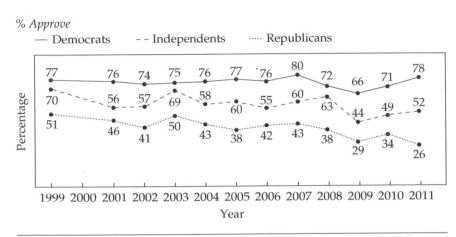

% *Approve*
— Democrats   - - Independents   ····· Republicans

Figure 2.4   Americans' Attitudes on the Future Strength
of Labor Unions, 2000 to 2012

*Thinking about the future, do you think labor unions in this country will become
stronger than they are today, the same as today, or weaker than they are today?*
— Stronger   - - Same   ····· Weaker

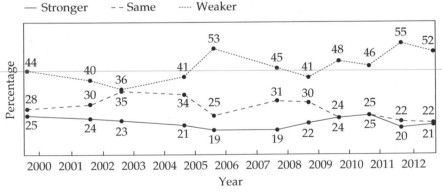

formation of the Congress of Industrial Organizations (CIO) suggest that a much larger proportion of Americans thought unions were the future rather than the past in the 1930s than was the case in the 2010s.

Americans have also soured on other economic and political institutions beyond unions in the past three decades. Reviewing diverse opinion polls, David Madland and Karla Walter (2010) report a drop in "favorable attitudes" toward and "confidence" in business from the 1970s and 1980s that exceeds the comparable loss of favorableness or confidence in labor. Since the Great Recession, a sizable proportion of Americans now believe that the country is headed in the wrong direction.[15] In 2011 the public rated lobbyists, major corporations, and financial institutions as the top institutions with "too much power" and placed unions in the middle of the pack, on par with state government and the legal system. The average responses, however, mask the partisan divide in attitudes toward unions. Republicans place unions just below the arch-villain federal government in their list of institutions with too much power, while Democrats place unions at the bottom of their list.[16] But regardless of where unions fit in the public perception of institutions with too much power, they are the only institution under such continuous attack as to face near-extinction unless they find new ways to operate.

LABOR ORGANIZATIONS WITHOUT COLLECTIVE BARGAINING

With the percentage of workers covered by collective bargaining steadily shrinking, activists inside and outside of unions have sought new ways to represent worker interests and maintain organized labor as the voice of workers in U.S. capitalism. In 2000, Joni Hersch, Larry Mishel, and I organized a National Bureau of Economic Research (NBER) conference on "Emerging Labor Market Institutions for the Twenty-First Century," held August 4–5, to examine the degree to which non–collective bargaining institutions were beginning to fill the gap left by declining unionism (Freeman, Hersch, and Mishel 2004). Our group examined a wide range of organizations: anti-sweatshop human rights groups; living wage campaigns; law groups devoted to enforcing labor and employment law; Working Today, an organization that was beginning to provide portable benefits to freelance workers; occupational associations; and union-management and community-based intermediaries that provided training to workers outside their firm. The "Emerging Institutions" study found that none of the organizations had developed the depth or breadth to be capable of substituting for unions, but noted that "this volume is just the first chapter in what may be a long story of innovations by nonmember organizations, by professional and other nonunion organizations, and by unions to find the best way to represent the interests of labor in an economic environment where traditional unionism is greatly weakened" (Freeman and Hersch 2004, 11).

This section is the second chapter in that story. It gives a more positive reading of the ability of new organizational forms to mobilize workers and improve labor conditions than the 2000 conference. By 2012, more non–collective bargaining institutions were operating and having an impact on labor developments in novel ways than a decade earlier. The spread of low-cost, Internet-based information and communication tools had made it easier to mobilize citizens, organize demonstrations and campaigns, and identify and appeal to workers than in earlier years.

Table 2.1 lists eleven non–collective bargaining labor institutions that formed or developed their current structure in the late 1990s and 2000s, categorized into three groups:

1. Groups that target broad economic and social issues and do not deal with specific firms, occupations, or industries

2. Groups that target workers in particular occupations or industries, seeking to improve their economic situation without gaining collective bargaining contracts

3. Groups that seek to improve the economic situation of workers in particular firms or those working for particular employers without gaining collective bargaining contracts

Organizations Targeting Broad Economic and Social Issues

Bringing Attention to Big Problems: Occupy Wall Street   In September 2011, Occupy Wall Street protesters sat down in Zuccotti Park near Wall Street to demonstrate against economic inequality.[17] The disparate group of largely college graduates camped out under banners that read WE ARE THE 99% did more to bring the problem of inequality to U.S. policy discourse than academics or unions had done in the preceding two to three decades.[18] Occupy spawned protests not only in the United States but worldwide.[19] The U.S. Occupy groups ranged from Wall Street–savvy experts writing technical critiques of financial regulations (www.occupythesec.org) to city-based groups focused on local issues (www.occupyoakland.org) to university-based groups targeting campus issues—Goldman Sachs recruiting at Harvard, for instance (www.occupyboston.org).[20] With its nonpartisan orientation and stress on identifying problems rather than offering solutions, the Occupy movement has shown that modern information and communication technology and social media allow a small

Table 2.1 Eleven Innovative Non–Collective Bargaining Labor Organizations

Institution (beginning date, numbers involved, dues)	Organization	Problem Addressed	Method of Influencing Outcome
Based on Social and Economic Issues			
Occupy movement (2011, thousands)	Diverse; many college graduates	Inequality; finance issues; varies by region	Publicity; demonstrations
Change.org, Internet petition site (2007, thousands of petitions, 123 million signatures, 20 million users)	For-profit business	User determined	Publicity via petitions
Working America (2003, 3 million)	AFL-CIO community affiliate	Local issues; electoral information; links to Union Plus benefits	Ballot box
Based on Occupation or Industry			
Worker centers (partner with AFL-CIO; 2006, 139 centers servicing less than 500 members but service more people)	NGO; religious foundations; fund-raising; dues	Workplace issues; accessing benefits; immigrant rights	Help with "grievances"; expose bad practices; advocacy; targeting employers
National Domestic Workers Alliance (2007, 10,000 persons in 35 local, membership-based organizations)	NGO	Pay and work conditions of domestic workers	Publicity; extension of labor laws to domestic workers; affiliated work centers to help workers with problems
New York Taxi Workers Alliance (1998, 15,000 members, $100/year dues)	First non–collective bargaining member of NYC Central Labor Council	Pay and benefits in taxi industry	Helping members with workplace problems; legal and political advocacy for drivers; discounted benefits

(Table continues on p. 60.)

Table 2.1   *(Continued)*

Institution (beginning date, numbers involved, dues)	Organization	Problem Addressed	Method of Influencing Outcome
Freelancers Union (2003, created from Working Today, 170,000 members, no dues)	Worker health insurance	Worker health insurance; wage arrears problems	Provide health insurance benefits; information
Employer-Based Alliance@IBM (1999, several hundred members, 5,000 subscribers, $10/month dues)	Communications Workers of America (CWA) local	Changes in employment practices and benefits	Internet information/publicity; petitions
WashTech (1998, $10–11/month dues)	CWA local	Changes in employment practices and benefits	Internet information/ publicity; petitions
OUR Walmart (2010, based on earlier UFCW campaigns, "several thousand" members, $5/month dues)	NGO, with UFCW support	Pay and work conditions in Walmart	Publicity; demonstrations
Public-sector unions in non–collective bargaining states (680,000 in 2011, 14.5 percent density)	Unions	Wages, benefits, work conditions	Politics; lobbying; meet-and-confer agreements

Source: Author's compilation. On Change.org, see "Start a Petition" (http://www.change.org/) and "About" (http://www.change.org/about) (accessed December 12, 2012); on the Freelancers Union, see "History" (http://www.freelancersunion.org/about/history.html); on Working Today, see Hersch (2004); on subscriber numbers for Alliance@IBM and on OUR Walmart, see Steven Greenhouse, "Wal-Mart Workers Try the Nonunion Route," *New York Times,* June 15, 2011; on public-sector unions, see Freeman and Han (2013).

group without much money or organization to come together and create ruckuses about social issues.[21]

Online Petition Sites: Change.org   Online petition sites provide a platform for citizens to use the historic mode of petitioning governments or other organizations to change policies.[22] Change.org, a for-profit, certified B-corporation,[23] is currently the world's leading petition site.[24] If you have Internet access, you can express easily your opinion on an issue. Go to the website and click the Start a Petition button. The script will ask you a set of questions: "Who do you want to petition?" "What do you want them to do?" "Why is this important?" Then you write your petition and submit it. The site alerts people who might be interested in your cause, who may then alert their friends, and . . . *pow!* the petition may go viral. Change.org makes money by selling its email database to charitable and other organizations that want to connect with people who have particular interests.

In the fall of 2011, two petitions begun by Molly Katchpole, a twenty-two-year-old college graduate working as a nanny, demonstrated the power of Internet petitioning. In October, the Bank of America (BOFA) began charging low-income customers monthly fees for using their debit cards.[25] Customer Katchpole placed a petition on Change.org, asking BOFA to rescind the policy (Colgrass 2011). It reads:

Brian T. Moynihan, President and CEO, Bank of America

I'm writing to express my deep concern over Bank of America's decision to charge customers $5 a month to use their debit cards when making purchases.

The American people bailed out Bank of America during a financial crisis the banks helped create. You paid zero dollars in federal income tax last year. And now your bank is profiting, raking in $2 billion in profits last quarter alone. How can you justify squeezing another $60 a year from your debit card customers? This is despicable.

American consumers can't afford these additional fees. We reject any claims by BofA that this latest fee is somehow necessary.

Please, do the right thing. Reverse your decision to charge customers $5 each month for using their debit cards to make purchases.

Sincerely,
[your name][26]

The petition was signed by 300,000 people, including President Barack Obama. U.S. Senator Richard Durbin of Illinois responded to the petition on Twitter. Congress decided to "look at legislation for out-of-control banking fees."[27] Most important, the media gave the petition national exposure, and people responded. Some customers left the Bank of America. Others threatened to leave. Faced with furious customers, the Bank of America dropped its banking fee.

Two months later, Verizon announced that customers paying telephone bills online had to pay a $2 fee. Customer Katchpole wrote a petition protesting the Verizon fee. Within hours, her petition gathered over 130,000 signatures. The Federal Communications Commission (FCC), which regulates telecommunications, announced that it would investigate. But there was no need for regulators. As Katchpole's petition gained signatures, Verizon withdrew the fee (Frellick 2012).

Change.org petitions rarely gain as much attention as Molly Katchpole's petitions and do not always end so successfully. In 2012, Rachel Voorhies at Dosha Salon Spa in Oregon petitioned her employer to bargain with the union the workers had chosen in an NLRB election the previous year. This petition had 595 signatories as of February 22, 2012, but signatures increased so rapidly in the ensuing months that in May 2012 change.org made the following announcement: "After over 17,000 signed Rachel Voorhies' petition . . . the owners have agreed to sit down with Rachel and her coworkers. In June 2012, Dosha and representatives of the union representing Rachel and her co-workers will begin mediation to settle their disputes and agree on ways to address workers' concerns like wages, health and safety, vacation time and benefits."[28] But the petitions did not in fact pressure management to compromise with the workers. Two months later, faced with a decertification election by workers who recognized that the union lacked the power to improve their situation, the union disclaimed interest, effectively dissolving itself.[29] Petitions can move firms to change their behavior, but seemingly only if they carry with them a viable threat of imposing economic costs on the firm, such as loss of customers, which the Dosha petition did not do.

The Occupy demonstrations and change.org and other Internet petition drives arise from grassroots individual behavior, using modern Internet-based technology and social media communication. Viewed through the lens of economics, these movements either create new markets or modernize older ways for people to come together and press society on issues that matter to them. Demonstrations and petitions succeed if the issues they target meet the market test of getting enough individuals involved and if they put significant pressure on the "powers that be" to rethink decisions.

Political Influence: Working America   Created by the AFL-CIO, Working America (WA) is a non–collective bargaining "community affiliate" that connects the federation to non-union workers, largely for the purpose of extending union political influence beyond its declining membership (for a detailed description, see Freeman and Rehavi 2009). Canvassing people in their homes to join, WA recruited about 2 million members in 2007 in states that it viewed as politically important in the 2008 national election, such as Ohio, Pennsylvania, and Virginia. It also obtained a national membership by gaining 135,000 members online, and by 2012 WA reported having about 3 million members. The organization offers involvement in a social movement focused on "the priorities that matter most to working people . . . [that can] . . . make a difference for your community, for America and for your working family," but its primary goal is to encourage members to become politically active and to vote for union-endorsed candidates. Until the Supreme Court's *Citizens United* decision in 2010, unions could not use their resources to proselytize nonmembers in political campaigns and thus needed an organization like WA to be able to target nonmember voters.[30] By allowing all organizations to use their funds for political purposes, *Citizens United* has eliminated this rationale for unions funding WA.

With local offices in many areas and a large membership, Working America could evolve into much more than a Washington-run organization seeking to influence citizens to vote in favor of unions, but without collective bargaining. WA could decentralize its structure, develop procedures for members to elect leaders in local chapters, and encourage chapters to experiment with their own ways of engaging the public and targeting workplace issues. Harold Meyerson (2012) reports that Working America "began some small-scale efforts in 2012 to have its members raise issues in their workplaces," but WA has a long way to go to become a freewheeling, member-driven, emerging labor institution.

Organizations Based on Occupation, Industry, or Community

Community-Based Advocacy: Worker Centers   Worker centers are community-based organizations that support low-wage workers, mostly from immigrant communities, outside of collective bargaining (for the most detailed analysis; see Fine 2006). The centers give legal assistance to individual workers facing wage arrears (delayed or unpaid wages) and other problems and educate workers and their communities about ways to campaign and lobby for improved work conditions. The number of worker centers increased rapidly from a handful in the 1990s to perhaps 150 by the late 2000s (Marculewicz and Thomas (2012). The centers have coalesced into two national networks, the National Day Laborer Organizing Network (NDLON), which had forty-three member organizations in 2012, and the Interfaith Worker Justice (IWJ), which listed twenty-six worker centers that reached seventeen thousand workers in 2012 (Enriquez 2011). Impressed by the worker centers movement, the AFL-CIO entered into partnership with NDLON in 2006 to "work together for state and local enforcement of rights as well as the development of new protections in areas including wage and hour laws, health and safety regulations, immigrants' rights and employee misclassification . . . [and] . . . for comprehensive immigration reform that supports workplace rights . . . and against punitive, anti-immigrant, anti-worker legislation" (AFL-CIO 2006).[31] The AFL-CIO also formed a partnership with the IWJ and entered similar agreements with two related immigrant-based organizations, the National Domestic Workers Alliance (NDWA) and the National Guestworker Alliance (NGA).

Since worker centers do not bargain collectively with single employers, they operate outside of the NLRA and seek to remain outside its jurisdiction, which would limit their ability to undertake secondary boycotts to assist workers outside of collective bargaining and would require them to file regular reports with the agency. Whether the centers can remain outside the NLRA is an area of controversy among labor lawyers. David Rosenfeld (2006, 469) argues that the definition of a labor organization is sufficiently broad that, "as they grow in number and scope, worker centers will have their development and effectiveness arrested by the very problem they were designed to avoid: the regulation of and restrictions on labor organizations under the National Labor Relations Act (NLRA)." Eli Naduris-Weissman (2009) argues the contrary—that as long as the centers limit themselves to settling individual employment claims, they will be exempt from the law.[32] Stefan Marculewicz and Jennifer Thomas (2012) claim that the worker centers are worker organizations by another name and thus subject to NLRA regulations.[33] That the centers prefer operating outside of the NLRA is a sign of how dysfunctional the U.S. labor code has become for workers seeking to better their economic condition.

Extending Labor Law to Domestic Workers: National Domestic Workers Alliance   The National Domestic Workers Alliance (NDWA) is a nongovernmental umbrella organization that provides information on the conditions of domestic workers and advocates for legislation to bring domestic workers under labor law.[34] Based on thirty-five local, membership-based affiliate organizations of over ten thousand nannies, housekeepers, and caregivers for the elderly located in nineteen cities and eleven states, the NDWA operates further outside the NRLB labor organizational form than worker centers. The NDWA's main legislative success was lobbying New York State to adopt the "Domestic Workers' Bill of Rights" to ensure basic labor protections for domestic workers. A similar bill that it pushed through the California legislature was vetoed by Governor Jerry Brown. It has pressed Congress to end exclusions of domestic workers from the nation's labor laws and to cover them under minimum wage and hours legislation. In 2011 the AFL-CIO endorsed the NDWA and sent a joint "open letter" with the group to trade unions and national centers around the world about the union movement's work with the NDWA (AFL-CIO/NDWA 2011).[35] *Time* magazine viewed the NDWA as sufficiently promising to name the group's founder, Ai-Jen Poo, one of the one hundred most influential people in the world in 2012—the only person on the list whose occupation was labor activist (Steinem 2012).

Advocacy for Taxi Drivers: New York Taxi Workers Alliance   The New York Taxi Workers Alliance (NYTWA) represents taxi drivers in the city as a trade union but without bargaining collectively with any single employer. Founded in 1998, the NYTWA reports having more than fifteen thousand members, who pay $100 a year in dues. It lists its successes as: gaining the first-ever living wage standard for U.S. taxi drivers; getting $15 million in federal disaster assistance for taxi drivers after the terrorist attacks of September 11, 2001; organizing short strikes of drivers in May 1998 and September 2007; recovering lost income due to unlawful license suspensions; defending drivers in civil court claims; lobbying for driver-friendly taxi industry policies and regulations. All of these successes, it claims, have raised drivers' incomes by 35 to 45 percent.

The NYTWA provides discounted or pro bono legal advice, financial management, and health services to its members. In September 2011, the AFL-CIO chartered the NYTWA as a member of the federation, making it the first nontraditional workers' organization chartered in over six decades. President Obama recognized the union for its success at a Washington, D.C., meeting hosted by the administration's Office of Faith-Based and Neighborhood Partnerships. The organization has inspired and assisted with the development of similar taxi driver worker alliances in twenty other areas of the United States and in several foreign countries. For creating a stable labor organization in an industry with high turnover, and in the absence of collective bargaining, the founder, Bhairavi Desai, has won various awards and been lauded for her success by President Obama and AFL-CIO head Richard Trumka.[36]

Obtaining Health Insurance: Freelancers Union   The Freelancers Union is a federation of independent workers that advocates for freelancers in the United States and operates a B-corporation insurance company to provide insurance benefits for independent workers in New York State at group health insurance rates. Initially, the Freelancers Union purchased insurance for its members from commercial insurance companies, but since 2008 it has done so through its wholly owned, for-profit subsidiary. The organization grew from about 35,000 members in the 1990s to close to 200,000 members as of January 2013. With support from New York City and New York State, it launched a freelancer medical center in Brooklyn in 2013, and with $340 million in federal funding, it is scheduled to expand its health coverage in New York, New Jersey, and Oregon in 2014. The Freelancers Union does no collective bargaining over wages or working conditions, but provides members with information about how to deal with wage arrears, which is a major problem for its members (Rodgers 2010). It also provides members with online tools, business management information, networking opportunities, group discount terms with various vendors or partners, and other assistance in working successfully as independents. It sponsored the Freelancer Payment Protection Act (S4129/A6698) in New York to grant freelancers the same wage protection as traditional employees and require the state department of labor to pursue freelancers' unpaid wages and hold deadbeat executives liable for up to $20,000 and jail time. The Freelancers Union receives considerable grant support from foundations, New York City, and New York State. In 2011 both *Forbes* and *Businessweek* named its founder, Sara Horowitz, to their lists of "top social entrepreneurs."

Employer-Based Organizations

Union Locals: Alliance@IBM and WashTech   Both Alliance@IBM and the Washington Alliance of Technology Workers (WashTech) are chartered locals of the Communication Workers of America (CWA). Information technology (IT) workers at IBM and Microsoft originally formed the groups as independent worker organizations and later affiliated with the CWA, which represents workers in telecommunications and related fields.

IT workers at IBM formed the Alliance@IBM in 1999 to protest the changes that IBM made to its pension system that harmed some future retirees. The protest succeeded in getting IBM to alter some parts of its planned changes. Recognizing that IBM management and the media would listen only if IBM employees had an organization of thousands, the Alliance@IBM initiated a membership drive for associate members, promising employees that their names would be confidential. When, at the end of 2012, IBM management changed the timing of the firm's match contribution to workers' 401(k) pension plans in ways that reduced the value of the plan to some employees, the Alliance@IBM used the change.org petition site to petition "to tell IBM to REVERSE their decision!"[37]

Microsoft contract employees in Redmond, Washington, formed the Washington Alliance of Technology Workers in 1998 to organize protests against the firm's overtime pay for contract employees. Because contract workers were hired by employment agencies rather than Microsoft and workers shifted employers frequently, WashTech, finding it unfeasible to represent only Microsoft workers (Bishop 2009), widened its scope to include high-tech industry workers in the Northwest more broadly. WashTech signed a collective bargaining contract with a company in 2003 and has negotiated and signed three more since with small employers. The organization tells workers, "Join WashTech today for as little as $11/month and enjoy Union Plus benefits," and it informs them that "you do not have to live in Washington State to join."

The CWA chartered both Alliance@IBM and WashTech as local unions even though neither has any possibility of gaining majority support from the IT giants. With minimal dues and modest membership, both organizations have remained alive and active for over a decade. Wayne Diamond and Richard Freeman (2002, 581) note that "even if workers at IBM, Microsoft and most other high tech firms never win an NLRB election, these sites make the union a part of the company in a way that was impossible prior to the Internet." But even with low-cost modern modes of communication, the organizations need more than a few activists to remain viable. In March 2013, Alliance@IBM reported on its website that "we can not continue to do our work if we don't have dues paying members. At this point we are on life support. Our membership has dropped and we are not gaining new members. In order to keep the Alliance going we need *you* to help out."[38]

A Union-Supported NGO: OUR Walmart   In the early 2010s, announcing that "the best thing the UFCW can be is a catalyst to help associates build an organization," the United Food and Commercial Workers (UFCW) undertook a novel campaign to help the "associates" at Walmart (also known as employees) develop a non–collective bargaining organization to improve wages and working conditions.[39] The design for Organization United for Respect at Walmart (OUR Walmart) was based on research by the public strategy group ASGK, which used Facebook to identify Walmart employees and tested messages that would appeal to them. The organization developed a twelve-point declaration that asked Walmart to improve conditions and to "provide wages and benefits that ensure that no Associate has to rely on government assistance" and to share profits and treat associates as partners.[40]

OUR Walmart burst to national attention in the fall of 2012, when members struck for a day at a California warehouse and then undertook a one-day protest/strike on "Black Friday," the post-Thanksgiving sales day. Though the number of workers who struck on Black Friday was minuscule compared to Walmart's 1.4 million U.S. employees, the strike received national attention.[41] Some analysts derided the strike as a failure, since it neither interfered with the operation of stores nor harmed company sales. Other analysts claimed that the strike succeeded in that it gained the attention of Walmart management. The company sought an NLRB injunction against the strike, held anti-union meetings in many stores to convince workers it was not in their interests to join OUR Walmart, and offered workers an extra discount on their Walmart purchases on Black Friday. Some workers joined the organization or went out on strike in response to management pressures.[42] Walmart was sufficiently bothered by the various protests that in March 2013 it sued the UFCW in a Florida court to "protect our customers and associates from further disruptive tactics associated with their continued, illegal trespassing."[43]

In 2012, OUR Walmart reported that it had about 4,000 members, who paid dues of $5 per month, and it also reported 2,229 signatures to its declaration. By raising issues and protesting conditions, OUR Walmart has proven that it can force management to respond. If it grows its membership, it is possible that Walmart will improve its human resource policies and wages and benefits to choke off further growth of the organization as well as to seek legal redress from protests. Whether OUR Walmart can go beyond that and become an organization that the firm feels compelled to "meet and confer" with over employee issues depends not only on its ability to galvanize workers but also to gain support from the store's customers.

Public-Sector Unions in States That Ban Public-Sector Collective Bargaining   Five states—Georgia, North Carolina, South Carolina, Texas, and Virginia—ban collective bargaining by state and local public employees. Several other states, such as Mississippi and Arizona, allow public-sector bargaining but have traditions that make it difficult for unions to obtain contracts. In both settings, many state and local workers join unions and gain some improvements in work conditions without collective bargaining contracts. For example, a majority of teachers in Georgia, Texas, and Virginia are union members.

How do unions succeed in representing their members without collective bargaining? Non–collective bargaining unions sign meet-and-confer agreements with local governments, lobby legislatures on laws regarding employment and budgets, and campaign for candidates favorable to their members—in short, in much the same way as some of the private-sector non–collective bargaining groups. The effects of the public-sector unions appear to be larger the higher their level of density (Freeman and Han 2012).

In short, union activity does not cease in the absence of collective bargaining, nor do work organizations become unable to affect the conditions of labor.

CONCLUSION

Since the turn of the twenty-first century, a wide range of groups—from freewheeling "occupiers," petition sites, and worker centers to alliances of freelancers or taxi drivers to the union-initiated, non-union worker organization OUR Walmart—have experimented with non–collective bargaining modes of representing workers' interests inside and outside companies. Some of these organizations fit the "open source union" model that Joel Rogers and I proposed over a decade ago to engage workers outside of collective bargaining (Freeman and Rogers 2002, 2006). Some have gone beyond what we envisaged as the ways in which groups can press for change have multiplied with the expansion of the Internet and the development of social media. Traditional unions have begun to move in the same direction, either to support innovative non-union groups or to learn from them how best to navigate an economic environment in which collective bargaining is in abeyance. In 2013, for the first time, the top leadership of the AFL-CIO went public in recognizing that the business model of representing workers through collective bargaining has failed and it is time to rebuild the labor movement around a different model. In a set of media interviews, AFL-CIO president Richard Trumka admitted that the basic system of workplace representation has failed "miserably to meet the needs of America's workers," and he called on unions to embrace new models of representation and to restructure their organizations to take as members "people who want to join," regardless of whether their employers accept collective bargaining.[44] Whether or not the unions can take up Trumka's charge to reinvent themselves and rebuild the U.S. labor movement, the "second chapter" in the story of labor organizations and activists seeking to help workers in nontraditional ways holds considerable promise. The implosion of Wall Street, the Great Recession, and the sluggish job recovery have brought the weaknesses of the U.S. economy to the fore and produced widespread dissatisfaction with the U.S. brand of capitalism. It is difficult to imagine the country successfully addressing its labor problems—income inequality, stagnant real wages, poverty-level earnings for low-paid workers, continued high rates of joblessness—without a strong labor movement of some kind. With a great social need and a growing pool of committed activists developing innovative ways to represent workers and fight for improvements in their living conditions, it is also difficult to imagine the present situation continuing ad infinitum. If the AFL-CIO or the Change to Win unions cannot do the job, I expect that other groups will forge ahead. At the risk of tempting some future scholar to cite my shortsightedness about where society may be heading—as I have cited Barnett's 1932 prediction—I see reason to believe that the diverse forms of social experimentation described here will give labor a more potent influence on society than it has today.

NOTES

1. George Barnett, American Economic Association presidential address, December 1932. For the relevance of these remarks today, see Eduardo Porter, "Unions' Past May Hold Key to Their Future,." *New York Times*, July 18, 2012.

2. The situation facing unions is so dire that I expect that NLRB policy changes such as the 2012 decision to speed up representation elections will have no noticeable effect on union density. See Steven Greenhouse, "Labor Board Adopts Rules to Speed Unionization Votes," *New York Times*, December 22, 2011.

3. See "Times Topics: United Automobile Workers," *New York Times*, available at: http://topics.nytimes.com/top/reference/timestopics/organizations/u/united_automobile_workers/index.html (accessed September 2013).

4. Bill Vlasik, "UAW Makes Concessions to Help Automakers," *New York Times*, December 3, 2008.

5. When GM earned its highest profits in history in 2011, its 47,000 blue-collar UAW workers received about $7,000 each in bonuses. Chrysler paid about $1,500 in bonuses to its 23,000 hourly workers. Ford paid $3,252 each to its 40,600 UAW workers based on half a year's profits, which put it in line for making annual bonus payments in 2011 of $6,000 to $7,000. For a discussion of Ford sharing the wealth, see Alisa Priddle, "Ford Sharing Wealth of Recent Gains," *Chicago Tribune*, January 20, 2012; on GM's 2011 profit-sharing, see United Automobile Workers (2012).

6. Motor vehicles and motor vehicles manufacturing data are for census code industry 3570, which covers many more firms than the Big Three.

7. Steven Greenhouse, "More Lockouts as Companies Battle Unions," *New York Times*, January 23, 2012; Wojcik (2012).

8. In 2011, the NFL and NBA locked out players to force them to accept lower shares of industry receipts. In August 2011, American Crystal Sugar locked

out its Minnesota employees, whom it replaced with temporary workers. This dispute was sixteen months long without resolution as of December 2012; see Mike Hughlett, "Crystal Sugar Workers Reject Contract Again," *Star Tribune*, December 2, 2012. In January 2011, the financially troubled New York City Opera locked out its orchestra and singers and won deep cuts in labor compensation; see Daniel J. Wakin, "New York City Opera Ratifies Agreement," *New York Times*, January 19, 2012. In 2012, the NFL locked out referees, and the NHL locked out its players.

9. See "The Union Membership and Coverage Database from the Current Population Survey: Union Membership, Coverage, Density, and Employment Among Public-Sector Workers, 1973–2011," constructed by Barry Hirsch and David Macpherson, available in the Index of Tables at: www.unionstats.com (accessed November 21, 2013).

10. In March 2009, John Kasich of Ohio, who would be elected governor in 2010, talked about the need to "break the back of organized labor in the schools" (ModernEsquire 2010). Many conservatives had long believed that it was illegitimate for government to bargain with unions in a democracy on the grounds that voters rather than bargaining should set the terms of work (McHugh 2011).

11. Earlier, Republican governors in Indiana, Kentucky, and Missouri had revoked executive orders that allowed state employees to bargain (Malin 2009). To make sure future governors did not restore the right to bargain, the Indiana legislature required legislative approval of any future executive decision.

12. Michael A. Fletcher and Sean Sullivan, "Michigan Enacts Right-to-Work Law, Dealing Blow to Unions," *Washington Post*, December 11, 2012.

13. Adam Berinsky and his colleagues (2011) have developed weights to turn the quota-sampling procedures used in the early public opinion surveys into population-weighted estimates. These show huge approval for unions from the 1930s through 1942.

14. In 2009, 51 percent believed that unions harm nonmembers, compared to 36 percent in 2006; for all of the Gallup poll results, see http://www.gallup.com/poll/12751/labor-unions.aspx (accessed September 2013).

15. The proportion who see the country as going in the wrong direction varies with economic and political developments, but it has been high since the implosion of the finance industry and the ensuing recession. See Real Clear Politics, "Direction of Country," based on 707 polls, available at: http://www.realclearpolitics.com/epolls/other/direction_of_country-902.html (updated December 5, 2012; accessed February 18, 2012).

16. The difference in the proportion of Republicans and Democrats who view unions as having too much power was a huge forty-nine points. This contrasts with modest partisan differences for other entities, save for the federal government (a forty-one point difference); see Saad (2011).

17. "OWS's main issues are social and economic inequality, greed, corruption and the perceived undue influence of corporations on government" (Dilek 2013).

18. In September 1981, unions organized a mass solidarity march on Washington to protest the emerging recession spurred by the economic policies of the Federal Reserve and by the Reagan administration's effort to curb inflation.

19. For a link to the Google spreadsheet showing 747 activities in the fall of 2011 under the Occupy banner, see Simon Rogers, "Occupy Protests Around the World: Full List Visualised." *The Guardian*, DataBlog: Facts Are Sacred, November 14, 2011, available at: http://www.guardian.co.uk/news/datablog/2011/oct/17/occupy-protests-world-list-map#data (accessed September 2013).

20. For an analysis of the Occupy movement at Harvard University, see Mercer R. Cook and Hana N. Rouse, "Did Occupy Matter?" *Harvard Crimson*, May 24, 2012; for a more critical view, see Wyatt N. Troia, "Why Occupy Harvard Failed," *Harvard Crimson*, February 21, 2012. Examples of these different kinds of Occupy groups can be found at the following websites: for a critique of financial regulations, see www.occupythesec.org (accessed September 2013); for a city-based group focused on local issues, see www.occupyoakland.org (accessed September 2013); and for a university-based group targeting Goldman Sachs recruiting at Harvard, see www.occupyboston.org (accessed September 2013).

21. See Occupy Wall Street, "About," available at: http://occupywallst.org/about/ (accessed September 2013); see also Take the Square (2011).

22. In imperial China, petitions were an accepted way for people to inform the government of problems and seek changes. The Petition Clause of the First Amendment to the U.S. Constitution guarantees the right of the people "to petition the Government for a redress of grievances"; see Wikipedia, "Petition," last revised March 13, 2013 (accessed March 29, 2013), available at: http://en.wikipedia.org/wiki/Petition (accessed September 2013).

23. In 2010, U.S. states beginning with Maryland instituted a charter for a benefit- or B-corporation, which commits itself to do more than seek profit maximization for shareholders.

24. The same technology has spawned many other sites, such as labourstart.org (accessed September 2013), a pioneer in gathering and publishing labor news from around the world that regularly asks users to sign petitions when union leaders or members are arrested or endangered. Facebook has pages that organize petitions as well.

25. The Federal Reserve had capped the amount that banks can charge merchants for processing debit card purchases, so BOFA and other large banks decided to make up the money by charging low-income consumers.

26. Change.org, "Tell Bank of America: No $5 Debit Card Fees," petition by Molly Katchpole, available at: http://www.change.org/petitions/tell-bank-of-america-no-5-debit-card-fees?utm_source=share_petition&utm_medium=url_share&utm_campaign=url_share_before_sign (accessed September 2013).

27. Wikipedia, "Change.org," last revised January 14, 2013 (accessed January 21, 2013), available at: http://en.wikipedia.org/wiki/Change.org (accessed September 2013).

28. Change.org, "Economic Justice: Start a Petition," available at: http://www.change.org/topics/economicjustice (accessed September 2013); see also Change.org, "Dosha Salon Spa: Respect Salon Workers," petition by Rachel Voorhies, available at: http://www.change.org/petitions/dosha-salon-spa-respect-salon-workers (accessed September 2013).

29. "Dosha Union Effort Comes to an End," nwLaborPress.org, August 21, 2012, available at: http://nwlaborpress.org/2012/08/dosha-9/ (accessed September 2013). The Dosha case is representative of some of the problems facing workers who seek to unionize in the United States. Dosha brought in an anti-union consultant, a former chairman of the Oregon Republican Party, who rejected union proposals to change the way the spa operated. Dosha violated the NLRA, including firing union activists, and paid fines for violations.

30. Wikipedia, "Citizens United v. Federal Election Commission," last revised January 14, 2013 (accessed January 16, 2013), available at: http://en.wikipedia.org/w/index.php?title=Citizens_United_v._Federal_Election_Commission&oldid=532943287 (accessed September 2013).

31. AFL-CIO, "AFL-CIO and NDLON, Largest Organization of Worker Centers, Enter Watershed Agreement to Improve Conditions for Working Families" (press release), August 6, 2006, available at: http://www.aflcio.org/Press-Room/Press-Releases/AFL-CIO-and-NDLON-Largest-Organization-of-Worker (accessed September 2013).

32. Naduris-Weissman (2009) believes, however, that if a worker center seeks to resolve a workplace dispute in sustained back-and-forth dealings with an employer, the NLRB and the courts are more likely to view it as being governed by the NLRA.

33. Marculewicz and Thomas (2012, 1) note that the head of the Restaurant Opportunities Center was opposed to NLRB coverage because it would have required spending time and money arbitrating worker grievances under the duty of fair representation to workers and would have restricted secondary picketing and protracted recognitional picketing.

34. In 2012 the NDWA published *Home Economics: The Invisible and Unregulated World of Domestic Work* by Linda Burnham and Nik Theodore; based on a survey of some two thousand nannies, caregivers, and housecleaners in fourteen metropolitan areas, *Home Economics* attained some media attention. The NDWA has also posted forty-two videos on YouTube telling the stories of domestic workers.

35. AFL-CIO and NDWA, "Open Letter from the AFL-CIO and National Domestic Workers Alliance (USA) to Trade Unions and National Centers Around the World," May 18, 2011.

36. Lizzie Widdicombe, "Our Local Correspondents: Thin Yellow Line: The Taxi Driver's Advocate," *The New Yorker*, April 18, 2011; "President Obama at the White House Diwali Event," October 29, 2011, available at: http://www.youtube.com/watch?feature=player_embedded&v=O7paNg2PP3M#!

(accessed September 2013); "Richard Trumka (AFL-CIO) Thanks Bhairavi Desai," published August 29, 2012, available at: http://www.youtube.com/watch?v=op7IauPe_WI (accessed September 2013).

37. The petition gained 1,030 supporters before it closed in 2013. See http://www.change.org/petitions/international-business-machines-ibm-usa-ibm-must-reverse-the-decision-changing-the-ibm-match-401-k-contribution (accessed March 29, 2013).
38. Alliance@IBM, available at: http://www.endicottalliance.org/newsupdate.htm (accessed March 29, 2013).
39. Dan Schlademan, UFCW official, quoted in Steven Greenhouse, "Wal-Mart Workers Try the Nonunion Route," *New York Times*, June 15, 2011.
40. OUR Walmart, "Declaration for Respect," available at: http://forrespect.nationbuilder.com/sign_the_declaration (accessed September 2013).
41. Walmart reports 2.2 million employees worldwide and 1.4 million in the United States "alone." See http://corporate.walmart.com/our-story/locations (accessed January 7, 2013).
42. Joel Griffith (2012) gives the case for the protests as failure, while Josh Eidelson (2012a, 2012b, 2012c), who live-blogged the Black Friday strike, gives the case for its success.
43. "Walmart Sues Grocery Workers Union, Others Who Have Protested at Florida Stores," Reuters, March 25, 2013, available at: http://www.huffingtonpost.com/2013/03/25/walmart-sues-protesters-florida-stores_n_2950992.html (accessed September 2013).
44. Peter Wallsten, "AFL-CIO's Trumka Looks to Remake U.S. Labor Movement," *Washington Post*, March 27, 2013. For other reports on the AFL-CIO's search for new initiatives in unionization, see Michael Bologna, "AFL-CIO's Trumka Calls for Change in the Labor Movement," *BNA Daily Labor Report*, March 11, 2013; "Richard Trumka, AFL-CIO Chief, Reflects on Unions' Thinning Ranks, Calls for New Strategies," *Huffington Post: Politics*, March 30, 2013; "AFL-CIO's Richard Trumka Admits Union in 'Crisis,' " *Washington Times*, February 28, 2013.

REFERENCES

AFL-CIO. 2006. "AFL-CIO and NDLON, Largest Organization of Work Centers, Enter Watershed Agreement to Improve Conditions for Working Families." August 9. Available at: http://www.aflcio.org/Press-Room/Press-Releases/AFL-CIO-and-NDLON-Largest-Organization-of-Worker (accessed September 2013).

Berinsky, Adam J., Eleanor Neff Powell, Eric Schickler, and Ian Brett Yohai. 2011. "Revisiting Public Opinion in the 1930s and 1940s." *Political Science and Politics* 44(3, July): 515–20.

Bishop, Todd. 2009. "Why WashTech Isn't Trying to Organize Microsoft Contractors." *Puget Sound Business Journal*, March 3 (updated September 5, 2009).
Available at: http://www.bizjournals.com/seattle/blog/techflash/2009/03/Why_
WashTech_isnt_trying_to_organize_Microsoft_contractors_40682137.html?s=
print (accessed September 2013).

Burnham, Linda, and Nik Theodore. 2012. *Home Economics: The Invisible and Unregulated World of Domestic Work*. New York: National Domestic Workers Alliance.

Colgrass, Neal. 2011. "How a College Grad Helped Sink BofA's Debit Card Fee."
Newser, November 7. Available at: http://www.newser.com/story/132782/how-
molly-katchpole-sunk-bank-of-americas-debit-card-fee.html (accessed September 2013).

Combs, Robert. 2012a. "Labor Stats and Facts: Lockout Rates Continue to Surge."
Bloomberg BNA, Labor and Employment Blog, October 17. Available at: http://
www.bna.com/labor-stats-facts-b17179870280/ (accessed September 2013).

———. 2012b. "Labor Stats and Facts: Lockouts Last Longer Than Strikes." *Bloomberg BNA*, Labor and Employment Blog, November 8. Available at: http://www.
bna.com/labor-stats-facts-b17179870766/ (accessed September 2013).

Diamond, Wayne J., and Richard B. Freeman. 2002. "Will Unionism Prosper in Cyber-
space? The Promise of the Internet for Employee Organization." *British Journal of
Industrial Relations* 40(3): 569–96.

Dilek, Emine. 2013. "Occupy Movement: What? Who? Why?" The Progressive Press,
January 12. Available at: http://www.progressivepress.net/occupy-movement-
what-who-why/ (accessed September 2013).

Eidelson, Josh. 2012a "With Biggest Strike Against Biggest Employer, Walmart
Workers Make History Again." *The Nation*, November 23. Available at: http://
www.thenation.com/blog/171435/biggest-strike-against-biggest-employer-
walmart-workers-make-history-again (accessed September 2013).

———. 2012b. "Why Walmart Failed to Suppress Black Friday Strikes." *The Nation*,
November 26. Available at: http://www.thenation.com/blog/171447/josh-eidelson-
walmarts-failing-strike-suppression# (accessed September 2013).

———. 2012c. "OUR Walmart Organizers Promise Multi-Pronged December." *The
Nation*, November 29. Available at: http://www.thenation.com/blog/171528/
walmart-organizers-promise-multi-pronged-december (accessed September
2013).

Eisenhower, Dwight D. 1955. "Telephone Broadcast to the AFL-CIO Merger Meet-
ing in New York City." December 5. Available at the American Presidency
Project, http://www.presidency.ucsb.edu/ws/index.php?pid=10394 (accessed
September 2013).

Enriquez, Dianne. 2011. "IWJ Worker Center Network Census 2011." Workers'
Center Network: Interfaith Worker Justice. Available at: http://files.www.iwj.
org/worker-center-network/labor-law/2011_WCN_Census.pdf (accessed September 2013).

Fine, Janice. 2006. *Worker Centers: Organizing Communities at the Edge of the Dream.* Ithaca, N.Y.: EPI/Cornell University Press.

Freeman, Richard B. 1998. "Spurts in Union Growth: Defining Moments and Social Processes." In *The Defining Moment: The Great Depression and the American Economy in the Twentieth Century,* ed. Michael D. Bordo, Claudia Goldin, and Eugene N. White. Chicago: University of Chicago Press for the National Bureau of Economic Research.

Freeman, Richard B., and Eunice Han. 2012. "The War Against Public-Sector Bargaining in the U.S." *Journal of Industrial Relations: Annual Review of Industrial Relations* 54(3, June): 386–407.

———. 2013. "Public-Sector Unionism Without Collective Bargaining." Unpublished paper. Cambridge, Mass. (January 6).

Freeman, Richard B., and Joni Hersch. 2004. "Introduction." In *Emerging Labor Market Institutions for the Twenty-First Century,* ed. Richard B. Freeman, Joni Hersch, and Lawrence Mishel. Chicago: University of Chicago Press for National Bureau of Economic Research.

Freeman, Richard B., Joni Hersch, and Lawrence Mishel, eds. 2004. *Emerging Labor Market Institutions for the Twenty-First Century.* Chicago: University of Chicago Press for National Bureau of Economic Research.

Freeman, Richard B., and Marit Rehavi. 2009. "Helping Workers Online and Offline: Innovations in Union and Worker Organization Using the Internet." In *Studies of Labor Market Intermediation,* ed. David H. Autor. Chicago: University of Chicago Press for National Bureau of Economic Research.

Freeman, Richard B., and Joel Rogers. 2002. "Open Source Unionism: Beyond Exclusive Collective Bargaining." *WorkingUSA* 5(4, March): 8–40.

———. 2006. *What Workers Want.* Ithaca, N.Y.: ILR Press for Russell Sage Foundation.

Frellick, Marcia. 2012. "Verizon Drops Fees Amid Consumer Protest." CreditCardGuide, January 4. Available at: http://www.creditcardguide.com/credit-cards/verizon-drops-fees-amid-consumer-protest.html#ixzz1n9xLs3Nn (accessed September 2013).

Godard, John, and Carola Frege. 2010. "Union Decline, Alternative Forms of Representation, and Workplace Authority Relations in the United States." November 10. Available at: http://ssrn.com/abstract=1729768 (accessed September 2013).

Griffith, Joel. 2012. "Walmart Strike: Why the Black Friday Labor Protests Were an Epic Failure." Policymic. Available at: http://www.policymic.com/articles/19550/walmart-strike-why-the-black-friday-labor-protests-were-an-epic-failure (accessed September 2013).

Hersch, Joni. 2004. "A Workers' Lobby to Provide Portable Benefits." In *Emerging Labor Market Institutions for the Twenty-First Century,* ed. Richard B. Freeman, Joni Hersch, and Lawrence Mishel. Chicago: University of Chicago Press for National Bureau of Economic Research.

Jones, Jeffrey N. 2011. "Approval of Labor Unions Holds Near Its Low, at 52%: Republican, Democratic Approval Ratings Diverge." Gallup.com, August 31. Available at: http://www.gallup.com/poll/149279/approval-labor-unions-holds-near-low.aspx (accessed September 2013).

———. 2012. "In U.S., Labor Union Approval Steady at 52%," Gallup Politics, August 31. Available at: http://www.gallup.com/poll/157025/labor-union-approval-steady.aspx (accessed September 2013).

Madland, David, and Karla Walter. 2010. "Why Is the Public Suddenly Down on Unions?" Washington, D.C.: Center for American Progress Action Fund, American Worker Project (July). Available at: http://www.americanprogressaction. org/wp-content/uploads/issues/2010/07/pdf/union_opinion.pdf (accessed September 2013).

Malin, Martin H. 2009. "The Paradox of Public-Sector Labor Law." Indiana Law Journal 84(4, article 10): 1369–99.

Marculewicz, Stefan J., and Jennifer Thomas. 2012. "Labor Organizations by Another Name: The Worker Center Movement and Its Evolution into Coverage Under the NLRA and LMRDA." Engage 13(3, October): 64–83. Available at: http://www.fed-soc.org/doclib/20121119_WorkerCenterEngage13.pdf (accessed September 2013).

McHugh, Jack. 2011. "Commentary: Government Collective Bargaining Inherently Corrupting, Should Be Outlawed." CapCon: Michigan Capitol Confidential, Mackinac Center for Public Policy, June 10. Available at: http://www.mackinac. org/article.aspx?ID=15197&print=yes (accessed September 2013).

Meyerson, Harold. 2012. "For Unions, It Was a Very Bad Year." The American Prospect, December 24. Available at: http://prospect.org/article/unions-it-was-very-bad-year (accessed September 2013).

ModernEsquire. 2010. "John Kasich on Public Unions: 'I Want to Break the Back of Teachers Unions.'" Plunderbund, September 27. Available at: http://www. plunderbund.com/2010/09/27/john-kasich-on-public-unions-i-want-to-break-the-back-of-teachers-unions/ (accessed September 2013).

Naduris-Weissman, Eli. 2009. "The Worker Center Movement and Traditional Labor Law: A Contextual Analysis." Berkeley Journal of Employment and Labor Law 30(1): 232–38.

Rodgers, William M., III. 2010. "The Threat of Nonpayment: Unpaid Wages and New York's Self-Employed." Report for the Heldrich Center for Workforce Development. New Brunswick, N.J.: Rutgers University, Bloustein School of Planning and Public Policy (June). Available at: https://fu-res.org/pdfs/advocacy/2010-unpaid-wages-report.pdf (accessed September 2013).

Rosenfeld, David. 2006. "Worker Centers: Emerging Labor Organizations—Until They Confront the National Labor Relations Act" (review essay). Berkeley Journal of Employment and Labor Law 27(2): 469.

Saad, Lydia. 2011. "Americans Decry Power of Lobbyists, Corporations, Banks, Feds." Gallup Politics, April 11. Available at: http://www.gallup.com/poll/147026/

americans-decry-power-lobbyists-corporations-banks-feds.aspx (accessed September 2013).

Schneider, Christian. 2011. "How the Wisconsin Senate Passed Walker's Bill." National Review Online, March 9. Available at: http://www.nationalreview.com/corner/261804/how-wisconsin-senate-passed-walkers-bill-christian-schneider (accessed September 2013).

Silver, Nate. 2009. "As Unemployment Rises, Support for Organized Labor Falls." FiveThirtyEight: Politics Done Right, September 7. Available at: http://www.fivethirtyeight.com/2009/09/as-unemployment-rises-support-for.html (accessed September 2013).

Steinem, Gloria. 2012. "The World's 100 Most Influential People, 2012: Ai-jen Poo: Labor Organizer." Time, April 18. Available at: http://www.time.com/time/specials/packages/article/0,28804,2111975_2111976_2112169,00.html (accessed September 2013).

Take the Square. 2011. "Quick Guide on Group Dynamics in People's Assemblies." July 31. Available at: http://takethesquare.net/2011/07/31/quick-guide-on-group-dynamics-in-peoples-assemblies/ (accessed September 2013).

United Automobile Workers. 2012. "Statement from UAW Vice President Joe Ashton on GM 2011 Profit Sharing." February 16. Available at: http://uaw.org/articles/statement-uaw-vice-president-joe-ashton-gm-2011-profit-sharing (accessed September 2013).

U.S. Department of Labor. Bureau of Labor Statistics. 2013. "Economic News Release: Union Members Summary: Union Members—2012." January 23. Available at: http://www.bls.gov/news.release/union2.nr0.htm (accessed September 2013).

Wojcik, John. 2012. "In Their War Against Workers, Corporations Increasingly Choose Lockouts." People's World, January 25. Available at: http://peoplesworld.org/in-their-war-against-workers-corporations-increasingly-choose-lockouts/ (accessed September 2013).

Part II | Workers on the Edge: Marginalized and Disadvantaged

Chapter 3 | Connecting the Disconnected: Improving Education and Employment Outcomes Among Disadvantaged Youth

Peter B. Edelman and Harry J. Holzer

EVEN BEFORE THE Great Recession began at the end of 2007, employment outcomes among disadvantaged and less-educated youth, and especially among young men, had been deteriorating over time. Both their levels of earnings and their employment and labor force participation rates had decreased for a few decades. Among young black men, the declines in employment and labor force activity have been particularly pronounced, while their rates of incarceration have risen dramatically. As a result, the percentage of these young men who are "disconnected" from school and work has risen.

Unfortunately, the Great Recession appears to have worsened these outcomes. Since 2007, employment rates have declined the most among young, less-educated, and/or minority men—in other words, mostly the same groups whose employment and earnings had already been worsening earlier. The recession has been not only severe but also very persistent; nearly five years after it began, relatively little labor market recovery has been observed. Therefore, the worsened employment outcomes we see for disadvantaged youth will last for many years and for many young people may lead to "scarring"—that is, their future earnings may be permanently lower.

In this chapter, we briefly review recent trends in employment outcomes for disadvantaged youth, focusing specifically on those who have become "disconnected" from school and the labor market, and discuss the reasons for these trends. We then review a range of policy prescriptions that might improve those outcomes, including: efforts to enhance

81

education and employment outcomes among both in-school youth who are at risk of dropping out and becoming disconnected and out-of-school youth who have already done so; policies to increase earnings and increase motivation among youth to participate in the labor force, such as expanding the eligibility of childless adults (and especially noncustodial parents, or NCPs) for the Earned Income Tax Credit (EITC); and specific policies to reduce the barriers to employment faced by ex-offenders and noncustodial parents.

Since these policy prescriptions tend to focus on either labor supply forces or the skills and behavior of the youth themselves, we also consider policies that target the demand side of the labor market. Looking at efforts to spur the willingness of employers to hire these young people and perhaps improve the quality of jobs available to them, we specifically suggest an initiative—almost surely impracticable under current fiscal and political realities—to create transitional employment in national and community service targeted mostly at those young people who have the greatest difficulty finding stable employment.

For both supply-side and demand-side policy prescriptions, we review the evaluation evidence and identify programs and policies that have had significant impacts on the employment outcomes of disadvantaged youth. If done together and at sufficient scale, we believe that a combination of supply- and demand-side policies could have a substantial positive impact on employment among our disconnected youth. At the same time, we are well aware of the deeper problems in our society that must be addressed if we are to create truly equal opportunities for all of our young people. The intersection of race (and ethnicity) and poverty features disproportionately in low-quality schools, in disproportionate incarceration, and in continuing discrimination based on race and ethnicity.

Finally, we discuss the implications of recent developments in education and labor market policy for this population. Although there has been some significant innovation in K-12 education (spurred by the Race to the Top funds and other initiatives) and some temporary funding under the American Recovery and Reinvestment Act (ARRA) of 2009 for training and public employment, there has been no broader effort to improve education or employment outcomes for at-risk or disconnected youth. The American Graduation Initiative proposed by the Obama administration in 2009, which would have funded a range of efforts at community colleges, might have provided a vehicle for such efforts, but funding for the proposal has been extremely limited. And proposed innovation funds for youth in the Workforce Investment Act (WIA) of 1998 remain limited as well. With its dismal fiscal situation, the nation's resources for any such efforts in the future are likely to be very limited and perhaps reduced. We discuss these developments in the recent past and their implications for disconnected youth over the next several years.

RECENT TRENDS IN OUTCOMES AND THEIR CAUSES

We begin by reviewing trends in employment among less-educated youth over the past three decades and recent changes in these trends during the Great Recession. In table 3.1, we present full-time school enrollment and employment rates, as well as hourly wages, among less-educated youth (defined as those with only a high school diploma or less but including those currently enrolled in higher education), age sixteen to twenty-four, at three points in time: 1979, 2007, and 2010. Employment rates are calculated for all young people in the sample, as well as only for those not enrolled in school full-time. Since 1979 and 2007 were both peak years for the U.S. economic business cycle, comparing outcomes between those years enables us to infer secular trends in these outcomes over the past three decades, and since 2010 represented the trough of the recession (in terms of unemployment and other labor market effects), comparing outcomes for 2007 and 2010 allows us to gauge the effects of the Great Recession. All results appear separately by gender and race.[1]

Several notable findings are reported in table 3.1 including some that are already known while others are not. The most striking finding is the dramatic rise between 1979 and 2007 in full-time school enrollment rates among youth, which nearly doubled for this group. Enrollment generally rose more among females than males and more among whites than minorities. Although the rise in enrollment rates is encouraging, other evidence indicates that rates of college *attainment*—the fraction of Americans who complete their courses of study and earn postsecondary degrees and credentials—have risen much less rapidly than enrollment (see, for example, Goldin and Katz 2008), especially among young people from lower-income backgrounds.

But, quite importantly, we also note that much of the increase in enrollment comes at the expense of employment—and much more so among less-educated young men than women. In other words, employment rates for young men who are not enrolled full-time in school—whom we might consider part of the potential youth labor force among the less-educated—have fallen quite sharply over time.[2] These employment declines among potential workers are quite pronounced among both young white men and young black men, though the declines for black men are larger in percentage terms (in other words, as a proportion of their employment rates in 1979, which started off much lower than those of whites). And if we adjust these numbers to include those who are or have been incarcerated,

Table 3.1   Employment and Education Outcomes, by Race and Gender, Among Less-Educated Youth, 1979, 2007, and 2010

	1979	2007	2010
Enrolled full-time			
All	25.0%	48.0%	50.5%
White male	24.2	48.8	50.1
Black male	30.8	49.9	49.5
Hispanic male	21.7	34.9	40.7
White female	24.7	53.3	55.7
Black female	28.2	49.3	52.1
Hispanic female	19.9	39.9	45.4
Employed but not enrolled full-time			
All	47.3	30.6	24.0
White male	55.8	33.9	26.7
Black male	38.5	26.1	18.8
Hispanic male	54.9	43.7	32.0
White female	45.3	26.8	22.7
Black female	27.5	24.0	19.6
Hispanic female	37.4	29.2	21.2
Neither employed nor enrolled full-time			
All	22.7	18.9	23.0
White male	12.1	13.7	19.3
Black male	23.7	22.8	30.8
Hispanic male	14.2	15.7	20.8
White female	27.9	18.6	20.5
Black female	42.2	26.5	27.9
Hispanic female	39.8	29.7	32.4
Employed (of potential youth labor force)			
All	67.6	61.8	51.0
White male	82.1	71.2	58.0
Black male	61.9	53.3	37.9
Hispanic male	79.5	73.5	60.6
White female	61.9	59.1	52.5
Black female	39.4	47.5	41.2
Hispanic female	48.5	49.6	39.6

(Table continues on p. 85.)

Table 3.1   (Continued)

	1979	2007	2010
Mean hourly wage			
All	$10.00	$10.50	$10.30
White male	12.30	11.30	11.20
Black male	10.90	10.30	10.20
Hispanic male	11.40	11.70	10.70
White female	9.40	9.50	9.50
Black female	9.20	9.40	9.60
Hispanic female	9.20	9.30	9.50

Source: Authors' calculations based on Current Population Survey, Outgoing Rotation Groups (U.S. Census Bureau, 1979–2010).
Notes: The sample is restricted to ages sixteen to twenty-four. It excludes anyone who has earned a postsecondary educational degree. It also excludes those employed in agriculture or the military and those who are self-employed. Individuals with real hourly wages below $2 or above $5,000 are not included.

the downward trend for young black men would look considerably worse.[3] We also note that trends in average hourly wages roughly parallel those of employment: real wages for young less-educated women have grown slightly over three decades, while real wages have fallen for young men, many of whom may have dropped out of the labor market as a result (Juhn 1992).

Finally, we note the apparent effects of the Great Recession, which seems to have led to modest rises in school enrollment for this population and very steep declines in employment, which, again, have been greatest among less-educated men. This recession has been not only severe but very persistent: as of early 2013, over five years after the recession began, the recovery observed so far in the labor market has been very modest, and virtually all economists expect that the recovery will proceed quite slowly over the next several years. This implies that young people are likely to be "scarred" by a loss of work experience over several years and a lack of upward mobility through different jobs (von Wachter 2010; Kahn 2010).[4]

What other outcomes for young people vary by race and gender in ways that might reflect differences in the opportunities they face? In table 3.2, we present tabulations of a range of outcomes by race and gender for a national sample of young people in their early twenties.[5] We include measures of academic achievement (for example, grade point average and test scores) and amount of schooling attained (dropping out of high school or

Table 3.2 Educational and Behavioral Outcomes of Youth, 2004 to 2005

	Males			Females		
	White	Black	Hispanic	White	Black	Hispanic
Not enrolled in school						
High school dropout/GED	13.4%	27.6%	20.8%	12.0%	19.0%	20.6%
Bachelor's degree	12.8	5.6	3.6	18.2	6.9	5.5
Enrolled in school						
Four-year college	17.2	9.7	10.1	19.0	14.4	13.2
Unmarried, has children	9.9	30.8	17.9	17.3	47.5	29.6
Ever incarcerated	7.6	14.8	9.6	2.7	3.1	2.4
High school grade point average	2.5	1.9	2.1	2.7	2.2	2.3
ASVAB	57.3	28.1	39.4	58.2	32.0	38.8

Source: National Longitudinal Survey of Youth (NLSY97), round 8, October 2004 to July 2005.
Notes: Samples include respondents age twenty-two to twenty-four at the time of the interview. Enrollment is measured in the month of November.
The Armed Services Vocational Aptitude test (ASVAB) score is measured as a percentile of the overall distribution of scores.

finishing a bachelor's degree), as well as having children outside marriage and having ever been incarcerated.[6]

The results show continuing large gaps by race, and some by gender, along all of these dimensions. In general, women outperform men in academic achievement and attainment, while minorities continue to lag behind whites. Black women report the most children outside of marriage, while black men are most frequently incarcerated, as is widely known.[7] Disturbingly, young black men do worse on virtually every outcome measure than any other race or gender group.

What might account for these ongoing gaps in employment and educational outcomes as well as other personal measures, and for the differential rates of progress that we see? Why have young women gained relative to men on most outcomes, even surpassing them in education, while less-educated young men, and especially black men, lag so far behind?

A full treatment of these issues clearly lies beyond the scope of this chapter. Gaps in educational achievement and attainment by gender and race (as well as family income) have been much discussed elsewhere (see, for example, Cornwell, Mustard, and Van Parys 2011; Jacob 2002; Magnuson and Waldfogel 2008), as have been the labor market gains of women relative to men in recent years (Blau and Kahn 1997) and racial patterns in unwed childbearing and incarceration (Western 2006; Wolfe and Wu 2001).

For our purposes, we limit ourselves to the following observations. First, there is little doubt that less-educated young men, and black men in particular, have been very negatively affected by changes in the economy that limit the demand for their labor. The structural changes that have reduced relative demand for less-skilled labor have mostly been induced by two forces: *globalization*, including rising imports of goods and services, offshoring of production activities, and immigration; and *technological change*, which is "skill-biased" (since it reduces employment more for less-educated than for more-educated workers). Together, these forces have almost certainly hurt less-educated men more than women, who seem to adapt better to many service-sector jobs, and they have hurt black men most of all, especially in the industrial Midwest as good-paying manufacturing jobs have disappeared (Bound and Freeman 1992; Bound and Holzer 1993).[8] Institutional changes that reduce compensation for lower-wage jobs—such as declining rates of unionization and lower real levels of the minimum wage—have probably contributed to these problems, though economists continue to debate the extent to which market or institutional forces account for these trends (Autor, Katz, and Kearney 2008; Card and Dinardo 2007). And the recent recession has clearly hurt less-educated young men more than any other group, because it has reduced

Figure 3.1   Effects of Adverse Labor Demand Shifts and Labor Supply
Response Among Less-Educated Young Men

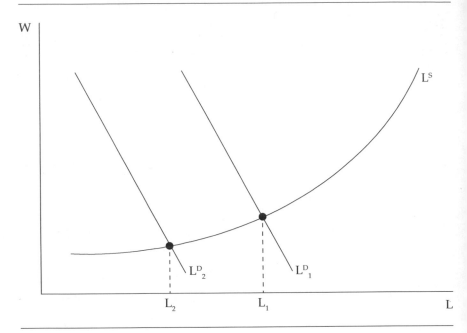

Source: Authors' figure based on Holzer (2009).

the demand for their labor (especially in cyclical industries like construction and manufacturing) more than the demand for the labor of others.

Second, we believe that some youth—especially black youth—who are now "disconnected" from both school and the labor market have responded to what appears to them to be a decline in long-run employment opportunities by giving up on mainstream possibilities and institutions. This is especially true not only for those who have dropped out of school and the labor market but also for the very large numbers of those who have become incarcerated or noncustodial parents: one-third of all young black men become incarcerated by age thirty-five, and up to one-half father children outside marriage. We have described this process more fully in our earlier book (Edelman, Holzer, and Offner 2006).

Figure 3.1 depicts these changes in employment and education outcomes. The figure shows an adverse (or inward) shift in labor demand, of the type that has probably affected less-educated men because of the economic forces just described. This demand shift leads to a withdrawal of labor force activity along a supply curve that is quite "elastic," or responsive to perceived (negative) changes in rewards. In other words, as young men perceive diminishing rewards to their labor in the market, they have less incentive to participate in that market, and so they withdraw from it. To the extent that some less educated young men also remain in the labor market but have trouble finding jobs at market wages (especially during recession periods), the result is high unemployment and low labor force participation.[9]

Along with this withdrawal from the legal or formal labor market, we also have seen the growing participation of young men in illegal activities. Almost certainly this withdrawal began for young black men during the 1970s and 1980s, when the relative rewards they faced for legal work were declining and the perceived rewards for illegal work were growing (Freeman 1992). Since that time, crime has fallen markedly but incarceration has risen very dramatically, especially among less-educated African American men. Besides the many pernicious effects of incarceration on low-income individuals, their families, and their communities (see, for example, Alexander 2010; Western 2006), very large numbers of young men are now "marked" with criminal records that further reduce the willingness of employers to hire them (Holzer 2009; Pager 2007). In addition, some aspects of the child support system (such as the large fractions who are in arrears on payments and therefore face very stiff penalties on legal earnings) further discourage the legal or reported work effort of these young men (Holzer, Offner, and Sorensen 2005).

Of course, some have argued that it is not so much economic realities as behavioral or cultural factors that explain these shifts.[10] In our view, these explanations are not mutually exclusive; if anything, we believe that broader behavioral or cultural patterns are largely responses to declines in perceived opportunities (see Wilson 2009). Others might object that the labor market imperatives to improve one's educational attainment are clearly stronger now than before and should therefore have led to improved outcomes; these incentives alone are not enough, however, to lead to major improvements in educational outcomes among disadvantaged youth absent a broader set of changes to help them overcome the barriers to success that develop early in life and last throughout their childhood and teen years (Duncan and Murnane 2011).

To address these issues we lay out a set of policy alternatives in the next section. The first set focuses on the labor supply of disadvantaged young people and attempts to encourage better educational and employment outcomes for them through improvements in their skills and work experiences so that they can more effectively respond to long-term changes on the demand side of the labor market. In this category, we also advocate for improving the pecuniary incentives for youth to take low-wage jobs and reducing the barriers and disincentives that tend to discourage work among ex-offenders and noncustodial parents. But given the major changes that have occurred in labor demand—especially during the recent downturn—we explore a set of demand-side policies as well.

POLICY PROPOSALS FOR DISADVANTAGED YOUTH

Improving the Skills and Work Incentives of Youth

There seems to be little doubt that disadvantaged and disconnected young people need higher levels of education and skills to better meet the demand for labor in jobs that still pay well in the United States.

We remain concerned about the decline of good-paying jobs in the U.S. economy. But contrary to recent claims that the middle of the labor market is collapsing, we believe that the longer-term demand for labor will remain fairly substantial in the United States at the "middle-skill" level, which we define as the set of jobs requiring more than a high school diploma but less than a full BA degree (Holzer 2010; Holzer and Lerman 2007).[11] The retirements of baby boomers over the next few decades and the need for replacements will enhance such demand. More broadly, Harry Holzer and his colleagues (2011) show that the labor market has continued to produce good-paying jobs over time, but that the nature of those jobs is changing rapidly—with many fewer in manufacturing and more in a range of sectors (including construction, health care, professional or management services, and even retail trade) that require a broader skill set than before.[12]

Moreover, the labor market returns to a range of certificates and associate's degrees are quite strong, especially in particular fields (Carnevale, Smith, and Strohl 2010; Jacobson and Mokher 2009). The secular employment prospects of poor and minority youth will brighten if more of them graduate from high school and can complete at least some kind of post-secondary certification, however remote this possibility seems while the recent downturn keeps labor markets depressed. Even for young minority men with weak academic outcomes (relative to whites and females in their own racial or ethnic group), middle-skill jobs in certain sectors or occupations—like construction, health technician work, or installation and repair of mechanical systems—hold particular promise.

A great deal has been written elsewhere on the "achievement gaps" that develop early in childhood between poor youth and others and on the need for reforms in the K-8 years. Here we focus instead on the years during which youth become disconnected from school and fail to connect to the labor market: the high school years and beyond. We therefore consider a set of policies designed to: (1) prevent disconnection and dropout among at-risk youth who are still in school and improve their pathways to postsecondary education and work; and (2) encourage those who have already dropped out to reconnect to school or the labor market.

What works to achieve these goals for young people most cost-effectively? While the overall evaluation evidence on employment and training programs has been mixed at best, we also believe that programs and curricula that offer a combination of skill development and paid work experience have often shown the strongest results at improving employment outcomes for these youth (Heinrich and Holzer 2011). If the best of these approaches could be replicated and brought to sufficient scale, in combination with other policies identified later in this chapter, we think that the impacts on disadvantaged youth in America could be positive and sizable. For in-school youth, perhaps the strongest evidence on effective combinations of education and work experience for youth appears in the recent random assignment evaluation of career academies (Kemple 2008). These programs often enroll a few hundred students within larger and more comprehensive high schools; they take general academic courses but also receive occupational training specific to a sector of the economy (such as health care, information technology, or financial services) along with work experience in the summer or during the school year.

The evaluation evidence on career academies shows that the subsequent earnings of at-risk young men were nearly 20 percent higher than earnings for those in the control group as many as eight years after entering the program. Indeed, impacts for at-risk young men were significantly larger than those for young women. More broadly, high-quality career and technical education (CTE) offers the promise of higher graduation rates and better labor market performance among youth (Hoffman 2011; Symonds et al. 2011), especially if we can build a range of "pathways" to good careers that combine strong academic preparation, applied technical instruction, and work experience for all students in secondary and postsecondary schools around the country.

For these programs to achieve their goals, they must not be perceived as "tracking" low-income or minority youth away from postsecondary education. The career academies succeeded in avoiding such tracking: those who attended the academies later enrolled in postsecondary education at the same rates as those in the control group. The goal is thus for high-quality CTE to expand career possibilities, not to deter young people from higher education. And career academies fit the model of "small schools of choice," which have generated much improved high school graduation rates recently in New York City (Bloom, Thompson, and Unterman 2010).[13]

For youth who are out of school, the sectoral training program Year Up offers similar evidence that skill development and paid work experience can improve youth outcomes (Roder and Elliott 2011).[14] Geared for recent high school graduates who have not yet gone on to postsecondary education, Year Up provides several months of training for work, mostly in the information technology and business management fields. It requires its enrollees to have a high school diploma or General Educational Development (GED) degree before joining the program, so those who have dropped out would have to at least clear that hurdle.

Among programs that seek to help young dropouts attain a high school diploma, the National Guard ChalleNGe program, a residential program based on a strict military model, stands out. In an evaluation using randomized controlled trials (RCTs), about 72 percent of participants earned a high school diploma or GED within three years of program entry, compared to 56 percent among controls (Millenky et al. 2011). The various programs in New York's Office of Multiple Pathways to Graduation (OMPG) offer longer-term and quite intensive remediation for youth with more serious skill deficiencies in a variety of nontraditional settings, while the Gateway to College program, which is now in thirty colleges in sixteen states, offers a quicker route to community college for those who have dropped out but have decent basic skills. The OMPG programs and Gateway to College remain to be evaluated, but look promising to date.

Out-of-school youth can also benefit from training and paid work experience in a residential setting. For instance, the latest evaluation of the Job Corps (Schochet, Burghardt, and McConnell 2008) shows some evidence of fadeout of early gains, but the program remains cost-effective for older youth (those age twenty to twenty-four).[15] Among nonresidential programs, YouthBuild provides training and construction experience for youth who work at rehabilitating low-income housing projects; it has not yet generated rigorous evaluation evidence (though an RCT evaluation is under way), but it has led to substantially higher earnings for thousands of out-of-school youth nationwide relative to the earnings of young people from similar backgrounds and demographics who were not enrolled. These programs are based on the view, widely held among practitioners, that paid work motivates young people to remain in programs and also generates opportunities for "contextual learning" that are not often available in the classroom.

For those who enter postsecondary education, our primary challenge is to reduce the enormous rates of noncompletion that prevail today, especially among the disadvantaged (Haskins, Holzer, and Lerman 2009). Many initiatives have been funded by the Gates Foundation and others—such as Achieving the Dream and Breaking Through—at community colleges around the country; these initiatives fund the provision of a range of supportive services and new curricula design, as well as efforts to improve links to the workforce by making courses of study more responsive to local labor market trends. Evidence of gains from these efforts is modest to date, though much more evaluation work remains to be done.

Still, some evidence exists that the kinds of supports provided in the Opening Doors demonstration can improve community college perfor mance and persistence (Richburg-Hayes 2009); these supports include the formation of small "learning communities" among student peer groups, additional financial aid (above and beyond Pell grants) tied to academic performance (such as maintaining a minimum grade point average), and certain kinds of mandatory counseling for students with weak perfor- mance. In addition, some recent evidence suggests that remedial education at community colleges can be improved by integrating the remediation into substantive education or training classes rather than keeping it on a separate track, from which so many students drop out before they even enter their primary course of study. Specifically, the Integrating Basic Education and Skill Training (I-BEST) program in Washington State has generated some evidence of higher rates of credit attainment and course completion in a recent non-experimental study (Jenkins, Zeidenberg, and Kienzl 2009).

Finally, we believe it is important to develop more systematic and com- prehensive approaches for youth, rather than rely on a series of isolated and fragmented programs, so that fewer of them fail. Some evidence that such approaches raise the enrollment and employment rates of disadvan- taged youth can be found in an evaluation of the Youth Opportunities program, which funded thirty-six comprehensive youth systems in low- income neighborhoods at the end of the Clinton administration (Decision Information Resources 2008). Among the most promising examples of a similar effort at the level of a large city is the Philadelphia Youth Network, which brings programs for in-school and out-of-school youth together into a single system.[16] It is critical that we make such systemic efforts, rather than continue with "siloed" programs, if we want to achieve widespread impacts at scale for disconnected young people.

IMPROVING WORK INCENTIVES: EXPANDING THE EARNED INCOME TAX CREDIT FOR CHILDLESS ADULTS

For those young people whose skills will remain limited and who will therefore face only the prospect of fairly low-wage employment, it would be helpful to supplement their meager wages with tax credits—in the hope of improving their earnings and also giving them incentives to work more. Indeed, as long as their labor supply is elastic, higher net wages should generate higher work effort.[17] The national experience with the

EITC over the past few decades has demonstrated the potential of "make work pay" programs to raise employment levels while improving earnings and income among the poor (Meyer and Rosenbaum 2001; Scholz 2007).

The EITC provides a *refundable* tax credit for workers with low family incomes—in other words, even those with little or no federal tax liability receive a tax credit anyway. It is most generous for low-income single mothers with two or more children, providing a credit of roughly 40 percent for each dollar of earned income up to a maximum of about $13,000.[18] The credit is constant over the next $4,000 of income and then is gradually phased out at a rate of about 20 percent per dollar of income over $17,000. But while the EITC currently is very generous to custodial parents of children, who are usually single mothers, it provides only very meager benefits to childless adults and especially noncustodial parents, who are often fathers. For this group, maximum benefits are only $475 per year.[19]

Accordingly, we have developed proposals to expand the EITC for childless adults (Edelman et al. 2006; Edelman et al. 2009). Subsidy rates, at 15 or 20 percent, would be well below the roughly 40 percent now available to low-income parents with custody of their children, but much more generous than they are today for childless adults. Special provisions would be needed to avoid large "marriage penalties" among pairs of workers who are individually eligible for the EITC but whose combined incomes would reduce or eliminate such eligibility; efforts would also need to be made for noncustodial fathers to receive payments, even those in arrears on their current support orders.[20]

More broadly, efforts to "make work pay" could have substantial positive effects not only on parents but on poor children as well. The best evidence of these potential positive effects can be found in the New Hope pilot program in Milwaukee, which provided a set of wage supplements and guaranteed benefits for those who accepted low-wage jobs, as well as public-service jobs for those who could not find a job in the private sector. The program significantly improved employment outcomes among adult participants during the period of the program and even for a few years afterwards, while also generating improved schooling and behavior outcomes among their children (Duncan, Huston, and Weisner 2007). Efforts to scale up this program and to test the replicability of its positive effects deserve support.

IMPROVING INCENTIVES AND REDUCING BARRIERS FOR EX-OFFENDERS AND NONCUSTODIAL PARENTS

Given the very large numbers of disconnected young (and especially African American) men who have criminal records and/or child support orders, it is also critical that efforts be made to reduce their barriers to employment and improve their incentives to accept and remain at low-wage jobs.

The best thing we can do in this regard would be to incarcerate fewer young men to start with, especially for nonviolent drug offenses. Recent efforts to incarcerate fewer young people have been centered on various alternatives to prison, such as drug courts, "smart" probation, community corrections, and a range of efforts commonly referred to as "justice reinvestment" and "restorative justice" (Office of National Drug Control Policy 2013). Reducing the number of parolees who recidivate owing to technical parole violations would help as well (Western 2008).

We should also limit the barriers to legitimate work associated with having a criminal record. States could be encouraged to review their laws that limit job opportunities for felons, to make efforts to define and limit employer discrimination against felons, and to expunge records after several years in which no re-offense has been committed. Several states, including New York, have made substantial progress to date in adopting such low-cost policies that can do much to raise employment for this population (Legal Action Center 2009).

Programmatic efforts to raise employment among ex-offenders have a mixed record to date. Early evidence on "transitional jobs" programs from the Center for Employment Opportunity (CEO) in New York was quite positive in terms of reducing recidivism, but little impact on post-program employment was observed (Redcross et al. 2009).[21] And more recent evidence on the impacts of a range of other transitional jobs programs has been even weaker (Bloom et al. 2010). Still, efforts to provide paid work experience to those behind bars before their release and/or to provide them with education and job training might still have some payoff and need more exploration (Holzer 2009; Mead 2011). Also showing promise are efforts to manage or even forgive portions of arrears for those keeping up with their current payments and to provide a range of employment services for those who need them plus EITC eligibility (Sorensen 2011).[22]

BUT WHAT ABOUT LABOR DEMAND?

All of these proposals focus almost exclusively on the supply side of the labor market—that is, on the youth themselves—while paying scant attention to developments on the demand side of the market. Given the severity of labor demand constraints on youth in the wake of the Great Recession, policies to generate more demand for their labor must be part of any youth policy agenda.

What kinds of demand-side policies make the most sense? We can distinguish between two categories of policy: efforts to stimulate job creation for youth in the short term, while the effects of the Great Recession remain pronounced; and efforts to improve the quantity or quality of the jobs available to disadvantaged youth in the longer term.

Efforts to stimulate demand in the short term could include various kinds of subsidized private or public employment and grants for building schools and infrastructure and preserving state and local public jobs, as well as tax credits for private-sector employers who hire more workers. Indeed, the American Jobs Act proposed by the Obama administration in 2011contained most of these ideas in various forms, but given the political polarization and deadlock that have characterized the federal government in the past few years, virtually none have been implemented as of mid-2013, and it seems unlikely that they will be implemented anytime soon.

The recent success of the Emergency Contingency Fund under the Temporary Assistance for Needy Families (TANF) program, which created about 250,000 jobs in the public and private sectors for the disadvantaged within a short time frame (Lower-Basch 2011), illustrates the potential of subsidized employment. More generally, public-service employment programs that are carefully designed and well targeted toward those in need can not only raise employment rates in the short term but generate valued services for communities as well (Ellwood and Welty 2000; Johnson 2010).

Ideal, but hardly practicable in the current fiscal and political climate, would be a large-scale initiative (building on Americorps and other efforts ranging back to the New Deal) to engage young people in transitional employment in community and national service, with particular emphasis on youth who are disconnected or at risk of becoming disconnected. They could be engaged in work on infrastructure, caregiving, conservation projects, and numerous other possibilities. The work could be combined with education and training so that participants would emerge far more prepared for successful transitions to either work or additional education.

The case for building schools and infrastructure in particular is strong; such work would contribute to a quicker recovery of employment in the construction sector while making much-needed improvements to capital that has been deteriorating. Although of the many trained construction workers who are now unemployed would be the most obvious workers to benefit, opportunities to develop apprenticeships for disadvantaged youth would also be available. More broadly, publicly funded apprenticeships, work-study programs, and other forms of on-the-job training are good ways to combine short-term work experience with longer-term skill and credential improvements that increase the earnings capacities of the disadvantaged over time.

Tax credits to private employers who create more jobs could also benefit youth to a large extent. The best design for such credits would be a temporary and generous "marginal" credit for employers whose payrolls rise by more than some base rate (Bartik 2010). More targeted credits for the hiring of youth or other disadvantaged groups would be aimed not at expanding overall employment but at shifting it toward these disadvantaged groups; recent evidence on the effectiveness of the Work Opportunity Tax Credit (WOTC) for several disadvantaged groups has been less promising (Hamersma 2011).[23]

And how might we encourage the private sector to improve the *quality* of jobs available to disadvantaged youth over the longer term? Historically, federal and state minimum wage statutes have been the most obvious tool for doing so. We continue to support periodic increases in the federal statutory minimum over time, though not so much and so quickly as to deter job creation by employers (especially in our currently weak labor markets).[24]

Similarly, collective bargaining has been an important tool for raising job quality over time, but it has generally been less prevalent in the service sector, where most disadvantaged youth ultimately gain employment, than in more traditional industrial sectors. Some recent successes of the Service Employees International Union (SEIU) at unionizing hotel workers and others in the low-wage sector are a hopeful sign, but private-sector unionization rates more broadly continue to decline and are now very low (about 6 percent nationally). Organizing sectors that are youth-intensive would be particularly challenging, given their very high turnover rates and lower commitments to the labor force. And the need for unionized jobs to survive in more competitive product and labor markets remains a challenge for them as well (Hirsch 2008).[25]

But better jobs for young people may result from encouraging employers—through technical assistance and tax credits—to build high-performance work systems with greater promotion possibilities for their workers. Some promising recent examples of employers being assisted in upgrading the quality and content of their jobs while remaining, or even becoming, more competitive appear in Osterman and Shulman (2011).[26] These approaches certainly merit further exploration and experimentation, along with greater public support.

YOUTH POLICY SINCE 2008

Our focus in this chapter has been on improving education and employment outcomes among disadvantaged youth. Youth policy also includes areas like Americorps and other community service opportunities, juvenile and criminal justice, aging out of foster care, teen pregnancy, runaway and homeless youth, sexual trafficking, and more. So our subject is less than the totality of youth policy, but education and employment outcomes are significantly related to everything else.

The story of youth policy since President Obama took office is mixed — in part because the new administration has offered fewer proposals than expected, and in part because of the remarkable partisan hostility that has been even more pronounced than anticipated.

In 2008–2009, we developed some policy proposals that included many of the ideas described in this chapter (Edelman et al. 2009). In the broadest sense, our hope was that there would be a new partnership for disadvantaged youth that cut across all relevant federal agencies, but especially the U.S. Department of Education and the U.S. Department of Labor. The salient characteristic of this partnership, as we have argued here, would have been bringing the worlds of education and employment closer together for those young people who would benefit from such a connection. The continuum would begin in high school and continue through adolescence into young adulthood and stable attachment to the labor market.

For the school- and community college–based portion of the contin-uum, our idea was that the Department of Education would play the lead role, in part because its fiscal capacity dwarfs the resources commanded by the Department of Labor, which we envisioned as using its funds to play a role in organizing and promoting the employer side of the partner-ship. And we saw the Labor Department playing the larger role in serving those young people who were both out of school and not employed, to get them back into some kind of setting with educational content as well as preparation for work. Overall, our proposals would have provided sig-nificant new resources to this issue, with an emphasis on replicating and scaling the best recent models of both programs and systems for youth and with the full set of complementary policies described here.

The partnership and policy as we envisioned it did not develop. Bits and pieces of the needed policies happened in the Department of Education — through Race to the Top, the community college initiative that fell short of full fruition, and, very modestly, through the Promise Neighborhoods pro-gram. And some of these policies were put in place at the Department of Labor through its innovation funds and other competitive grants, though changes in youth policy more broadly have been caught up in the snail's pace of reauthorization of the Workforce Investment Act.

Finally, we note again that a range of efforts could have been under-taken to raise job creation rates in the aftermath of the Great Recession and to target them toward disadvantaged youth. But political polarization and paralysis at the federal level, as well as the dismal fiscal situations in which states and localities have found themselves, have prevented the implementation of these kinds of proposals, thus prolonging the effects of the recession and worsening the "scarring" encountered by some disadvantaged young people (and others more broadly). While the federal paralysis continues, perhaps such policies could be implemented in the more pragmatic political atmospheres of some states. If state fiscal environments continue to improve as the economic recovery proceeds, there is a greater likelihood that some states will make this effort. This would give us the opportunity to learn more about what works and what does not, so that any ultimate action by the federal government would be even better informed by recent experience.

Beyond steps that can practicably be taken at all levels of government and in the private sector, we need as a nation and in communities across the country to tackle the structural and other problems that block full inclusion in our economy and our society for far too many young people. Issues of race and poverty still matter in fundamental ways. Making our public schools perform at a level of excellence for every child is a challenge that underlies everything we have discussed. Ending the disproportionate and destructive impact of our law enforcement system on young people of color is vital. Ensuring truly equal opportunity in the labor market is an objective still to be fulfilled. Communities across the country need to harness all of the relevant actors to create school-to-work pathways and systems that deliver in the inner city as well as they do in the wealthiest suburb.

As we continue to lose too large a portion of each cohort of young people as they come along, especially young people of color, we know more about what to do than about how to put our knowledge to work. We have to do more.

NOTES

1. These computations are drawn from the outgoing rotation groups of the Current Population Survey (CPS-ORG). We thank Marek Hlavac for generating this table for us.

2. Though part of this decline might represent the fact that the average skill levels of those who remain non-enrolled are likely to fall as enrollment rates rise, this does not appear to explain the overall trend (Holzer and Offner 2006).

3. Employment rates for less-educated young men calculated using the standard definitions of labor force participation and overall enrollment show greater declines since 1979 among blacks than whites (Holzer and Offner 2006). Furthermore, the incarcerated are generally not included in measures of the "non-institutional population" that are calculated from CPS data, and low-income men tend to be undercounted more generally even when not

incarcerated. If the incarcerated were added to our population measures but not to employment counts, our estimated employment rates for the population would be lower for all groups of men, but especially for less-educated black men, who have the highest incarceration rates in the United States (as well as the worst population undercounts); their employment declines over time would also be more severe than what we observe. Unfortunately, we do not have access to group-specific incarceration rates (or undercount rates) that would enable us to correct these measures.

4. While the nation's unemployment rate dropped by about two percentage points (from just over 10 percent to below 8 percent) between 2010 and 2012, most of this drop was caused by falling labor force participation rather than rising employment rates. Employment rates among youth have only barely improved in this time period. We have also seen a dramatic reduction in voluntary employment changes (quits) in this recession, which usually enable young workers to increase their wages and salaries by moving into better jobs early in their careers.

5. These tabulations are based on young people age twenty-two to twenty-four in the 1997 cohort of the National Longitudinal Survey of Youth (NLSY97). See Hill, Holzer, and Chen (2009) for a fuller description and analysis.

6. Most of these results are based on self-reports of respondents except for incarceration, which is often determined from whether or not the individual was incarcerated at the time of the interview. Self-reports on incarceration between interviews or having children outside marriage might still be downward-biased.

7. Since many fewer men than women report having children outside marriage, the differences might reflect the effects of custody on these self-reports or indicate that fathers tend to be older and outside the relevant age group.

8. Before the current decade, most economists believed that technological change was a more powerful force than globalization in raising inequality. This view has changed somewhat since 2000, given the rising imports of manufactured goods from China as well as the growth of offshoring of production jobs more broadly (Hanson 2012; Haskel et al. 2012). Economists have also debated the extent to which immigration reduces the employment or earnings of native-born workers (Borjas 2003; Card 2005). The general consensus is that these impacts are mostly quite modest, but somewhat more negative for high school dropouts and for the least-skilled workers more generally (Holzer 2011).

9. If wages were downwardly "rigid" when labor demand shifts in figure 3.1, then we could observe involuntary unemployment. As drawn, the figure merely shows lower employment and labor force activity at the second "equilibrium" point in the labor market after demand has shifted away from these workers.

10. See, for example, Mead (2011): see also Orland Patterson, "A Poverty of the Mind," *New York Times*, March 26, 2006.

11. For instance, David Autor (2010) usually defines middle-skill jobs—many of them good-paying production and clerical jobs for high school graduates—as those whose average occupational wages as of 1980 were in the middle of the wage spectrum. Though jobs in these particular categories have shrunken dramatically in number, other categories of jobs for technicians and moderately skilled employees in many sectors have grown over time in ways that are not well captured by these data. Although these middle-skill job categories shrank significantly during the Great Recession, especially in construction and manufacturing, we believe that at least a significant portion of these jobs will return when the labor market recovers.

12. Using longitudinal micro data on both employers and workers from the Longitudinal Employer Household Dynamics (LEHD) data at the Census Bureau, Holzer and his colleagues (2011) were able to measure both worker and firm quality over time and how workers of different skills are matched to jobs of different quality in various years.

13. For a review of efforts to reduce high school dropout rates or to recover dropouts, see Tyler and Lofstrom (2010).

14. Sheila Maguire and her colleagues (2010) report very strong evidence on the success of sectoral training programs for working poor adults, though youth participated in these programs to some extent as well. These researchers found that earnings were about $4,000 higher for a randomly assigned participant group than for controls, up to twenty-four months after the training began. Ann Roder and Mark Elliott's (2011) estimated impacts for Year Up, based on randomized control trials, were similar in magnitude.

15. Unfortunately, the residential component of the program also makes it quite expensive, with annual costs of approximately $20,000 per participant.

16. For descriptions of citywide efforts to help youth in several major cities in the United States, see Martin and Halperin (2006).

17. Evidence on the positive labor supply elasticities of the disadvantaged is summarized in Katz (1998).

18. Maximum dollar amounts of the credit were just over $5,200 for families with two children and just over $5,800 for those with three or more in 2012.

19. This maximum represents a tax credit of 7.6 percent on earned income up to $6,250 per year.

20. See Edelman et al. (2009) for discussions of both sets of issues. The marriage penalty could be lessened by counting only half of the lower earner's income when calculating total income for purposes of eligibility. NCPs who are currently paying support and whose previous child support debts (or "arrears") are being "managed" (as discussed later in the chapter) would be eligible to keep their EITC payments.

21. For instance, arrest rates among CEO participants in the second year following program entry were about five percentage points lower (23 versus

28 percent) than among control group members. The fact that employment effects faded more quickly than recidivism effects suggests that the transitional jobs and other services did not transmit lasting improvements in workplace skills that were valued by the labor market, but these jobs and services may have influenced personal motivation or social networks in ways that improved behavioral outcomes.

22. The state of New York was one of the first to make noncustodial fathers paying child support eligible for the EITC. But take-up rates have been very low, owing to the fact that those in arrears will have any such additional payments garnished. The need to combine EITC eligibility with arrears management and default orders adjustment is clearly illustrated in the New York experience.

23. The WOTC, which replaced the earlier Targeted Jobs Tax Credit (TJTC), provides tax credits for up to a year for the hiring of workers from a range of specific disadvantaged populations, such as ex-offenders and long-term welfare recipients. But take-up rates are generally low, as employers seem to be either unaware or uninterested in the credits, apparently preferring to pay more for employees whom they expect to perform well on their jobs. These credits can also create windfalls for employers who simply hire the same workers with or without the credits. Hamersma (2011) shows that impacts on the employment of current and former welfare recipients while the credit is in effect are very modest and that they disappear once individual eligibility for the credits expire.

24. For some recent evidence on the extent to which minimum wage increases might reduce employment among the young, see Neumark and Wascher (2009). A more sanguine view, arguing that the evidence of falling employment in response to minimum wage increases is quite thin, appears in earlier work by Card and Krueger (1997).

25. If anything, even the modest reductions in employment that might be generated if union wage increases were not offset by productivity increases might hurt youth the most, as they are the most marginal workers in any setting.

26. These include many sectoral training programs, such as those run by Local 1199c in health care and Project Quest in San Antonio, where intermediaries help employers build career ladders and pathways and invest more in training frontline workers for better jobs on these pathways.

REFERENCES

Alexander, Michelle. 2010. *The New Jim Crow: Mass Incarceration in the Age of Color-blindness*. New York: New Press.

Autor, David. 2010. "The Polarization of Job Opportunities in the U.S. Labor Market." Washington, D.C.: Center for American Progress.

Autor, David, Lawrence F. Katz, and Melissa S. Kearney. 2008. "Trends in U.S. Wage Inequality: Revising the Revisionists." *Review of Economics and Statistics* 90(2): 300–323.

Bartik, Timothy. 2010. "Not All Job Creation Tax Credits Are Created Equal." Washington, D.C.: Economic Policy Institute

Blau, Francine, and Lawrence Kahn. 1997. "Swimming Upstream: Trends in the Gender Wage Differential in the 1980s." *Journal of Labor Economics* 15(1): 1–42.

Bloom, Howard, Saskia Levy Thompson, and Rebecca Unterman. 2010. "Transforming the High School Experience: How New York City's New Small Schools Are Boosting Student Achievement and Graduation Rates." New York: MDRC.

Borjas, George. 2003. "The Labor Demand Curve *Is* Downward Sloping: Reexamining the Impacts of Immigration on the Labor Market." *Quarterly Journal of Economics* 118(4): 1335–74.

Bound, John, and Richard Freeman. 1992. "What Went Wrong? The Erosion of Relative Earnings and Employment Among Young Black Men in the 1980s." *Quarterly Journal of Economics* 107(1): 201–32.

Bound, John, and Harry J. Holzer. 1993. "Industrial Structure, Skill Levels, and the Employment Rates of White and Black Males." *Review of Economics and Statistics* 75(3): 387–94.

Card, David. 2005. "Is the New Immigration Really So Bad?" *Economic Journal* 115(506): 300–323.

Card, David, and Jonathan Dinardo. 2007. "The Impact of Technological Change on Low-Wage Workers: A Review." In *Working and Poor: How Economic and Policy Changes Are Affecting Low-Wage Workers*, ed. Rebecca M. Blank, Sheldon H. Danziger, and Robert F. Schoeni. New York: Russell Sage Foundation.

Card, David, and Alan Krueger. 1997. *Myth and Measurement: The New Economics of the Minimum Wage*. Princeton, N.J.: Princeton University Press.

Carnevale, Anthony, Nicole Smith, and Jeffrey Strohl. 2010. "'Help Wanted': Projections of Jobs and Education Requirements Through 2018." Washington, D.C.: Georgetown University, Center for Education and the Workforce.

Cornwell, Christopher, David Mustard, and Jessica Van Parys. 2011. "Non-Cognitive Skills and Gender Disparities in Test Scores and Teacher Assessments: Evidence from Primary School." Working Paper 5973. Bonn, Germany: Institute for the Study of Labor (IZA).

Decision Information Resources, Inc. 2008. "Evaluation of Youth Opportunities Program." Report to the Employment and Training Administration. Washington: U.S. Department of Labor.

Duncan, Greg J., Aletha C. Huston, and Thomas S. Weisner. 2007. *Higher Ground: New Hope for the Working Poor and Their Children*. New York: Russell Sage Foundation.

Duncan, Greg, and Richard Murnane, eds. 2011. *Whither Opportunity? Rising Inequality, Schools, and Children's Life Chances*. New York: Russell Sage Foundation.

Edelman, Peter, Mark Greenberg, Steve Holt, and Harry Holzer. 2009. "Expanding the EITC to Help More Low-Wage Workers." Washington, D.C.: Georgetown University, Center on Poverty, Inequality, and Public Policy.

Edelman, Peter, Harry J. Holzer, and Paul Offner. 2006. *Reconnecting Disadvantaged Young Men*. Washington, D.C.: Urban Institute Press.

Ellwood, David, and Elisabeth Welty. 2000. "Public Service Employment and Mandatory Work." In *Finding Jobs: Work and Welfare Reform*, ed. David Card and Rebecca Blank. New York: Russell Sage Foundation.

Freeman, Richard. 1992. "Crime and the Employment of Disadvantaged Youth." In *Urban Labor Markets and Job Opportunity*, ed. George E. Peterson and Wayne Vroman. Washington, D.C.: Urban Institute Press.

Goldin, Claudia, and Lawrence Katz. 2008. *The Race Between Education and Technology*. Cambridge, Mass.: Harvard University Press.

Hamersma, Sarah. 2011. "Why Don't Eligible Firms Claim Hiring Subsidies? The Role of Job Duration." *Economic Inquiry* 49(3): 916–34.

Hanson, Gordon. 2012. "The Rise of Middle Kingdoms: Emerging Economies in Global Trade." *Journal of Economic Perspectives* 26(2): 41–64.

Haskel, Jonathan, Robert Lawrence, Edward Leamer, and Matthew Slaughter. 2012. "Globalization and U.S. Wages: Modifying Classic Theory to Explain Recent Facts." *Journal of Economic Perspectives* 26(2): 65–90.

Haskins, Ron, Harry Holzer, and Robert Lerman. 2009. "Promoting Economic Mobility by Increasing Postsecondary Educational Attainment Among the Disadvantaged." Washington, D.C.: Pew Trusts, Economic Mobility Project.

Heinrich, Carolyn, and Harry Holzer. 2011. "Improving Education and Employment Among Disadvantaged Young Men: Proven and Promising Strategies." *Annals of the American Academy of Political and Social Science* 635: 163–91.

Hill, Carolyn, Harry Holzer, and Henry Chen. 2009. *Against the Tide: Household Structure, Opportunities, and Outcomes Among White and Black Youth*. Kalamazoo, Mich.: W. E. Upjohn Institute for Employment Research.

Hirsch, Barry. 2008. "Sluggish Institutions in a Dynamic World: Can Unions and Industrial Competition Coexist?" *Journal of Economic Perspectives* 22(1): 153–76.

Hoffman, Nancy. 2011. "A Fresh Look at Career and Technical Education." Paper presented to the conference on "Preparing Youth for the Jobs of Tomorrow." University of Pennsylvania Graduate School of Education, Philadelphia, May 25.

Holzer, Harry. 2009. "Collateral Costs: Effects of Incarceration on Employment and Earnings of Young Workers." In *Do Prisons Make Us Safer? The Benefits and Costs of the Prison Boom*, ed. Steven Raphael and Michael A. Stoll. New York: Russell Sage Foundation.

——. 2010. "Is the Middle of the Job Market Really Disappearing? Comments on the Polarization Hypothesis." Washington, D.C.: Center for American Progress.

———. 2011. "Immigration Policy and Less-Skilled Workers in the United States: Reflections on Future Directions for Reform." Washington, D.C.: Migration Policy Institute (January).

Holzer, Harry, Julia Lane, David Rosenblum, and Fredrik Andersson. 2011. *Where Are All the Good Jobs Going?* New York: Russell Sage Foundation.

Holzer, Harry, and Robert Lerman. 2007. "America's Forgotten Middle-Skill Jobs: Education and Training Requirements for the Next Decade and Beyond." Washington, D.C.: Workforce Alliance.

Holzer, Harry, and Paul Offner. 2006. "Trends in the Employment of Less-Educated Young Men." In *Black Males Left Behind*, ed. Ronald Mincy. Washington, D.C.: Urban Institute Press.

Holzer, Harry, Paul Offner, and Elaine Sorensen. 2005. "Declining Employment Among Less-Educated Young Black Men: The Role of Incarceration and Child Support." *Journal of Policy Analysis and Management* 24(2): 329–50.

Jacob, Brian. 2002. "Where the Boys Aren't: Non-Cognitive Skills, Returns to School, and the Gender Gap in Higher Education." Working Paper 8964. Cambridge, Mass.: National Bureau of Economic Research (May).

Jacobson, Louis, and Christine Mokher. 2009. "Pathways to Boosting the Earnings of Low-Income Students by Increasing Their Educational Attainment." Arlington, Va.: Hudson Institute Center for Employment Policy/CNA Analysis & Solutions (January).

Jenkins, Davis, Matthew Zeidenberg, and Gregory Kienzl. 2009. "Building Bridges to Postsecondary Training for Low-Skill Adults: Outcomes of Washington State's I-BEST Program." Working paper. New York: Columbia University, Center for Research on Community Colleges (May).

Johnson, Cliff. 2010. "Publicly Funded Jobs: An Essential Strategy for Reducing Poverty and Economic Distress Throughout the Business Cycle." Washington, D.C.: Urban Institute.

Juhn, Chinhui. 1992. "Declining Labor Force Participation Among Young Men: The Role of Declining Market Opportunities." *Quarterly Journal of Economics* 107(1): 79–121.

Kahn, Lisa. 2010. "The Long-Term Labour Market Consequences of Graduating from College in a Bad Economy." *Labour Economics* 17(2): 303–16.

Katz, Lawrence. 1998. "Wage Subsidies for the Disadvantaged." In *Generating Jobs*, ed. Richard Freeman and Peter Gottschalk. New York: Russell Sage Foundation.

Kemple, James. 2008. *Career Academies: Long-Term Impacts on Earnings, Educational Attainment, and the Transition to Adulthood*. New York: MDRC.

Legal Action Center. 2009. *After Prison: Roadblocks to Reentry, 2009 Update*. New York: Legal Action Center.

Lower-Basch, Elizabeth. 2011. "Rethinking Work Opportunity: From Tax Credits to Subsidized Job Placements." Washington, D.C.: Spotlight on Poverty and Opportunity (November 8).

Magnuson, Katherine, and Jane Waldfogel, eds. 2008. *Steady Gains and Stalled Progress*. New York: Russell Sage Foundation.

Maguire, Sheila, Joshua Freely, Carol Clymer, Maureen Conway, and Deena Schwartz. 2010. "Tuning in to Local Labor Markets: Findings from the Sectoral Employment Impact Study." Philadelphia: Public/Private Ventures.

Martin, Nancy, and Samuel Halperin. 2006. "Whatever It Takes: How Twelve Communities Are Reconnecting Out-of-School Youth." Washington, D.C.: American Youth Policy Forum.

Mead, Lawrence. 2011. *Expanding Work Programs for Poor Men*. Washington, D.C.: American Enterprise Institute.

Meyer, Bruce, and Daniel Rosenbaum. 2001. "Welfare, the EITC, and the Labor Supply of Single Mothers." *Quarterly Journal of Economics* 116(3): 1063–1114.

Millenky, Megan, Dan Bloom, Sara Muller-Ravett, and Joseph Broadus. 2011. "Staying on Course: Three-Year Results of the National Guard Youth ChalleNGe Evaluation." New York: MDRC.

Neumark, David, and William Wascher. 2009. *Minimum Wages*. Cambridge, Mass.: MIT Press.

Office of National Drug Control Policy. 2013. "Alternatives to Incarceration." Washington: Executive Office of the President. Available at: http://www.whitehouse.gov/ondcp/alternatives-to-incarceration (accessed December 2011).

Osterman, Paul, and Beth Shulman. 2011. *Good Jobs America*. New York: Russell Sage Foundation.

Pager, Devah. 2007. *Marked: Race, Crime, and Finding Work in an Era of Mass Incarceration*. Chicago: University of Chicago Press.

Redcross, Cynthia, Dan Bloom, Gilda Azurdia, Janine Zweig, and Nancy Pindus. 2009. "Transitional Jobs for Ex-Prisoners: Implementation, Two-Year Impacts, and Costs of the Center for Employment Opportunities (CEO) Prisoner Reentry Program." New York: MDRC.

Richburg-Hayes, LaShawn. 2009. "Rewarding Persistence: Impacts of a Performance-Based Scholarship Program on Low-Income Parents." New York: MDRC.

Roder, Ann, and Mark Elliott. 2011. "A Promising Start: Year Up's Initial Impacts on Low-Income Young Adults' Careers." New York: Economic Mobility Corporation.

Schochet, Peter, John Burghardt, and Sheena McConnell. 2008. "Does Job Corps Work? Impact Findings from the National Job Corps Study." *American Economic Review* 98(5): 1864–86.

Scholz, J. Karl. 2007. "Employment-Based Tax Credits for Low-Wage Workers." Washington, D.C.: Brookings Institution, Hamilton Project.

Sorensen, Elaine. 2011. "New York Initiative Helps Fathers Increase Earnings and Child Support." Policy Brief. Washington, D.C.: Urban Institute.

Symonds, William, et al. 2011. "Pathways to Prosperity: Meeting the Challenge of Preparing Young Americans for the 21st Century." Cambridge, Mass.: Harvard University, Graduate School of Education (February).

Tyler, John, and Magnus Lofstrom. 2010. "Finishing High School: Alternative Pathways and Dropout Recovery." *The Future of Children* 19(1): 77–103.

U.S. Census Bureau. 1979–2010. *Current Population Surveys, Outgoing Rotation Groups*. Washington: U.S. Census Bureau.

Von Wachter, Till. 2010. "Responding to Long-Term Unemployment." Testimony before the Joint Economic Committee of the U.S. Congress. May 25.

Western, Bruce. 2006. *Punishment and Inequality in America*. New York: Russell Sage Foundation.

———. 2008. "From Prison to Work: A Proposal for a National Prisoner Reentry Program." Washington, D.C.: Brookings Institution, Hamilton Project.

Wilson, William J. 2009. *More Than Just Race: Being Black and Poor in the Inner City*. New York: W. W. Norton.

Wolfe, Barbara, and Lawrence Wu, eds. 2001. *Out of Wedlock: Causes and Consequences of Nonmarital Fertility*. New York: Russell Sage Foundation.

Chapter 4 | Mending the Fissured Workplace

David Weil

DURING MUCH OF the twentieth century, the critical employment relationship was between large businesses and workers, but that is no longer the case. Large businesses with national and international reputations operating at the top of their industries continue to focus on delivering value to their customers and investors. However, they no longer directly employ legions of workers to make products or deliver service. Like a rock that has developed a fissure that deepens and spreads with time, the workplace over the last three decades has broken apart as employment has been shed by lead businesses and transferred to a complicated network of smaller business units.

In the fissured workplace, employment is no longer a clear relationship between a well-defined employer and its employees. The basic terms of employment—hiring, evaluation, pay, supervision, training, coordination—are now distributed across multiple organizations, and responsibility for working conditions has become blurred. Fissuring has also had serious impacts on the bedrocks that workers depend on from employment: the share of the economic pie available to them and their families; their exposure to health and safety and other risks each day at work; and employer compliance with the most basic labor standards set out by law.

The fissured workplace has spread across sectors and organizational forms. Several examples are indicative of the scope of change. In 1960 most hotel employees worked for the brand whose name appeared over the hotel entrance. Today more than 80 percent of hotel staff are employed by owners and supervised by separate management companies that bear no relation to the hotel brand name of the property where they work. Twenty years ago, workers in the distribution center of a major manufacturer like Hershey's or a retailer like Walmart would be hired, supervised, evaluated, and paid by that company. Today many workers receive a paycheck from a labor supplier and are managed by the personnel of a large logistics company, but follow the detailed operating standards of the nationally known retailer or consumer brand serviced by the facility. And whereas IBM in its ascendency directly employed workers to produce its computers, from designers and engineers to the people on the factory floor, Apple, now our economy's most highly valued company, directly employs only 63,000 of the more than 750,000 workers globally responsible for designing, selling, manufacturing, and assembling its products.

Many of the industries we associate with low wages, precarious employment, high rates of violation of basic labor standards, and dangerous working conditions are also the industries in which fissuring is most advanced.[1] These include eating and drinking businesses, janitorial services, many sectors of manufacturing, residential construction, and services. But fissuring also has spread to industries in retailing, the telecommunications and IT sectors, hospitals, and business services. In fact, employment fissuring represents an organizational format that has spread across many sectors of the economy and assumes many different forms.

Fissured employment has three fundamental impacts on society. First, moving employment from lead employers to other businesses providing services for them has repercussions for how wages are set and economic surplus is shared. Gains once shared between lead businesses and their workforce have shifted increasingly to investors and in some cases consumers. Wage stagnation and the worsening nature of work for many can be seen as a consequence of this change.

Second, shifting employment outward necessitates changes in how work is coordinated. Problems arise when there are many hands in a kitchen and inadequate oversight. So too in the workplace. As fissured employment blurs lines of responsibility and liability (intentionally so in some cases), oversight of important activities like health and safety may fall through the cracks. In the worst cases, breakdowns in lines of responsibility lead to workplace fatalities, as seen in petrochemicals, coal mining, cell towers, and manufacturing.

Finally, fissuring's third impact on society has been to undermine compliance with labor standards. Fissuring creates "orbits" of subsidiary businesses revolving around a central lead company. Competition is intense in each orbit—and often becomes more so the further out the orbit is from the lead business. Since competition is often price-based, the pressure to reduce costs becomes intense, leading these subsidiary businesses to lower wages, allow more precarious employment conditions, and, in many cases, subvert or even violate workplace laws and labor standards.

The fissured workplace compels us to rethink our basic definitions of employment. An economy in which much employment has been shifted outside of the boundaries poses grave questions about the efficacy of the traditional approach to workplace regulation. The problems are magnified for low-wage and vulnerable workers working at the "outer orbits" of fissured employment structures.

This chapter begins with a discussion of the elements of employment fissuring and the "recipe" that underlies it. It then examines the limitations of current law with respect to fissured employment, as well as the inherent problems of traditional approaches to enforcement. The central part of the chapter discusses a number of initiatives undertaken by the Obama administration that suggest ways in which new enforcement methods might persuade lead business organizations to rethink their decisions that lead to the fissured workplace, including a focus on the top of a fissured structure and an end to forms of the fissured workplace that are expressly designed to avoid basic employer obligations.

THE FISSURED "RECIPE"

Fissured employment represents the intersection of three business strategies—a focus on revenues, a focus on costs, and the "glue" that makes the overall strategy operate effectively.[2] These areas of focus arise not from employment per se, but from the demands by capital markets that leading companies focus on the "core competencies" that produce value to investors and consumers by building brands, creating innovative products and services, capitalizing on true economies of scale and scope, or coordinating complex supply chains. But focusing on core competencies has also led to shifting out activities once considered central to operations to other organizations in order to convert employer-employee relationships into arm's-length market transactions. Fissuring weds these potentially contradictory activities together through the "glue" of creating, monitoring, and enforcing standards on product and service delivery made available through new information and communication technologies and enabled by organizational models like franchising, labor brokers, and third-party management.

The first element of fissuring, the broad movement urging companies to focus on core competencies, began in the late 1970s, when investors, lenders, and general capital market pressures increasingly compelled the senior management of leading companies to focus attention on those activities that added the greatest value (such as product design, product innovation, cost or quality efficiencies, and other unique strengths) while farming out work to other organizations not central to their core mission. This strategy led companies to focus their key strategies and their workforces on developing brands and strong customer identification with their goods or services, building the capacity to introduce new products or designs, and creating true economies of scale or scope in production and operation. Activities outside of this core were shifted away.[3]

The second element of fissuring, the focus on costs, leads companies to respond to the drive to develop core competencies by breaking apart the elements of producing a good or providing a service and shifting to other parties those elements that are not central to its profit model. Even in the 1930s, the Ford Motor Company, a pioneer in the vertical integration of production, realized the limits of integration: the automaker discovered, for instance, that it did not benefit from trying to supply its own steel or leather (Chandler 1977; Williamson 1985). It could shift that work to others and use the market to acquire those inputs. The evolving auto industry has pushed that concept further and further as major producers have shifted off more and more production to other suppliers. But assessments of the proper boundaries of a firm have not been limited to manufacturing.

For a variety of reasons, the large employers that dominated the economy and labor market of the last century required unified personnel and pay policies and internal labor markets: to take advantage of administrative efficiencies; to create consistency in corporate policies; and to reduce exposure to violations of laws. In large firms employing everyone from engineers and clerical employees to line workers and janitors, unified human resource policies reduced potential friction among the diverse workforce by creating standard wages and benefits within jobs as well as across different jobs. This had the effect of raising wages at the lower end of the wage distribution (such as for janitors in an automobile factory) and, as a result, the average wages of large employers relative to smaller employers. Fissuring the provision of service to other firms has had the impact of allowing lead companies to lower their costs, since externalizing activities to other firms (particularly those operating in more competitive markets) eliminates the need to pay the higher wages and benefits typically provided by large enterprises, as well as the need to establish consistency in human resource policies, which are no longer uniformly relevant inside the firm.[4]

Clearly, there is a tension between the first two elements of fissured strategies: by shifting the provision of services to other businesses, companies that have created brands may jeopardize them if quality standards are not adhered to closely. Similarly, coordination economies do not persist if the suppliers that a firm depends on fail to live up to them or to provide the services required in a timely manner. The third element of a fissured strategy is therefore developing clear, explicit, and detailed standards that provide the blueprint for the enterprises at lower levels to follow. But detailed standards are not enough: the lead organization must also create contracts or develop organizational structures that allow it to monitor the affiliated companies and impose real costs if they fail to abide by them.

It is not coincidental, then, that the growth of fissuring has been accompanied by the creation of many different forms of standard setting and monitoring, from the promulgation of bar codes, electronic standards, GPS, and other methods of tracking products through supply chains and the monitoring of the provision of services to customers (Baker and Hubbard 2003). At the same time, organizational forms that were once restricted to a few industries like fast food, such as franchising, have become omnipresent, spanning sectors from janitorial and landscaping services to home health care (see generally Blair and Lafontaine 2005).

Taken together, these elements of fissuring have created a model for industries—and for an overall economy—that is wired differently from the model it has gradually replaced. Large corporations, where value creation, market power, and notably employment were concentrated, dominated the economic system for much of the twentieth century. The fissured economy still is powerfully affected by the large corporation, with this concentration of value creation and economic power. But employment now has been split off; shifted to a range of secondary players that function in more competitive markets, and separated from the locus of value creation.

WORKPLACE LAWS AND DEFINITIONS OF EMPLOYMENT

Although the modern employment relationship bears little resemblance to the relationship assumed in the core U.S. workplace regulations, there are some desirable aspects of the fissured world—consumers benefit, for instance, when companies try to market goods and services that conform to their tastes—as well as productivity gains when firms focus on core competencies.[5]

Franchise manuals, performance contracts, delivery standards and systems, and monitoring arrangements directly affect the day-to-day and often hour-by-hour operation of lower-level businesses, thereby influencing the tasks, pacing, and outcomes of work. The prices paid by lead companies to lower-level businesses, whether in the form of service contracts, franchise agreements, or pay packages for subcontractors, correspondingly determine the operating margins of those entities providing services. Yet despite the resulting influence wielded by lead companies, they regularly profess a lack of knowledge about the work conditions that result and often absent themselves from some coordination functions that might compromise their arm's-length status.

Thus arises a fundamental question framing workplace policies. Current public policies, premised on simple employer-employee models, implicitly bundle operational control with responsibility, but fissuring splits that bundle apart, allowing lead companies to set the terms of a wide range of workplace practices yet eschew responsibility for their consequences, which are left on the shoulders of the lower-level businesses operating under more demanding conditions. Given the social consequences of these arrangements, *should lead companies be allowed to have it both ways?*

Turning back the clock to an earlier time, in the hope that lead employers will reemploy the large and varied workforce of previous times, is not only unlikely to happen but in some respects would be undesirable. Instead, public policies should attempt to influence the internal balancing carried on by lead companies when they create fissured relationships in their organizations. To see how this could be done, we start by briefly reviewing how workplace laws currently treat employment. This review will bring into sharper relief the outlines of a more fruitful policy to change the dynamics that bring on many of the problems of the low-wage workplace.

Who's in Charge? Defining Employers in the Fissured Workplace

Workplace laws and the court opinions interpreting them generally start with the definitions of employers and employees arising from the common law.[6] The common law bases its views of employment relationships on whether there is a master-servant relationship between the parties, where the master (or principal) employs the servant (acting as the master's agent) to undertake some action for its benefit. The master in the relationship directs and controls the servant in his or her activities. Under tort law regarding the liability of the master for the actions of the servant, courts apply a "direct and control" test to ascertain whether those tasks have been sufficiently defined, monitored, and rewarded to establish employment. The question of whether a party oversees the means (that is the way that work is actually done) or only the outcomes has important implications as to whether the party undertaking the work activity is an employee or an independent contractor. But the important point is that the test itself can impose a fairly high standard in showing that the principal has a significant role in setting out the tasks and activities it expects of its agent.[7]

The Fair Labor Standards Act (FLSA) defines an employee as "any individual who is employed by an employer" and as someone whose "employ includes to suffer or permit to work." This obscure phrase offers perhaps the broadest definition of employee of any federal statute. It goes beyond the definition offered by the common law focus on the degree of actual control of the employee. Instead, courts have noted that the phrase "to suffer or permit" implies that even an employer's broad knowledge of the working being done on its behalf is sufficient to establish a relationship. Given the wide latitude implied by this definition, courts have applied an economic reality test to evaluate the particular economic situation surrounding a worker and employer or employers. Although the language makes possible interpretations that capture the complexities of the modern workplace, courts have historically tended to hew to relatively narrow definitions of employment.[8]

At the other end of the spectrum, the National Labor Relations Act (NLRA), the federal statute governing union organizing and collective bargaining, uses a restrictive definition and a narrow economic reality test for defining employment that adheres more closely to common law notions. Originally, the Supreme Court, in ruling on the NLRA's employer-employee definitions, deferred to the National Labor Relations Board (NLRB). In NLRB v. Hearst Publications Inc., the Court explicitly stated that the employment definition was not confined to common law definitions but could legitimately look to whether "as a matter of economic fact, to the evils the Act was designed to eradicate." In this particular case, the Court upheld an NLRB ruling that "newsies" (boys who sold newspapers in the street on commission) were in fact employees of the Hearst publishing empire, despite Hearst's contention that they were formally independent contractors who purchased papers from Hearst but sold them on their own as "entrepreneurs." The NLRB decision and Supreme Court affirmation of it led enraged conservatives in Congress to amend the NLRA in 1947 to specifically exempt independent contractors.[9] This moved the NLRB and the courts to apply the tests for employment created by common law in deciding on issues of coverage under the act.[10]

The Occupational Safety and Health Act (OSHA) of 1970 defines an "employer" as "a person engaged in a business affecting commerce who has employees." The act requires that an employer "shall furnish to each of his employees employment and a place of employment which are free from recognized hazards that are causing or are likely to cause death or serious physical harm to his employees."[11] Although this definition of employer reflects the act's focus on ensuring that safe conditions prevail in the workplace, it creates obvious problems in that, with the many forms of fissuring, the party that creates the conditions of work might not actually have "employees." For example, AT&T does not directly employ cell tower maintenance workers (although it once did, before the demand for iPhones exponentially expanded the need for cell tower capacity), but uses multiple layers of subcontractors to undertake this work. As a result, fatality rates on AT&T cell towers and those of other carriers are ten times the level of those for construction in general.[12]

Other federal and state statutes offer their own definitions of employment that are similarly rooted in common law definitions of agency, but tailored to the particular aims of the statutes. For a large swath of employment in the economy, subtle definitions did not matter much for many decades: it was relatively clear who the employer was and who the employee was, and the boundaries of the firm were equally clear. The more the workplace has fissured, however, the more the subtleties presented by the common law and the specific definitions embodied in statutes have come to matter. In effect, what was at one time located at the edges of legal disputes regarding either idiosyncratic occupations (newsies) or historically fissured industries (construction and garments) has become a mainstream problem of employment; as a result, the subtleties of these statutes are more central to achieving the objectives of workplace laws.[13]

Rethinking Employment Boundaries

The balancing that is a basic part of the fissured recipe creates incentives for the employer to further distance itself from the employment relationship.[14] To bring existing workplace statutes into closer alignment with the arrangements in many fissured workplaces, legislation would need to broaden the responsibility of lead organizations in the realm of employment to make it consistent with the roles they play in their other relationships with subordinate businesses. The principle here would be one of parallelism: if a company exerts minute control over aspects of quality, production, and delivery of services, that control should extend more fully to the domain of employment as well—all these being aspects of the business that are directly valuable to the company.

Similarly, if a firm sits at the top of a complicated process of production in which its pricing, technical standards, and quality requirements fundamentally affect the returns available to the network of businesses operating within that firm, public policies should increase this firm's incentives to oversee coordination of the system it has created by virtue of its position (particularly with respect to health and safety issues). In effect, such public policies would recognize that if lead businesses can create effective systems to achieve quality, price, and scheduling objectives, they should be required to bring that expertise to the employment realm and ensure workplace and public safety as well.

A number of legal scholars have put forward proposals with respect to rethinking employment boundaries. One set of proposals focuses on broadening employer responsibility for violations of workplace standards and increasing liability for those companies that benefit from various fissured forms. Several proposals build on the model created under a current provision of the Fair Labor Standards Act, referred to as the "hot cargo" provision. The hot cargo provision allows the U.S. Department of Labor's Wage and Hour Division to embargo goods in transit if investigations find that the law has been violated at any earlier point of production. This provision allows the department, for example, to hold the delivery of a manufacturer's clothing shipment if it finds that a subcontractor violated minimum wage standards.

Brishen Rogers (2010) proposes a broad expansion of the hot cargo provision to workplace legislation generally through the creation of a duty-based test that would expand employer responsibility to end-user firms that fail to exercise due care in ensuring that suppliers have complied with labor standards. Timothy Glynn (2011) goes a step further, arguing that the nature of "disaggregated" employment requires abandoning fine-grained arguments over immediate or extended employer liability. He argues instead that "commercial actors would be held strictly liable for wage and hour violations in the production of any goods and services they purchase, sell, or distribute, whether directly or through intermediaries" (Glynn 2011, 105). Expanding liability to include upstream producers would certainly affect important elements of fissured employment decisions, as the prior discussion of the factors underlying vicarious liability indicates.

Successful legislation to address the problems arising from fissured employment would require lead businesses to include social as well as private benefits and costs in making their balancing decisions on employment. With laws changed so that lead businesses cannot "have it both ways," some companies might choose to keep employment "inside" the organization. But that is not the only outcome that legislation should seek. Lead businesses might still choose to shift employment outward through contracting, franchising, third-party management, or other organizational forms. But they might do so with greater scrutiny in the selection, monitoring, and coordination of those subordinate organizations, given their heightened responsibility.

There are compelling reasons for making substantial changes to individual federal workplace statutes as well as state laws that are similarly out of synch with workplace realities. It is equally important to rethink the assignment of liability in the workplace, as well as other public outcomes (environment, consumer safety, public health) affected by the changed relationships of fissured employment. However, the battlefield of workplace legislation in the last two decades is littered with failure. Given the political climate in Washington, sweeping changes to the definitions of employer liability or even more modest changes to definitions of joint employment seem unlikely for the foreseeable future.[15]

A more promising approach to mending the fissured workplace focuses on using existing laws to create the incentives for lead businesses to rethink decisions that lead to fissured workplaces. Focusing on enforcement and implementation of minimum wage, overtime, health and safety, and anti-discrimination laws affords opportunities to address workplace problems immediately. Using scarce political resources to create innovative tools and approaches for enforcement can produce more significant results in a shorter amount of time than focusing solely on new legislation. We turn to the possibilities in this regard in the next section, drawing on the experiences of enforcement initiatives that are already under way.

STRATEGIC ENFORCEMENT FOR THE FISSURED WORKPLACE

Traditional enforcement strategies assume that enforcement should be focused at the level where workplace violations occur. Yet the forces driving noncompliance in many industries with large concentrations of low-wage workers arise from the organizations located at higher levels of industry structures. Enforcement policies seeking to improve compliance and conditions among low-wage workers need to be informed by an understanding of the fissured workplace and should focus more strategically on the higher-level business organizations that affect compliance behavior "on the ground," where vulnerable workers are actually found.

Agencies responsible for enforcing the law where fissured workplaces are common should begin by "mapping" the business relationships underlying a sector, carefully tracking all of the different players that have an impact on workplace conditions. Improving conditions in the eating and drinking industry, for example, could include investigations not only of outlets with violations (such as those arising from worker complaints) but also of other units owned by the particular franchisee. Such a strategic enforcement strategy would require a systematic analysis of all other investigations of the franchisor (brand) in question to detect the presence of multiple instances of violations at other franchisees. Finally, the strategy could entail contacting the brand itself about the results of these investigations if it is clear that significant violations extend beyond the boundaries of any one franchisee or owner group.[16]

This approach implies a very different orientation: the government would focus its efforts, not necessarily on the employer of record, but on the portion of the industry that is driving the conditions that have resulted in compliance problems. Reorienting enforcement attention in this way would alter the behavior of the various parties up and down industry structures to become more compatible with better workplace conditions.

A top-focused enforcement strategy would target lead organizations that have a documented history of systemic violations among their subordinate units (such as franchisees, subcontracted entities, or workplaces monitored through third-party arrangements). These lead players could be identified through evaluation of past investigation records.[17] Once identified, workplace agencies could undertake broad and coordinated investigations in different locations and across multiple franchisees in order to establish the extent of systemwide violations and pursue statutory penalties for those violations. As part of its process of resolving the violations, agencies could negotiate a comprehensive agreement that would cover all outlets and properties and include provisions for outreach, education, and monitoring.

Beyond direct enforcement, outreach could also be geared toward lead firms in their role—whether as a brand, a major logistics coordinator, or a third-party manager—as a promulgator of standards and practices among subsidiary units. Cooperative approaches could entail reaching out to lead companies with positive employment reputations and favorable records of systemwide compliance and working with them to help ensure compliance with workplace policies across their systems of franchisees or subordinate organizations. Cooperative agreements could include a commitment by the lead organization to cascade information through the units that operate under its umbrella (for example, both company-owned and franchised properties and outlets in branded systems, or supplier networks in distribution and logistic coordinators). These agreements could also integrate workplace practices and expectations into the basic fabric of the standards used by the lead organization.

Several recent examples illustrate these approaches in practice.

Mending a Fissured Construction Company

Construction has always drawn on a contractor-subcontractor model of organization. In many respects, this is a natural method of production given that different skills (business and worker) are required for different durations in the process of building. Some of these skills are needed throughout the course of building (carpentry and basic laborers), while others are needed for relatively short durations (for example, roofing or sheet metal contracting).

In sectors of construction like major commercial and public construction, a lead contractor takes on the responsibility of coordinating construction activities and is typically responsible for ensuring that the project is completed on time and within budget. In prior decades, the lead "general" contractor played this role and also directly employed the workers who would be present throughout the project, while subcontracting specialty trades to others. In more recent times, the lead player strictly plays a coordinating role ("project manager"); as a result, even the basic trades functions are undertaken by subcontractors.

Residential construction has historically been more decentralized than other sectors of the industry, owing in large part to the smaller size of the end users (homeowners). In recent years, however, the industry has experienced significant consolidation because of the scale advantages arising from access to capital and land development. In addition, the "branding" of home-builder companies became an important tool for improving profitability. Just prior to the home-building bust in 2007, the top ten builders accounted for close to 25 percent of new single-family homes constructed.[18] Despite their scale and important role in the industry, even the largest home-builders eschew the role of direct employer of workers, relying instead on contractors and subcontractors. Thus, growth in the size of national home-builders has been accompanied by more fissuring rather than less.

One impact of this industry restructuring is that some large-scale contractors have arisen in various trades to provide construction services to home-builders. An OSHA settlement with one of these national players—Nations Roof LLC—provides an example of an enforcement agreement focused on the top. The case involved a group of roofing contractors, all under the general umbrella of Nations Roof LLC, but operating as seventeen affiliated companies.

In the past, OSHA enforcement procedures would have led it to deal with the various companies affiliated with Nations Roof as essentially independent and separate entities, each with responsibility for its own construction decisions. As part of a wider "enterprise-level" effort, however, OSHA treated violations documented at different affiliated companies as if they were all part of one common enterprise. As part of the complaint associated with the inspection, OSHA cited Nations Roof's own website as evidence of the coordinating role it exercised and proof of the operational control it exercised over its affiliates:

This is a company that owns all its locations, not an affiliation of independents; it is one company that can deliver consistently and on time. . . .

Nations Roof does not support separate and redundant overhead in multiple locations and business unit presidents are highly motivated owner-partners in the company.

A direct implication of treating the affiliated companies as part of a common business was that violations found in multiple places could be treated as "repeat" violations and therefore subjected to higher penalties. For example, by considering the various affiliates part of the national company, OSHA could reclassify citations for inadequate protections against roof falls (employees exposed with no protection to falls between twenty and twenty-six feet) from "serious" violations to "repeat" violations, thereby increasing the associated penalty from $2,100 to $35,000.[19]

A settlement agreement between OSHA and Nations Roof contains a number of novel features that require the parent organization, Nations Roof LLC, to take on the role of the party responsible for overall safety and health across the sixteen affiliated businesses.[20] First, in exchange for a reduction in penalties, the agreement requires that the management development program for the business managers of all sixteen affiliates be amended to include training on safety and health policies, practices, and standards. Second, it requires that each affiliate appoint a manager to be the health and safety director with specific responsibilities and accountability for the creation and administration of a health and safety policy, and that each affiliate engage in specific activities such as weekly inspections of construction sites.[21] Third, the settlement requires Nations Roof, LLC, to review "on a regular basis (for example, annually, semi-annually, etc.) . . . the performance of each Business Unit Owner/Manager with respect to matters affecting occupational safety and health." Performance criteria include the number and severity of occupational injuries and illnesses at the company's construction sites; the quantity and quality of inspections conducted by the company; and other factors related to the adequacy of the company's safety and health programs. Fourth, the agreement lays out very specific and stringent requirements for general health and safety procedures, job site inspections, trainings, daily "tool box talks" about safety issues, and the development of site-specific safety plans on an ongoing basis.

Finally, the settlement agreement requires Nations Roof, LLC, to "perform random, unannounced inspections of the active jobsites of every Nations Roof Affiliate. . . . Except as otherwise provided in this Section 4(I)(iii), Respondent Nations Roof, LLC shall conduct four Parent Inspections of each Nations Roof Affiliate every calendar year." The oversight activities required of Nations Roof make clear the responsibility of the parent organization in overseeing the health and safety activities of affiliates (just as its website describes its role as ensuring the delivery of services "consistently and on time"). The agreement therefore rebalances the relationship of lead and affiliate organizations in a way that favors greater scrutiny of activities at the construction work site so as to promote better health and safety outcomes.[22]

Mending a Fissured Company in the Cable Industry

If organized like many twentieth-century businesses, large telecommunication companies in the cable industry acting as service providers would be responsible for the provision and installation of cable services for their customers. By 2011, however, companies like TimeWarner had fissured much of the process of installing cable hardware in customers' homes to other providers.

Typical is the case of Cascom Inc., a company that contracted with TimeWarner Cable to install cable for residential customers in the Dayton, Ohio, area. Cascom completed thousands of cable installations for TimeWarner for residential customers. It employed virtually no workers. Instead, it hired cable installers as independent contractors, who were paid on the basis of each installation performed (rather than an hourly rate).[23]

The problem with this arrangement was that the workers were employees in almost every other sense: they received their work orders from Cascom; they could be removed for failing to meet production targets or for quality complaints by customers; they purchased (leased) their equipment from Cascom; they were not allowed to set the rates for installation; and they could not hire employees to work with them (which of course would be permissible if they were truly independent contractors). In essence, by fissuring employment, TimeWarner paid Cascom, which, in turn, could pay workers (as independent contractors) according to their individual productivity rather than having to set a single common wage for all installers.[24]

In fact, this practice is common to many cable installers working for TimeWarner. Two recent cases brought by the Labor Department's Wage and Hour Division (WHD) involving the cable installation companies Cascom in Ohio and Integral Development Solutions LLC in Texas are particularly important. Cable installers working for Cascom and Integral Development Solutions were paid on a piece-rate system for hours worked as contractors and were therefore not compensated for overtime. The Cascom case resulted in a U.S. District Court ruling that the installers were covered by the FLSA and entitled to back wages. In the Integral Development Solutions case, the WHD assessed the company for more than $270,000 in overtime back wages as well as for failing to maintain accurate records of hours and wages. In settling the case, the company agreed to pay all back wages due and committed to future FLSA compliance.[25]

More importantly, in both cases TimeWarner Cable instructed its contracted units to reclassify cable installers as FLSA-covered employees and to comply with the act. Although TimeWarner did not bring this work back within the walls of the company, it did exert its powerful role at the head of this telecommunication system to alter the behavior of key players at the secondary levels of the industry.

Transparency, Reputation, and Striking a New Balance

A complementary strategy to top-focused policies like the examples discussed here is to act on one of the key components underlying fissuring: brand reputation. Business strategies based on reputation and the maintenance of quality standards are pervasive for a reason: they make good business sense. By creating strong consumer allegiances or by ensuring tight quality standards (or the combination of the two), businesses can create margins through higher pricing. As I have stated throughout, this is a legitimate business aim that is often beneficial to consumers and the public.

However, these business strategies based on maintaining brand reputation lead to great sensitivity to any form of threat to image or disruption of carefully crafted standards. These threats—private, public, or otherwise—lead businesses to put in place private systems to preempt any loss of reputation among consumers or, more ominously for them, onerous public interventions. Whether one looks at Nike's response to accusations that its shoes were made in sweatshops or Walmart's responses to any number of labor, environment, or consumer campaigns, it is obvious that lead businesses are sensitive to reputational attacks (Locke 2013).

Targeted transparency—organizations' disclosure of standardized information regarding their performance to serve a regulatory purpose—has become widespread (Fung, Graham, and Weil 2007). Efforts focused on the disclosure of information regarding workplace practices in fissured industries could use the power of transparency to create incentives for the creation of alternative methods to address problems arising in those industries. Although disclosed information may lead some consumers with a particular interest in working conditions to avoid companies with poor records, this need not be the only response to such disclosures. If violations are perceived as indicators—or reasons—for compromised food or service quality, disclosure creates incentives for lead firms to change practices in order to protect the brand. This includes preemptive responses, which are frequently the result of mandatory disclosure policies.

An interesting example of a public policy revealing variations in the performance of franchisees is the impact of transparency on restaurant hygiene in Los Angeles County. Ginger Jin and Philip Leslie (2009) show that, prior to the imposition of mandated restaurant disclosure, franchisees within a brand had worse hygiene performance than company-owned outlets in the same brands. In 1998, L.A. County required restaurants to publicly post grades, based on restaurant hygiene inspections, on their front window. This public disclosure gradually led to the elimination of these discrepancies in intrabrand hygiene performance. In this case, free-riding was eliminated as a consequence of consumer behavior. But it was also a result of an overall threat to reputation that caused brands to put greater internal pressure on their franchisees.

One initiative of the Obama administration picks up on the opportunities to use transparency as a regulatory instrument. As part of its larger effort to promote transparency across executive agencies, the Department of Labor has promoted the development of new apps, such as the "DOL-Timesheet" app, to assist workers in assessing whether they have been paid according to FLSA standards.[26] The department has also sponsored development contests to create apps that use WHD and OSHA data to provide end users with information on past compliance behavior. The winner of the first app contest, "Eat/Shop/Sleep," provides this information in a format similar to consumer search apps like Yelp. Such initiatives could increase the salience and impact of enforcement data generally, but especially enforcement data connected with regulatory efforts in fissured industries.[27]

Stopping Egregious Fissuring

Some forms of fissuring are clearly end-run attempts to evade basic employment responsibilities, such as deliberately classifying workers as independent contractors who by all recognizable standards are employees. Many states became aware of this problem in the last decade, and multiple state-level statutes were passed that expressly address misclassification. In 2011 the U.S. Department of Labor also announced a major enforcement initiative focused on misclassification, in concert with the Internal Revenue Service (IRS) and a number of state labor agencies.

These efforts are aimed at stopping forms of fissuring that not only are illegal but have the secondary effect of creating competitive conditions that undercut legitimate service providers in an industry. The case of the janitorial service industry is indicative. Franchising has become a dominant form of fissuring in the janitorial sector in recent years. This particular franchise structure inherently places franchisees in a position that undermines their ability to obey workplace laws and requirements. An analysis of the underlying costs of a typical franchise structure, comparing those costs to prevailing prices for janitorial services in those markets, reveals that a franchisee faces one of two options: either underpay the workforce or fail to receive returns high enough to sustain the franchise (Weil forthcoming).

The presence of a tier of franchised janitorial service providers that in many markets cannot be financially viable without cutting corners has repercussions on the equilibrium prices in the market as a whole. The large demand for services and the elastic supply of janitorial service providers create market conditions that push prices for services down toward the lowest costs of the existing supply base for a given quality tier. The ready supply of would-be franchisees therefore drives prevailing market prices down toward a level below that necessary to meet minimum labor standards for their workforce.

In effect, by being the lowest-cost suppliers in many commercial markets, franchisees set a baseline price for services that, in turn, makes them unable to sustain their businesses within state or federal wage and hour requirements (and undoubtedly other requirements such as workers' compensation, unemployment insurance, and even the payment of payroll taxes to state and federal governments). The high rates of noncompliance in janitorial services arise from the interaction of the competitive conditions driving the market and the impact of a pervasive form of business organization on the behavior of individual players and, in turn, the market price on the margin.

Any effort to improve compliance in this industry must begin with the market dynamics clearly in mind. Traditional approaches to enforcement—focusing on the individual enterprise—will certainly bring to light case after case of violations of the laws governing minimum wages, overtime pay, and off-the-clock work and other statutes. But if not wedded to a larger strategy that attempts to change the market forces driving this behavior, enforcement will not make the problem less prevalent. Enforcement efforts and other public policies (including those protecting potential investors in franchises) must evaluate whether these forms of business organization not only create conditions inherently disadvantageous to franchisees but undermine broader public policy objectives by driving down prevailing price levels and, in turn, the ability of employers to meet workplace obligations.

MENDING THE FISSURED WORKPLACE

Accounts of low-wage work often emphasize workplace restructurings—outsourcing, temporary agencies, contingent work, misclassification—explanations that are rooted almost exclusively on the cost side of the business income statement. Fissured employment arises from a coordinated strategy that businesses have increasingly chosen to take. Its motivation arises from both revenue and cost considerations. In particular, lead companies use branding and other strategies to secure customer allegiance to their products or services in order to generate for themselves more inelastic demand and capture price premiums in addition to the devoted customers. These companies then focus only on activities related to core functions, while allocating to other entities the production of products or provision of services. Lead firms thereby become the coordinator of other organizations rather than the vertically integrated company that most employment laws assume.

The coherent strategy underlying fissured employment makes it clearer why it is often difficult to alter the decisions made by companies in this regard. Since fissured employment is a reflection of larger integrated strategies, enforcement that responds to their effects as if they were only an expression of labor cost avoidance will be unsuccessful. Unwinding the labor cost strategy is difficult if it does not address the revenue side strategy.

A path forward can be found in understanding the boundaries of lead businesses in the economy and the ways in which modern employment has changed and crafting public and private policies based on that understanding. Fissuring strategies are based in decisions that balance the need to protect and expand core competencies against the benefits of shifting out the employment problem to others. Businesses weigh that balance carefully and fashion sophisticated systems to establish standards, monitor performance, and reward or punish compliance.

Some companies, having experienced the private benefits and costs of overseeing subordinate businesses, are already following this alternative pathway; others are doing so because collective agreements with unions require it, or because their leaders have made commitments to socially responsible behavior. But many companies do not and will not abandon fissuring strategies until public policies that change the private calculus underlying fissured employment decisions are put in place.

Requiring lead businesses to more fully incorporate the social costs of shedding employment into the standards and systems they use to monitor the network of businesses they rely on or the prices they pay to subsidiary organizations working on their behalf would have ripple effects on the wider network of workplaces. Whether measured in terms of wages, access to benefits, or daily treatment at work, conditions in many low-wage workplaces have been worsening over the last few decades. Realigning the incentives that drive the lead businesses in our economy could move the standards upward once again, making the underlying network of workplaces better places for workers at all levels of skill and education, even as companies enjoy the advantages of harnessing new ways of organizing production.

Lead organizations lack neither the capacity to monitor and oversee behavior nor the technologies and systems to do so. They simply lack sufficient regulatory and legal pressure to include the social consequences of fissuring when they weigh these decisions. Public policies that require lead businesses to factor in the social costs borne by low-wage workers can rebalance those choices and begin to mend the fissured workplace.

NOTES

1. See, for example, Osterman and Shulman (2011), Kalleberg (2011), Bernhardt et al. (2009), and Milkman (2008). More popular accounts can be found in Bobo (2011), Greenhouse (2008), and Ehrenreich (2001).

2. This section summarizes a much larger analysis of the roots, mechanisms, and consequences of fissuring by the author. The complete discussion is contained in Weil (forthcoming).

3. For early academic discussion of core competency, see Prahalad and Hamel (1990), who discussed the idea with respect to the changing fortune of companies in the high-tech sector of the 1980s.

4. As the social scientists Sidney Webb and Beatrice Webb (1897, 281) pointed out at the turn of the last century, "The most autocratic and unfettered employer spontaneously adopts Standard Rates for classes of workmen, just as the large shopkeeper fixes his prices, not according to the haggling capacity of particular customers, but by a definite percentage on cost." Ernst Fehr and Klaus Schmidt (2007) argue that this is fundamentally related to fairness considerations in wage-setting. The impact of fairness concerns on wage determination in large firms from the 1960s to the late 1980s is documented by Fred Foulkes (1980) and Truman Bewley (1999). Empirical evidence is also consistent with findings about this impact. The well-established premium paid by larger employers that is not explained by skills, education, or productivity differences between workers is consistent with the impact of wage-setting done "inside" versus "outside" firm boundaries (see Brown, Hamilton, and Medoff 1989), as well as with the diminishing size of the premium over time in recent years (Hollister 2004). Recent studies also show that wages for particular janitorial and security jobs are higher when set inside firms than when set by contractors to those firms (see Abraham and Taylor 1996; Berlinski 2008; Dube and Kaplan 2010). I develop this argument in detail in Weil (forthcoming).

5. The tension between fair pay and conditions for workers and low prices for consumers is certainly not a new issue. At the turn of the last century, B. L. Hutchins and Amy Harrison (1926, xii) described this tension as it played out in the passage of early factory legislation in England: "Unfortunately, in

the absence of regulation, the evil tends to increase and the sweated trades to spread. In the all-pervading competition of the modern world market, each industry is perpetually struggling against every other industry to maintain and to improve its position . . . tempting the consumer by cheapness continually to increase his demand for its commodities, inducing the investor by swollen profits to divert more and more of the nation's capital in its direction, and attracting, by large salaries, more and more the nation's brains to its service."

6. This section does not attempt to provide a detailed analysis of the statutory, judicial, or academic writing in this area, nor even to provide a basic overview. Instead, it simply seeks to paint an overall picture that the definitions of employment relationships are grounded. Excellent discussions can be found in Davidov (2006) and in other essays from the same edited volume (Davidov and Langille 2006), as well as in the legal writing cited later in this section.

7. The multi-factor test of whether an individual is an employee or an independent contractor examines attributes of the relationship, including the extent of control exercised by the principal; whether the agent is in a distinct occupation or business; whether the type of work involved is generally done under the direction of employers elsewhere; the degree of skill required for the work; whether the agent supplies his or her own tools; the length of employment; the method of payment (by time or by job); and whether the work is part of the regular business of the employer. As Micah Jost (2011) and others have pointed out, the seeming precision of the multi-factor test evaporates in practice where the different factors must be weighed against one another in deciding on the presence of a legitimate employment relationship.

8. See Fair Labor Standards Act, 29 U.S.C. §§ 201–19 (1994). The Supreme Court in its Rutherford Food Corp. v. McComb decision (331 U.S. 722 [1947] at 728–29) affirmed the idea of a broad definition given that the FLSA "contains its own definitions comprehensive enough to require its application to many persons and working relationships which, prior to this Act, were not deemed to fall within an employer-employee category." This still leaves a great deal of room for applying the economic reality test. For example, the Sixth Circuit Court applied such a test to conclude that migrant pickle workers were excluded from FLSA coverage because of the temporary nature of their employment relationship, farmers' "lack of control" over migrant workers given that they were paid on a piece-rate basis, and the skill of those workers (Donovan v. Brandel, 736 F.2d 1114 [6th Cir. 1984]). In 1987, however, the Sixth Circuit Court reached an opposite result with similar case facts in Secretary of Labor v. Lauritzen, 835 F.2d 1529 (6th Cir. 1987). See Goldstein et al. (1999) and Ruckelshaus (2008) for detailed discussions of the employer-employee definition under the FLSA.

9. NLRB v. Hearst Publications, Inc., 322 U.S. 111 (1944). The case was the basis of Newsies, a Disney movie, play, and, most recently, Broadway musical. Undoubtedly, more high school students have been exposed to a memorable

moment in U.S. labor history through local performances of *Newsies* than in the scant treatment of the topic in most history curricula. See Zatz (2008) for a discussion of this case and an overview of the debate on employer-employee definitions under the NLRA.

10. For example, in NLRB v. United Insurance (390 U.S. 254 [1968] at 256), the Supreme Court held that "there is no doubt we should apply the common-law agency test here in distinguishing an employee from an independent contractor." A recent opinion of the D.C. Circuit Court in FedEx Home Delivery Inc. v. NLRB (563 F.3d 492 [D.C. Cir. 2009]), however, seems to apply a new test for independent contracting that is quite different from the one used under the common law: does the contractor have significant "entrepreneurial opportunity for gain or loss"? For a discussion of this new line of reasoning and its potential to further expand the legal underpinning for the use of independent contractors, see Jost (2011).

11. Employers are defined in the OSHA at 29 U.S.C. 652; employer and employee duties are specified at 29 U.S.C. 654.

12. The investigative reporters Ryan Knutson and Liz Day (2012), of *Frontline* and ProPublica, respectively, have documented the AT&T and cell tower story extensively, showing the lethal impact of subcontracting the service and maintenance of the towers.

13. For related discussions, see Estlund (2010), Jost (2011), Stone (2006), and Rogers (2010).

14. The common law further reinforces the incentives to shift out work via fissured employment. "Vicarious liability" refers to liability imposed on one party because of the actions of another. Under tort law, an organization is not liable for the torts of an independent contractor hired by it. Central to the determination of liability is whether the principal party had the ability to directly control the action of the subordinate organization. This creates incentives for a business contracting with another to avoid practices that might be construed by courts as exerting control (thereby making it vicariously liable for the other's actions), such as training of subcontractors, direct operational monitoring or supervision, or explicit direction of the work of subcontractors. Vicarious liability therefore may lead an organization to underinvest in activities that would otherwise be socially efficient for them (Arlen and MacLeod 2005).

15. Over the past quarter-century, significant federal workplace legislation has been passed. Although support for workplace legislation among business groups is rare, segments of the business community have had reason to move from a position of strict opposition to one of negotiation. In these cases, and in the presence of a broad coalition of legislative advocates, Congress has been able to pass legislation such as the Worker Adjustment and Retraining Notification (WARN) Act of 1988 (which cushions workers during plant closings), the Family and Medical Leave Act of 1993, and the Lilly Ledbetter Fair Pay Act

of 2009. The history of the political coalitions necessary to pass these laws provides insight into how to pass legislation in the future. On the passage of social legislation generally, see Skocpol (1992), and on workplace policies in particular, see Fishback and Kantor (2000), Fishback (2007), Bernhardt et al. (2008), and Weil (2008).

16. Alternatively, in an industry like residential construction, greater attention should be paid to systemic violations among contractors working under the umbrella of a national home-builder, which typically employs a minimal number of construction workers directly but rather contracts and subcontracts work. The enforcement strategy could focus investigations on contractors to look for patterns of violations; if violations are present, investigations could widen to include the home-builder's division or, if more wide-scale violations are uncovered, multiple divisions of projects undertaken by the home-builder's national office.

17. For example, MinWoong Ji and David Weil (2012) find significantly higher back wage violations among particular brands in the fast-food sector, even after statistically holding constant other factors that might also explain non-compliance. In particular, compared to typical McDonald's outlets (which had the best overall compliance record among the top twenty branded companies studied), Subway, Domino's Pizza, and Popeye's Chicken were all found to owe back wages that were substantially higher.

18. Even more, the top five home-builders accounted for much more than one-third of single-family homes built in major metropolitan markets like Las Vegas, Houston, and Dallas at the peak of the building boom in 2005 and 2006. See Abernathy et al. (2012) for a discussion of the emergence of national home-builders in the years leading up to the housing bust.

19. See Secretary of Labor v. Nations Roof of New England, LLC, and Nations Roof LLC, Occupational Safety and Health Review Commission, docket 10-1674, region 1, inspection 311593180, December 3, 2010.

20. The following terms are taken from the settlement agreement reached between representatives of Nations Roof of New England, LLC, and Nations Roof LLC and the U.S. Solicitor of Labor. See Secretary of Labor v. Nations Roof of New England, LLC, and Nations Roof LLC, docket 10-1674, region 1, inspection 311593180, Settlement Agreement, July 28, 2011. The full settlement is available at http://op.bna.com/env.nsf/id/jstn-8lbru3/$File/NationsRoof.pdf (accessed September 2013).

21. The agreement also stipulates that the designated safety and health director at each affiliate spend at minimum one-third of his or her time on safety and health activities.

22. OSHA, in conjunction with the Solicitor's Office of the U.S. Department of Labor, has signed a series of corporate-wide agreements since 2010. A compendium of them can be found at: http://www.osha.gov/pls/oshaweb/owasrch.

search_form?p_doc_type=CWSA&p_toc_level=0&p_keyvalue=&p_status=
CURRENT (accessed February 16, 2013).
23. See U.S. Department of Labor, Wage and Hour Division, "News Release: Judge Rules Ohio-Based Cascom Employees Misclassified as Independent Contractors, Denied Overtime Pay in Suit Brought by U.S. Labor Department," October 4, 2011, available at: www.dol.gov/opa/media/press/whd/WHD20111425.htm (accessed November 15, 2011); and Bill Pokorny, "Cable Installers Employees, Not Independent Contractors," Wage & Hour Insights, October 10, 2011, available at: http://www.wagehourinsights.com/independent-contractors/court-cable-installers-employees-not-independent-contractors/ (accessed November 15, 2011).
24. The U.S. District Court held in favor of the Department of Labor's position that the 250 installers were in fact employees and not independent contractors. As a result, they were entitled to overtime pay for their work, amounting to over $800,000 and an equal amount of liquidated damages (also paid to the affected workers). See Solis v. Cascom Inc. et al., Civil Action No. 3:09-CV-00257, U.S. District Court, Southern District of Ohio, Western Division at Dayton. See generally General Accountability Office (2009).
25. See U.S. Department of Labor, Wage and Hour Division, "Cable Installers in Plano, Texas, to Receive More Than $270,000 in Overtime Back Wage Following U.S. Labor Department Investigation," press release 11-484-DAL, May 16, 2011.
26. The DOL-Timesheet app is available via Apple iTunes; see: http://itunes.apple.com/us/app/ dol-timesheet/id433638193?mt=8.
27. For more on the Labor Department's development contest, and on the "Eat/Shop/Sleep" app, see: http://informaction.challenge.gov/submissions/4585-eat-shop-sleep (accessed February 16, 2013).

REFERENCES

Abernathy, Frederick, Kermit Baker, Kent Colton, and David Weil. 2012. *Bigger Isn't Necessarily Better: Lessons from the Harvard Home Builder Study.* Lanham, Md.: Lexington Books.

Abraham, Katherine, and Susan Taylor. 1996. "Firms' Use of Outside Contractors: Theory and Evidence." *Journal of Labor Economics* 14(3): 394–424.

Arlen, Jennifer, and W. Bentley MacLeod. 2005. "Beyond Master-Servant: A Critique of Vicarious Liability." In *Exploring Tort Law*, ed. Stuart Madden. New York: Cambridge University Press.

Baker, George, and Thomas Hubbard. 2003. "Make Versus Buy in Trucking: Asset Ownership, Job Design, and Information." *American Economic Review* (September): 1328–53.

Berlinski, Samuel. 2008. "Wages and Contracting Out: Does the Law of One Price Hold?" *British Journal of Industrial Relations* 46(1): 59–75.

Bernhardt, Annette, Heather Boushey, Laura Dresser, and Chris Tilly. 2008. *The Gloves-Off Economy: Workplace Standards at the Bottom of America's Labor Market*. Champaign, Ill.: University of Illinois for the Labor and Employment Relations Association.

Bernhardt, Annette, Ruth Milkman, Nik Theodore, Douglas Heckathorn, Mirabel Auer, James DeFillipis, Ana Luz Gonzalez, Victor Narro, Jason Perelshteyn, Diana Polson, and Michael Spiller. 2009. *Broken Laws, Unprotected Workers: Violations of Employment in Labor Laws in America's Cities*. Chicago and Los Angeles: University of Illinois–Chicago, Center for Urban Economic Development, National Employment Law Project and the UCLA Institute for Research on Labor and Employment.

Bewley, Truman. 1999. *Why Wages Don't Fall During a Recession*. Cambridge, Mass.: Harvard University Press.

Blair, Roger D., and Francine Lafontaine. 2005. *The Economics of Franchising*. New York: Cambridge University Press.

Bobo, Kim. 2011. *Wage Theft in America: Why Millions of Americans Are Not Getting Paid and What We Can Do About It*, rev. ed. New York: New Press.

Brown, Charles, James Hamilton, and James Medoff. 1990. *Employers Large and Small*. Cambridge, Mass.: Harvard University Press.

Chandler, Alfred D. 1977. *The Visible Hand: The Managerial Revolution in American Business*. Cambridge, Mass.: Harvard University Press.

Davidov, Guy. 2006. "The Reports of My Death Are Greatly Exaggerated: 'Employee' as a Viable (Though Overly Used) Legal Concept." In *Boundaries and Frontiers of Labour Law: Goals and Means in the Regulation of Work*, ed. Guy Davidov and Brian Langille. Oxford: Hart Publishing.

Davidov, Guy, and Brian Langille, eds. 2006. *Boundaries and Frontiers of Labour Law: Goals and Means in the Regulation of Work*. Oxford: Hart Publishing.

Dube, Arandajit, and Ethan Kaplan. 2010. "Does Outsourcing Reduce Wages in the Low-Wage Service Occupations? Evidence from Janitors and Guards." *Industrial and Labor Relations Review* 63(2): 287–306.

Ehrenreich, Barbara. 2001. *Nickel and Dimed: On (Not) Getting by in America*. New York: Holt.

Estlund, Cynthia. 2010. *Regoverning the Workplace: From Self-regulation to Co-regulation*. New Haven, Conn.: Yale University Press.

Fehr, Ernst, and Klaus Schmidt. 2007. "A Theory of Fairness, Competition, and Cooperation." *Quarterly Journal of Economics* 97(2): 817–68.

Fishback, Price. 2007. "Seeking Security in the Postwar Era." In *Government and the American Economy: A New History*, ed. Price Fishback. Chicago: University of Chicago Press.

Fishback, Price, and Shawn Kantor. 2000. *Prelude to the Welfare State: The Origins of Workers' Compensation*. Chicago: University of Chicago Press.

Foulkes, Fred. 1980. *Personnel Policies in Large Non-Union Workplaces.* Englewood Cliff, N.J.: Prentice-Hall.

Fung, Archon, Mary Graham, and David Weil. 2007. *Full Disclosure: Perils and Promise of Transparency.* New York: Cambridge University Press.

General Accountability Office. 2009. *Employee Misclassification: Improved Coordination, Outreach, and Targeting Could Better Ensure Detection and Prevention.* GAO-09-717. Washington, DC.: GAO.

Glynn, Timothy. 2011. "Taking the Employer Out of Employment Law? Accountability for Wage and Hour Violations in an Age of Enterprise Disaggregation." *Employee Rights and Employment Policy Journal* 15(1): 101–35.

Goldstein, Bruce, Marc Linder, Laurence Norton, and Catherine Ruckelshaus. 1999. "Enforcing Fair Labor Standards in the Modern American Sweatshop: Rediscovering the Statutory Definition of Employment." *UCLA Law Review* 46(4): 983–1106.

Greenhouse, Steven. 2008. *The Big Squeeze: Tough Times for the American Worker.* New York: Knopf.

Hollister, Matissa. 2004. "Does Firm Size Matter Anymore? The New Economy and Firm Size Wage Effect." *American Sociological Review* 69(5): 659–76.

Hutchins, B. L., and Amy Harrison. 1926. *A History of Factory Legislation,* 3rd ed. London: Frank Cass & Co.

Ji, MinWoong, and David Weil. 2012. "Does Ownership Structure Influence Regulatory Behavior? The Impact of Franchisee Free-Riding on Labor Standards Compliance." Working paper. Boston: Boston University.

Jin, Ginger, and Philip Leslie. 2009. "Reputational Incentives for Restaurant Hygiene." *American Economic Journal: Microeconomics* 1(1): 237–67.

Jost, Micah Prieb Stoltzfus. 2011. "Independent Contractors, Employees, and Entrepreneurialism under the National Labor Relations Act: A Worker-by-Worker Approach." *Washington and Lee Law Review* 68(1): 313–73.

Kalleberg, Arne. 2011. *Good Jobs/Bad Jobs: The Rise of Polarized and Precarious Employment Systems in the United States, 1970s to 2000s.* New York: Russell Sage Foundation.

Knutson, Ryan, and Liz Day. 2012. "Anatomy of a Cell Tower Death." *Frontline,* June 6, 2012. Available at: http://www.pbs.org/wgbh/pages/frontline/social-issues/cell-tower-deaths/anatomy-of-a-cell-tower-death/ (accessed October 10, 2012).

Locke, Richard. 2013. *Improving Labor Rights in a Global Economy.* New York: Cambridge University Press.

Milkman, Ruth. 2008. "Putting Wages Back into Competition: Deunionization and Degradation in Place-Bound Industries." In *The Gloves-Off Economy: Workplace Standards at the Bottom of America's Labor Market,* ed. Annette Bernhardt, Heather Boushey, Laura Dresser, and Chris Tilly. Champaign, Ill.: University of Illinois for the Labor and Employment Relations Association.

Osterman, Paul, and Beth Shulman. 2011. *Good Jobs America: Making Work Better for Everyone.* New York: Russell Sage Foundation.

Prahalad, C. K., and Gary Hamel. 1990. "The Core Competence of the Corporation." *Harvard Business Review* (May–June): 79–91.

Rogers, Brishen. 2010. "Toward Third-Party Liability for Wage Theft." *Berkeley Journal of Employment and Labor Law* 30(1): 1–64.

Ruckelshaus, Catherine K. 2008. "Labor's Wage War." *Fordham Urban Law Journal* 35(2): 373–404.

Skocpol, Theda. 1992. *Protecting Soldiers and Mothers: The Political Origins of Social Policy in the United States.* Cambridge, Mass.: Harvard University Press.

Stone, Katherine. 2006. "Legal Protections for Atypical Employees: Employment Law for Workers Without Workplaces and Employees Without Employers." *Berkeley Journal of Employment and Labor Law* 27(2): 251–81.

Webb, Sidney, and Beatrice Webb. 1897. *Industrial Democracy.* London: Macmillan.

Weil, David. 2008. "Mighty Monolith or Fractured Federation? Business Opposition and the Enactment of Workplace Legislation." In *The Gloves-Off Economy: Workplace Standards at the Bottom of America's Labor Market,* ed. Annette Bernhardt, Heather Boushey, Laura Dresser, and Chris Tilly. Champaign, Ill.: University of Illinois for the Labor and Employment Relations Association.

———. Forthcoming. *The Fissured Workplace: Why Work Became So Bad for So Many and What Can Be Done to Improve It.* Cambridge, Mass.: Harvard University Press.

Williamson, Oliver. 1985. *The Economic Institutions of Capitalism.* New York: Free Press.

Zatz, Noah. 2008. "Working Beyond the Reach or Grasp of Employment Law." In *The Gloves-Off Economy: Workplace Standards at the Bottom of America's Labor Market,* ed. Annette Bernhardt, Heather Boushey, Laura Dresser, and Chris Tilly. Champaign, Ill.: University of Illinois for the Labor and Employment Relations Association.

Chapter 5 | Holding the Line on Workplace Standards: What Works for Immigrant Workers (and What Doesn't)?

Jennifer Gordon

IMMIGRATION POLICY IS a peripheral subject for most scholars of labor and employment in the United States. Yet any coherent discussion of how to improve low-wage work in this country, where over 1 million new legal immigrants arrive each year and the population of undocumented immigrants surpasses 11 million, requires an understanding of the impact of immigration regulations and enforcement on low-wage workers' ability to claim their rights. Likewise, few immigration scholars have in-depth knowledge of the law and policy of the workplace. Yet work remains the principal force drawing newcomers to the United States. How immigrants do once they reach this country is intimately related to the floor for treatment on the job set by workplace protections. Whether and how that floor can be enforced vis-à-vis undocumented or guest workers—the most vulnerable newcomers—are critical questions. In this chapter, I explore the U.S. immigration policies that have impeded workers' ability to defend their rights over the past twenty-five years—roughly the period between the 1986 Immigration Reform and Control Act (IRCA) and Congress's 2013 comprehensive immigration reform endeavor—and the sources of support in institutional structures and workplace law and policy that have been important in overcoming those impediments during the same period.

The U.S. employment law regime assigns most of the same workplace protections to undocumented workers as to citizens. Nonetheless, as I argue in the first part of this chapter, government enforcement of immigration

134

regulation (and employer manipulation of that regulation) became a central factor impeding undocumented workers' capacity to enforce the law and raise working standards during the decades following IRCA's creation of employer sanctions. Because the treatment of the most vulnerable workers in a job category sets the standard for all workers in that segment of the industry, this is a serious concern for all those employed in labor markets where undocumented workers and other recent immigrants are concentrated, including the service, agriculture, food processing, and construction sectors in most of the country.

Advocates seeking to improve conditions at the bottom of the labor market rightly demand an end to immigration restrictions on worker mobility and to immigration enforcement in the workplace, calling instead for freer movement in a context of equal workplace rights. To see what a free movement regime might look like in practice from an immigrant workers' rights perspective, I turn in the second part of the chapter to the United Kingdom, where new European Union (EU) citizens from much lower-wage countries in Eastern and Central Europe have been permitted since 2004 to enter at will and do any job they can find. Although the situation is too new, and my research too preliminary, to draw definitive conclusions, the available data and anecdotal reports indicate that during the first six years following accession "free movers" continued to face more abuse than their native counterparts in the same low-wage jobs in the United Kingdom, and that there was less worker activism among these newcomers in the United Kingdom than among new immigrants in the United States. More than mobility appears to be required to ensure that immigrants are in a position to access their rights and to join with other low-wage workers to demand better wages and working conditions.

What that something more might be is suggested by a return look at the United States in the last part of the chapter. Although immigration regulation in this country has impeded immigrant workers' access to their rights, it has not always derailed their willingness to act to improve their wages and working conditions, nor determined their ultimate ability to prevail. Despite the punitive regime in place during this period, many undocumented immigrants and their coworkers have exercised agency and courage in demanding respect for baseline workers' rights and in organizing through unions and worker centers. Together with those organizations, they have drawn on workplace rights as resources and have sought and often received the support of workplace regulators. These new institutional forms, strategies, and alliances have emerged in the United States in the past twenty-five years, roughly parallel to the implementation of employer sanctions but with opposite effect. Their development offers valuable lessons moving forward.

IMMIGRATION LAW IN THE WORKPLACE

U.S. Labor Immigration Policy as of 2012

The permanent immigration scheme in the United States is heavily weighted toward family reunification rather than employment needs. Of the 1,062,000 immigrants admitted to the United States as new green-card holders in fiscal year 2011, 688,000 were sponsored by family members. Only 139,000 were admitted through the employment-based immigration program. Of these, the vast majority were highly skilled immigrants. Just 10,000 immigrants per year are granted permanent residence through the one category that does not require a bachelor's degree or skill training.[1] The waiting list for this category is currently between five and ten years long, and the list for workers with a bachelor's degree is close to four years, both longer than most employers are willing to hold a job open (Monger and Yankay 2012, 3, table 2; U.S. Department of State 2012).

The preferential treatment of highly skilled immigrants is in accord with a consensus among economists that immigrant professionals are a nearly unmitigated asset for the United States (Holzer 2011, 1, 3; Somerville and Sumption 2009, 23, 29, 32). But that consensus does not address the large supply of less-skilled workers seeking to immigrate to the United States for work, nor the large demand among U.S. employers for their labor. A small amount of the overflow is managed through the approximately 200,000 to 300,000 temporary low-skilled work visas that the United States issues per year (Monger 2012, 4, table 2).[2] Although such visas are supposed to be limited to agricultural and seasonal jobs (the H-2A and H-2B visa programs, respectively), there is evidence that employers have also begun to import labor using temporary visas never intended as guest worker programs (Costa 2011).

Temporary visas address only a minor part of the demand for low-wage immigrant workers. The bulk is met by undocumented immigrants, approximately 11.2 million of whom now reside in the United States and 8 million of whom are working (Passel and Cohn 2011, 1). The undocumented make up 5 percent of the U.S. labor force (Passel and Cohn 2010, iv).[3]

The Enforcement of Immigration Law in the Workplace

Economists have long disagreed about whether these newcomers compete with legal residents for jobs. Although a full exploration of this question is beyond the scope of this chapter, at the current stage of the economic debate it appears that most negative effects of such competition—largely invisible in national-level studies of the economy as a whole—are felt by earlier immigrants rather than by natives (Catanzarite 2003, 77, 88; Manacorda,

Manning, and Wadsworth 2006, 17–18, 27–28; Shierholz, 2010 3). With regard to natives, a negative impact on wages appears more likely in localized areas that are newly experiencing immigration and in occupations where native workers tend to have less than a high school education and the immigrants in question are guest workers or undocumented workers (Gentsch and Massey 2011, 891; Shierholz 2010, 19). In these contexts, it is urgent to understand the impact of immigration status and other immigration laws on immigrant workers' rights and their ability to access the workplace protections available to them.

The interaction between immigration law and access to workplace rights is complex. Both temporary legal migrants and the undocumented share many rights with U.S. workers—on paper. Indeed, most temporary labor migration programs require that employers pay a higher rate than the applicable minimum wage, and they offer migrants benefits and guarantees not provided to workers hired through the local labor market.[4] For their part, the undocumented are technically covered by the minimum wage and overtime protections of the Fair Labor Standards Act (FLSA),[5] the safe and healthy workplace provisions of the Occupational Safety and Health Act (OSHA) (Smith et al. 2007, 12), in most federal courts by antidiscrimination laws,[6] and in most states by workers' compensation programs for on-the-job injury.[7] Although in the 2002 Hoffman Plastics Compounds case the Supreme Court denied undocumented immigrants back pay or reinstatement if they are fired for supporting a union in violation of the National Labor Relations Act (NLRA), it explicitly reiterated that undocumented individuals are "employees" covered by that act and are permitted to form and join unions.[8]

Nonetheless, both legal temporary labor migrants and undocumented immigrants face numerous practical impediments to exercising these rights.

Temporary Visa-Holders and the Employer as Sponsor The core problem for holders of the H-2A and H-2B temporary visas is that their permit to remain in the United States is tied to continuing employment by the employer that sponsored them. If a worker is fired because she complains about the treatment she receives on the job or attempts to enforce her rights, her visa immediately terminates and she must return home. She also risks being put on a blacklist that would bar her future return through the program. Workers in these programs frequently see their rights violated. A report by the U.S. Government Accountability Office (GAO) (2010) notes multiple examples of employers flouting H-2B protections, including payment of wages of $3.00 per hour and cases of servitude and bondage, reinforced by fraud, conspiracy, and threats of violence to keep workers compliant. The

Southern Poverty Law Center (2007, 15–16 passim) reports numerous cases of serious abuse in both H-2A and H-2B programs, including employers that explicitly seek to deter workers by threatening to report to immigration authorities those who stand up for their rights. Lawsuits over the past few years on behalf of tree planters, traveling fair workers, welders, and others have alleged that guest workers suffered grave abuses, including economic deprivation, serious injuries, threats of retaliation, and in some cases trafficking, captivity, and forced labor.[9] In all cases, workers faced the loss of their visa if they were fired after coming forward to complain.

Undocumented Workers and Employer Sanctions   Undocumented workers also face a different, but equally debilitating, dynamic. Since their presence in the country is illegal, many fear that any effort they make to defend their rights will result not only in getting fired but in being reported to Immigration and Customs Enforcement (ICE, the immigration agency that replaced the Immigration and Naturalization Service, or INS, in 2003 as the enforcer of immigration laws inside the United States) and subsequently deported. This has long been a concern for those working without legal papers, but the picture became more complicated—and ironically, employers gained another tool for the intimidation of undocumented workers—with Congress's passage of employer sanctions in 1986, and then again with administrative efforts to beef up the enforcement of those sanctions beginning in 2006.

Prior to 1986, there was no federal scheme to penalize employers who hired the undocumented. In that year, in passing the Immigration Reform and Control Act (IRCA), Congress enacted employer sanctions as part of a carrot-and-stick package that also included a large-scale legalization program. The law requires employers to verify both the identity and the work authorization of all new hires. Penalties for violations range from small fines for paperwork offenses to felony charges for intentional flouting of the law.[10]

Other than a brief burst of enforcement in the few years after employer sanctions passed, the law was barely used by the federal government for nearly twenty years. During that time, few employers were penalized for noncompliance (U.S. Government Accountability Office 2005, 12–16; Wishnie 2007, 209). Indeed, in testimony to Congress in 2005, the then-director of Homeland Security and Justice within the GAO reported that the Department of Homeland Security had issued only three employers a "notice of intent to fine" under the employer sanctions law in the previous year (U.S. Government Accountability Office 2005, 15).

While employers were largely unscathed during this time, workers suffered greatly under the first twenty years of the sanctions regime. To the extent that inspections related to sanctions did take place, government enforcement actions penalized far more workers, who were often arrested and deported, than employers, who were rarely fined (U.S. Government Accountability Office 2005, 15; Wishnie 2007, 209; Smith, Avendaño, and Ortega 2009, 10). Discrimination has also been an ongoing side effect of employer sanctions (U.S. General Accounting Office 1990, 37–79; Bacon and Hing 2010, 87). Most detrimentally, during this period employers found that the law put a useful tool in their hands for controlling immigrant workforces seeking to organize unions or assert their workplace rights (Smith, Avendaño, and Ortega 2009; Bacon and Hing 2010; Gordon 2005, 41–43, 68; Lee 2009, 1119–23; Wishnie 2007). Unscrupulous employers would either ignore employer sanctions at the time of hire or fill out forms perfunctorily. If workers sought to organize a union or raise a complaint about a violation of their rights, the employer would suddenly become concerned about sanctions, firing workers who could not produce a work authorization (Wishnie 2007, 215–16). This cloaked retaliation in the shroud of compliance with employer sanctions. In some cases, employers themselves called INS (or later ICE) to raid the workplace to derail organizing campaigns that appeared likely to succeed (Smith, Avendaño, and Ortega 2009, 15–29).

By late 2006, Congress had concluded several fruitless years of debate over comprehensive immigration reform without passing legislation. The question of immigration enforcement remained in the spotlight, and the government's inattention to employer sanctions drew public attention. Faced with the political fallout from these revelations, and seeking to quell the firestorm on undocumented immigration, the Bush administration began an initiative to increase enforcement of immigration law within the borders of the United States, with a focus on aggressively enforcing sanctions through inspections of employers combined with immigration raids on workplaces (Migration Policy Institute 2009, 9–10).

Images of flashing sirens, workers fleeing in panic and chaos, and families torn apart by the abrupt deportations that accompanied a raid became commonplace in the media (Smith, Avendaño, and Ortega 2009, 23–29). The terror that these raids induced in immigrant workers increased the pressure to keep their heads low and ignore abuses at work, in order to avoid drawing the attention of their employer or the authorities. While a long-standing memorandum of understanding between ICE and the U.S. Department of Labor seeks to discourage ICE intervention at a company with an ongoing workplace dispute or allegations of violations of the law under investigation (U.S. Immigration and Naturalization Service, U.S. Department of Justice, and U.S. Department of Labor 1998; U.S. Department of Homeland Security, Immigration and Customs Enforcement 1996;

U.S. Department of Homeland Security and U.S. Department of Labor 2011; National Immigration Law Center 2009), this agreement has been ignored in a number of cases (Wishnie 2003, 390–92; Smith, Avendaño, and Ortega 2009, 23–29).[11]

Examples abound. In 2007, on the eve of an election in which two unions sought to represent the same group of workers, the New York City grocery delivery company Fresh Direct notified employees that it was undergoing an ICE audit; it required that workers prove their employment eligibility to remain in their jobs. Over one hundred of the company's nine hundred workers, many of them union supporters, left. When the election was held less than two weeks later, the unions lost.[12] In 2008, in a case that received considerable publicity, ICE raided the Agriprocessors slaughterhouse in Postville, Iowa, arresting over six hundred workers. At the time, the United Food and Commercial Workers Union had an organizing campaign under way, and state and federal agencies were actively investigating allegations of workplace violations at the plant.[13]

We are now in a transitional moment with regard to immigration enforcement in the workplace. The Obama administration vigorously enforces employer sanctions.[14] In fiscal year 2011, ICE inspectors began investigations at over three thousand employers and issued 331 final administrative fine orders, compared to 18 in fiscal year 2008, the last under the Bush administration. In fiscal year 2010, ICE worksite investigations levied over $40 million in a range of penalties against employers related to worksite enforcement (U.S. Department of Homeland Security, Immigration and Customs Enforcement 2011).

Under President Obama, however, ICE has made numerous changes in its enforcement approach, many of which appear to respond directly to advocates' critiques of the Bush administration's policies. In response to concerns about the terrorizing effect of raids, it has sharply decreased conventional raids on workplaces and instead has initiated thousands of employer audits (sometimes called silent raids) and investigations (U.S. Department of Homeland Security, Immigration and Customs Enforcement 2011; Preston, "A Crackdown on Employing Illegal Workers"; Bacon and Hing 2010, 79–84).[15] If the government finds missing I-9 forms or forms with expired or missing documents, the firm is given a period of time for the workers to rectify the situation; if that is not possible, the firm is told to fire the workers or face penalties. This shift away from a focus on targeting workers for deportation and toward holding the employer liable is evident in the fact that arrests of workers in relation to workplace enforcement of immigration law have dropped precipitously. So have criminal convictions against workers on charges related to work. Meanwhile, recently released data demonstrate much higher fines against firms, as well as criminal indictments, convictions, and jail time for employers, under the Obama administration (Preston, "A Crackdown on Employing Illegal Workers"; U.S. Department of Homeland Security, Immigration and Customs Enforcement 2011).

Despite these reforms, there remains cause for concern. The Obama administration has stated that it intends to focus on firms that are "egregious" offenders in both the labor and immigration arenas. Nonetheless, high-profile targets in the first few years of its policy included companies with reputations as decent employers, including American Apparel, Chipotle, and unionized building service company ABM (Bacon and Hing 2010, 82–84; Jamieson 2011, 3–4; Kaye 2011, 9).[16] And what the Obama approach has illustrated most of all is that without legalizing the undocumented immigrants already present in the country, enforcing employer sanctions only makes the goals of improving pay and working conditions in low-wage industries and increasing the jobs available to legally authorized workers harder to attain. Although far fewer workers are being deported, many thousands have been fired (Bacon and Hing 2010, 81). The undocumented workers fired as a result of worksite enforcement do not appear to be leaving the country in large numbers, as some had hoped; rather, most remain and seek other work, eventually taking jobs at even lower pay, with a greater sense of vulnerability and increased reluctance to speak up against abuses and risk attracting government attention (Bacon and Hing 2010, 81; Jamieson 2011, 3; Kaye 2011, 7).

Although an underlying principle of sanctions is that in the face of a strict enforcement of the regime employers will hire legal workers at higher wages than they paid the undocumented, whether this is actually happening in practice is unclear (Flora, Prado-Meza, and Lewis 2011, 14; Jamieson 2011, 3). Some employers may be turning to guest worker programs in response to increased enforcement of sanctions, rather than seeking out native workers (or because they have been unable to recruit or retain them at the wages they are willing to offer).[17] Hiring guest workers under the current regime represents a shift to an equally problematic situation in terms of workers' rights, for all of the reasons outlined earlier.

Far from having been effective in addressing undocumented migration, sanctions have coincided with a time of tremendous growth in the undocumented population, from 3.2 million in 1986, when IRCA was passed (Wasem 2012), to an estimated 11.2 million in 2010 (Passel and Cohn 2011, 1). In response to this fact, and to the harm that sanctions have done to workers' ability to enforce their basic rights, advocates have argued vociferously for the repeal of sanctions. The major success of this advocacy project came over a decade ago, when the AFL-CIO, a supporter of sanctions at the time of their passage, shifted to a position advocating their repeal in 2000.[18] Otherwise, the calls have fallen on deaf ears. Reformed, enhanced, and better-enforced sanctions have been a feature— indeed, a centerpiece—of all of the comprehensive immigration reform proposals given serious consideration by Congress in the past decade. In addition, following the Supreme Court's 2011 ruling in Chamber of Commerce v. Whiting upholding Arizona's law mandating that employers in the state participate in E-Verify, increasing numbers of states are adopting similar provisions.[19]

MIGRANT WORKERS WITHOUT IMMIGRATION RESTRICTIONS: REFLECTIONS ON THE U.K. EXPERIENCE IN THE WAKE OF ACCESSION

In the United States, the repeal of employer sanctions is currently politically inconceivable, and as this book goes to press, a limited version of the "full mobility, fully equal rights" model of temporary labor migration is contemplated for only a very small number of guest workers in the reform proposals on the table.[20] Meanwhile, however, the European Union has a policy of free movement for work among EU nations, although through the framework of EU citizenship rather than a work visa. In this section, using the United Kingdom as an example, I will set out what is known about the working conditions of Eastern and Central European nationals in the United Kingdom in the first six years following the EU's 2004 enlargement to include those countries. Although these workers are better off than migrants to the United Kingdom from *outside* the EU who are undocumented or who hold restrictive temporary work visas, they still appear to suffer high rates of workplace abuse relative to their native counterparts, and they have been slow to bring complaints against their employers for violations of the law and resistant to invitations to join trade unions. The experience of these "free movers" supports the idea that more than the immigration regime must change for migrants to be able and willing to access their rights.

In 2004 the European Union incorporated eight new Eastern and Central European (ECE) countries, including Poland, Lithuania, and Latvia (the group was collectively referred to as the "A8"). In 2007 it grew to include Bulgaria and Romania (the "A2"). At the time of the 2007 accession, the wage disparity between the highest- and lowest-wage countries in the EU was about sixteen-to-one (European Commission 2012), compared to roughly seven-to-one between the United States and Mexico (Jus Semper Global Alliance 2011, 8). The guarantee of free movement between EU member states permits a citizen of any EU country to move between EU countries and to work freely in any other EU country, without limitations on length of stay or on mobility between jobs, regions, or nations. Although at the time of enlargement existing member states were permitted to limit labor market access to citizens of new member states to seven years, as of May 2011 all restrictions on A8 nationals' labor mobility has been lifted.

Breaking with the rest of Europe, the United Kingdom and Ireland (together with Sweden) chose to grant full labor market access to A8 nationals immediately in 2004. Because the United Kingdom opened its labor market to A8s earlier than most EU countries, and because there are many similarities between the U.K. approach to labor regulation and that of the United States, it is a useful place to look for insights about the implications of a more open labor migration regime in this country.[21] A few key observations follow. Over the first five and a half years after accession, an estimated 1.5 million ECE nationals arrived in the United Kingdom (Sumption and Somerville 2010, 9). Flows slowed considerably in 2008 and remained low during the recession, but appeared to be increasing in 2010 and 2011 (McCollum and Findlay 2011, 11; Vargas-Silva 2012, 5). Many of these newcomers have seen their stay in the United Kingdom as temporary and have returned home after working for a period of time (Sumption and Somerville 2010, 18–20; Vargas Silva 2012, 4). Most have relatively high levels of education and training—for example, Polish A8 migrants to the United Kingdom have an average of over thirteen years of education (Drinkwater, Eade, and Garapich 2006, 24). Nonetheless, they overwhelmingly work in low-wage "undesirable" jobs such as food processing, patient and elderly care, hospitality, and construction. As with immigration to the United States, economists have found little negative effect on the labor market for native workers from this influx of newcomers.

Highly skilled, English-speaking A8 migrants have been particularly successful in reaping the benefits of access to the U.K. labor market. Full mobility—between employers, industries, regions, and indeed the United Kingdom and A8 migrants' home countries—appears to have been key. For a significant subset of non-English-speaking A8 workers, however, genuine mobility and decent treatment on the job have remained out of reach. The problems they have faced include illegal deductions, unsafe working conditions, and long hours for low pay (Gordon 2011, 7–8).

It is important to recognize that *most* workers suffer high rates of workplace violations in the low-wage labor markets that these migrants are entering. In other words, the mistreatment of migrants is not anomalous exploitation, but the product of a business model that relies on the subcontracting of labor as a profit-generating mechanism (Trades Union Congress Commission on Vulnerable Employment 2008, 39). (As an aspect of this model, some employers seek to subcontract only the most recent group of migrants, favoring them over newcomers with a few years of experience; see MacKenzie and Forde [2009, 142].) In the United Kingdom, where the government's approach to the enforcement of basic workplace protections is frequently characterized as balkanized, underfunded, and ineffective, violations of basic laws are commonplace and frequently go undetected by regulators (Pollert 2008, 225; Holgate et al. 2010; Trades Union Congress Commission on Vulnerable Employment 2008, 40; Poinasamy 2011, 22). While one antidote might be an effective complaint-based system or private enforcement of the law, non-union workers in the United Kingdom (a group in which immigrants, including A8s, are overrepresented) have few sources of support in bringing workplace claims to the government's attention—and little hope of prevailing without that assistance (Anderson, Clark, and Parutis 2007, 3; Markova and Black 2008, 29; Tailby et al. 2009).

Nonetheless, low-wage A8 migrants in the United Kingdom appear to have faced obstacles to enforcing their rights even beyond those encountered by native workers. Obvious impediments include their lack of language skills and their unfamiliarity with U.K. law, labor markets, and institutions (Gordon 2011, 8). The negative role played by private recruitment agencies, which employ up to 50 percent of A8 migrants in the United Kingdom (Blanchflower and Lawton 2008, 5), also appears to be an important contributing factor. Agency practices encourage—indeed, in many cases require—applicants to work below their level of training and education. Common agency abuses include overcharging, dubious lending practices, and inaccurate promises about placements. Agencies limit migrant mobility by making placements in isolated areas and by fomenting the fear among agency workers that if they pursue their rights they will be fired or denied future placements (Gordon 2011, 8–9).

Also notable is the fact that despite the full EU citizenship of A8 migrants and their ostensible mobility and equal access to workplace rights, there appear to have been fewer organizing successes to date among this population in the United Kingdom than among guest workers and undocumented immigrants in the United States, despite the much less favorable legal environment that the latter face. Although unions in the United Kingdom have sought to reach out to A8 and other migrant workers and have experimented with approaches ranging from creating a migrant workers branch to hiring organizers from Polish unions to creating a short-term internal "migrant worker support unit," migrants do not appear to have joined U.K. unions in significant numbers (Fitzgerald and Hardy 2010, 139, 145; Gumbrell-McCormick 2011). Several union staff and leaders whom I interviewed in 2010 attribute this to the fact that U.K. union membership rules and structures do not correspond to the reality of A8 migrant life, in that they require year-round membership in a single-industry union branch that corresponds to one location, while migrants are likely to move frequently between jobs, regions, and their home countries and the United Kingdom.[22] Although there is interest in the United Kingdom in the worker center model, it has not yet taken hold.

There are unquestionably lessons in this account of the U.K. experience for advocates in the United States. One is the need to begin to think seriously about the regulation of recruitment. Although the United States has some experience with the phenomenon of foreign labor recruiters in low-wage work in the context of guest work visas and in a few other industries, the undocumented status of so many low-wage migrants has bred more illegal than legal intermediaries. Should we move toward expanding opportunities to enter the United States for temporary work, we should expect that intermediaries will grow exponentially. This will require new kinds of regulation and demand a deeper understanding of the functioning of agencies in this market. In this regard, the United Kingdom's innovative Gangmasters Licensing Authority, an agency that since 2006 has held both recruiters and ultimate employers responsible for violations of a range of workplace laws, is a model worthy of further consideration (Gordon 2011, 10–11, 13).

Beyond this, the experiences of EU migrants in the United Kingdom suggest that even were the United States to implement the most positive of changes to the structure of labor immigration policy—say, a worker visa program that permits people from lower-wage countries entirely free movement between employers and regions and grants these migrants full and equal labor rights—this alone would be insufficient to deter employers whose business model relies on the exploitation of the newest arrivals, nor would it provide adequate support to low-wage immigrant and migrant workers in coming forward to defend their rights.

WHAT WORKS FOR IMMIGRANT WORKERS?

Despite the frequency with which immigration enforcement in the United States has derailed workers' efforts to stand up for their rights, there are powerful examples in very recent times of undocumented immigrants and guest workers organizing to demand better wages and working conditions, sue their employers, and join unions despite the forces arrayed against them. Union organizing campaigns involving undocumented workers are now under way throughout much of the country. Indeed, both activists and scholars have argued that immigrants, including the undocumented, are often more receptive to the idea of organizing than their native counterparts (Delgado 1993, 10–11; Milkman 2006, 126–40).

Receptivity on its own, however, is clearly not enough. In this section, I briefly highlight two developments in the United States over the past two decades that have enabled immigrant workers to defend their rights despite the restrictions created by their immigration status.[23] One is institutional: the emergence of worker centers and their networks, as well as unions' experimentation with new organizing approaches uniquely tailored to the needs and perspectives of undocumented and temporary workers. These new or reshaped institutions have provided immigrants with sustained support and a home base that remains constant whatever industry—indeed, in some cases, whatever country—they are working in.

The other development is, in a broad sense, legal, in that it embraces the idea of workers' rights as a central framework for the discussion of immigrants in the workplace (rather than the delegitimizing frame of immigration status), relies on creative litigation and legislative initiatives in the arena of workers' rights, and engages directly with government actors to advance the enforcement of those rights.

New Institutions and Strategies

Some part of the labor movement has always sought to organize immigrants—just as there has always been another segment that has rejected them (Burgoon et al. 2011). In the past twenty years, however, unions in industries such as hospitality, building services, health care, and food processing have come to recognize that if they do not make a priority of organizing the immigrants who now dominate those workplaces, they will quite simply cease to exist. An early and iconic effort was the Service Employees International Union (SEIU) "Justice for Janitors" campaign, which has brought tens of thousands of immigrant cleaning workers into unions all over the country over the two decades since its inception (Milkman 2006, 155–62; Meyerson 2001). Today the United Food and Commercial Workers Union, the Hotel Employees and Restaurant Employees Union, and numerous other service industry unions are equally involved in immigrant-organizing campaigns.

Many of the innovations of these campaigns and the lessons they offer have been comprehensively addressed elsewhere, and I list but a few here.[24] Successful immigrant-organizing unions have developed the capacity to reach workers in their own languages, and with reference to their own cultures, via organizers who share their ethnicities. They have built alliances with community organizations, religious groups, and worker centers (addressed later in the chapter). They have piloted associate membership programs to reach immigrants before there is an organizing campaign under way in their workplace. And perhaps most importantly, they have been attentive to and willing to spend political capital on the defense of undocumented workers in the face of employers' efforts to use their lack of status as a pretext for firing them.[25]

Meanwhile, worker centers have grown in number, from five in 1992 to an estimate of over two hundred nationwide in 2011 (Fine 2011, 607, 615). Such centers have been key actors in many of the victories involving undocumented workers over the past two decades. They deploy a range of strategies, from education and outreach to legal and policy advocacy to membership-based organizing, to support low-wage, largely immigrant workers. The greatest successes of worker centers have been in the policy arena. For example, the New York City–based Domestic Workers United succeeded in passing the historic New York "Domestic Workers' Bill of Rights" in 2010, and it and fellow member organizations of the National Domestic Workers Alliance (NDWA) played a critical role in the 2011 adoption by the International Labor Organization (ILO) of the "Convention Concerning Decent Work for Domestic Workers." Worker centers have also had successes in raising wages and improving working conditions in specific workplaces. One illustration here is the work of the Restaurant Opportunities Center (ROC-NY), founded in New York and now part of a national network of such centers. ROC-NY has targeted high-end restaurants in Manhattan for protest and litigation regarding wage theft, and has succeeded in winning settlement agreements that include paid breaks, access to training and promotions, and grievance resolution mechanisms (Fine 2006, 16–18; Fine 2011, 609, 613–14, 616; Ashar 2007, 1881; Jayaraman 2005).

In recent years, a number of worker centers have moved from a purely local focus to a regional or national outlook. Several centers have opened branches in new cities, and national networks have emerged. The National Day Labor Organizing Network, the National Domestic Worker Alliance, the Restaurant Opportunity Center-United, and the International Taxi Workers Alliance are prominent examples. Most recently, the United Workers Congress was founded by a coalition of those networks and additional unions and organizations to put forward an affirmative agenda to demand the right for all workers to organize (Fine 2011; Goldberg and Jackson 2011, 54–59).[26] These networks, as well as a few individual centers, have also formed alliances with the AFL-CIO, SEIU, LIUNA (Laborers International Union of North America), and other unions.[27]

Beyond undocumented workers, guest workers—long thought to be unorganizable because of their temporariness and the vulnerability induced by the tie between their visas and particular employers—have also been successful in organizing for better conditions, despite the restrictions attached to their visas. With the support of a few unions and worker centers—

including most recently the National Guestworker Alliance (NGA), a project of the New Orleans Workers' Center for Racial Justice—they have walked off the job and led campaigns to reform the programs in which they work.

Because far less attention has been paid to guest-worker organizing than to that of the undocumented, I offer several examples here. The National Guestworker Alliance (NGA) first came into the limelight for the campaign it initiated in 2008 with one hundred welders working on H-2B visas for Signal Shipbuilding. The guest workers left the camps where they were being held captive and began a sustained public protest, including a march to Washington, a twenty-nine-day hunger strike, a lawsuit, and a trafficking investigation by the Department of Justice, among other strategies. They eventually won the right to remain in the United States and succeeded in publicizing the conditions facing guest workers across the country.[28] More recently, in 2011, NGA supported an organizing campaign involving three hundred workers on J visas (a visitor exchange program being used as a low-wage guest-worker visa) who held a walkout at the Hershey distribution plant where they had been made to work for a net wage of less than $3.00 per hour.[29] In 2012 crab pickers who worked for a Walmart supplier on H-2B visas won concessions from Walmart, again with NGA's support.[30]

NGA is not a traditional union. It is a membership organization that joins with guest workers to expose the conditions under which they labor, through a series of campaigns. To date, the campaigns have resulted in discrete benefits for the guest workers involved, including legal immigration status and the payment of money owed; changes in U.S. government policy affecting all workers in a particular visa category; and perhaps most importantly, a vast increase in public awareness of the existence of guest workers and their use and abuse in a wide range of industries.

In another remarkable development in the past decade, the Farm Labor Organizing Committee (FLOC) has unionized H-2A temporary agricultural workers and negotiated contracts with their employers, a previously unheard-of achievement. FLOC's collective bargaining agreement with the North Carolina Growers Association, which since 2004 has covered over six thousand H-2A agricultural guest workers in North Carolina, is the most sustained and successful example of guest-worker unionization in this country's history.[31] In the absence of a stable workforce that could itself make demands, FLOC relied on consumer pressure to bring the North Carolina Growers Association to the table and to agree to bargain. Its ongoing organizing strategy has been successful in part because of the union's capacity to adapt its structures to the realities of guest work. For example, FLOC opened an office in Monterrey, Mexico, to remain in contact with its members while they are at home, and it has also functionally taken on some of the roles played by labor contractors under the terms of the agreement (Gordon 2007, 574–76; Hill 2008).

FLOC and NGA offer two models for raising workplace standards for the most vulnerable immigrant workers.

Workers' Rights as a Central Feature

The second factor I highlight is the importance of the legal framework of workers' rights. In the United States, where many workplace protections have been extended to both undocumented and temporary workers, advocates have used these laws in many ways to support immigrants who seek better working conditions. Workers' rights provide an alternative framework for the rhetoric about immigration ("respect for all workers' rights" as a counter to "get illegals out of the workplace") and an alternative solution for poor working conditions ("enforce basic workplace rights" as an alternative to "enforce immigration laws in the workplace") (Gordon 2012, 134–35). Workers' rights have also offered advocates tools to be deployed creatively through litigation and expanded through legislation (often on a state or local level). Worker advocates' emphasis on workplace rights has grown alongside, and more recently interacted with, an increased interest on the part of the U.S. Department of Labor and some state attorney general's offices and labor departments in the strategic enforcement of workplace laws in a way that is crafted to mirror the reality of the industry in question and is sensitive to the concerns of immigrant workers.

This confluence of interests has led some worker organizations and some agencies to explore public-private collaborations to further enforcement goals. In an earlier article, Janice Fine and I called for robust partnerships between workers' organizations and state and federal departments of labor, which would share responsibility for outreach, the investigation of complaints, and the design of proactive, industry-specific enforcement strategies (Fine and Gordon 2010, 561–62). Although such collaborations have struggled at times to resolve conflicts between the law enforcement perspective of government agencies and the organizing perspective of unions and worker centers, they also draw on the complementary strengths of both parties. In particular, we note that workers' organizations "have access to information about sectors that are otherwise hard for the government to penetrate, knowledge about industry structures, and the capacity to reach workers and document complicated cases" (575–76). We highlight three partnerships that have been sustained over time: two involve the building trades in Los Angeles, and one links SEIU and the California Department of Labor Standards Enforcement.

The Obama administration has also explored options for strategic enforcement of workplace laws, drawing in part on the work of labor standards enforcement expert David Weil (2010) and the work of a coalition of advocacy groups led by the National Employment Law Project (2010). The administration's efforts have included substantially increasing the number of labor inspectors; targeting industries with high concentrations of immigrants; establishing relationships with the consulates of immigrants' countries of origin; creating and distributing engaging multilingual outreach materials on workers' rights through the Web and other media; initiating a system to refer people with wage and hour claims to private attorneys in the plaintiffs' bar; and taking small—albeit politically controversial—steps to initiate partnerships with community organizations (Bobo 2011; Weil 2012, 12).

An ongoing campaign among car-wash workers in Los Angeles, many of whom are undocumented, illustrates the interaction of many of the innovations highlighted in this chapter, including the insistence on baseline workers' rights (usually seen as the purview of worker centers) as the framework for a union organizing campaign (Hill 2010). The Los Angeles "CLEAN Car Wash Campaign" has been the product of coordination among legal advocates, a union, community allies, and government agencies. In its early stages, legal cases and a successful campaign for a California car-wash workers' law exposed the abuses endemic to the industry. In 2008 the United Steel Workers (USW) union formed its Carwash Workers Organizing Committee, and the CLEAN Car Wash Campaign was formally launched.[32] With the new law in place and an organizing campaign under way, the California Department of Labor Standards Enforcement became involved, initiating a spate of targeted and well-publicized enforcement actions that made clear the consequences of a low-road business model. In late 2011 and early 2012, following years of organizing by the USW and collaborations with groups as diverse as the Sierra Club and the religious group Clergy and Laity United for Economic Justice, workers voted for union representation at three car washes around L.A., among the first examples of unionization in the industry. All three businesses are now governed by collective bargaining agreements.[33]

The victories by undocumented immigrant and guest workers noted in this chapter were hard-fought, and most at some point encountered employers seeking to use immigration law to derail the campaigns. That they could eventually be won illustrates that even in an atmosphere of fear generated by immigration enforcement targeting the workplace, and even after adverse legal rulings such as Hoffman Plastics Compounds, there are times when the impediments of immigration law and status can be

overcome by worker bravery, solidarity, institutional support from workers' organizations, and an insistence on the enforcement of baseline workplace rights.

CONCLUSION: LOOKING TO THE FUTURE

The presence of immigration law in the workplace, whether in the form of
mobility restrictions incorporated in temporary worker visas or employer
sanctions and immigration raids in the context of undocumented workers, has proven to be a serious obstacle to the enforcement of basic
workers' rights. In practice, employer sanctions offer employers a ready
cover for retaliatory firing, guest workers are effectively bonded to their
employers, immigration priorities often eclipse employment protections
when it comes to government strategies, and migrant and immigrant
workers fear coming forward to report abuse because of the immigration
consequences that may ensue. For these reasons, advocates have long
called for the elimination of the requirement that a guest worker remain
with her sponsoring employer, the repeal of employer sanctions, and a
government emphasis on compliance with worksite protections rather
than on the enforcement of immigration law in the workplace. These
demands are right on target, in great part because they understand that it
is not enough to remove immigration law from the workplace if it is not
replaced with a determination to make workplace protections real for all
workers.

As important as this prescription is, it would be wrong to conclude
that changes in legal policy are adequate to ensure that immigrant workers who want to advocate for their rights are able to do so. As in the post-
enlargement United Kingdom, where a legal regime permitting EU citizens
free movement and equal rights has not resulted in a noticeable surge of
organizing among such workers, all low-wage labor migrants—even those
who travel with unprecedented freedom for transnational migrants—are
likely to face higher levels of rights violations and less organizing success
than their native counterparts. One key force that appears to be depressing
their working standards is the intervention of labor recruiters, who have
re-created through private means many of the concerns that arise in the
United States as a result of the immigration laws. Another is the weakness
in the U.K. regime of basic workplace protections and its enforcement,
including a failure to collaborate between government actors and worker
advocates. A final factor is a gap between migrants' needs and perspectives
and the institutional support available to them in the United Kingdom,
whether because trade union structures and strategies have not adapted
to migrant realities in the way they have begun to in the United States or

because of the lack of alternative structures, such as worker centers, in all but the most embryonic form.

This contrast graphically illustrates that for low-wage migrants, greater mobility and equal rights on paper are important elements in the fight for decent work, but do not alone guarantee a positive outcome. Past proposals for comprehensive immigration reform did not address many of the elements I have argued are important for success. To be sure, such bills included legalization, which would have brought many undocumented workers out of the shadows. But they also included "future flow" programs that would have re-created the flaws in our current guest-worker scheme and mandated increased reliance on employer sanctions and E-Verify. As this book goes to press, the outcome of the 2013 immigration reform debate in Congress remains to be seen.

What would be the features of an immigration policy reflecting the insights I highlight in this chapter? Legalization is an essential background condition. If a guest-worker program is part of the policy, it must also allow the migrants to whom it grants visas the freedom to move between employers. In the realm of temporary work visas, however, we must think beyond mobility and consider how to create the incentives and support necessary for migrants to stand in defense of their rights. I have suggested elsewhere that this might be done through a regime I call "transnational labor citizenship" (Gordon 2007).

Under transnational labor citizenship, visas would be allocated to low-wage migrant workers not through the traditional route of employer sponsorship, but on the basis of the would-be visa holders' promise to refuse employment from any firm that does not comply with workplace standards and to report any employer that seeks to hire them on illegal terms. The migrants would enter the program through membership organizations in their home countries with a commitment to advocacy for workers' and immigrants' rights. On arrival, they would also become members in worker centers, unions, or other workers' organizations in the industry or geographical area where they found work. This transnational network would be supported by advocates and labor enforcement specialists in both countries. In this way, migrants would be labor citizens at home and abroad, with the institutional support and incentives they need to make sure that they are paid and treated in accordance with the law.

Transnational labor citizenship remains more of a thought experiment than a concrete proposal in the current political context. But whether immigration reform is eventually done piecemeal or Congress passes a comprehensive proposal, it is crucial that the goal of achieving decent work for immigrant and native workers alike be at its center.

NOTES

1. Immigration and Nationality Act § 203(b)(3) (2006).
2. The figure varies by year; the 200,000 to 300,000 annual number reflects admissions under H-2A and H-2B visas for the past three fiscal years.
3. Foreign-born workers as a whole make up 15.9 percent of the U.S. labor force (U.S. Department of Labor, Bureau of Labor Statistics 2012). In other words, the undocumented make up about one third of the immigrant workforce. This is in slightly greater proportion to their representation in the immigrant population as a whole, a number recently estimated at 28 percent (Passel and Cohn 2011, 9).
4. For example, the H-2A program requires that employers pay whatever is higher: the adverse effect wage rate (AEWR), the applicable prevailing wage, or the federal minimum wage; see 8 U.S.C. § 1188(a)(1)(A), (B) (2000); 20 C.F.R. § 655.107(b) (2002). In 2012 the AEWR ranged from $9.30 to $12.26 per hour, depending on the state (U.S. Department of Labor, Employment and Training Administration 2011). In all cases the AEWR is higher than the federal minimum wage. The employer must also provide H-2A workers with meals and housing and must pay the worker for at least three-fourths of the time promised in the contract, even if there is not enough work to keep the worker busy during that time (U.S. Department of Labor, Wage and Hour Division 2010).
5. See Patel v. Quality Inn South, 846 F.2d 700, 706 (11th Cir. 1988).
6. See Rivera v. NIBCO, Inc., 364 F.3d 1057 (9th Cir. 2004); Iweala v. Operational Techs. Servs., 634 F. Supp. 2d 73, 80 (D.D.C. 2009); and Escobar v. Spartan Sec. Serv., 281 F. Supp. 2d 895, 897 (S.D. Tex. 2003); but see Egbuna v. Time-Life Libraries, Inc., 153 F.3d 184, 187–88 (4th Cir. 1998).
7. Workers' compensation for on-the-job injuries suffered by undocumented immigrants is limited in a few states and under dispute in others, although most states and the District of Columbia still guarantee coverage to the undocumented. See Visoso v. Cargill Meat Solutions, 778 N.W.2d 504, 511 (Neb. Ct. App. 2009); and Asylum Co. v. Dep't of Emp't Servs., 10 A.3d 619, 626 (D.C. 2010); but see Sanchez v. Eagle Alloy Inc., 658 N.W.2d 510, 519 (Mich. Ct. App. 2003).
8. Hoffman Plastics Compounds v. NLRB, 535 U.S. 137, 152 (2002).
9. Chuck Bartels, "Migrant Forest Workers Get $2.75M Wage Settlement," Seattle Times, February 12, 2010; see also U.S. Equal Employment Opportunity Commission, "EEOC Files Its Largest Farm Worker Human Trafficking Suit Against Global Horizons, Farms" (press release), April 20, 2011, available at: http://www.eeoc.gov/eeoc/newsroom/release/4-20-11b.cfm (accessed September 2013); and Southern Poverty Law Center (2007).
10. INA § 274(b).
11. In June 2012, ICE for the first time stayed an enforcement action it had initiated at a workplace with a unionization campaign and a strike under way, consistent with the revised memorandum of understanding; see Steven Greenhouse and Steven Yaccino, "Fight over Immigrant Firings," New York Times, July 28, 2012.

12. Nina Bernstein, "Warehouse Workers Quit in Immigration Inquiry," *New York Times*, December 13, 2007, and "Groceries on the Computer, and Immigrants in the Cold," *New York Times*, December 22, 2007; Sewell Chan, "Pressure Mounts as FreshDirect Turmoil Rises; Union Vote Fails," *New York Times*, City Room (blog), December 21, 2007 (updated December 23), available at: http://cityroom.blogs.nytimes.com/2007/12/21/pressure-mounts-as-freshdirect-turmoil-rises/?scp=25&sq=Fresh%20Direct&st=cse (accessed September 2013).

13. Julia Preston, "After Iowa Raid, Immigrants Fuel Labor Inquiries," *New York Times*, July 27, 2008; see also Smith, Avendaño, and Ortega (2009), 23–24.

14. Julia Preston, "A Crackdown on Employing Illegal Workers," *New York Times*, May 30, 2011; see also Kaye (2011).

15. The administration has not, however, eliminated workplace raids; see Greg Hardesty and Cindy Carcamo, "ICE Agents Raid Manufacturer in Fullerton," *Orange County Register*, June 30, 2010; see also American Civil Liberties Union (2011, 4–5). Some workers continue to be arrested and deported under the new approach. In one recent restaurant "sweep," for example, forty-two undocumented immigrants were arrested and thirteen were detained or deported; see Preston, "A Crackdown on Employing Illegal Workers."

16. See also Julia Preston, "U.S. Shifts Strategy on Illicit Work by Immigrants," *New York Times*, July 3, 2009.

17. Most evidence that employers are responding to sanctions is circumstantial or anecdotal. For example, journalists Edgar Sandoval and John Marzulli report an increase in H-2B applications for racetrack workers, long a job held by undocumented laborers; Edgar Sandoval and John Marzulli, "Belmont Stable Owners Insist Foreign Workers Are Needed for Dirty Jobs That NYers Refuse to Do," *New York Daily News*. October 18, 2011. Kerstin Gentsch and Douglas Massey (2011, 891), noting that the use of guest worker programs in 2008 was ten times higher than in 1996, argue that this was at least in part the result of increased enforcement of immigration law inside the United States.

18. Today there are signs that some unions in the AFL-CIO are reconsidering this change in position (AFL-CIO Building and Construction Trades Department 2009, 1–2).

19. 131 S. Ct. 1968 (2011).

20. This section is adapted and updated from Gordon (2011).

21. It is important to recognize a number of divergences between the U.S. and U.K. contexts as well (Gordon 2011, 11–12).

22. Donna Reeve (organizing department campaign support and secretary, UNITE), interview with the author, London, February 16, 2010; Sean Bamford (policy officer, European Union and Trades Union Congress International Relations Department), telephone interview with the author, February 11, 2010; see also Gumbrell-McCormick (2011).

23. It is important to remember, however, that until undocumented immigrants gain legal status, they remain vulnerable to retaliatory firings even once unionized, and there is little they or their unions and worker centers can do to get their jobs back, however courageous the workers and creative the organizations.
24. Readers interested in in-depth case studies should see *Organizing Immigrants* (Milkman 2000), Working for Justice (Milkman, Bloom, and Narro 2010), and *Immigrants, Unions, and the New U.S. Labor Market* (Ness 2005).
25. Greenhouse and Yaccino, "Fight over Immigrant Firings"; Albor Ruiz, "Contract Protects Immigrant Hotel Workers," *New York Daily News*, March 4, 2012; see also Sherman and Voss (2000, 90–92).
26. For more on the United Workers Congress, see the website at: http://www. excludedworkerscongress.org (accessed September 2013).
27. AFL-CIO, "Worker Center Partnerships," available at: http://www.aflcio.org/ About/Worker-Center-Partnerships (accessed September 2013); see also Fine (2011, 615).
28. Julia Preston, "Workers on Hunger Strike Say They Were Misled on Visas," *New York Times*, June 7, 2008; see also Ness (2011, 102–9).
29. Julia Preston, "Pleas Unheeded as Students' U.S. Jobs Soured," *New York Times*, October 17, 2011; see also Human Rights Delegation 2011).
30. Steven Greenhouse, "Wal-Mart Suspends Supplier of Seafood," *New York Times*, June 30, 2012.
31. For a copy of the collective bargaining agreement between FLOC and the North Carolina Growers Association, go to: http://ncgrowers.org/ncgas-union-agreement/ (accessed September 2013), and click on the link to the agreement.
32. See the website for the CLEAN Carwash Campaign at: http://www.cleancar washla.org/ (accessed September 2013); the campaign launch was announced in a March 27, 2008, press release ("Coalition Launches Campaign to Clean Up LA Carwash Industry"), http://laborweb.aflcio.org/sites/Open5/carwash/ index.cfm?action=article&articleID=d60266f6-9338-4560-949d-959bdad14be7 (accessed September 2013). See also Sam Quinones, "Carwash Workers Celebrate Union Contract," *Los Angeles Times*, October 26, 2011; Alana Semuels, "Union Forges a New Alliance with Carwash Workers," *Los Angeles Times*, February 22, 2012; and Garea and Stern 2010.
33. Quinones, "Carwash Workers Celebrate Union Contract"; Semuels, "Union Forges a New Alliance with Carwash Workers."

REFERENCES

AFL-CIO Building and Construction Trades Department. 2009. "The Building and Construction Trades Department's Statement of Principles on Comprehensive Immigration Reform." May 13. Available at: http://www.bctd.org/BCTD/

media/Documents/Newsroom/Policy%20Statements/BCTDStatement.pdf (accessed September 2013).

American Civil Liberties Union. 2011. "ICE Worksite Enforcement: Up to the Job?" Statement submitted to House Committee on the Judiciary, Subcommittee on Immigration Policy and Enforcement, 112th Congress, January 26.

Anderson, Bridget, Nick Clark, and Violetta Parutis. 2007. "New EU Members? Migrant Workers' Challenges and Opportunities to U.K. Trade Unions: A Polish and Lithuanian Case Study." London: Trades Union Congress. Available at: http://www.tuc.org.uk/extras/migrantchallenges.pdf (accessed September 2013).

Ashar, Sameer M. 2007. "Public Interest Lawyers and Resistance Movements." *California Law Review* 95(5): 1879–1925.

Bacon, David, and Bill Ong Hing. 2010. "The Rise and Fall of Employer Sanctions." *Fordham Urban Law Journal* 38(1): 77–105.

Blanchflower, David G., and Helen Lawton. 2008. "The Impact of the Recent Expansion of the EU on the U.K. Labour Market." Discussion Paper 3695. Bonn, Germany: Institute for the Study of Labor (IZA) (September). Available at: http://ftp.iza.org/dp3695.pdf (accessed September 2013).

Bobo, Kim. 2011. "Examining Regulatory and Enforcement Actions Under the Fair Labor Standards Act." Testimony before House Committee on Education and the Workforce, Subcommittee on Workforce Protections, 112th Congress, November 3.

Burgoon, Brian, Wade Jacoby, Janice Fine, and Daniel Tichenor. 2011. "Immigration and the Transformation of American Unionism." *International Migration Review* 44(4): 933–73.

Catanzarite, Lisa. 2003. "Occupational Context and Wage Competition of New Immigrant Latinos with Minorities and Whites." *Review of Black Political Economy* 31(1): 77–94.

Costa, Daniel. 2011. "Guest Worker Diplomacy: J Visas Receive Minimal Oversight Despite Significant Implications for the U.S. Labor Market." Briefing Paper 317. Washington, D.C.: Economic Policy Institute (July 14). Available at: http://www.epi.org/files/2011/BriefingPaper317.pdf (accessed September 2013).

Delgado, Héctor L. 1993. *New Immigrants, Old Unions: Organizing Undocumented Workers in Los Angeles.* Philadelphia: Temple University Press.

Drinkwater, Stephen, John Eade, and Michal Garapich. 2006. "Poles Apart? EU Enlargement and the Labour Market Outcomes of Immigrants in the U.K." Discussion Paper 2410. Bonn, Germany: Institute for the Study of Labor (IZA) (October). Available at: http://ftp.iza.org/dp2410.pdf (accessed September 2013).

European Commission. 2012. "Eurostat Table." Available at: http://epp.eurostat. ec.europa.eu/tgm/refreshTableAction.do;jsessionid=9ea7d07e30dbe4df21cadb 5543078b41b9ebffeee3f3.e34MbxeSahmMa40LbNiMbxaMbhyTe0?tab=table&p lugin=1&pcode=tps00173&language=en (accessed September 2013).

Fine, Janice. 2006. *Worker Centers: Organizing Communities at the Edge of the Dream.* Ithaca, N.Y.: Cornell University Press.

———. 2011. "New Forms to Settle Old Scores: Updating the Worker Centre Story in the United States." *Industrial Relations* 66(4): 604–30.

Fine, Janice, and Jennifer Gordon. 2010. "Strengthening Labor Standards Enforcement Through Partnerships with Workers' Organizations." *Politics and Society* 38(4): 552–85.

Fitzgerald, Ian, and Jane Hardy. 2010. "'Thinking Outside the Box'? Trade Union Organizing Strategies and Polish Migrant Workers in the United Kingdom." *British Journal of Industrial Relations* 48(1): 131–50.

Flora, Jan L., Claudia M. Prado-Meza, and Hannah Lewis. 2011. "After the Raid Is Over: Marshalltown, Iowa, and the Consequences of Worksite Enforcement Raids." Special report. Washington, D.C.: Immigration Policy Center (January). Available at: http://www.ilw.com/articles/2011,0310-ipc.pdf (accessed September 2013).

Garea, Susan, and Sasha Alexandra Stern. 2010. "From Legal Advocacy to Organizing: Progressive Lawyering and the Los Angeles Car Wash Campaign." In *Working for Justice: The L.A. Model of Organizing and Advocacy,* ed. Ruth Milkman, Joshua Bloom, and Victor Narro. Ithaca, N.Y.: Cornell University Press.

Gentsch, Kerstin, and Douglas S. Massey. 2011. "Labor Market Outcomes for Legal Mexican Immigrants Under the New Regime of Immigration Enforcement." *Social Science Quarterly* 92(3): 875–93.

Goldberg, Harmony, and Randy Jackson. 2011. "The Excluded Workers' Congress: Reimagining the Right to Organize." *New Labor Forum* 20(3): 54–59.

Gordon, Jennifer. 2005. "Lack of Worksite Enforcement and Employer Sanctions." Testimony before House Committee on the Judiciary, Subcommittee on Immigration, Border Security, and Claims, 109th Congress, June 21.

———. 2007. "Transnational Labor Citizenship." *Southern California Law Review* 80(3): 503–88.

———. 2011. "Free Movement and Equal Rights for Low-Wage Workers? What the United States Can Learn from the New EU Migration to Britain." Issue brief. Berkeley: University of California–Berkeley Law School, Chief Justice Earl Warren Institute on Law and Social Policy (May). Available at: http://www.law.berkeley.edu/img/Gordon_Issue_Brief_May_2011_FINAL.pdf (accessed September 2013).

———. 2012. "Tensions in Rhetoric and Reality at the Intersection of Labor and Immigration." *University of California Irvine Law Review* 2(1): 125–46.

Gumbrell-McCormick, Rebecca. 2011. "European Trade Unions and 'Atypical' Workers." *Industrial Relations Journal* 42(3): 293–310.

Hill, Jennifer. 2008. "Binational Guestworker Unions: Moving Guestworkers into the House of Labor." *Fordham Urban Law Journal* 35(2): 307–38.

———. 2010. "Can Unions Use Worker Center Strategies? In an Age of Doing More with Less, Unions Should Consider Thinking Locally but Acting Globally." *FIU Law Review* 5(2): 551–92.

Holgate, Jane, Janroj Keles, Leena Kumarappan, and Anna Pollert. 2010. "Help and Representation for Problems at Work: What Has Happened to Support Networks and Advice Centres?" London: Working Lives Research Institute. Available at: http://www.workinglives.org/londonmet/fms/MRSite/Research/wlri/Photo%20 gallery/Project%20final%20report.pdf (accessed September 2013).

Holzer, Harry J. 2011. "Immigration Policy and Less-Skilled Workers in the United States: Reflections on Future Directions for Reform." Washington, D.C.: Migration Policy Institute (January). Available at: http://www.urban.org/uploadedpdf/1001488-immigration-policy.pdf (accessed September 2013).

Human Rights Delegation. 2011. "Report of the August 2011 Human Rights Delegation to Hershey, Pennsylvania." September 8. Available at: http://www.guest workeralliance.org/wp-content/uploads/2011/09/Human-Rights-Delegation-Report-Hershey-Reissue-September-8.pdf (accessed September 2013).

Jamieson, Dave. 2011. "Chipotle, Undocumented Workers, and the Trouble with 'Enforcement-Only' Immigration." Huffington Post, May 11 (updated July 11, 2011). Available at: http://www.huffingtonpost.com/2011/05/11/chipotle-immigration-reform_n_860565.html (accessed September 2013).

Jayaraman, Sarumathi. 2005. " 'ROCing' the Industry: Organizing Restaurant Workers in New York." In The New Urban Immigrant Workforce: Innovative Models for Labor Organizing, ed. Sarumathi Jayaraman and Immanuel Ness. Armonk, N.Y.: M. E. Sharpe.

Jus Semper Global Alliance. 2011. "Mexico's Wage Gap Charts." December. Available at: http://www.jussemper.org/Resources/Labour%20Resources/WGC/Resources/WagegapsMex2006.pdf (accessed September 2013).

Kaye, Jeffrey. 2011. "Deeper into the Shadows: The Unintended Consequences of Immigration Worksite Enforcement." Special report. Washington, D.C.: Immigration Policy Center (February). Available at: http://www.ilw.com/articles/2011,0324-kaye.pdf (accessed September 2013).

Lee, Stephen. 2009. "Private Immigration Screening in the Workplace." Stanford Law Review 61(5): 1103–46.

MacKenzie, Robert, and Chris Forde. 2009. "The Rhetoric of the 'Good Worker' Versus the Realities of Employers' Use and the Experiences of Migrant Workers." Work, Employment, and Society 23(1): 142–59.

Manacorda, Marco, Alan Manning, and Jonathan Wadsworth. 2006. "The Impact of Immigration on the Structure of Male Wages: Theory and Evidence from Britain." Discussion Paper 2352. Bonn, Germany: Institute for the Study of Labor (IZA) (October). Available at: ftp://repec.iza.org/RePEc/Discussion paper/dp2352.pdf (accessed September 2013).

Markova, Eugenia, and Richard Black. 2008. "The Experiences of 'New' East European Immigrants in the U.K. Labour Market." Journal of Poverty and Social Justice 16(1): 19–31.

McCollum, David, and Allan Findlay. 2011. "Trends in A8 Migration to the U.K. During the Recession." Population Trends 145(1, Autumn): 1–13. Available at:

http://www.cpc.ac.uk/resources/downloads/2011%20poptrends145%20A8%20 migration.pdf (accessed September 2013).

Meyerson, Harold. 2001. "A Clean Sweep." *The American Prospect*, December 19. Available at: http://prospect.org/article/clean-sweep (accessed September 2013).

Migration Policy Institute. 2009. "DHS and Immigration: Taking Stock and Correct ing Course." Presentation, February 11. Available at: https://secure.migration policy.org/images/2009.2.11_Presentation-1.pdf (accessed September 2013).

Milkman, Ruth, ed. 2000. *Organizing Immigrants: The Challenge for Unions in Con temporary California*. Ithaca, N.Y.: Cornell University Press.

———. 2006. *L.A. Story: Immigrant Workers and the Future of the U.S. Labor Movement*. New York: Russell Sage Foundation.

Milkman, Ruth, Joshua Bloom, and Victor Narro, eds. 2010. *Working for Justice: The L.A. Model of Organizing and Advocacy*. Ithaca, N.Y.: Cornell University Press.

Monger, Randall. 2012. "Nonimmigrant Admissions to the United States: 2011." *Annual Flow Report* (July). Washington: U.S. Department of Homeland Secu- rity. Available at: http://www.dhs.gov/xlibrary/assets/statistics/publications/ni_ fr_2011.pdf (accessed September 2013).

Monger, Randall, and James Yankay. 2012. "U.S. Legal Permanent Residents: 2011." *Annual Flow Report* (April). Washington: U.S. Department of Homeland Secu- rity. Available at: http://www.dhs.gov/xlibrary/assets/statistics/publications/ lpr_fr_2011.pdf (accessed September 2013).

National Employment Law Project. 2010. "Just Pay: Improving Wage and Hour Enforcement at the United States Department of Labor." Available at: http:// www.nelp.org/page/-/Justice/2010/JustPayReport2010.pdf?nocdn=1 (accessed September 2013).

National Immigration Law Center. 2009. "Issue Brief: Immigration Enforcement During Labor Disputes." Available at: http://www.nilc.org/genworkenf.html (accessed September 2013).

Ness, Immanuel. 2005. *Immigrants, Unions, and the New U.S. Labor Market*. Phila- delphia: Temple University Press.

———. 2011. *Guest Workers and Resistance to U.S. Corporate Despotism*. Urbana: Uni- versity of Illinois Press.

Passel, Jeffrey S., and D'Vera Cohn. 2010. "U.S. Unauthorized Immigration Flows Are Down Sharply Since Mid-Decade." Washington, D.C.: Pew Hispanic Cen- ter (September 1). Available at: http://www.pewhispanic.org/files/reports/126. pdf (accessed September 2013).

———. 2011. "Unauthorized Immigrant Population: National and State Trends, 2010." Washington, D.C.: Pew Hispanic Center (February 1). Available at: http:// pewhispanic.org/files/reports/133.pdf (accessed September 2013).

Poinasamy, Krisnah. 2011. "When Work Won't Pay: In-Work Poverty in the U.K." Discussion paper. Oxford: Oxfam (November). Available at: http://policy- practice.oxfam.org.uk/publications/when-work-wont-pay-in-work-poverty- in-the-uk-197010 (accessed September 2013).

Pollert, Anna. 2008. "Injustice at Work: How Britain's Low-Paid Non-Unionised Employees Experience Workplace Problems." *Journal of Workplace Rights* 13(3): 223–44.

Sherman, Rachel, and Kim Voss. 2000. "Organize or Die: Labor's New Tactics and Immigrant Workers." In *Organizing Immigrants*, ed. Ruth Milkman. Ithaca, N.Y.: Cornell University Press.

Shierholz, Heidi. 2010. "Immigration and Wages: Methodological Advancements Confirm Modest Gains for Native Workers." Briefing Paper 255. Washington, D.C.: Economic Policy Institute (February 4). Available at: http://www.epi.org/page/-/bp255/bp255.pdf (accessed September 2013).

Smith, Rebecca, Ana Avendaño, and Julie Martínez Ortega. 2009. "ICED OUT: How Immigration Enforcement Has Interfered with Workers' Rights." New York: National Employment Law Project (October 27). Available at: http://nelp.3cdn.net/75a43e6ae48f67216a_w2m6bp1ak.pdf (accessed September 2013).

Smith, Rebecca, Amy Sugimori, Ana Avendaño, and Marielena Hincapie. 2007. "Undocumented Workers: Preserving Rights and Remedies After Hoffman Plastic Compounds v. NLRB." New York: National Employment Law Project (February 23). Available at: http://nelp.3cdn.net/b378145245dde2e58d_0qm6i6i6g.pdf (accessed September 2013).

Somerville, Will, and Madeleine Sumption. 2009. "Immigration and the Labor Market: Theory, Evidence, and Policy." Washington, D.C.: Migration Policy Institute (March). Available at: http://www.migrationpolicy.org/pubs/Immigration-and-the-Labour-Market.pdf (accessed September 2013).

Southern Poverty Law Center. 2007. "Closer to Slavery: Guestworker Programs in the United States." Montgomery, Ala.: Southern Poverty Law Center (March). Available at: http://www.splcenter.org/sites/default/files/downloads/Close_to_Slavery.pdf (accessed September 2013).

Sumption, Madeleine, and Will Somerville. 2010. "The U.K.'s New Europeans: Progress and Challenges Five Years After Accession." Washington, D.C.: Migration Policy Institute. Available at: http://www.equalityhumanrights.com/uploaded_files/new_europeans.pdf (accessed September 2013).

Tailby, Stephanie, Anna Pollert, Stella Warren, Andy Danford, and Nick Wilton. 2009. "Under-funded and Overwhelmed: The Voluntary Sector as Worker Representation in Britain's Individualised Industrial Relations System." *Industrial Relations Journal* 42(3): 273–92.

Trades Union Congress Commission on Vulnerable Employment. 2008. "Hard Work, Hidden Lives: The Short Report of the Commission on Vulnerable Employment." London: Trades Union Congress (May 7). Available at: http://www.vulnerableworkers.org.uk/files/CoVE_short_report.pdf (accessed September 2013).

U.S. Department of Homeland Security. Immigration and Customs Enforcement. 1996. "Questioning Persons During Labor Disputes." Operating Instructions 287.3a, December 4. Available at: http://www.uscis.gov/ilink/docView/SLB/HTML/SLB/0-0-0-1/0-0-0-53690/0-0-0-61072/0-0-0-61097.html (accessed September 2013).

——. 2011. "Oversight Hearing on U.S. Immigration and Customs Enforcement: Priorities and the Rule of Law." Statement of John Morton, Director, before House Committee on the Judiciary, Subcommittee on Immigration Policy and Enforcement, 112th Congress, October 12. Available at: http://www.dhs.gov/ynews/testimony/20111012 morton icc oversight.shtm (accessed September 2013).

U.S. Department of Homeland Security and U.S. Department of Labor. 2011. "Revised Memorandum of Understanding Between the Departments of Homeland Security and Labor Concerning Enforcement Activities at Worksites." December 7. Available at: http://www.dol.gov/asp/media/reports/DHS-DOL-MOU.pdf (accessed September 2013).

U.S. Department of Labor. Bureau of Labor Statistics. 2012. "Foreign-Born Workers: Labor Force Characteristics—2011." Available at: http://www.bls.gov/news.release/archives/forbrn_05242012.htm (accessed September 2013).

——. Employment and Training Administration. 2011. "2012 Adverse Effect Wage Rates" (map). Available at: http://www.foreignlaborcert.doleta.gov/pdf/aewr_map_2012.pdf (accessed September 2013).

——. Wage and Hour Division. 2010. "Fact Sheet 26: Section H-2A of the Immigration and Nationality Act (INA)." Available at: http://www.dol.gov/whd/regs/compliance/whdfs26.htm (accessed September 2013).

U.S. Department of State. Bureau of Consular Affairs. 2012. "Visa Bulletin for August 2012." Travel.State.Gov. Available at: http://www.travel.state.gov/visa/bulletin/bulletin_5749.html (accessed September 2013).

U.S. General Accounting Office. 1990. *Immigration Reform: Employer Sanctions and the Question of Discrimination.* Report to Congress, March 29. GAO/GGD-90-62. Available at: http://archive.gao.gov/d24t8/140974.pdf (accessed September 2013).

U.S. Government Accountability Office. 2005. "Immigration Enforcement: Preliminary Observations on Employment Verification and Worksite Enforcement Efforts." Statement of Richard M. Stana, Director of Homeland Security and Justice of GAO, submitted to House Committee on the Judiciary, Subcommittee on Immigration, Border Security, and Claims, 109th Congress, June 21, GAO-05 822T. Available at: http://www.gao.gov/new.items/d05822t.pdf (accessed September 2013).

——. 2010. "H-2B Visa Program: Closed Civil and Criminal Cases Illustrate Instances of H-2B Workers Being Targets of Fraud and Abuse." Report to House Committee on Education and Labor, 111th Congress, September 30, GAO-10-1053. Available at: http://www.gao.gov/assets/320/310640.pdf (accessed September 2013).

U.S. Immigration and Naturalization Service, U.S. Department of Justice, and U.S. Department of Labor. 1998. "Memorandum of Understanding Between the Immigration and Naturalization Service, Department of Justice, and the Employment Standards Administration, Department of Labor." November 23. Available at: http://bender.lexisnexis.com/us/lpgateway.dll?f=templates$fn=tools-contents.htm$cp=325j%2F8%2F9%2F322$tt=document-frame.htm$tf=main$3.0 (accessed September 2013).

Vargas-Silva, Carlos. 2012. "Migration Flows of A8 and Other EU Migrants to and from the U.K." Migration Observatory Briefing. Oxford: Oxford University, Centre on Migration, Policy, and Society (January). Available at: http://www.migrationobservatory.ox.ac.uk/sites/files/migobs/Migration%20Flows%20of%20A8%20and%20other%20EU%20Migrants%20to%20and%20from%20the%20UK.pdf (accessed September 2013).

Wasem, Ruth Ellen. 2012. "Unauthorized Aliens Residing in the United States: Estimates Since 1986." Washington, D.C.: Congressional Research Service (December 13). Available at: http://www.fas.org/sgp/crs/misc/RL33874.pdf (accessed September 2013).

Weil, David. 2010. "Improving Workplace Conditions Through Strategic Enforcement: A Report to the Wage and Hour Division." May. Available at: http://www.dol.gov/whd/resources/strategicEnforcement.pdf (accessed September 2013).

———. 2012. " 'Broken Windows,' Vulnerable Workers, and the Future of Worker Representation." *The Forum* 10(1): 9.

Wishnie, Michael J. 2003. "The Border Crossed Us: Current Issues in Immigrant Labor." *New York University Review of Law and Social Change* 28(3): 389–96 (accessed September 2013).

———. 2007. "Prohibiting the Employment of Unauthorized Immigrants: The Experiment Fails." *University of Chicago Legal Forum* 2007: 193–218.

CASES

Asylum Co. v. Dep't of Emp't Servs., 10 A.3d 619 (D.C. 2010)
Chamber of Commerce v. Whiting, 131 S. Ct. 1968 (2011)
Egbuna v. Time-Life Libraries, Inc., 153 F.3d 184 (4th Cir. 1998)
Escobar v. Spartan Sec. Serv., 281 F. Supp. 2d, 895 (S.D. Tex. 2003)
Hoffman Plastics Compounds v. NLRB, 535 U.S. 137 (2002)
Iweala v. Operational Techs. Servs., 634 F. Supp. 2d 73 (D.D.C. 2009)
Patel v. Quality Inn South, 846 F.2d 700 (11th Cir. 1988)
Rivera v. NIBCO, Inc., 364 F.3d 1057 (9th Cir. 2004)
Sanchez v. Eagle Alloy Inc., 658 N.W.2d 510 (Mich. Ct. App. 2003)
Visoso v. Cargill Meat Solutions, 778 N.W.2d 504 (Neb. Ct. App. 2009)

STATUTES

8 U.S.C. § 1188(a)(1)(A), (B) (2000)
Immigration and Nationality Act § 203(b)(3) (2006)
Immigration and Nationality Act § 274(b) (2006)
20 C.F.R. § 655.107(b) (2002)

Part III | Innovative Labor
          Market Interventions

Chapter 6 | Career Ladders in the Low-Wage Labor Market

Paul Osterman

FAR TOO MANY jobs in the United States fall below the standard that most people would consider decent work. If we ask only about wages (hence being conservative by ignoring health insurance, pensions, and other attributes of decent work) and focus only on adults age twenty-five to sixty-four, then in 2011, 19 percent of adult workers earned an hourly wage below that necessary (working full-time/full-year) to raise a family of four above the poverty line of $10.96 an hour.[1] This is a very conservative estimate because it is widely accepted that the poverty line is flawed and underestimates what it takes to maintain a basic living standard. Indeed, a recent study that estimated a basic needs budget for a family of four found that 44 percent of adults fall below the standard (Wider Opportunities for Women 2011).

One might argue that even for adults, low-wage work is transitory and a great many will find ways to climb up the ladder into better jobs. However, the unfortunate fact is that this is not true: most low-wage workers remain trapped.[2] There is also extensive evidence that low incomes have negative effects on families in terms of the health of the adults and the educational achievement of the children (Wilkinson and Pickett 2009). In a deeper sense, people who are scrambling to hold themselves and their families together economically cannot be fully functioning citizens or participants in society.

The extent of bad jobs touches directly on broader challenges. There is widespread dismay at growing inequality, and while some of this can be attributed to excesses at the very top, it is clear that any real solution must address the labor market circumstances of millions of Americans in low-paying work. In addition, middle-class Americans in good jobs are confronting the reality of losing work and being forced, if they are lucky, to take employment in the low-wage labor market. Improving these jobs is in their interest too.

A FRAMEWORK FOR THINKING ABOUT POLICY

The goal of this chapter is to discuss the potential and the challenges of a specific policy to address low-wage jobs: training programs and, more specifically, labor market intermediaries. Before turning to these policies, however, it is useful to think about the larger policy universe. A wide variety of tools are available for influencing how firms organize their employment systems, and a framework or classification system is helpful for understanding them. One important distinction is between what might be termed "standard-setting" policies, on the one hand, and "programmatic interventions," on the other. Examples of the former include unionization, minimum and living wage legislation, and community benefit agreements. Examples of the latter are sectoral training programs, labor market intermediaries, and variants of manufacturing extension services.

A second useful distinction is between interventions aimed at improving the quality of existing jobs ("making bad jobs good") and interventions aimed at creating, or retaining, more good jobs. Examples of the first set of policies are efforts to raise wages or create job ladders in the existing job base—for example, in the retail, health, or hospitality industries. Examples of the second category are economic development programs that utilize labor market tools to attract good jobs or to help existing firms compete more effectively and hence maintain the base of good jobs that already exists. Figure 6.1 organizes possible policy levers in terms of these distinctions.

The distinctions in this chart are to some extent arbitrary (for example, some unions run substantial training career ladder programs, as noted later), but they do represent a useful way of thinking about the universe of policy interventions on the demand side. This chapter focuses on programs in the upper right quadrant: programmatic interventions that work with firms to improve careers within the organization.

TRAINING AND CAREER LADDERS

Before turning to training programs, we must ask the following question: will there be good jobs that low-wage workers can aspire to, or is the trajectory of technological change creating a situation in which the only jobs available will be either very low-skill or very high-skill, with few opportunities in the middle? This is an important question, and a recent line

Figure 6.1   A Typology of Intervention Strategies

	Standard-setting	Programmatic
Make bad jobs good	Minimum wage Living wages Unionization	Career ladders Intermediaries Sectoral programs
Create more good jobs	Community benefit agreements Managed tax incentives	Extension services Sectoral programs

Source: Author's figure.

of research has claimed that the latter situation, dubbed "polarization," characterizes our future.

The polarization story emerged as an explanation for the apparent failure of earlier models linking education to inequality. These models worked well in explaining the patterns in the 1980s, but significant problems began to emerge in the 1990s. People with a high school degree or less have held their own relative to the median wage, a reversal of the pattern in the 1980s, when the bottom fell out of the high school labor market. In addition, however, and very problematic for the education story, is that the wages of those with just a college degree (as opposed to an advanced degree) have stagnated.[3]

The explanation that emerged was grounded in ideas about the impact of computer technologies.[4] The argument was that computers eliminate routine work that can be adequately captured by algorithms and that these tend to be middle-skilled jobs (for example, clerical work or assembly-line work). What is left is a growing demand for service work at the bottom, which cannot be computerized (think washing floors or caring for the elderly) and highly skilled work at the top (think senior managers or investment bankers). Hence, jobs grow at the bottom and the top of the skill distribution, wages at the bottom hold their own relative to the middle, and wages at the top pull away from the middle.

There is certainly some truth to this story. In particular, service-sector jobs are growing as a proportion of the economy, although it should also

Table 6.1   Replacement Hiring, 2010 to 2020

Occupation	Net Change in Employment, 2010 to 2020	Openings Due to Replacement, 2010 to 2020
Installation, maintenance, repair	+800,200	+1,225,600
Production	+356,800	+1,874,400
Entire economy	+20,468,900	+34,318,500

Source: Author's adaptation of U.S. Department of Labor, Bureau of Labor Statistics (2012).

be noted that this growth does not prove the argument about computers. The demand for service occupations could be growing for numerous reasons, such as the aging of the population and the changing demand for services. It also seems a bit awkward to argue that people with a college degree—who reaped huge wage gains in the 1980s and early 1990s—are suddenly doing routine work and hence experiencing stagnant earnings.

Nonetheless, whatever one thinks of the technological version of the polarization idea, it is simply not the case that there will be few new job openings for middle-skill work (Holzer and Lerman 2009). According to projections by the U.S. Bureau of Labor Statistics (BLS), only 23 percent of all job openings projected between 2008 and 2018 will require a college degree or more (Lacey and Wright 2009). Examples of good jobs that are attainable with less than a four-year degree include numerous health care technician jobs, skilled blue-collar work, computer support jobs, truck drivers, biotechnology technicians, and so on. Other projections suggest that there will be a substantial number of new jobs available for skilled blue-collar work (machine maintenance, technicians, repair jobs, and the like) and that these too require education in the "some college" or associate's degree range.

The continued importance of middle-skill jobs is also based on projected hiring to replace the retiring generation of baby boomers. The importance of this is apparent in table 6.1: even in blue-collar jobs, which in net terms will grow very slowly or actually decline, there will be considerable hiring going forward. These projections may be delayed by deferred retirements caused by the Great Recession, but they cannot be avoided. The bottom line is that middle-skill openings will be accessible to career ladder initiatives.

THE SUBSTANCE OF PROGRAMS

Career ladder programs, and the training that accompanies these efforts, are important in large measure because low-wage workers typically receive very little training from their employers. Good data on training inside

Table 6.2   Employees Receiving Employer-Provided Training, 1995 and 2001

	1995	2001
High school degree or less	22.2%	19.8%
Some college	44.1	44.5
BA degree or higher	50.0	54.1
Lowest earnings quintile	27.1	22.0
Next earnings quintile	31.3	33.7
Next highest earnings quintile	42.1	46.7
Highest earnings quintile	49.3	48.8

Source: Author's adaptation of Mikelson and Nightingale (2004).

firms are hard to find, but table 6.2 tells the basic story. Employees with low levels of education receive far less training than do their better-educated colleagues, and in the same vein, low-paid employees receive much less training than do better-paid workers. These practices represent savings for employers and to some extent may be reasonable in that workers with low-skill jobs presumably need less training to do their work than do employees with more complex tasks. However, the paucity of training also reflects a state of mind—that some workers simply cannot learn and that improvements in the quality of their work or in their career trajectories are not feasible. Typical is the observation of an evaluation team that interviewed firms participating in a set of activities organized by the National Association of Manufacturers (NAM) and aimed at helping them upgrade their production practices: "Employers knew they had problems of absenteeism, turnover, skill deficiencies, and low productivity but accepted them fatalistically as 'facts of life,' feeling that not much could be done about them" (Whiting 2005, 19).

Program models, termed "intermediaries" or "sectoral programs," vary along a number of dimensions: target groups, the auspices under which the programs are managed, and the nature of the services that are provided. What is striking, however, is that they have also coalesced around a common set of what might be termed "best practices" elements. It is these elements that move these innovations beyond the traditional approach of job training programs and make these new programs distinctive and important.

The most important of these elements is an understanding that employment and training efforts work best if they connect effectively to both sides of the labor market—that is, to employers as well as to clients. To accomplish this, the programs work hard to become knowledgeable about the human resource needs of their target group of firms and, in some cases, also seek to understand how they can contribute to the competitive success of the firms. In short, these programs attempt to appeal to firms as a business proposition, not as a charity, public relations, or welfare effort.

The second feature is that best practice programs make substantial investments in their clients. They reject the quick and dirty training, short-term investments, and simple job search assistance models that characterize much of the traditional employment and training system. The new programs' investments take a variety of forms: long training periods, more sustained involvement with firms, and higher levels of support to clients in terms of financial assistance and counseling.

There are, however, important differences across the programs. Many programs rely on community colleges for training and focus their own efforts on supporting the trainees and working with employers. Other programs, albeit a minority, have invested in their own training capacity. Program auspices vary and include community groups, unions, community colleges, employer organizations, and state governments. The programs also vary in the extent to which they work with incumbent workers versus job-seekers.

Programs that work with firms to improve the quality of the jobs focus on two main strategies. The first is redesigning jobs to create career ladders or to enlarge the content of existing jobs. These strategies imply working with management to restructure work and provide training and support to employees so that they can meet the additional responsibilities and move up in the workplace. The second, simpler approach is to encourage firms to increase the quantity of training that they make available to lower-paid employees in the hope that this will lead to career advancement.

Programs in Action

An anchor of the Boston economy is the presence of world-class hospitals that, taken together, are the largest source of jobs in the region. Add to these hospitals the numerous nursing homes and other health facilities and the importance of this sector to the region is obvious. Researchers, doctors, and highly skilled nurses are central to delivering quality health care and world-class innovation, but they are not alone. Just as is true throughout the country, a large low-paid workforce labors at the core of this industry. These are the kitchen staff, the orderlies, the cleaners, the certified nursing assistants (CNAs) and patient care technicians (PCTs), the laundry workers, and many others without whom the system would break down. These people come from all parts of the world and speak different languages, but they do have some things in common. They work very hard, and they are poorly paid. Some of the very best examples of what can be done in cooperation with employers to improve the quality of jobs can be found in health care.

In the spring of 2010, a graduation was held in the auditorium of Children's Hospital for employees from several hospitals who had just finished a program supported by the employers and by several foundations and managed by Jewish Vocational Services (JVS). Some had completed the final step in their English for speakers of other languages (ESOL) program, and others had completed a college bridge program aimed at getting them ready to enter a community college. Attending were the employees, their families, the program staff, and hospital managers. It was a happy and proud event, and the most moving talks were given by employees, who spoke about how hard they had worked, how they could not have achieved what they had without the program's support, and the kinds of jobs or education to which they now aspired. For these people, it was clear that bad jobs were being transformed into better ones.

Jewish Vocational Services is a large agency that operates a wide range of education and training programs in the Boston area. It works with the Russian Jewish immigrant community to facilitate their settling in the area. It has a program with CVS Pharmacy to help people from the community obtain entry-level sales jobs and, for the lucky and ambitious, move into positions like pharmacy technicians. JVS is also beginning to work with a local community organization with roots in the Haitian community to establish a college preparatory program for adults. But its largest effort is aimed at health care employers. The graduation described here was for employees in multiple hospitals in the area, but JVS also works with nursing homes, which have an even higher proportion of low-wage workers because of the nature of the business (largely daily care and maintenance of elderly residents).

All of the organizations with which JVS collaborates speak highly of the quality of the agency's instruction, but our point goes beyond this. In a variety of ways, JVS has enhanced what might be termed the "education and training" culture within the employer workplaces. In part it accomplishes this by encouraging small but significant changes in policies, such as when it worked with Children's Hospital to enable prepayment of tuition assistance, a change that opened up opportunities for people whose family budgets could not accommodate tuition bills. JVS also hosts monthly meetings of the human resources staff of all its client employers in which it diffuses best practices. In some organizations, JVS has innovated in pedagogy—for example, by shifting its ESOL teaching away from chalk-and-talk and toward experiential activities. This innovation has led to greater success rates, which in turn have encouraged the organizations to expand the amount of training they give their employees. In addition, because JVS is an important actor that operates at some scale, it can effectively link employers to other actors, such as community colleges or state funding agencies. In short, our interviews with these health care providers provided convincing testimony that the amount of training they provide to their employees has increased owing to their relationships with JVS.

JVS is not alone in working to improve job quality in the health care industry. Several hospitals and nursing homes in Philadelphia are part of a very large career ladder and training program rooted in a collective bargaining agreement with Local 1199C. The program is funded by a contribution from the employers set at 1.5 percent of the wage bill and is organized and managed by the union in cooperation with the employers. Unlike many career ladder efforts, this one is large enough to merit its own facility and is housed in a cheerful building in the city's downtown.

More than eleven thousand employees pass annually through this program seeking services that range from the simple processing of tuition assistance payments to assessment—such as General Educational Development (GED) testing—and taking a broad range of classes. Over three thousand employees are in education or training programs. Employees in low-level positions—cleaners, orderlies, licensed practical nurses (LPNs) who wish to become registered nurses (RNs), and so on—are given some released time and tuition assistance by their employer, and the counselors and faculty at the program assist them in meeting the education requirements they need to move up.

One woman told us that she had wanted to be a nurse but was discouraged by a college counselor. She dropped out of school, passed through a series of casual jobs, and then landed employment as a nurse's aide. She connected with the program and entered LPN training, achieved that, and is now in an RN program part-time while working. We also met a young man who was, in his words, "educated on the street." He heard about the assessment center, came in, did the foundation courses, became a CNA, and is now in an LPN program. His friends told us that during a major snowstorm he had walked three miles to get to work because he felt he had a commitment to his job. Another woman we met was a ninth-grade dropout and entered via the GED program.

Health care providers are an attractive venue for training and career ladder programs because they provide many middle-level job opportunities that low-wage workers can aspire to and because they are more vulnerable than many other employers to public pressure to play ball. That said, there have been significant initiatives in other industries, including several in hotels and in manufacturing.

Hotels represent a greater challenge than health care because of the nature of the jobs. There is a large low-wage base of room cleaners as well as laundry and kitchen workers. The problem is that there are proportionally fewer jobs in the middle level of the organization to which these workers can aspire. Nonetheless, because there are so many low-wage workers employed in hotels, a number of efforts have been made to provide training opportunities for incumbent workers and open career pathways for them.

One flagship hotel program in Las Vegas is the product of a collective bargaining agreement between the "Strip" hotels and the Culinary Workers Union, local 226 of UNITE HERE. The contract with the Strip hotels funds a large union-run training center that commits the hotels to using it as a hiring source for good middle-level jobs in kitchens and in customer-facing functions. We interviewed employers, trainers, and workers at this center just as the recession was beginning to bite hard and hiring had slowed down considerably. Nonetheless, it was clear that the center was successful in opening mobility pathways for employees. At the time of our visit, the center trained about three thousand employees per year in a wide range of skills. Our interviews with employees provided numerous examples of upward mobility.

Is this effort unique, however, in that its existence rests on the special circumstances of Las Vegas and the relationship of the union to large employers in that city? Another union-based program, this one in Boston, provides some reassurance on this score.

The Boston hotels program was organized by the local union UNITE HERE Local 26, which represents over half of the eleven thousand hotel workers in Boston (Mikelson and Nightingale 2004).[5] In 2004 the union created an on-call banquet server training program in which longtime servers trained other union members so that they could pick up extra shifts during busy periods. The union negotiated with the hotels to ensure that the spots would first be offered to members who had gone through the training. Once the banquet training was established, the union worked with hotel managers to determine whether there were other needs that a union-run training program could fill. A training program opened to union members in 2006 and again in 2008 with additional funds from the state Workforce Competitiveness Trust Fund led to the formation of the Hotel Training Workforce Partnership, which has provided training to people seeking entry into jobs at union hotels as well as to incumbent workers seeking training in general skills such as computer and English language skills. The union worked with the hotels to develop a professional busser/food server certificate. Additionally, the program offers certification courses in food safety and the handling of alcohol. Across all of its components, the program served 267 union members in 2007 and 416 in 2008.

The trainings and certificates combined with guidance from a career coach are intended to create several career tracks within union hotels. Career pathways were developed by program managers working jointly with the union and hotel managers to identify competencies and evaluation criteria for different positions within three departments: food and beverage, guest services, and culinary.

These career pathways are relatively new, and it is too soon to tell whether they have made an impact on the hotels' promotion practices. That said, the program's atmospherics were good. All of the human resources managers we spoke with felt that the program has been responsive to the needs of the hotels. One manager reported that it had "been a win all around," with no unforeseen costs. No one felt that it was time-consuming to work with the program. "The relationship has been far better than any of us could have imagined," said one manager.

Programs for incumbent workers in manufacturing have a different feel than those in hotels or in health care. The focus is less on upward mobility and more on upgrading the skills of incumbent workers and providing technical assistance to firms so that they can operate more efficiently. This latter emphasis is driven by the difficult economic circumstances of manufacturing enterprises, which are much more at risk than health care providers or hotels. Another key difference is that manufacturing programs focus much more on small and medium-size firms that lack the internal capacity to think systematically about their human resource needs.

An example of a sustained effort to work with small manufacturers to improve the training and advancement opportunities of low-wage employees was the Retention and Advancement Demonstration Program, which was managed nationally between 2001 and 2004 by the National Association of Manufacturers and locally in three states by state-level employers' associations in Connecticut, Michigan, and Pennsylvania (Whiting 2005).

The associations that worked with the employers were consistently struck by the poor quality and stressed-out nature of the human resources (HR) systems they encountered and by the limited expectations that HR staff and supervisors held out for their entry-level or low-wage workers. An important part of the effort was an attempt to change both these expectations and these conditions. With respect to the HR systems, a staff person in one of the business associations commented, "Even though company managers usually expressed their top priority as skills upgrading, we usually had to work our way toward the frontline workforce, fixing up various HR systems along the way. It would do little good, and probably be impossible anyway, to mount effective training initiatives if the underlying HR systems and supervisory practices wouldn't support or take advantage of such efforts." This observation speaks directly to the suboptimal nature of the operation of many firms and the scope for improvement. This is a central point because it shows that there is room for productivity gains that benefit low-wage employees as well as employers.

Once the HR systems were in place, the local associations either provided or brokered training. The topics included business writing, blueprint reading, quality control, customer relations and customer service, basic plant metrics, statistical process control, laser technology, plastics molding, machinist skills, lean manufacturing, continuous improvement, Adobe Photoshop and Illustrator, process certification, basic computer skills, and English as a second language (ESL).

Performance and Challenges

What is the evidence that intermediaries are successful? Observers tend to be positive, but the number of careful evaluations is limited. For the JVS health care program, internal data through December 2011 show that 384 incumbent workers received services, of whom 124 enrolled in postsecondary education and 43 completed a postsecondary degree. Of these employees, 220 received pay increases and 61 received promotions.

Two major national random assignment evaluations are currently under way (one funded by the Mott Foundation and the other by the U.S. Department of Health and Human Services), but for now we have to be content with a few careful studies of specific programs. That said, the evidence is positive. One example is the random assignment evaluation of three sectoral programs that provided entry-level training in specific industries (in this case, health care, manufacturing, and information technology) for people who experienced multiple barriers to employment and who averaged less than $10,000 annual earnings prior to the program (Maguire et al. 2010). After completion of the program, the treatment group earned over $4,000 more than the control group.

Another powerful example is Project QUEST in San Antonio, Texas. This program has several features that are consistent with what has come to be seen as best practice. It works with employers to identify future job needs and often involves them in designing training; it provides a good deal of support to trainees in the form of counseling and small amounts of financial assistance; and it is relatively long term and hence makes real investments in people. One participant whom we interviewed said that "they believed in me and made me feel ten feet tall," while another said that "there was opportunity at a time when I needed a lifeline." Formal evaluation results support these observations: participants gained nearly

$5,000 in annual income relative to a comparison group (Osterman and Lautsch 1998). Similar outcomes were found for a sister program in Austin called Capital Idea (King, Carter Smith, and Schroeder 2009).

Several efforts in manufacturing programs were evaluated, at least through careful narratives if not formal random assignment. The National Association of Manufacturers program described earlier involved one thousand employees, and according to the evaluation report, a total of twenty-eight salary increases and fourteen promotions were attributed to the program. These low outcomes numbers were somewhat offset by the evaluator's opinion that the program improved the overall operation of the firms and hence held out the prospect of more employee gains going forward. This view was supported by numerous comments by the employers, who praised the effort and pointed to the gains that they experienced. Although these observations are optimistic, it is also important to acknowledge that measureable gains to employees after an intervention that lasted three full years were very limited.

A second manufacturing assessment comes from a program that began in 2002 in Massachusetts and was aimed at working with firms to increase training and develop career paths for low-skill and low-wage incumbent workers in three industries: health care, financial services, and manufacturing (FutureWorks 2004). Over two thousand employees were involved, with a bit over 40 percent in manufacturing. The program devoted substantial resources to working with employers to design career pathways and provide training to employees. As the evaluation noted, "With its emphasis on incumbent workers, career pathways, integrated curricula and employer involvement, [the initiative] incorporated new 'best practices' of workforce development into program design." Employers displayed very little interest in developing career ladders and, when the program staff laid out possible pathways, very little interest in implementing them. The evaluators commented that

it remains unclear whether limited demand for career path models across industry sectors is due to lack of information (i.e. employers are simply unfamiliar with the concept and need better/more information about career path models), lack of time and resources (i.e. employers don't have the internal resources to develop and implement the approach) or . . . employer perceptions regarding entry-level workers (i.e. employers have difficulty viewing entry-level workers as future skilled labor). (FutureWorks 2004, 28)

The experience was more positive with respect to training. Both employers and employees were happy to receive additional training resources and to participate in the programs. It turned out that the level of basic skills needs was considerably larger than expected, and in the end over half of all training resources went into ESL and other basic skills subjects (as opposed to training more directly aimed at job-related skills). The implication was that even if career paths were created, there was going to be a long haul involved in moving people up through them In addition, interviews with employees showed that many of them were interested in the ESOL and other basic skills training as a pathway to improving the quality of their lives and their self-confidence rather than as a way to advance their career.

Taken as a whole, these evaluations should be seen as "existence proofs" that well-designed programs that work with employers can be effective, although it is also clear that not all efforts succeed. But it should be remembered that there is a distribution of outcomes for training programs, as with other policies, and too often the discussion ignores evidence that success is possible. Rather than giving up, we should learn lessons from best practices and aspire toward these. This is what has happened in the charter school debate—a broad range of advocates focus on best practice cases rather than on the outcomes in the average program—and there is no reason why the same attitude should not prevail for training low-wage employees.

Challenges

A core challenge facing intermediary programs is obtaining employer buy-in. Why should firms want to participate in these programs? The health care sector provides the clearest case for participation, and hence it is not surprising that most programs are found in this sector. Health care providers suffer from high turnover and labor shortages in some of the technician positions that are often targets of these programs. So employers should benefit from a higher level of commitment and effort on the part of their employees, as well as from a lower turnover rate and the associated reduced costs of recruitment. At the same time, health care providers are vulnerable to pressure to improve jobs. This is obvious in the case of employers with union contracts but is also true more generally. Hospitals and other providers are quasi-public in the sense that even private ones rely very heavily on public funding and hence are sensitive to pressure. Their reliance on numerous regulatory decisions also helps make them responsive to these programs. In addition, the shape of the job structure means that there are multiple levels of employment—for example, numerous technician jobs—that represent reasonable targets for the upward advancement of low-wage workers. For these reasons, more career ladder programs can be found in health care than in any other industry.

All this said, there has been resistance, arising from broad-based managerial attitudes. The twin problems are skepticism about training and the players in the organization—senior management, the human resources department, program operators, and line supervisors—often not being on the same page.

An example of managerial skepticism emerged in a conversation with the head of a nursing home that was part of a chain. This leader worked with the Philadelphia 1199C program (even though he was non-union); by creating some career paths, he had reduced turnover of CNAs from 60 percent to 10 percent. Yet despite this success, he was unable to convince his colleagues, the leaders of other nursing homes in the organization, to participate. He attributed this failure to inertia and to a lack of belief in training for this population of employees.

Within the larger non-union hospitals, the sources of resistance tend to be found in the HR departments and among some line supervisors. The advocates are senior management, who have a strong interest in community relations, and the program staff. The HR staff, on the other hand, are often committed to their own routines of recruitment and assessment, and supervisors are focused on what is easiest in terms of staffing (which is often hiring from the outside) as opposed to creating opportunities for lower-level employees to move up. The puzzle is why senior management does not simply insist on cooperation and execution, but the answer lies in the multiple pressures and interests of top management. While these leaders appear to have a genuine interest in the programs, they also confront a myriad of other problems, and forcing their middle managers out of their routines in order to create career ladders or to expand training opportunities is often seen as relatively low-priority and disruptive, no matter how much the top management likes the idea in principle. Hence, the programs remain relatively small-scale in the larger organizational context.

An additional challenge facing these programs stems from a hard fact of life: it is difficult for many employees to obtain the education and skills it takes to move up job ladders in hospitals. Virtually all of the target jobs require at least a community college–level certificate, and many require a two-year degree. Set against this is the unfortunate reality that many, if not most, of the employees with aspirations to move out of low-wage jobs have something like an eighth-grade educational attainment, and many also face challenges with English. In addition, employees' family circumstances can pose significant obstacles. Put in terms of our earlier discussion, there are clear human capital challenges as well as organizational and structural barriers, and it is naive to deny or ignore this. As a consequence of these barriers, the path from, say, working as a Certified Nursing Assistant to an LPN or a technician job can take five or more years. This is a long haul, and many do not make it.

In the study of the Massachusetts manufacturing program mentioned earlier, a final, and somewhat discouraging, finding was that although employers expressed satisfaction with the training, they also explicitly stated that they were satisfied in large part because it was costless. The firms did not continue making the training available when the subsidy ended. The more positive side was that as long as the training was subsidized, employers were willing to let public programs through their doors, something that is not always easy to accomplish. Similar efforts in other parts of the country have also demonstrated that involving employers in subsidized training interventions is quite feasible (Pindus et al. 2004).

One interpretation of the foregoing is that the career ladder idea is flawed. The basis for this view is that there is very little evidence in any of the cases that new job paths have been created that operate at any scale. That is, firms have not fundamentally reorganized their promotion ladders in order to create new rungs (that is, new jobs or reconfigured tasks) that enable low-wage workers to more easily move up. This would be a possible reading, but it is too pessimistic: even though ladders have not been reshaped, the programs do indeed demonstrate that employers can be encouraged, incentivized, and supported to increase the amount of training they provide to their incumbent workforce. This is clear from the work of JVS in Boston, 1199C in Philadelphia, and the several hotel projects we reviewed, and to a lesser extent it can be seen in the manufacturing examples as well. This is important for two reasons. First, as we have seen, one of the markers of bad jobs is that they provide little training. We saw this in the data that demonstrated that low-wage workers receive far less firm-based training than do their more advantaged colleagues. Increasing training is also important because it enables employees to move up existing job paths. Even if the job paths remain the same, more training can improve the prospects of those at the bottom, and in this sense the nature of low-level jobs changes. Instead of being dead-end, they now lead somewhere.

The path to progress is not easy. The internal politics of organizations can be problematic. Multiple organizational actors—top executives, HR staff, line supervisors, and staff charged with running the actual programs—have different priorities, and these are not always congruent. We also saw that small employers often lack the managerial or human resources staff capacity to take full advantage of the programs. On top of all this, these efforts take a long time. With the difficulties faced by low wage workers, in terms of both skills and family issues, it is a long haul to get the training needed and to move up the job ladder. It is naive to expect easy and rapid improvements.

All this said, there are more positive lessons. In virtually all cases, employees are eager participants. Their level of motivation and desire to improve themselves is very strong and provides a strong basis for moving forward. Finally, it does seem clear that well-designed programs can help change the culture of an organization and move it toward one in which the training and education of low-wage workers is seen as a good way of doing business. This is an important step forward in improving the quality of these jobs.

An Aside on Community Colleges

Many of the career ladder programs use community colleges for skill training. Beyond this, it is important to recognize that community colleges are the most important source of skill acquisition for low-wage adults. There are roughly 1,200 community colleges that enroll over 7 million students in credit-bearing courses.[6] We are not sure how many students are enrolled in noncredit community college courses—studying topics that range from the directly vocational to the recreational—because not all states keep data on these enrollments, but experts agree that the numbers are very close to those in credit courses. Hence, in the range of 12 million Americans are enrolled in community colleges. Among students who are enrolled for credit, most are in degree programs, but a substantial minority seek certificates.

Public community college students do not resemble the traditional image of a college student. Nearly 40 percent are over age twenty-four, and 60 percent attend part-time. Indeed, the rhetoric regarding the diminishing importance of the traditional college student is really about community college students. By contrast, among undergraduates in four-year institutions, 79.5 percent attend full-time, and about 70 percent are under age twenty-four (National Center for Education Statistics 2009, table 1). Community college students are more likely to be minority, are more likely to be self-supporting, and are more likely to be first-generation college students (Kazis 2002).

For students who obtain a credential, either a certificate or an associate's degree, community colleges perform well and are an excellent investment. The first widely noted research on rates of return to community college credentials reported positive results (Kain and Rouse 1995), and more recent research has updated these findings while managing to control for a large range of personal and family variables (Marcotte et al. 2005).[7] The rates of return range from 13 percent for men who obtain an associate's degree to a remarkable 38.9 percent for women. In general the results are more robust for women across all specifications, but for both genders the overall positive message is clear for those who manage to obtain a credential.

Thus far the news has been good. However, when we ask what proportion of students who enroll in community college obtain a degree or certificate, or even accomplish a full year of attendance, the picture darkens considerably. Although there is controversy about the precise failure rates, all agree that they are much too high.[8] This failure rate is without question the greatest challenge confronting community colleges.

It is clear from this discussion that community colleges by dint of their scale and the nature of the students who enroll are central training institutions for the people who are at the core of this chapter's interest. It is also clear that, as shown by the gains achieved by people who obtain community college credentials, these institutions hold considerable promise. All this said, the high rates of failure point to the need to take significant steps to improve these institutions, and the question of how to do so is addressed in the final section.

CONCLUSION

As noted at the beginning of this chapter, it is important to understand that a serious effort to reduce the prevalence of low-wage work will require a range of initiatives of which career ladders and training are only one component. Nevertheless, career ladders are certainly worth pursuing. But how do we make them more effective? And what more do we need to know about them?

Improving community college performance is obviously one crucial step. Important experiments are under way to simplify the choices facing students and restructure remedial education so that those choices are both faster and better integrated into the credit curriculum. In addition, despite their importance, community colleges receive far less funding than do four-year schools, and the gap cannot be fully explained by the broader mission of the better-funded institutions. This low level of funding for community colleges has consequences in terms of the prevalence of part-time faculty and the absence of significant counseling and support functions.

Resources are in fact a more general concern. To date, a great deal of intermediary and career ladder funding as well as programmatic initiatives for career ladder programs have come from foundations. The federal government has played a role—for example, resources in the American Recovery and Reinvestment Act (ARRA) of 2009 were set aside for programs aimed at careers in green jobs—but in general federal funding has been inadequate and declining. U.S. Department of Labor Workforce Investment Act (WIA) funding has declined since 2004 and is at major risk, owing to the current budgetary and political difficulties. It is unreasonable to assume that foundations can continue to be a major source of support, and in any case, they will never be able to provide resources at scale. The uneven and declining federal commitment is a source of real concern.

There are also important issues regarding how best to structure support for career ladder programs. As described earlier, in some firms the notion of creating new pathways for upward mobility makes sense, while in other situations the more realistic objective would be to increase employer investment in training for existing career ladders. Indeed, inadequate levels of employer training for low-wage workers is a major challenge. This points in the direction of designing matching programs, and perhaps tax incentives, to stimulate additional training by firms.

We have in hand a set of tools, described earlier in figure 6.1, that we know are effective in reducing the extent of low-wage employment. This is encouraging because it means that the problem is not intractable, that we can make considerable progress should we wish. What is worrying, of course, is that so little has happened. The political challenges are clearly more daunting than are the programmatic ones.

NOTES

1. This calculation is based on the Current Population Survey Outgoing Rotation Group (CPS-ORG). The data are for people age twenty-five to sixty-four in civilian employment. For more information on how the data are analyzed, see Osterman and Shulman (2011).

2. One study found that among low-earners over six years, starting in the early 1990s—a period of remarkable economic strength—only 27 percent raised théir income enough to rise consistently above the poverty line for a family of four (Holzer 2004). A more recent study looked at low-earners in the years 1995 to 2001 and found that 6 percent of those working full-time and 18 percent of those working part-time in any year had dropped out of the labor force by the next year. Among those who did stay in the workforce, 40 percent experienced either a decrease or no change in their earnings (Theodos and Bednarzik 2006.) Using yet a third data source, this time tracking mobility from 2001 to 2003, researchers found that 44 percent of the employees at poverty wages in 2001 had no better wages in 2003; moreover, an additional 22 percent were not even employed (Lopreste et al. 2009).

3. Among working adults in the census ORG data between 2000 and 2009, the hourly wage of those with a college degree increased by a total of 0.3 percent, while the hourly wage of those with only a high school degree grew by 1.9 percent and the hourly wage of those with a graduate degree grew by 2.7 percent.

4. For a discussion of the technology story, see Autor, Levy, and Murnane (2003). For the application of this story to explain recent trends in wages, see Autor, Katz, and Kearney (2008); see also Autor (2010).

5. The account in this session is based on fieldwork by Elizabeth Chimienti.

6. For the number of community colleges, see American Association of Community Colleges, "Fast Facts from Our Fact Sheet," available at: http://www.aacc.nche. edu/AboutCC/Pages/fastfactsfactsheet.aspx (accessed April 2013). Among community colleges, 17 percent have enrollment of at least ten thousand, and 12 percent have enrollment of five hundred or less. Twenty-three percent of community colleges are in California (National Center for Education Statistics 2008, 3).

7. The estimates were for year 2000 wages for students who were in the eighth grade in 1988 and no longer in school when the earnings data were collected. Because the data source—the National Educational Longitudinal Survey (NELS)—is quite rich, the authors were able to control for high school performance as well as a wide range of parental characteristics. These controls substantially reduce concerns regarding selection bias in driving the results.

8. The federal government collects data on graduation rates through its Integrated Post-Secondary Data System (IPEDS); according to the most recent figures, only 22 percent of public community college students who entered in 2005 had obtained a degree or certificate within 150 percent of the expected time, that is, by 2008. However, the problem with these data is that they refer only to full-time students, whereas we saw that a strong majority attend part-time. Another federal source, the Post-Secondary Longitudinal Students Survey, includes both full- and part-time students. In these data, among students who enrolled in the fall of 2003, by June 2006 5.5 percent had obtained a certificate, 10.0 percent had earned an associate's degree, 39.8 percent were still enrolled, and 44.6 percent were no longer enrolled. In other words, the three-year success rate, as measured by a credential, was an even lower 15.5 percent, presumably reflecting worse outcomes for part-time students.

These outcomes are more than a little discouraging. However, many observers would point out that they are also somewhat unfair. Given the substantial fraction of part-time students, focusing on a three-year completion rate may be too stringent. The U.S. Department of Education does not collect outcomes for a longer enrollment period; however, a recent effort, executed by Jobs for the Future as part of the Lumina Foundation Achieving the Dream initiative, did collect detailed outcome data from six states for a six-year period since enrollment. These data paint a brighter picture than do the three-year federal figures, but the assessment is still grim. Even assuming that the story for transfer students has a uniformly happy ending, at best only four out of ten students reach their goals within six years of enrolling, and in most states the results are even worse; see National Center for Education Statistics (2010, table 5) and National Center for Education Statistics (2003–2004).

REFERENCES

Autor, David. 2010. "The Polarization of Job Opportunities in the U.S. Labor Market: Implications for Employment and Earnings." Washington, D.C.: Center for America Progress (April).

Autor, David, Lawrence F. Katz, and Melissa S. Kearney. 2008. "Trends in U.S. Wage Inequality: Revising the Revisionists." *Review of Economics and Statistics* 90(2, May): 300–323.

Autor, David, Frank Levy, and Richard Murnane. 2003. "The Skill Content of Recent Technological Change: An Empirical Investigation." *Quarterly Journal of Economics* 118(November): 1279–1333.

FutureWorks. 2004. "Building Essential Skills Through Training (BEST): Final Evaluation Report." Boston: The Commonwealth Corporation (September).

Holzer, Harry. 2004. "Encouraging Job Advancement Among Low-Wage Workers: A New Approach." Policy Brief 30. Washington, D.C.: Brookings Institution (May).

Holzer, Harry, and Robert Lerman. 2009. "America's Forgotten Middle-Skill Jobs." Washington, D.C.: Workforce Alliance.

Kain, Thomas, and Cecelia Rouse. 1995. "Labor Market Returns to Two- and Four-Year Colleges." *American Economic Review* 85(3): 600–614.

Kazis, Richard. 2002. "Community Colleges and Low-Income Populations." Boston: Jobs for the Future (March).

King, Christopher T., Tara Carter Smith, and Daniel G. Schroeder. 2009. "Evaluating Local Workforce Investments: Results for Short- and Long-Term Training in Austin (TX)." Austin: University of Texas, LBJ School of Public Affairs, Ray Marshall Center for the Study of Human Resources. Presented to the 31st annual research conference of the Association for Public Policy Analysis and Management (APPAM). Washington, D.C. (November 2009).

Lacey, T. Alan, and Benjamin Wright. 2009. "Occupational Employment Projections to 2018." *Monthly Labor Review* 132(11, November): 82–123.

Lopreste, Pamela, Gregory Acs, Caroline Ratcliffe, and Katie Vinopal. 2009. "Who Are Low-Wage Workers?" ASPE Research Brief. Washington: U.S. Department of Health and Human Services, Office of the Assistant Secretary for Planning and Evaluation (February).

Maguire, Shelia, Joshua Freely, Carol Clymer, Maureen Conway, and Deena Schwartz. 2010. "Tuning In to Local Labor Markets: Findings from the Sectoral Employment Study." Philadelphia: Public/Private Ventures.

Marcotte, David E., Thomas Bailey, Carey Borkoski, and Greg S. Kienzl. 2005. "The Returns of a Community College Education: Evidence from the National Education Longitudinal Survey." *Educational Evaluation and Policy Analysis* 27(Summer): 157–75.

Mikelson, Kelley, and Demetra Nightingale. 2004. "Estimating Public and Private Expenditures on Occupational Training in the United States." Washington,

D.C.: Urban Institute, for U.S. Department of Labor Employment and Training Administration (December).

National Center for Education Statistics. 2003–2004. "Beginning Postsecondary StudentsLongitudinalStudy:FirstFollow-up."BPS:04/06.Availableat:http://nces. ed.gov/das/library/tables_listings/showTable2005.asp?popup=true&tableID= 3786&rt= (accessed September 2013)

———. 2008. "Community Colleges: Special Supplement to the Condition of Education." NCES 2008-033. Washington, D.C.: NCES.

———. 2009. *Enrollment in Postsecondary Institutions, Fall 2007 — First Look*. NECS 2009-155. Washington, D.C.: NCES.

———. 2010. *Enrollment in Postsecondary Institutions, 2008: First Look*. NECS 2010-152. Washington, D.C.: NCES.

Osterman, Paul, and Brenda Lautsch. 1998. "Changing the Constraints: A Successful Employment and Training Strategy." In *Jobs and Economic Development*, ed. Robert Giloth. Thousand Oaks, Calif.: Sage Publications.

Osterman, Paul, and Beth Shulman. 2011. *Good Jobs America: Making Work Better for Everyone*. New York: Russell Sage Foundation.

Pindus, Nancy M., Carolyn O'Brien, Maureen Conway, Conaway Haskins, and Ida Rademacher. 2004. "Evaluation of the Sectoral Employment Demonstration Program." Washington, D.C.: Urban Institute (June).

Theodos, Brett, and Robert Bednarzik. 2006. "Earnings Mobility and Low-Wage Workers in the United States." *Monthly Labor Review* (July): 34–47.

U.S. Department of Labor, Bureau of Labor Statistics. 2012. "Table 1.2, Employment by Detailed Occupation, 2010 and Projected 2020." Available at: http://www.bls.gov/emp/ep_table_102.htm (accessed September 2013).

Whiting, Basil. 2005. "The Retention and Advancement Demonstration Project (RAD): A 'Win-Win' for Manufacturers and Their Workers at Entry and Near-Entry Levels." Washington, D.C.: National Association of Manufacturers (NAM), Manufacturing Institute, Center for Workforce Success (August).

Wider Opportunities for Women. 2011. *The Basic Economic Security Tables For the United States, 2010*. Washington, D.C.: Wider Opportunities for Women.

Wilkinson, Richard G., and Kate E. Pickett. 2009. "Income Inequality and Social Dysfunction." *Annual Review of Sociology* 35: 493–511.

Chapter 7 | Employment Subsidies to Firms and Workers: Key Distinctions Between the Effects of the Work Opportunity Tax Credit and the Earned Income Tax Credit

Sarah Hamersma

CLASSIC ECONOMIC THEORY suggests that an employment subsidy will increase the number of jobs and the take-home pay of workers regardless of whether it is received by firms or workers, but the targeting and implementation of each type of subsidy program can differ substantially, resulting in widely varying outcomes. In this chapter, I examine the key distinctions between these two styles of subsidies as they have been implemented in the United States, most recently via the Work Opportunity Tax Credit (WOTC), a firm subsidy, and the Earned Income Tax Credit (EITC) a worker subsidy. Both programs boast low federal administrative costs relative to typical transfer programs, and both offer the promise of increased work and income for disadvantaged individuals. However, despite many shared goals, these two programs have different eligibility requirements, firm and worker administrative burdens, and payment schemes. As a result, participation rates in the programs differ, as does their measured effectiveness in improving outcomes. This chapter synthesizes the existing literature on these findings, suggests possible explanations for the differences in effectiveness, and provides new estimates of recent participation rates in the expanding Work Opportunity Tax Credit program.

Figure 7.1   Labor Market Effects of a Subsidy

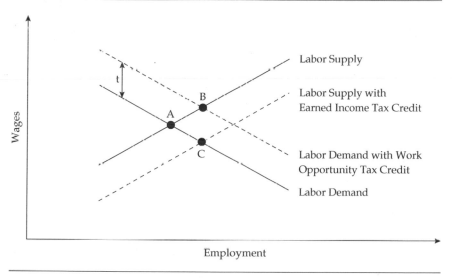

Source: Author's illustration.

A THEORY OF TAX CREDIT INCIDENCE

Economists model tax credits as negative taxes, allowing the use of general tax incidence theory to evaluate their predicted effects. Figure 7.1 illustrates the framework for this theory, with the market equilibrium in the absence of a tax credit program labeled as point A. An employer tax credit of size t is expressed as a rightward shift of the labor demand curve, such that at a given wage a firm is willing to hire additional workers. The resulting equilibrium, labeled B, indicates an increase in employment and an increase in wages paid to workers (but a decrease in wages paid by firms, with the difference reflecting the value of the credit). A worker tax credit is expressed as a rightward shift of the labor supply curve, such that at a given wage there are more people willing to work. The resulting equilibrium, labeled C, indicates an increase in employment and a decrease in wages paid by firms (but an increase in wages received by workers when the tax credit value is included in the wage). For a given size of tax credit, the effect on employment, take home wage, and firm-paid wage is the same regardless of whether the tax credit is given to the worker or the firm.

Of course, this model is simplified relative to reality. First, it assumes that the tax credit applies to all workers in the market. Under the current worker subsidy program (the Earned Income Tax Credit), the tax credit applies only to workers with positive but low family earned income, and it applies to different degrees depending on the level of that income and the size of the family. The current employer subsidy program (the Work Opportunity Tax Credit) applies to firms hiring workers who have (typically) been connected with public assistance programs. Although these populations surely overlap, neither of them necessarily represents the whole relevant labor market.

The theory of tax incidence also assumes that the financial aspects of the programs are the only ones relevant for understanding their likely effects. It assumes that any party that would financially benefit from a subsidy will claim it. However, participation in both types of programs is not universal; employer subsidies in particular have had historically low participation rates among eligible firms (Hamersma 2003). With the exception of a model by Stacy Dickert-Conlin and Douglas Holtz-Eakin (2000) that incorporates worker stigma, there has been little attempt to model this incomplete participation.

Finally, this model makes predictions for the consequences of subsidies when markets are in equilibrium. In a time of recession, with substantial unemployment, it is hard to imagine a worker-side subsidy promoting much job growth, since it depends on the idea of increasing the labor supply (which is not helpful if there is already a surplus of workers). Similarly, if unemployment is very low, we may not find firms increasing employment in response to a subsidy since there is likely to be a labor shortage already. Thus, the larger economic climate—and the political response to that climate—are important for understanding these programs in context.

This chapter continues with an overview of the existing relevant programs and then considers how they have played out in the past and may play out in the future in our broader policy context.

EXISTING EMPLOYMENT TAX CREDITS

The Earned Income Tax Credit

The Earned Income Tax Credit (EITC) was signed into law in 1975 under the Ford administration (in the spirit of earlier proposals developed by the Nixon administration) and has since grown to be the largest cash assistance program in the country. The credit is applied based on family earned income and the number of qualified children.[1] The credit provides an earnings supplement and an incentive for nonworkers to begin working.

Figure 7.2   Federal Earned Income Tax Credit Benefits

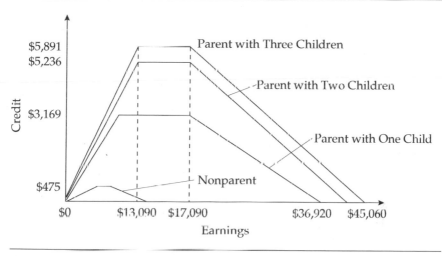

Source: Author's illustration based on Tax Policy Center (2013).
Notes: The numbers labeled on the *y*-axis represent the maximum credit for each group. These rates apply to single individuals, with or without children. Taxpayers who are married filing jointly have higher beginning and ending points of the phaseout range (that is, the range over which they receive maximum benefits is larger). In 2012 these points were $5,210 higher (on the *x*-axis) than those shown in the figure. For details of the parameters graphed here, see Urban Institute and Brookings Institution, Tax Policy Center, "Tax Facts: Earned Income Tax Credit Parameters, 1975–2013," available at: http://www.taxpolicy center.org/taxfacts/displayafact.cfm?Docid=36 (accessed September 2013).

It does this by subsidizing wages by a large percentage when earnings are low and then capping and gradually phasing out the subsidy. The top line on figure 7.2 shows the pattern of the tax credit for a single-mother family with three children in 2012. Earnings in this case are increased by 45 percent for the first $13,090 of earnings until the maximum credit of $5,891 is reached. At this point, the mother can still earn more money without losing any benefits. Only when earnings exceed $17,090 does the credit begin to phase out, at a rate of 21 percent. Those with earnings above $45,060 do not qualify for the credit. Benefit amounts are smaller for those with fewer or no children, as shown on the lower lines in figure 7.2.

The EITC is administered by the Internal Revenue Service (IRS). While the credit could technically (until recently) be claimed smoothly over a year, most recipients have received it as a lump sum upon filing annual federal income taxes. The EITC is a refundable credit, so it is possible for filing units to get refund checks that exceed the amount they have paid in federal income tax. Because of this feature of the program, there are some individuals who would not otherwise be obligated to file who can benefit from filing because of the EITC.

Issues of EITC compliance have been a major concern in recent years (U.S. Treasury Inspector General for Tax Administration 2011). Recent estimates suggest that about one-fourth of EITC claims are made inappropriately. The primary confusion for recipients (and their tax preparers) seems to be the issue of the appropriate number of children to claim (Hotz and Scholz 2003). The definition of a "qualifying child" under EITC includes an age, relationship, and residency test and has not always been the same as that used for other tax credits (Hamel 2009). The IRS has engaged in a number of outreach strategies to claimants and tax preparers to help improve rates of compliance (U.S. Treasury Inspector General for Tax Administration 2011).

The overall cost of the EITC program has increased substantially over the years due to both eligibility expansions and benefit increases. Table 7.1 provides the annual number of participants and total cost of the program. In recent years, the annual cost has been over $55 billion. This far exceeds the 2009 spending on cash assistance—Temporary Assistance for Needy Families (TANF)—of about $6 billion and is on par with the 2009 cost of the Supplemental Nutrition Assistance Program (SNAP), which grew by 42 percent relative to 2008.[2] The cost of EITC benefits shown in table 7.1 does not include administrative costs, although these are relatively small for tax credits relative to transfer programs, for which close to 20 percent of costs can be administrative (Olson 2011).

The Earned Income Tax Credit has received fairly consistent political support since its inception, with major expansions enacted in 1986, 1990, and 1993. V. Joseph Hotz and John Karl Scholz (2003) provide a detailed discussion of the nature of each of the early expansions. The most recent changes in the EITC have been a higher subsidy rate for those with three or more children as well as an increase in the beginning of the phaseout range for couples filing joint returns (introduced via the American Recovery and Reinvestment Act of 2009 and extended through 2017 via the American Taxpayer Relief Act of 2013).[3] In addition, the IRS continues to develop outreach methods to improve compliance, since consistently poor compliance (whether real or perceived) could make the EITC less politically palatable than it has historically been.

The Work Opportunity Tax Credit

The Work Opportunity Tax Credit (WOTC) was introduced in 1996 as part of the Small Business Job Protection Act. The WOTC was designed

Table 7.1   Earned Income Tax Credit: Number of Recipients and
             Amount of Credit, 1975 to 2009

Year	Number of Recipient Families (in Thousands)	Total Amount of Credit (in Millions of 2009 Dollars)	Refunded Portions of Credit (in Millions of 2009 Dollars)	Average Credit per Family (in 2009 Dollars)
1975	6,215	$4,984	$3,588	$801
1976	6,473	4,882	3,355	754
1977	5,627	3,989	3,115	708
1978	5,192	3,448	2,635	665
1979	7,135	6,063	4,122	851
1980	6,954	5,170	3,566	745
1981	6,717	4,512	3,016	673
1982	6,395	3,945	2,716	618
1983	7,368	3,866	2,776	482
1984	6,376	3,382	2,399	531
1985	7,432	4,162	2,988	560
1986	7,156	3,932	2,895	550
1987	8,738	6,403	5,532	850
1988	11,148	10,691	7,719	959
1989	11,696	11,408	8,020	976
1990	12,542	12,378	8,642	986
1991	13,665	17,489	12,887	1,280
1992	14,097	19,918	15,226	1,413
1993	15,117	23,064	17,855	1,526
1994	19,017	30,547	24,023	1,607
1995	19,334	36,533	29,316	1,889
1996	19,464	39,407	31,658	2,025
1997	19,391	40,613	32,604	2,094
1998	20,273	42,558	35,761	2,099
1999	19,259	41,073	35,541	2,132
2000	19,277	40,229	34,633	2,086
2001	19,593	40,424	35,176	2,064
2002	21,703	45,546	40,226	2,098
2003	22,024	45,065	39,650	2,046
2004	22,270	45,448	40,084	2,041
2005	22,752	46,579	41,148	2,047

(Table continues on p. 192.)

Table 7.1   (Continued)

Year	Number of Recipient Families (in Thousands)	Total Amount of Credit (in Millions of 2009 Dollars)	Refunded Portions of Credit (in Millions of 2009 Dollars)	Average Credit per Family (in 2009 Dollars)
2006	23,042	47,228	41,572	2,049
2007	24,584	50,226	43,984	2,043
2008	24,757	50,481	44,096	2,039
2009	27,041	60,932	55,524	2,194

Source: Author's compilation based on Tax Policy Center (2012).
Note: The nominal version of this table was generated by the Tax Policy Center using Internal Revenue Service, Statistics of Income Division, "table 1, Individual Income Tax Returns: Selected Income and Tax Items for Tax Years 1999–2009." The 2009 estimates are preliminary. I have adjusted by the CPI to convert to 2009 dollars. The nominal table is available at: http://www.taxpolicycenter.org/taxfacts/displayafact.cfm?DocID=37&Topic2id=30&Topic3id=39.

to increase access to the labor market for people facing barriers to employment; in this sense, the legislation was complementary to the major welfare reform passed in the same year, the Personal Responsibility and Work Opportunity Reconciliation Act, which was intended to reduce dependence on cash welfare programs. The WOTC is a tax credit claimed by firms, with the amount dependent on the number of workers the firm has gotten "certified" as eligible (at the time of hire) and the number of hours worked by those employees. A similar credit, called the Welfare-to-Work Credit, was introduced in 1997 and recently rolled into the WOTC.[4]

Although the program is not explicitly directed to poor families, most eligible groups have low income. The two largest groups have historically been welfare recipients and young food stamp recipients, with other eligible groups including disability income recipients, residents of disadvantaged neighborhoods, low-income ex-felons, vocational rehabilitation participants, and others.[5] Similar to the EITC, the credit increases with hours worked up to a maximum credit; unlike the EITC, the WOTC is time-limited to one year per worker. Figure 7.3 shows the pattern of benefits for a firm with a certified worker earning $8 an hour. There is no cap on the total number of workers a firm can claim each year, though there is a per-worker dollar-value cap and the total credit cannot exceed 90 percent of a company's annual income tax liability (Scott 2011). The largest participating firms claim a significant share of all credits; a study of

Figure 7.3   Work Opportunity Tax Credit Benefit Structure

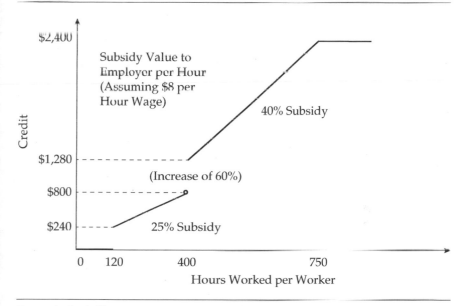

Source: Author's illustration using parameters from U.S. Department of Labor (n.d.).

California and Texas in 1997 and 1999 found that 3 percent of participating firms accounted for 83 percent of WOTC certifications. This study found that in 1997 the top 5 percent of firms in terms of size (gross receipts) claimed two-thirds of all WOTC dollars (U.S. General Accounting Office 2001a). Another study found that temporary help services (THS) firms make up a disproportionate share of participating firms; THS firms in Wisconsin made up 26 percent of WOTC applications in 2002 (Hamersma and Heinrich 2008). This brings up policy concerns about job quality for WOTC recipients, given the limited legal obligations of THS firms to the workers they place.[6]

An important difference between the EITC and WOTC is that the WOTC is given only when a minimal hours-of-work requirement is met: workers must remain with the employer for at least 120 hours, and to reach the maximum subsidy rate the duration needs to exceed 400 hours. The credit is capped for most targeted groups at $2,400 per worker. Though national data are not available, an analysis of the population of Wisconsin WOTC certifications over a period of two and a half years indicated that about one-third of certified workers did not reach the 120-hour threshold, and that another one-third were between 120 and 400 hours. Elsewhere (Hamersma 2011) I have suggested that there is evidence that the hours requirement is one explanation for low participation in the credit.

Another important difference between the EITC and WOTC is the refundability of the credits. The WOTC, like most tax credits but unlike the EITC, is not refundable. Firms whose credit eligibility exceeds their tax liability do have the option of carrying over the value of the subsidy to future years, which makes the lack of refundability a bit less relevant, but it does not overcome the exclusion of nonprofit firms from the program. Low-income workers in, for instance, charity-funded hospitals would not qualify the employer for a credit, even as their EITC eligibility is unaffected by the nature of their employment.

Compliance issues in the WOTC program are very different from those in the EITC, in large part because the WOTC system of administration is unique. The WOTC is jointly administered by the U.S. Department of Labor (working through state-level offices) and the IRS. Applications for the WOTC are submitted by firms at the time of hire to the state office, and certifications are granted (or not) by that state office based on documentation either submitted by the firm or gathered by the office from government databases. There is a 10 percent required audit rate of these certifications to assess the accuracy of eligibility determinations (though I am unaware of any reports related to these audits). The certification or denial, once sent to a firm, marks the completion of the role of the Department of Labor and grants permission to the firm to claim this worker on its IRS tax forms the following year. However, because the credit amount depends on work hours as well, it is the responsibility of the IRS to assess whether a claim made—even on behalf of a certified worker—is accurate. To my knowledge, there has been no public information about IRS auditing related to this concern. The IRS form submitted by firms, in fact, contains only the aggregate WOTC claim of the firm, making it impossible for researchers (even if we were armed with IRS WOTC data, which we are not) to understand much about compliance.

The lack of compliance concerns with the WOTC seems incongruent with the substantial attention paid to EITC compliance, but the reason may be related to the much smaller size of the WOTC program relative to the EITC. Table 7.2 provides the number of certifications for each year of the program along with estimates of the tax cost of these certifications. For most of its history, the WOTC has cost $300 million to $400 million per year; in very recent years, it has expanded dramatically to just over $1 billion. Much of the latest growth appears to be due to a recent expansion in

Table 7.2 Work Opportunity Tax Credit and Welfare-to-Work Certification Patterns, 1997 to 2008

Fiscal Year	Number of WOTC Certifications	Number of WtW Certifications	Number of Total Certifications	Total FY Cost (Million)	Distribution of Certifications Across Target Groups Within WOTC (Dollars)
1997	123,407	—	123,407	$110	60 percent AFDC/TANF, 21 percent food stamp youth, 19 percent other (Levine 1998)
1998	285,322	46,580	331,902	$185	54 percent AFDC/TANF, 20 percent food stamp youth, less than 8 percent each for other groups (U.S. GAO 2001a)
1999	335,707	104,998	440,705	$305	
2000	370,835	154,608	525,443	$440	40 percent AFDC/TANF, 27 percent food stamp youth, 13 percent high-risk youth, 6 percent supplemental security income, 5 percent vocational rehab, 6 percent ex-felons (Levine 2005)
2001	383,357	97,072	480,429	$390	
2002	377,310	46,652	423,962	$460	
2003	403,243	33,068	436,311	$490	
2004	244,445	15,601	260,046	$340	45 percent food stamp[a], 28 percent TANF, 8 percent high-risk youth, 7 percent ex-felons, 6 percent supplemental security income (Levine 2008)
2005	598,101	32,817	630,918	$230	
2006	325,178	13,859	339,037	$290	
2007	612,052	21,771	633,964	$450	

(Table continues on p. 196.)

Table 7.2 (Continued)

Fiscal Year	Number of WOTC Certifications	Number of WtW Certifications	Number of Total Certifications	Total FY Cost (Million)	Distribution of Certifications Across Target Groups Within WOTC (Dollars)
2008	668,214	24,207	692,421	$570	61 percent food stamp, 14 percent TANF, 11 percent designated community residents[b], 7 percent ex-felons, 4 percent supplemental security income, 3 percent vocational rehab, less than 3 percent each for other groups (Scott 2011)
2009	702,312	17,502	719,814	$870	74 percent food stamp, 10 percent TANF, 3 percent designated community residents, 6 percent ex-felons, less than 3 percent each for other groups (Scott 2013)
2010	849,044	65,447	914,491	$1,110	59 percent food stamp, 6 percent TANF, 8 percent designated community residents, 4 percent ex-felons, 18 percent disconnected youth[c], less than 3 percent each for other groups (Scott 2013)

2011	1,081,158	79,365	1,160,523	$1,110	63 percent food stamp, 5 percent TANF, 6 percent designated community residents, 3 percent ex-felons, 19 percent disconnected youth, less than 3 percent each for other groups (Scott 2013)
2012	820,907	71,407	892,314	$1,130	73 percent food stamp, 6 percent TANF, 6 percent designated community residents, 3 percent ex-felons, 5 percent disconnected youth, 4 percent veterans, less than 3 percent each for other groups (Scott 2013)

Source: Author's compilation certification totals for 1997–2007 are from Levine (2008); for 2008–2012, from Scott (2013). Dollar values are from the U.S. Office of Management and Budget (various years) using the most recent available estimate for each year from 1999 to 2014. The target-group distribution is reported only in some years, with the appropriate reports cited where relevant.

[a] The "food stamp youth" category was expanded to include those up to age thirty-nine hired after January 1, 2007 and thus is renamed "food stamp" for the remainder of the table.

[b] The "high-risk youth" category of eighteen- to twenty-four-year-old enterprise zone, empowerment community, or rural renewal community residents was renamed "designated community residents" and expanded through thirty-nine-year-olds as of May 25, 2007 (http://www.gpo. gov/fdsys/pkg/PLAW-110publ28/html/PLAW-110publ28.htm).

[c] The "disconnected youth" category was a new temporary target group created for hires during 2009 and 2010. This group included sixteen- to twenty-four-year-olds who were neither working nor in school in the previous six months and who lacked job skills.

eligibility that changed the "food stamp youth" target group (ages eighteen to twenty-four) to the "food stamp" group (ages eighteen to thirty-nine), combined with a recession that has resulted in unprecedented participation in food stamps. The program also expanded the age group for the geographically defined "high-risk youth" (and renamed them "designated community residents") and added a "disconnected youth" category for two years, resulting in a large new target group in those years.[7] Even in these recent years, however, the cost of the program is less than 2 percent that of the EITC and might be considered of second-order importance when it comes to auditing and compliance.

It could also be the case that less attention is dedicated to WOTC compliance than EITC compliance because of potential backlash from the large, influential firms that claim the vast majority of WOTC dollars. The individuals whose EITC claims are challenged are often low-income workers who are not equipped to appeal such challenges, while large firms have resources at their disposal and a significant amount of money at stake. Congressional testimony in favor of WOTC extension from corporations such as Marriott suggests that concern about the maintenance of WOTC benefits already has the attention of the large firms that participate.

The political history of the WOTC actually began long before the program itself. The first large programs for employer tax credits began in the late 1970s. The New Jobs Tax Credit (NJTC) of 1977 and 1978 provided tax credits to firms for expanding employment by a substantial amount without targeting particular workers. Upon expiration, the NJTC was replaced by the Targeted Jobs Tax Credit (TJTC), a program with target groups similar to those of the WOTC. Over the years, issues of stigma (due to the program's use of worker vouchers) and limited evidence of a net employment effect ultimately caused Congress to allow the credit to expire in 1994 (U.S. Department of Labor, Office of the Inspector General 1994). Perhaps surprisingly, two years later the WOTC, which differs only slightly from the TJTC, was introduced and passed around the same time as welfare reform.[8] Although the WOTC has not faced major political challenges since then, the dynamics of legislation have been more irregular than they have been for the more solidly supported EITC. The WOTC was initially legislated as a temporary program, and it is typically extended in one- to two-year increments, sometimes retroactively.[9] It has also developed a sort of "patchwork" structure as Congress authorizes new, narrowly defined target groups for specific time periods (for example, a Liberty Zone group related to the terrorist attacks of September 11, 2001, and later a Hurricane Katrina group). Several provisions related to veterans were introduced and expanded on November 21, 2011, in the Vow to Hire Heroes Act, and recently the American Taxpayer Relief Act of 2012 extended the WOTC through December 31, 2013.

BEHAVIORAL INCENTIVES AND EFFECTS OF THE EITC AND THE WOTC

Both the EITC and the WOTC generate complicated sets of incentives; some are by design and some are side effects of other program features. At the most basic level, each program provides incentives for employment among disadvantaged workers, one by providing individuals with subsidies for working and one by providing firms with subsidies for hiring. In theory, as noted earlier, both programs could generate the same outcomes, but their distinct structures make this unlikely.

The EITC provides unambiguous, positive work incentives only on the margin of the decision to work or not; for those already working, the incentives are less clear and even negative in some parts of the hours-of-work distribution. In particular, in the phaseout range of the credit a worker loses some EITC benefits for each additional hour worked, effectively reducing the wage for that hour of work. This phaseout, however, is a necessary component of a program that provides substantial help at the bottom; because the EITC is fundamentally an antipoverty program and not simply a work incentive program, some perverse incentives are unavoidable.

The WOTC provides firms with an incentive to hire and retain workers, but there are discontinuities in the benefit mechanism that make this incentive more or less salient at different places in the hours-of-work distribution illustrated in figure 7.3. The minimum-hours threshold of 120 hours means that there is no marginal gain per hour of retention if the worker does not stay for at least 120 hours. If the first threshold is met, the firm qualifies for a subsidy of 25 percent of wages and thus has an incentive to keep a worker as long as his or her productivity covers at least 75 percent of his or her wage.[10] This retention incentive becomes much stronger, however, as a worker approaches 400 hours of work, as the firm's total subsidy increases to 40 percent of the worker's wages if this threshold is met. To be clear, this is a change not in the marginal subsidy rate but in the total subsidy rate; with the large jump in the value of the subsidy at this point, even a worker with very low productivity may generate positive returns if the firm retains him or her until just past the 400-hour mark (for a numerical example, see Hamersma 2011). Finally, the subsidy cap of $2,400 and the one-year time limit (for most groups) curtail the subsidy's incentives rather abruptly, generating an incentive for the churning of qualified workers.

Empirical research on both the EITC and the WOTC has been mixed in terms of uncovering employment and earnings responses to the work incentives created by each program.[11] There is, however, a consistent finding that the perverse incentives in each program have not caused serious problems. In the case of the EITC, the research suggests that workers in the phaseout range of the EITC do not appear to respond to the subsidy by reducing earnings (Eissa and Hoynes 2006), and in general it appears that the kink points in the policy are fairly unnoticed by claimants, with the possible exception of the self-employed (Saez 2010). Even studies focusing on secondary earners do not find large reductions in hours worked (Eissa and Hoynes 2006; Heim 2007). Some new evidence from Raj Chetty and Emmanuel Saez (2013) does indicate, however, that workers are more likely to respond to the work incentives (including negative incentives) of the EITC when they are given specific information about their place in the EITC distribution by their tax preparer. Similarly, work on the WOTC has found neither evidence of firms churning workers whose subsidies have expired (U.S. General Accounting Office 2001a) nor any evidence that job separations bunch near the program's hours thresholds (Hamersma 2011).

A major difference appears in the evidence on positive effects for the two tax credits. The evidence on the EITC is encouraging: the incentive to join the workforce appears to have caused sizable increases in labor force participation among single mothers (for a summary of several studies, see Eissa and Hoynes 2006). For example, V. Joseph Hotz, Charles Mullin, and John Karl Scholz (2006) use the growing difference in EITC benefits to families with one child versus those with two children to identify the employment effects of the EITC; they find that the EITC increased relative employment of the latter group by as much as 3.4 percentage points. In contrast, the WOTC incentive for firms to hire additional disadvantaged workers does not appear to have taken hold, at least based on the limited research available. Elsewhere (Hamersma 2008) I have found very little evidence of an employment effect of the credit in Wisconsin. It appears that most hires under the program would have been hired anyway and merely created a financial benefit for firms that claimed the credit. Small employment effects of the WOTC are consistent with past experience with the TJTC (Katz 1998).

However, work on these programs has not exclusively examined employment. Economic theory predicts not just an employment effect but a wage effect of each program. In the case of the EITC, tax incidence theory tells us that we should expect to see a reduction in wages due to the new, lower reservation wage of those who are now willing to enter the labor market because of the wage supplement; in other words, some of the value of the subsidy passes through to the firm. Similarly, we would expect that some of the WOTC subsidy passes through to workers in the form of higher wages. There is indeed evidence that earnings at WOTC jobs are higher than we would otherwise predict (Hamersma and Heinrich 2008; Hamersma 2008), though these earnings benefits seems to be tied to the particular job rather than following a worker into the future. In this sense, the WOTC does not appear to provide a stepping-stone to better labor market outcomes. Work on the wage effects of the EITC suggests that a 10 percent increase in EITC generosity is associated with a 2 percent fall in wages for workers with only a high school diploma and a 5 percent fall in wages for high school dropouts—values consistent with most estimates of labor demand elasticity (Leigh 2010).

AT THE FOUNDATION: PROGRAM PARTICIPATION

For the EITC and the WOTC to have a meaningful impact on the labor market for disadvantaged workers—in either their present form or a modified form—there must be substantial participation by eligible workers (EITC) and firms (WOTC). Measuring participation in each of these programs is a nontrivial task, but even given some uncertainty about participation, it is clear that the patterns of participation in the two programs are very different. In this section, I detail the measurement issues involved, provide an overview of the historical patterns in participation, and look at the proposed explanations for these patterns in both programs.

The Earned Income Tax Credit

The total number of EITC claims is publicly available; the numbers shown in table 7.1 are reported by the Tax Policy Center based on IRS Statistics of Income data. However, there are two major difficulties in measuring participation in the EITC. The first is the challenge of identifying the full set of eligible tax units (the denominator of the participation rate). A typical approach to estimating the eligible population for a program is the use of national survey data, and for the EITC the best option seems to be the March Current Population Survey (specifically, the Annual Social and Economic Supplement [ASEC]).[12] There are a number of difficulties in identifying the EITC-eligible population in a survey that is not explicitly designed for that purpose. First, the household and family data in the CPS must be used to formulate tax units, a nontrivial process. Second, the rules for qualifying children for the EITC involve a residency requirement, but (within that) some flexibility in which taxpayers can claim the credit (for instance, in multigenerational households). This makes it impossible to definitively identify the number of eligible children in each tax unit.

Table 7.3   Earned Income Tax Credit Participation Rate
             Estimates, 1990, 1999, and 2005

Tax Year	Estimated EITC Participation Rate
1990	80 to 86 percent
1999	75 percent overall;
	86 percent with children
2005	75 percent overall;
	81 percent with children

Sources: Author's compilation. For 1990, Scholz (1994); for 1999, General Accounting Office (2001b); for 2005, Plueger (2009).

Third, citizenship status is not always available or reliable. Finally, the income variables in the survey must be used to estimate taxable income; unfortunately, there is a substantial (and increasing) amount of income imputation in the CPS that makes the income data less reliable (Hirsch and Schumacher 2004).[13]

The second challenge of measuring EITC participation is related to proper interpretation of the number of EITC claims. While one would be tempted to simply divide the number of EITC claims by the number of eligible tax units to estimate a participation rate, there is concern that some of the EITC claims are not in fact made by eligible tax units. If we are interested in the participation rate of eligible workers, the participants should in fact be eligible. As noted earlier, there is a good deal of controversy about compliance in the EITC program, with recent estimates suggesting that 23 to 28 percent of fiscal year 2009 claims were made in error, at a cost of $11 billion to $13 billion (U.S. Treasury Inspector General for Tax Administration 2011). The IRS is conducting data collection under its National Research Program that will provide new estimated compliance rates starting in 2012, to be updated annually from that point.[14]

A recent study by Dean Plueger (2009) provides participation rate estimates for the EITC using matched IRS and CPS data and handling as many of the aforementioned issues as possible. Table 7.3 provides his most recent estimates, as well as those from prior years from other researchers. Although no particular set of estimates would claim to be definitive, the pattern over time is roughly 80 to 85 percent participation among taxpayers with children (with lower aggregate participation in recent years being driven by low participation among nonparents).[15]

The explanations for incomplete participation in the EITC are fairly sensible, though not easily tested. Lower participation among childless eligibles could reflect their lower benefit levels; it is much more costly for a family with children to fail to claim the credit. Incomplete participation among those with children is harder to explain, but is likely to be due at least in part to nonfiling. Some families who are not required to file an income tax return because of their income could benefit from the EITC but may not be aware of the refundability of the credit (U.S. General Accounting Office 2001b).

The Work Opportunity Tax Credit

Measuring participation in the Work Opportunity Tax Credit has a distinct set of challenges relative to the EITC. Absent investigations of compliance (due in part to a lack of relevant data), estimates of participation rates must ignore the complication of ineligible recipients. However, the identification of eligible workers in survey data is incomplete and complex. It is incomplete in that neither of the data sets that have been used for this purpose—the March CPS and the (preferred) Survey of Income and Program Participation (SIPP)—contain the necessary information to identify more than a few target groups.[16] For instance, because both ex-felon status and detailed geographic location are missing, it is impossible to consider the size of the ex-offender and designated-community-resident target groups. Historically, the two groups obtaining the largest number of certifications have been the welfare and food stamp (or SNAP) groups, and fortunately, because program participation is available in these data sets, it is possible to assess participation rates among these two groups.

There are, however, some limitations in identifying eligible workers even in these groups. First, a fair amount of missing data on welfare and food stamp participation results in a range of participation rate estimates rather than point estimates (obtained by imputing either "receipt" or "nonreceipt" to all missing values to get the widest range of possibilities). Second, there is the potential for error in linking job-start dates to imputed WOTC eligibility in that same month; if there is any issue with timing, we may inaccurately assign eligibility (or ineligibility) of that job for the WOTC. Third, we cannot observe the nonprofit status of firms, so some workers who would appear to be eligible could not actually be claimed by their firms.

It is important to note that there are no survey data in which information on participation in the WOTC is collected. Therefore, existing estimates simply use the total number of certifications reported by the Department of Labor for the numerator and an estimate of the number of eligible workers for the denominator. The rates reported in table 7.4 use the SIPP (1996, 2001, and 2004 panels) to identify participation rates in selected years. The limited number of years for which estimates are

Table 7.4   Work Opportunity Tax Credit Participation Rate Estimates, 1997, 1999, 2003, and 2007

Year	Estimated WOTC Participation Rate
1997	Welfare: 1 to 7 percent
	Food stamp youth: 0.3 to 6 percent
1999	Welfare: 6 to 32 percent
	Food stamp youth: 0.7 to 17 percent
2003	Welfare: 6 to 49 percent
	Food stamp youth: 1.0 to 29 percent
2007	Welfare: 6 to 47 percent
	Food stamp: 0.8 to 31 percent

Source: Author's compilation. For 1997 and 1999, Hamersma (2003); for 2003 and 2007, new estimates by author.
Notes: The lower bounds listed here for the 1997 and 1999 welfare groups are slightly lower than those in the published paper owing to an adjustment for a minor programming error affecting only those two numbers. All estimates use SIPP data to estimate denominators and the data in table 7.2 for numerators. Note that as of January 1, 2007, the food stamp group began to include ages eighteen to thirty-nine instead of the previous eighteen to twenty-four; estimates for fiscal year 2007 reflect that change.

available reflects the combination of limited information on target group–specific certifications (see table 7.2) and the timing of SIPP surveys (as we need to "look back" up to eighteen months to assess welfare-group eligibility, so cannot use early months of the data in any panel). The 1997 and 1999 rates were previously published, while the 2003 and 2007 rates are reported here for the first time, using the same methodology.

Although the rate of WOTC participation clearly grew between the late 1990s and early 2000s, perhaps because of growing awareness of the program, there seems to have been a fair amount of stabilization in participation between 2003 and 2007. In both years, the upper bound on participation remained below 50 percent for the welfare target group and around 30 percent for the food stamp group. Moreover, the many missing observations related to eligibility determination cause the range from the lower bound to the upper bound to be wide; the more of these unknown-status people are eligible, the closer the true participation rate is to the lower bound. However, since it is more likely that most of the unknown-status observations are ineligible (assuming there is not extreme selection into having missing data), true participation rates are probably closer to the upper bound than the lower bound. Either way, participation is simply not high.

Although the number of certifications has risen substantially since 2007 (see table 7.2), particularly among the newly expanded food stamp group, unfortunately there is no data available with which to assess the more recent participation rates.[17] Moreover, the large increase in certifications among the food stamp group has happened alongside major increases in food stamp participation, indicating that we cannot assume that participation among eligibles has increased; the increased certifications could just reflect similar participation rates among the new, larger eligible population.

There has been substantial discussion in the WOTC literature (and the preceding literature on targeted tax credits) on the reasons for low participation rates. One possible culprit is the complexity of administration, as the program requires at least some small amount of administration from both the employer (which needs to send forms to the state employment agency) and the worker (who usually needs to provide basic documentation). This is in contrast to the EITC, in which only the individual and his or her tax preparer are likely to be aware of the claim.[18] The WOTC requires individuals to make known their eligibility, either voluntarily or with the prompting of a worksheet provided with the job application or new-hire packet. This requirement for the worker to interact with the firm (or at least the firm's tax consultant) regarding eligibility also raises the possibility of stigma that would make a worker unwilling to indicate eligibility, effectively forcing the firm into nonparticipation for that worker. Results reported in Burtless (1985) on the TJTC program suggested that stigma was a major issue when workers were given "eligibility vouchers" to be brought to their firm; this system, while still available under the WOTC, is seldom used now.

Basic firm administrative costs, while they have been reduced since the previous (TJTC) tax credit program, are also still potentially an issue, because of their timing. These costs are paid up-front by firms claiming the WOTC, as their application for a new worker must be submitted within twenty-eight days of hire, even though the firm does not yet know if the worker will meet minimum hours thresholds for subsidy qualification.

There are also some reasons for low WOTC participation that parallel those for the EITC. For instance, there is always the concern that the relevant parties do not have necessary information. In the case of the WOTC, firms may not be aware of the program, and in the case of the EITC, individuals who are not tax filers may be unaware of their potential benefits. There is also the very logical explanation that nonparticipants may be those with the least to gain from the program (implying that the "money left on the table" is not as much as the participation rate levels might suggest). Formal work on both the EITC and the WOTC supports this view. Plueger (2009) finds that EITC participation rates monotonically increase with the level of benefits available; participation is less than 50 percent for those qualifying for less than $200 in benefits, while it is over 85 percent for those qualifying for $2,000 or more.[19] Similarly, I have used Wisconsin administrative data to estimate WOTC participation rates by firms hiring disadvantaged workers with varying rates of potential tax credits (Hamersma 2011). For firms qualifying for less than $30,000 in credits, participation rates tend to hover around 15 percent; for those qualifying for $100,000 or more, the rate rises to nearly 60 percent.[20]

ASSESSING THE PROSPECTS FOR THE FUTURE

It is clear that while both the EITC and WOTC programs are designed to improve employment outcomes, they operate with substantially different scope and produce distinct effects in the labor market. Both eligibility for and participation in the EITC are higher than is the case with the WOTC, making the relative program costs substantial (more than $50 billion versus $1 billion). However, the EITC has produced employment improvements that have not been produced by the WOTC (which seems to primarily benefit firms). Many researchers have argued on these grounds for the superiority of the EITC for subsidizing employment.

Recent work by Eissa and Hoynes (2011) and Meyer (2010) uses policy simulations to examine different ways in which the EITC might be modified to meet various distributional, budget, and welfare goals. Among these modifications are the extension of a more generous credit to childless individuals, stronger targeting of low-income workers (by steepening the phaseout range in exchange for a higher maximum credit), and more universal eligibility (by flattening and extending the phaseout range in exchange for a lower maximum credit).

However, there is some concern that in times of recession modifications of the EITC may not be adequate for meeting employment goals. For instance, an extension of the EITC to childless individuals—many of whom are men—would not be likely to generate a large labor supply response because most men already work if they can find employment (Meyer 2010). The employment effects of the EITC are predicated on the notion that financial incentives encourage people to join the labor force, and there is clear evidence that this happened for single mothers in the boom of the late 1990s, but to the extent that the labor market is slack it is less clear that this incentive translates into additional jobs. This has led even strong supporters of the EITC to suggest an added role for employer-side subsidies in times of high unemployment and low job growth (see, for instance, Neumark 2011).

In light of concerns about labor demand, several researchers are revisiting options related to employer tax credits like the WOTC or other subsidized-job programs. A major concern with the WOTC is the low participation rate and the narrow targeting of eligible individuals. During a recession, one could argue that many unemployed workers who are not "disadvantaged" by traditional definitions may need assistance. This line of reasoning has brought David Neumark (2011) and John Bishop and Timothy Bartik (2009) to argue for the introduction of a less-targeted employer tax credit program. Such a program would be similar to the New Jobs Tax Credit of the late 1970s, providing tax credits to firms for marginal growth in the workforce, regardless of who is hired. One might be concerned that many of these workers would have been hired anyway, but net job creation at reasonably low per-job cost might be possible.

Bishop and Bartik (2009) argue that a temporary, well-designed "Job Creation Tax Credit" that refunds 10 to 15 percent of new wage costs could create 5 million jobs over two years.[21] Although this credit would be of substantial gross cost (estimated at nearly $150 billion over two years), their analysis of the spillover effects in terms of GDP and ultimately net federal revenue produces an estimated net cost of about $27 billion, or about $5,500 per job created.[22] Neumark (2011) is much more cautious about the potential for such low costs of job creation and generally prefers the EITC as a long-term strategy, but still argues that a temporary focus on this approach is merited in the midst of recession. One reason for this focus, he argues, is the potential benefits for men, who have been hit hard with unemployment but are less likely to benefit from the EITC due to its concentration on poor and low-income families. Neumark's second reason is his concern that the current economy is not in equilibrium but instead has suffered from a negative shift in labor demand in the presence of wage rigidities. This, he argues, implies that increasing labor supply through modification of the EITC would not influence total employment, as there are already excess workers available to work (but no jobs for them). From this view, labor demand must be directly influenced through a firm-side subsidy.

Thus far, there has been (to my knowledge) only a small move in the direction of a federal job creation tax credit, through the Hiring Incentives to Restore Employment (HIRE) Act of 2010. This legislation provided a 6.2 percent payroll tax incentive for firms (effectively exempting them from their share of Social Security payroll taxes) for newly hired, recently unemployed workers hired during 2010. It also provided a general tax credit of up to $1,000 to firms for workers retained for at least a year. The U.S. Treasury Department (2010) estimated that over 10 million workers were eligible to be claimed for the payroll tax exemption during the period February to October 2010, and the projected cost of the program was $13 billion. This program was only enacted for 2010, so it has since expired, though the retention credits continue to be claimed based on hires in 2010. There has not yet been a formal evaluation of this program's effectiveness.

Meanwhile, there has been substantial movement among states to implement state-level job creation tax credits or other programs. Robert Chirinko and Daniel Wilson (2010) note that by August 2009 twenty-four states had job creation tax credits in place. Their preliminary findings indicate very little net job creation from the credits. An alternative approach that states have used to generate jobs from the employer side utilizes government funds to directly and fully subsidize jobs. Elizabeth Lower-Basch (2011) describes subsidized job creation using funds made available through the 2009 American Recovery and Reinvestment Act's $5 billion TANF Emergency Fund. She reports that using this fund, thirty-nine states and the District of Columbia placed more than 260,000 individuals into jobs, mostly in the private sector. Although there is not yet a formal program evaluation of the employment effects of the program, Lower-Basch argues that the stronger incentives created by a larger subsidy (up to 100 percent of wages), the more intentional nature of the job matches, and the flexibility of states to design customized programs provide some hope of effectiveness that the WOTC has been shown to lack.

CONCLUSION

The important differences between worker-side and employer-side tax credits have driven remarkably different participation patterns and employment outcomes, despite many common goals and theoretical predictions. Based on the research thus far, the employer-side WOTC might be summarized as providing relatively few tax credits, at relatively low cost, with relatively minimal employment effects (with the important caveat that certifications have dramatically increased in the last few years but no new evaluations are yet available). The majority of credits are obtained by firms in the top 5 percent by size, with a disproportionate share going to temporary help agencies. The consequences to disadvantaged workers of taking jobs in temporary agencies is widely debated, making this prominent role of the WOTC in that sector potentially controversial as well. There may also be compliance issues with the WOTC, especially given the incentive structure to keep workers just past certain hours-of-work thresholds, but little attention has been paid to the potential for fraud.

Conversely, the EITC provides many tax credits, at relatively high cost, with relatively large employment effects. Researchers generally agree that there are positive effects of the program. However, concerns about the high and increasing costs of the program, combined with compliance issues, could bring new levels of scrutiny to the program despite its benefits. This is particularly true in the current fiscal environment. More-over, the EITC's power to create jobs is weakest when the economy is weak, and thus it would appear that new policy for job creation during downturns may be warranted. Although most researchers see the WOTC as an unattractive model for such an approach, there is ongoing discussion as to whether broad-based temporary job creation tax credits might have a role in alleviating recession-driven unemployment. These credits would not be targeted only at specific groups of workers, but would be widely available to firms willing to hire in difficult economic times. Alongside these programs, there may also be a role for direct subsidized-job pro-grams. Timely evaluation of existing state-level tax credit and subsidized-job programs would be helpful for designing successful federal programs along these lines.

NOTES

1. Technically, the relevant income is that of the tax-filing unit.
2. TANF data are from U.S. Department of Health and Human Services (2009), which shows the amount spent on assistance itself, apart from administration. SNAP data are from Oliveira (2010).
3. Interested readers can obtain up-to-date policy information on the website of the Center for Budget and Policy Priorities (www.cbpp.org).
4. The Welfare-to-Work Credit was specifically for long-term welfare recipients and has different hours thresholds and subsidy rates (even upon being rolled into the WOTC as of January 1, 2007). Details are available from the U.S. Department of Labor at: http://www.doleta.gov/business/incentives/opptax/ (accessed September 2013).
5. The fraction of the total certifications represented by each group is discussed in detail later in the chapter. The full list with detailed definitions of current eligible groups can be found at U.S. Department of Labor, Employment and Training Administration, "Work Opportunity Tax Credit," available at: http://www.doleta.gov/business/incentives/opptax/ (accessed September 2013).
6. For detailed discussion of these concerns, see Hamersma and Heinrich (2008) and Hamersma, Heinrich, and Mueser (forthcoming).
7. The designated community residents must reside in an Empowerment Zone, Enterprise Community, or Rural Renewal Community.
8. One key improvement relative to the TJTC was a reduction in the need for workers to initiate the credit; although vouchers are still available, they are seldom used. Another important change was a reduction in the paperwork burden for firms.
9. A detailed description of the legislative history of the program is in Scott (2013). Note that even with retroactive legislation, there are large dips in certifications

in years when the WOTC was (apparently) expired, such as in fiscal year 2004, when there was a nine-month hiatus, and in the fiscal year 2006 period, when there was a thirteen-month hiatus.

10. Making this assessment may be straightforward in settings with easily observable measureable productivity (such as sales or direct production of physical goods), but is more difficult in settings where this is not the case (such as service professions).

11. A variety of other outcomes—not directly related to employment levels or earnings—have also been examined by researchers of the EITC and the WOTC. For example, Bruce Meyer (2010) and Nada Eissa and Hilary Hoynes (2011) lay out the distributional effects of the EITC and address efficiency concerns. Other work has examined interactions of the EITC with the marriage penalties and bonuses in the tax code (Holtzblatt and Rebelein 2001). Work on the WOTC has examined its effects on job tenure (Hamersma 2008) and its distinct outcomes in the market for THS employment (Hamersma and Heinrich 2008). In the interest of brevity, I review only the findings on employment and earnings.

12. Dean Plueger (2009) provides a careful discussion of the most recent methodologies developed for estimating EITC participation using a combination of the March CPS and IRS data.

13. A typical March CPS has imputed earnings for about 20 percent of respondents.

14. The fiscal year 2009 estimates rely heavily on data from 2001 so are not fully reflective of current conditions. The new estimates will use fiscal year 2006 data, the latest iteration of the National Research Program data (U.S. Treasury Inspector General for Tax Administration 2011).

15. Nonparents were not eligible for the EITC until 1994, and even though they are now eligible, nonparents are still qualified for only a small maximum credit of $475; see Urban Institute and Brookings Institution, Tax Policy Center, "Tax Facts: Earned Income Tax Credit Parameters, 1975–2013," available at: http://www.taxpolicycenter.org/taxfacts/displayafact.cfm?Docid=36 (accessed September 2013).

16. The SIPP is preferred because its monthly panel structure allows more accurate assessment of past program participation, a necessary element for assessing WOTC eligibility. Details on CPS results are provided in a footnote in Hamersma (2003).

17. After the conclusion of the 2004 SIPP, a new panel began with interviews in September 2008. Because we require eighteen months of past information as well as a full fiscal year of data, the next possible year for which estimates could have been developed was fiscal year 2011. At the time this data work was done, sufficient SIPP data had not yet been released.

18. When an individual receives the EITC throughout the year as an addition to his or her paycheck, the employer would also be aware of the claim. The

possibility of the employer's knowledge leading to stigma may be one reason that very few recipients ever chose this option (which was eliminated as of tax year 2011).

19. These numbers were gleaned from combining categories reported in Plueger (2009), table 11.

20. All firms in the sample had at least ten eligible workers during the period July 1999 to December 2001. Firms that applied for the WOTC at some point, but did so for fewer than 20 percent of their eligible workers, after that point are excluded. See table 2 of Hamersma (2011) for further details.

21. Bishop and Bartik's (2009) specific estimates simulate a 15 percent subsidy in 2010 and a 10 percent subsidy in 2011.

22. Bishop and Bartik (2009) assume that about 18 percent of jobs receiving the credit would be newly created, while the other 82 percent would be subsidized but would have existed even in the absence of a subsidy. Details about their assumptions are provided in their paper.

REFERENCES

Bishop, John H., and Timothy J. Bartik. 2009. "The Job Creation Tax Credit: Dismal Projections for Employment Call for a Quick, Efficient, and Effective Response." Briefing Paper 248. Washington, D.C.: Economic Policy Institute.

Burtless, Gary. 1985. "Are Targeted Wage Subsidies Harmful? Evidence from a Wage Voucher Experiment." *Industrial and Labor Relations Review* 39(1): 105–14.

Chetty, Raj, and Emmanuel Saez. 2013. "Teaching the Tax Code: Earnings Responses to an Experiment with EITC Recipients." *American Economic Journal: Applied Economics* 5(1): 1–31.

Chirinko, Robert S., and Daniel J. Wilson. 2010. "Job Creation Tax Credits and Job Growth: Whether, When, and Where?" Working Paper 2010-25. San Francisco: Federal Reserve Bank of San Francisco.

Dickert-Conlin, Stacy, and Douglas Holtz-Eakin. 2000. "Employee-Based Versus Employer-Based Subsidies to Low-Wage Workers: A Public Finance Perspective." In *Finding Jobs: Work and Welfare Reform*, ed. David Card and Rebecca Blank. New York: Russell Sage Foundation.

Eissa, Nada, and Hilary Hoynes. 2006. "Behavioral Responses to Taxes: Lessons from the EITC and Labor Supply." Working Paper 11729. Cambridge, Mass.: National Bureau of Economic Research (November).

———. 2011. "Redistribution and Tax Expenditures: The Earned Income Tax Credit." *National Tax Journal* 64(2, pt. 2): 689–730.

Hamel, Jennifer S. 2009. "Is Anybody Home? The Relaxation of the Residency Requirement for Claiming a Qualifying Child Under the Earned Income Tax Credit After *Rowe v. Commissioner*." *Maine Law Review* 61(1): 219–39.

Hamersma, Sarah. 2003. "The Work Opportunity and Welfare-to-Work Tax Credits: Participation Rates Among Eligible Workers." *National Tax Journal* 56(4): 725–38.

———. 2008. "The Effects of an Employer Subsidy on Employment Outcomes: A Study of the Work Opportunity and Welfare-to-Work Tax Credits." *Journal of Policy Analysis and Management* 27(3): 498–520.

———. 2011. "Why Don't Eligible Firms Claim Hiring Subsidies? The Role of Job Duration." *Economic Inquiry* 49(3): 916–34.

Hamersma, Sarah, and Carolyn Heinrich. 2008. "Temporary Help Service Firms' Use of Employer Tax Credits: Implications for Disadvantaged Workers' Labor Market Outcomes." *Southern Economic Journal* 74(4): 1123–48.

Hamersma, Sarah, Carolyn J. Heinrich, and Peter Mueser. Forthcoming. "Temporary Help Work: Earnings, Wages, and Multiple Job Holding" *Industrial Relations*, forthcoming.

Heim, Bradley T. 2007. "The Incredible Shrinking Elasticities Married Female Labor Supply, 1978–2002." *Journal of Human Resources* 42(4): 881–918.

Hirsch, Barry T., and Edward J. Schumacher. 2004. "Match Bias in Wage Gap Estimates Due to Earnings Imputation." *Journal of Labor Economics* 22(3): 689–722.

Holtzblatt, Janet, and Robert Rebelein. 2001. "Measuring the Effect of the Earned Income Tax Credit on Marriage Penalties and Bonuses." In *Making Work Pay: The Earned Income Tax Credit and Its Impact on America's Families*, ed. Bruce D. Meyer and Douglas Holtz-Eakin. New York: Russell Sage Foundation.

Hotz, V. Joseph, Charles H. Mullin, and John Karl Scholz. 2006. "Examining the Effect of the Earned Income Tax Credit on the Labor Market Participation of Families on Welfare." Working paper 11968. Cambridge, Mass.: National Bureau of Economic Research (January).

Hotz, V. Joseph, and John Karl Scholz. 2003. "The Earned Income Tax Credit." In *Means-Tested Transfer Programs in the United States*, ed. Robert Moffitt. Chicago: University of Chicago Press.

Katz, Lawrence F. 1998. "Wage Subsidies for the Disadvantaged." In *Generating Jobs: How to Increase Demand for Less-Skilled Workers*, ed. Richard B. Freeman and Peter Gottschalk. New York: Russell Sage Foundation.

Leigh, Andrew. 2010. "Who Benefits from the Earned Income Tax Credit? Incidence among Recipients, Coworkers, and Firms." *The B.E. Journal of Economic Analysis and Policy* 10(1). Available at: http://www.bepress.com/bejeap/vol10/iss1/art45 (accessed September 2013).

Levine, Linda. 1998. "The Work Opportunity Tax Credit: A Fact Sheet." Report for Congress 96-356E. Washington: Congressional Research Service (April 2).

———. 2005. "The Work Opportunity Tax Credit (WOTC) and the Welfare-to-Work (WtW) Tax Credit." *Federal Publications* 189 (April). Available at: http://digitalcommons.ilr.cornell.edu/key_workplace/189 (accessed September 2013).

———. 2008. "The Work Opportunity Tax Credit." Report RL30089. Washington: Congressional Research Service.

Lower-Basch, Elizabeth. 2011. "Rethinking Work Opportunity: From Tax Credits to Subsidized Job Placements." CLASP: Big Ideas for Job Creation (November). Available at: http://www.clasp.org/admin/site/publications/files/Big-Ideas-for-Job-Creation-Rethinking-Work-Opportunity.pdf (accessed September 2013).

Meyer, Bruce D. 2010. "The Effects of the Earned Income Tax Credit and Recent Reforms." In *Tax Policy and the Economy*, vol. 24, edited by Jeffrey R. Brown. Chicago: University of Chicago Press, for the National Bureau of Economic Research.

Neumark, David. 2011. "How Can California Spur Job Creation?" San Francisco: Public Policy Institute of California.

Oliveira, Victor. 2010. "The Food Assistance Landscape: FY2009 Annual Report." Economic Information Bulletin EIB-6-7. Washington: U.S. Department of Agriculture, Economic Research Service (March). Available at: http://www.ers.usda.gov/Publications/EIB6-7/EIB6-7.pdf (accessed September 2013).

Olson, Nina E. (national taxpayer advocate). 2011. Statement before House Committee on Ways and Means, Subcommittee on Oversight, hearing on improper payments in the administration of refundable tax credits. May 25.

Plueger, Dean. 2009. "Earned Income Tax Credit Participation Rate for Tax Year 2005." IRS Research Bulletin: 151–15. Available at: http://www.irs.gov/pub/irs-soi/09resconeitcpart.pdf (accessed September 2013).

Saez, Emmanuel. 2010. "Do Taxpayers Bunch at Kink Points?" *American Economic Journal: Economic Policy* 2(3): 180–212.

Scholz, John Karl. 1994. "The Earned Income Tax Credit: Participation, Compliance, and Antipoverty Effectiveness." *National Tax Journal* 47(1): 63–87.

Scott, Christine. 2011. "The Work Opportunity Tax Credit (WOTC)." Report RL30089. Washington: Congressional Research Service.

———. 2013. "The Work Opportunity Tax Credit (WOTC)." Report RL-30089. Washington: Congressional Research Service.

Tax Policy Center. 2012. "Historical EITC Recipients." Available at: http://www.taxpolicycenter.org/taxfacts/displayafact.cfm?Docid=37&TopicID=30&TopicID=39 (accessed September 2013).

———. 2013. "Earned Income Tax Credit Parameters, 1975–2013." Available at: http://www.taxpolicycenter.org/taxfacts/displayafact.cfm?Docid=36 (accessed September 2013).

U.S. Department of Health and Human Services. Administration for Children and Families. 2009. Available at: http://archive.acf.hhs.gov/programs/ofs/data/2009/table_al_2009.html (accessed September 2013).

U.S. Department of Labor. Office of the Inspector General. 1994. "Targeted Jobs Tax Credit: Employment Inducement or Employer Windfall?" Washington: U.S. Department of Labor.

U.S. Department of Labor. n.d. "Work Opportunity Tax Credit." Available at: http://www.doleta.gov/business/incentives/opptax/ (accessed September 2013).

U.S. General Accounting Office. 2001a. "Work Opportunity Tax Credit: Employers Do Not Appear to Dismiss Employees to Increase Tax Credits." Report to the Chairman, House Committee on Ways and Means, Subcommittee on Oversight. GAO-01-329. Washington: GAO (March). Available at: http://www.gao.gov/new.items/d01329.pdf (accessed September 2013).

———. 2001b. "Earned Income Tax Credit Participation." GAO-02-290R. Washington: GAO (December 14). Available at: http://www.gao.gov/new.items/d02290r.pdf (accessed September 2013).

U.S. Office of Management and Budget. Various years (1999–2014). Budget of the United States. Washington: Executive Office of the President.

U.S. Treasury Department. 2010. "Updated Estimates of Newly Hired Employees Eligible for the HIRE Act Tax Exemption." December 8. Available at: http://www.treasury.gov/resource-center/economic-policy/Documents/12.8.10%20HIRE%20Act%20Report%20FINAL.pdf (accessed September 2013).

U.S. Treasury Inspector General for Tax Administration. 2011. "Reduction Targets and Strategies Have Not Been Established to Reduce the Billions of Dollars in Improper Earned Income Tax Credit Payments Each Year." February 7. Available at: http://www.treasury.gov/tigta/auditreports/2011reports/201140023fr.pdf (accessed September 2013).

Chapter 8 | Living Wages, Minimum Wages, and Low-Wage Workers

Stephanie Luce

MUCH HAS ALREADY been written about the modern U.S. "living wage" movement, which began in 1994 in Baltimore.[1] The movement was hailed as one of the most exciting, and most successful, efforts of labor and community organizations of the past several decades. Almost twenty years later, with over 125 ordinances or policies in place around the country, living wage activists are still fighting for higher wages in a handful of cities, on college campuses, and in other countries. The living wage concept is perhaps as popular as ever. A recent poll found that 74 percent of New York City voters support the idea, and a 2007 poll in California found that the same proportion supported a living wage proposal in Los Angeles.[2]

But as successful as the movement has been, it is not clear how much living wage ordinances help low-wage workers. The ordinances cover only a small proportion of workers, and although wage levels are a significant improvement over minimum wage, they are not necessarily high enough to raise workers out of poverty—and in fact, on average, the raises are less than the median wage increase that low-wage workers experience from unionization (37 percent) (Schmitt et al. 2007). Therefore, some might ask whether it is worth pursuing living wage campaigns at all.

Living wage organizers never promised that the ordinances would be sufficient for solving poverty or other issues related to the working poor; indeed, many of those organizers have also been heavily involved in other policy campaigns—such as minimum wage or the Earned Income Tax Credit (EITC) as well as efforts to organize workers into community organizations and unions. Many of them saw the living wage as a tool that could help build coalitions and develop the political power needed to pursue broader policy goals, expand outreach, influence public debate

215

on wages and economic development, and perhaps open space for new union organizing or strengthening bargaining power for existing unions. In some respects, the whole existence of the living wage movement can be seen as an indication of failure on the part of the labor movement and social movements to raise wages more broadly through national legislation and unionization. Therefore, living wage ordinances cannot be judged solely as policy tools for directly improving conditions for low-wage workers. A thorough evaluation must assess the indirect outcomes on building political power and increasing union density. Still, living wage proponents should examine ways to improve the coverage and impact of the ordinances.

This chapter reviews the research on living wage laws, focusing on their impact on low-wage workers. I first situate the living wage movement in the context of minimum wage laws, reviewing the relation between the two policies and summarizing recent academic research on the latter. I then discuss the challenges to establishing a more effective living wage and provide some ideas on how to expand the coverage of the ordinances.

LIVING WAGES AND MINIMUM WAGES

The most common form of living wage ordinance covers only workers employed by city service contractors; as such, the coverage is limited, though not because living wage activists prefer these more narrow ordinances to the broader minimum wage. In fact, many living wage activists have also been involved in efforts to raise state and federal minimum wages. The living wage movement grew in large part because activists felt that they lacked the power to pass the broader legislation. For this reason, living wage ordinances and minimum wage legislation should be seen as complements rather than as competing policies. Many activists saw the living wage movement as a way to build the political power and momentum needed to raise wages in a variety of ways, including the minimum wage.

Both the debate and the research on the living wage and the minimum wage are fairly similar. In both cases, opponents claim that establishing or raising wage standards will lead to unintended consequences—primarily job loss. Economists have debated the impact of minimum wage laws for decades. In the 1970s and 1980s, the dominant view was that an increase in the minimum wage would lead to job loss. But this work was based on neoclassical models and assumptions that have been proven to be inadequate for studying the low-wage labor market in particular. For example, the models assumed that workers can be hired and fired, or can quit and change jobs, without cost, and that both employers and workers have perfect information about the labor market. The models also assumed a competitive labor market, where wages are determined through negotiations between employer and employee. It assumed that employees have access to other jobs and that workers can withhold their labor if they are not paid an adequate wage (Fox 2006).

Economists began to study the impact of minimum wage increases through empirical studies rather than relying on standard models. For example, David Card conducted a series of studies examining the impact of state minimum wage increases, and these studies resulted in a number of pathbreaking publications, including his well-known work coauthored with Alan Krueger (2000). Card and Krueger surveyed fast-food restaurants near the state line of New Jersey and Pennsylvania, both before and after a 1992 minimum wage increase that happened in New Jersey alone. Their results were surprising: employment did not decline in New Jersey despite the higher wage—if anything, there was a slight increase in employment. Additional studies in other states and countries had similar results, and some economists tried to explain why the predicted job losses did not come to pass. First, as mentioned, the basic assumptions of the neoclassical model did not hold in most labor markets. Second, they suggested, the employers might have experienced some cost savings through "efficiency wage gains": with higher wages, they might have experienced higher productivity and lower turnover and absenteeism. Third, there might have been a multiplier effect: low-wage workers who received a wage increase were likely to spend most or all of that new income, putting money back into the economy. Finally, employers might have been covering the costs of the wage increase in other ways, such as through reduced CEO or managerial salaries or through a small amount of consumer pass-through. For example, Card and Krueger found in their study that the New Jersey fast-food restaurants increased the average cost of a hamburger by one cent.

In addition to empirical studies, economists advanced the field of minimum wage research by moving from the practice of time-series studies to a differences-in-differences methodology. This allowed researchers to replicate a form of experimental treatment and control groups: studying the changes in the treatment group (for example, those workers who received wage increases in New Jersey) with the changes in the control group (workers in Pennsylvania, where the minimum wage was not increased). This technique improved upon the time-series analysis, which attempted to control for a wide range of factors that might have an impact on employment.

The spate of research led to a large shift in the prevailing thinking in the field. By the 2000s, a number of prominent economists had changed their minds, acknowledging that serious research had raised doubts about the earlier held views. By 2006, over 650 economists, including five Nobel Prize winners and six past presidents of the American Economic Association, had signed a letter calling for an increase in the federal minimum wage, stating that it could "significantly improve the lives of low-income workers and their families, without the adverse effects that critics have claimed" (Economic Policy Institute 2006).

This is not to say that the debate is closed. Economists such as David Neumark continue to produce studies suggesting that minimum wage increases can have negative impacts on employment, though now the focus is on particular subsets of workers, particularly low-skilled workers, teenagers, and black workers (Neumark, Salas, and Wascher 2013). Neumark and others find that minimum wage increases lead to statistically significant disemployment effects of −0.1 to −0.3 for teenagers. This means that if the minimum wage is increased by 10 percent, the employment rate for teenagers would fall by 1 to 3 percent (Neumark and Wascher 2006). Other economists argue that the methodology behind these results is flawed, as it fails to take into account controls for spatial heterogeneity (Schmitt 2013). For example, Arindrajit Dube, William Lester, and Michael Reich (2010) and Sylvia Allegretto, Dube, and Reich (2011) argue that because teen employment patterns differ significantly by state and census region, it is difficult to compare aggregate data for states. They argue that researchers must include controls for census region and for state-specific trends. In work that compares contiguous counties, Dube and his colleagues (2010) find no negative outcomes from minimum wage increases. These researchers have advanced the field methodologically: previously there had been two different methodologies for studying minimum wage impact, a national approach and a case study approach, but their work combines the two. Improving the methodology in the national approach and generalizing the case study approach, they find no evidence of job loss. Perhaps surprisingly, their results hold even for a slack labor market, such as in the 2007 to 2009 recession. No matter whether unemployment is relatively high or low, Dube and his colleagues find no evidence that raising the minimum wage causes job loss (Heidi Shierholz, personal correspondence with the author, May 24, 2013).

While there remains some debate about the impact of minimum wage laws on teenagers, the vast majority of workers affected by minimum wage increases are not teenagers. As of 2012, more than three-quarters of workers who would be affected by a minimum wage increase were older than twenty. The Fair Minimum Wage Act of 2013 would increase the federal minimum wage from $7.25 to $10.10 in three stages and then index it to inflation; it would also increase the tipped minimum wage. Such an increase would affect 30 million workers. Over half of these workers work full-time, and 44 percent have completed some college. In addition, the average affected worker contributes about half of his or her family's income. One estimate finds that this wage increase would generate $51 billion in additional wages (Cooper and Hall 2013). The evidence seems strong that minimum wage policies have positive impacts for low-income workers (Cooper 2012). What about living wage laws?

What Do We Know About the Impact of Living Wage Laws on Low-Wage Workers?

Despite all the attention and research focused on living wage campaigns, there is little information on the number of workers actually covered or affected by the ordinances. There are several reasons for this gap. First, the ordinances themselves differ from city to city. Most cover service contractors, but some also cover city employees, subcontractors, economic development recipients, and concessionaires operating on city-owned property. In a few places, the "living wage" is more like a minimum wage, covering most workers within the city borders (in San Francisco and San Jose, California, Albuquerque and Santa Fe, New Mexico, and Washington, D.C.).[3] Some ordinances cover counties and county service contractors. A few universities have living wage policies that can apply to contractors, subcontractors, or university employees.

In many cities, the work done by service contractors was once done by public employees, but then subcontracted out in an effort to save money. Contracting practices differ widely by city and state; in most cases, contractors are not required to report the number of employees who work on contracts.[4] It can be difficult to acquire city contracts to review employment numbers.[5] It is even more difficult to get information on subcontracted employees, as contractors are usually not required to report anything about this aspect of their work.[6] Furthermore, the provision that covers economic development subsidy recipients applies only to future projects. These projects are often kept quiet for many years while in negotiation, and there is no way to easily estimate the number of workers who will be covered.

Another challenge is measuring indirect impacts of the ordinances. There is strong evidence that increasing wage floors leads to "ripple effects" within a firm. When employers raise the floor, they also tend to raise the wages of workers who were already making the new floor or close to it. Jeanette Wicks-Lim (see Pollin et al. 2008) has attempted to measure the size of the ripple effect of minimum wage and living wage laws, but this too varies given the size of the wage increase and the number of workers covered. Still, living wage opponents are quick to point out the ripple effects of living wage ordinances because they impose an additional cost on employers. Therefore, it seems appropriate to include these indirect recipients when measuring the coverage of the movement.

There may also be a "spillover effect": when employers raise wages in some firms, nearby employers may also raise wages because they are competing in the same geographic labor market. This effect is even more difficult to measure, but considering the relatively small coverage of living wage ordinances, it seems unlikely that it will have a major effect in most cities. Other workers have benefited from using the term "living wage" in contract negotiations—such as the National Education Association campaigns to raise the wages of para-educators—or to set employer policy but these do not result in living wage ordinances, and it is nearly impossible to track these cases and their coverage.

In addition to the basic challenges of estimating potential coverage of the laws, there is also the problem of enforcement. In my research, I found that many cities are doing a poor job of enforcing the ordinances once passed. Some city administrators refuse to implement the law or are generous with waivers; in a few cases, politicians have repealed the ordinances via city or state legislation. In other cases, the laws are on the books but weakly enforced, making it very difficult to estimate the number of workers who actually receive the higher wage. There have been a few cases where workers and/or unions filed charges with the city because of noncompliance; the fact that the city or courts have ruled in favor of the workers suggests that there may be other cases where employers are not in compliance with the law.[7]

Given these challenges, our efforts to estimate coverage of living wage laws are necessarily fairly loose. By 2002, we estimated, somewhere between 100,000 and 250,000 workers had directly benefited from living wage ordinances. Since that time, forty-seven more cities and counties have passed laws, including four cities that passed citywide laws and a Pueblo-wide law in Sandia Pueblo, New Mexico.[8]

Based on the initial estimate of coverage as of 2002, I took an average number of workers covered per "traditional" living wage ordinance, using a total of 175,000 workers (the midpoint between 100,000 and 250,000). That gives an average of 1,923 workers per ordinance. The 39 traditional living wage ordinances passed since 2002 would amount to an additional 75,000 workers covered. The four citywide and one Pueblo-wide ordinances are estimated to have had a direct impact on another 83,000 workers (Pollin 2005; Pollin et al. 2008; Reich and Latinen 2003). This would amount to approximately 333,000 workers covered directly. Living wage studies suggest that approximately 50 to 200 percent of directly covered workers benefit from the ripple effects of these increases. For example, if 500 people are directly covered, ripple effects will impact 250 to 1,000 workers. In the most generous estimate, we could assume that 666,000 workers receive ripple effect wage increases, bringing our total impact to about 1 million workers covered through living wage ordinances (see Pollin et al. 2008). Clearly, this is only a very small fraction of the total low-wage workforce. As of 2011, 28 percent of all workers in the United States—almost 37 million people—were earning poverty-level wages.[9]

Who Are the Workers?   Living wage ordinances vary a lot in terms of who is covered. The majority of ordinances cover city service contracts, and these workers may be found in janitorial services, security, laundry, landscaping, bus driving, and food service. The larger ordinances cover retail and restaurant workers in airports or in sports arenas, and the city-wide ordinances cover most all low-wage work.

There are at least three major studies of living wage ordinances that profile the covered workers. The economist David Fairris and Los Angeles Alliance for a New Economy researchers David Runsten, Carolina Brio nes, and Jessica Goodheart (2005) surveyed workers covered by the Los Angeles ordinance. University of California–Berkeley scholars Michael Reich, Peter Hall, and Ken Jacobs (2003, 2005) studied workers covered at the San Francisco airport, and Mark Brenner and Stephanie Luce (2005), economists at the Political Economy Research Institute (PERI), surveyed workers in Boston, where those covered worked predominantly in child care and educational services. Despite the different industries and occupations, all of these researchers came to some similar conclusions.

Contrary to the claims of some opponents, living wage recipients are not teenagers working for extra money. Workers covered by traditional living wage ordinances are in their thirties, support at least one family member on their income, and have been in their job for at least a few years. They are disproportionately people of color, and disproportionately from low-income households. For example, Boston workers are on average thirty-two years old and have 2.9 years of tenure in their current job. Almost two-thirds are people of color. Their median annual income in 2002 was $23,324. In Los Angeles, 58 percent of covered workers were age thirty-five or older, 86 percent worked full-time, and the covered workers had an average of twenty years in the workforce. Half were Latino, 29 percent African American, and 12 percent Asian. Over 75 percent of workers covered by the San Francisco airport ordinance were twenty-five years or older, and 86 percent were people of color.

The studies found some differences by location, which seem primarily explained by the type of work covered. While the Boston workers were 79 percent women (employed in child care and educational services), the

San Francisco airport workers were mostly men. Boston workers had a higher average education level, with 52 percent holding a two- or four-year college degree and another 11 percent having earned a master's degree. In contrast, 71 percent of covered workers in Los Angeles had a high school degree or less.

The Impact on Workers   What was the impact of the living wage increase on the covered workers? The Boston survey compared workers who had received a living wage increase to those who did not and found that, on average, the living wage increased hourly earnings by 25 percent and annual earnings by 60 percent. Annual earnings were higher because workers had more hours per week, and more weeks per year, than those not covered by the living wage. From this study, it appears that employers began to convert part-time jobs into full-time ones once they were mandated to pay the higher wage and provide some benefits. Most of the Boston workers were initially from poverty or near-poverty households. Although the living wage resulted in higher earnings, the increase was generally not enough to raise workers much above poverty, particularly when using more realistic measures of poverty.

The Los Angeles study found that, on average, workers who stayed in their jobs and received a raise due to the ordinance received an initial average raise of $1.48 per hour and an average annual increase of $2,590. However, 81 percent of workers surveyed said that the living wage was not enough to enable them to meet the basic needs of their families.

The San Francisco airport ordinance resulted in raises for almost 90 percent of the ground-based nonmanagement workers, with an average pay increase of 22 percent. Reich, Hall, and Jacobs (2003) estimate that this resulted in a total pay increase for all covered workers of $56.6 million in annual earnings. The pay increases greatly reduced the wage differentials between the in-house employees and the subcontracted employees.

Negative Outcomes?   Living wage opponents claim that while the ordinances may help some workers, they hurt other workers who are laid off or not hired as employers cut jobs to comply with the higher wage mandate. Much of the research in this area focuses on the impact of minimum wage laws, and another set of studies engages in a debate about the best methodology to use to measure the impact of living wage ordinances. Overall, the impact studies that use employer and worker surveys find little or no evidence of employment effects due to living wage ordinances. A set of studies authored primarily by economists David Neumark and Scott Adams do find some negative employment effects. However, their methodology has been extensively critiqued by PERI economists Mark Brenner, Robert Pollin, and Jeanette Wicks-Lim (Pollin et al. 2008).

Another critique of ordinances is that they can lead to labor-labor substitution—employers replacing one set of workers (predominantly people of color, or workers with less education) with another (more white workers, with higher education levels), thereby leading to the "unintended consequence" of hurting the most disadvantaged workers. The three major living wage impact studies have different findings on this point. In the Boston study, no employers reported a change in hiring standards as a result of the ordinance, suggesting that no labor-labor substitution occurred in that city. In Los Angeles, researchers compared employees hired before and after the ordinance was enacted and found slight changes: workers hired after the ordinance was in place were somewhat more likely to be Latino, to be male, and to have received formal training before being hired. Otherwise, there was no difference in those hired before and after by education level, age at hiring, native English speaker, or school attendance. In San Francisco, the ordinance covering the airport introduced a new requirement: workers in certain positions had to have completed a high school degree. Therefore, the finding that the percentage of workers without a high school degree fell after the ordinance is difficult to attribute to labor-labor substitution.

With few negative impacts and significant positive outcomes for those directly affected, living wage ordinances can be a valuable policy for raising the standard of living for low-wage workers. Is it possible to expand their scope so that more workers benefit?

THE CHALLENGES FOR EXPANSION

Living wage ordinances have had a significant impact on covered workers, but are limited in several ways. First, the ordinances cover a small proportion of low-wage workers, even when the four citywide ordinances are included. Second, the wage levels vary but in most cases are not enough to raise workers to a true living wage. Third, in addition to wage levels, not all workers are given full-time hours, so even with a higher wage they may not meet federal poverty thresholds.

A variety of reasons underlie these limitations. First, living wage activists have had to focus on the local level because of their weak political power. Living wage supporters would be likely to agree that the best strategy to raise wages would be a significant increase in the federal minimum wage, with the addition of an automatic annual adjustment for inflation. But they do not have the political power to make that happen. Their power is strongest at the local level, where they have more direct relations to elected officials and "people power" has a better chance to counter business lobbies and money. But even at the local level, more ambitious ordinances and those that would target large retailers or hotels have encountered much more resistance. The success rate for traditional ordinances affecting city contracts is much higher than the success rate for more ambitious ordinances covering more workers.

Depending on the state and "home rule" laws, legal restrictions also limit the ability of living wage activists to pass local laws. Only some states permit local governments to enact wage laws. In others (Louisiana, Wisconsin, Florida, and a handful of other states), the state legislature passed new legislation to repeal living wage or minimum wage laws or prevent localities from passing them. The federal Employment Retirement Income Security Act (ERISA) prevents local governments from passing laws mandating that employers provide health insurance to employees.

Another challenge for living wage campaigns is the level of the wage. Despite the term "living wage," the majority of ordinances win only an hourly wage that would raise a full-time worker with a family of three or four to the federal poverty line. There is a strong consensus among poverty scholars that the official poverty calculations are outdated and the levels are too low (Pollin et al. 2008). Therefore, the poverty line is not even an accurate measure of poverty, let alone a living wage. Several methodologies are available to measure a more accurate cost of living. These utilize government data to calculate the realistic costs of minimal expenses. For example, the Economic Policy Institute (EPI) developed a "basic family budget" calculator that accounts for housing, food, shelter, transportation, health care, taxes, and child care. It also adjusts for family size and region, which the federal poverty line does not do. The EPI budget numbers are usually much higher than the poverty line.

This suggests that the living wage rates of around $10 to $11 per hour are too low to meet even basic needs. This is not a surprise to living wage activists. The poverty line was chosen not because it was the best number but because it was politically feasible.[10]

The other alternative is for living wage activists to join in efforts to reduce the cost of living. Policies that increase affordable housing or reduce or make free health care, child care, and transportation would have a large impact on the cost of living and therefore reduce the wage levels needed to cover basic needs.

Putting aside larger campaigns to dramatically increase the federal minimum wage or reduce the cost of living through policies like single-payer health care or universal child care, what can living wage activists do to expand the impact of the movement? Here I focus on two main avenues to expand coverage and address limited hours of work.

Table 8.1   Union Density for Low-Wage Occupations, 2012

Occupation Title	Total Employment	Union Density	Union Members
Retail salespersons	4,340,000	1.1%	47,740
Cashiers	3,314,010	5	165,701
Combined food preparation and serving workers, including fast food	2,943,810	11.6	341,482
Waiters and waitresses	2,332,020	1.6	37,312
Laborers and freight, stock, and material movers, hand	2,143,940	14.7	315,159
Janitors and cleaners, except maids and housekeepers	2,097,380	15.2	318,802
Stock clerks and order fillers	1,806,310	9.3	167,987
Nursing assistants[a]	1,420,020	10.7	151,942
Security guards[a]	1,046,420	10.7	111,967
Cooks, restaurant[a]	1,000,710	4.2	42,030
Total	22,444,620	7.6	1,700,121

Source: Author's compilation based on Bureau of Labor Statistics (2013); Hirsch and Macpherson (2012).
[a]CPS occupation titles do not match OES titles exactly. For nursing assistants, I used "nursing, psychiatric, and home health aides" from Hirsch and Macpherson (2012). For security guards, I used "security guards and gaming surveillance officers." For cooks, restaurants, I used "cooks."

EXPANDING COVERAGE

In order to explore options to expand coverage, we should first look at where low-wage workers work. The 2012 poverty threshold for a family of four was $23,497, which means that, with two thousand hours of work per year, the living wage for a family of four was $12 per hour. According to tables I.1 and I.2, the largest low-wage occupations can be found in food service, health care, retail, and building services. There are unions and organizations working to organize some of these occupations, such as the Service Employees International Union in home health care, the National Domestic Workers Alliance on domestic work, and the Restaurant Opportunities Center on food preparation and serving. The United Food and Commercial Workers Union and Workers United represent some workers in retail. Overall, however, organization in these occupations is very low. Data on worker center membership are not available, but CPS data on union membership show that union density for these ten largest low-wage occupations ranges from 1.1 percent in retail sales to 15.2 percent among janitors and cleaners, except maids and housekeepers (table 8.1). Overall, the density for these occupations is 7.6 percent, accounting for just 1.7 million workers. In other words, over 20 million of those employed in low-wage occupations are not union members.

Therefore, the living wage movement might be seen as one way to find points of leverage or political hooks that could create an opening to raise wages and lay the groundwork for unionization. The campaigns could assist unionization in several ways. First, they could simply be a way for unions to do outreach among workers and create a positive image of unions as effective avenues for raising wages. After the Communication Workers of America helped pass a living wage ordinance in Tucson, Arizona, city workers contacted the union and said they wanted to form a union for themselves; they subsequently succeeded in doing so (Luce 2004).

The ordinances could also include a range of provisions to make unionization a little easier. For example, many ordinances contain "nonretaliation" language for workers who discuss their wage levels and rights on the job. Even though the National Labor Relations Act (NLRA) makes it illegal for employers to fire workers who organize in their workplace, employers do so frequently without much penalty. Living wage ordinances could provide another layer of protection for workers who talk about workers' rights in the workplace. A few ordinances allow municipal governments to deny economic benefits to firms with a history of labor law violations, on the grounds that the city wants to protect its investment and needs to ensure "labor peace."[11]

Unions have already targeted some of the occupations listed here for organizing, such as janitors and nursing home workers. It seems more likely that living wage campaigns could be targeted at the occupations with lower union density, where it is much harder to win an organizing drive or achieve gains of any kind. What are the possibilities for these kinds of campaigns? Living wage ordinances already cover a number of these occupations, although in a limited fashion. Many of the ordinances cover the janitorial and food service contractors who service city buildings, although this usually represents a small number of workers. The Boston ordinance covers child care workers hired through county contracts, and most ordinances apply to security and landscaping workers employed through city contracts.

Living wage ordinances also cover some retail, restaurant, and fast-food work. This is done directly through living wage ordinances that cover concessionaires in city-owned property (airports, stadiums, ports) or in a few designated geographic zones (such as the public Marina in Berkeley, California). Approximately fifty-six ordinances include a living wage requirement for economic development projects. However, most of these have either a high threshold or easy exemptions, so few cities have really implemented the living wage for economic development.

Would it be possible to expand the living wage policies to cover more of these low-wage occupations?

Home Health Care

A few living wage ordinances cover counties that administer contracts covering home health care work. These programs are funded through Medicaid and run by the state, although in some states the money goes through county contracts. The living wage ordinances that apply to home care workers are either in counties (for example, Dane County, Wisconsin) or in cities that happen to be contiguous with counties (for example, New York, New York, and San Francisco, California). But in some states the programs are not run through the counties. And even where they are, raising wages at the county level still requires lobbying the state to raise reimbursement rates. Thus, statewide campaigns to pass living wage policies covering home health care would be needed in these states, and those are much more difficult to win than local campaigns, because at the state level money plays a much larger role and local coalitions do not have the same access to legislators. Still, statewide policies to mandate living wages for home health care workers would have a major impact, particularly as this occupation has the largest predicted job growth through 2018.

Calculations using estimates of employment and union density show that currently there are potentially 825,712 non-unionized home health care workers who could be affected. However, not all home health care employees earn low wages. According to Occupational Employment Statistics (OES), the median hourly wage in the occupation is $9.91, and the seventy-fifth-percentile wage is $11.52. A living wage campaign using $11.52 an hour could cover up to 619,284 current home health care workers. Assuming that new jobs in the field remain at the same level of unionization and wages, the living wage could also affect another 308,755 workers.

The same dynamics exist for a few other social service programs that are funded with state and federal money, such as some child care and special education services. These are covered in only a few living wage ordinances. Living wage policies at the state level that cover all human services would also have an impact, although, unlike home health care, publicly funded child care accounts for a minority of child care work. About 30 percent of child care workers are self-employed, working from their homes or in other private homes (Bureau of Labor Statistics 2012). That is a working situation more similar to that of the occupation "maids and housekeeping workers."

Domestic Workers

Domestic workers include housekeepers, nannies, and elder care workers who work in private homes. There are a number of domestic worker organizations around the country, and most have come together to work through the National Domestic Workers Alliance, formed in 2007. In New York State, the Domestic Workers United proposed a "Domestic Workers' Bill of Rights" that set a minimum wage of $12 per hour, to have risen to $14 per hour by 2010, for domestic workers. The Bill of Rights eventually passed, but did not include the living wage provision. There is now a campaign for a Domestic Workers' Bill of Rights in California. It does not set a minimum wage level, but would mandate that domestic workers are entitled to annual cost-of-living increases.

If passed, these laws might be difficult to enforce, as workers tend to be working on their own, directly for an employer. Yet this is a possible avenue to begin to raise the floor for a large number of workers in the large low-wage categories of "maids and nannies" and "personal care," as well as one of the fastest-growing occupations, child care. As with home health care, we can take the total employment and subtract the unionized workers to get a potential 813,887 workers who might be affected. Then, if we take the 75 percent of workers who earn up to $11.39 per hour, we get 610,415 current workers who could be affected by a living wage law. This occupation is expected to grow at a pace slower than the national average, but still, 111,600 new jobs are predicted. Assuming new jobs in the field remain at the same level of unionization and wages, the living wage could also affect another 77,950.

Of course, activists already realize the need to raise wages for home health care and domestic workers. But these campaigns are hard to win, owing to the weak political power of the workers in these occupations, let alone the weakness of the labor movement more generally. Living wage campaigns have targeted city service contracts not because these are the most effective target to deal with conditions for low-wage workers, but because these campaigns have more chance of winning.

Economic Development

The campaigns to apply living wages to public economic development funding are perhaps easier to win than statewide living wage campaigns, both because activists can target economic development at the local level, where they have greater relative strength, and because they have found ways to hold up development projects through the city council. The campaigns may also generate greater support from those who desire greater government accountability on spending: even some conservatives believe that government should not give out large sums of money without attaching more stringent requirements in exchange for that money.

That means that the most likely path to expanding living wage coverage may be through policies to cover more economic development. Chicago attempted to do this through a "big-box" ordinance that would have applied to large retail stores, but it was vetoed by Mayor Richard Daley.[12] Still, big-box ordinances could have a significant impact on low-wage jobs. Despite the economic downturn, retail sales continue to grow, and national chains predict continued development in the years to come. Walmart's CFO recently stated that "WalMart has twice the opportunity to grow in Los Angeles or New York than the opportunity in India and China combined," and the vice chairman noted that Walmart is looking to grow in the fifty largest urban markets in the coming years (Kellerman and Luce 2011).

The big-box ordinance in Chicago would have applied to stores of 90,000 square feet or more; the average Walmart "Supercenter" (averaging 185,000 square feet) would have been covered, but not Walmart's smaller-format "Neighborhood Market" (averaging 42,000 square feet) or the new Walmart "Express Market" (which so far averages 15,000 square feet). A recent study estimated that Walmart will need to build up to eleven Supercenters in New York City in the coming years if it is to maintain its national market share (Kellerman and Luce 2011). At an average of 300 employees per store, this could create 3,300 new jobs (although research shows that net job gain is much smaller, as a new Walmart tends to drive neighboring stores out of business). Still, if a big-box ordinance were in place, 3,300 new jobs would be subject to the living wage ordinance. Critics may argue that with a big-box ordinance, Walmart would not build those eleven Supercenters, nor would other retailers add stores. That may be the case. Walmart may choose to build smaller stores not covered by the ordinance, or to not build at all. But if big-box ordinances were ubiquitous throughout the major urban areas, Walmart would have fewer options about where and how to build.

There are no publicly available estimates of Walmart's Supercenter plans, so I developed a crude estimate based on the New York estimate. Using a measure of GDP per metropolitan area for the top fifty urban centers, I took a ratio of GDP per city relative to New York and applied it to the eleven Supercenters in New York. This resulted in a possibility of six supercenters in Los Angeles, five in Chicago, four in Washington, D.C., and between one and three for the remaining forty-six urban areas, for a total of eighty-one new Supercenters (including New York) and a total of about 24,000 jobs. This is clearly not the strategy to cover large numbers of retail workers. Of course, big-box ordinances would affect not only Walmart but other retailers like Target and Home Depot. But Walmart is much larger than these other chains, so it is not likely that extending the coverage to the other stores would drastically change the estimates. As of 2011, Walmart had 3,014 Supercenters, 635 "Discount Stores," 167 Neighborhood Markets, and only a few test Express Markets. In comparison, Target has only 1,750 stores total, which includes 240 "SuperTargets." Home Depot has 2,200 stores. Other stores, like TJ Maxx, Staples, Best Buy, and Bed, Bath and Beyond, have much smaller stores—averaging between 20,000 and 45,000 square feet. A big-box ordinance would need to lower its size threshold to have any impact on many of these chains.

Therefore, extending the Walmart projections to Target and Home Depot would add another 30,000 workers, for a total of 54,000 workers potentially covered by ordinances applying to new big-box development. These workers are not unionized, but not all earn low wages. A recent study calculated that approximately 22 percent of Walmart workers earn below $9 per hour, and 64 percent earn below $12 per hour (Jacobs, Graham-Squire, and Luce 2011). If these proportions are similar for Target and Home Depot workers, we estimate that 11,880 workers would be affected by a big-box ordinance at $9 an hour, and 34,560 at $12 per hour.

Another model is from Los Angeles, which has a living wage policy that applies to Community Redevelopment Agency (CRA) projects. The living wage applies to the developer and any contractors and subcontractors whose primary work is at the development site, such as janitors, grounds-keepers, and security. The policy also applies to third-party tenants (such as retailers) if the land is owned or leased by the CRA. An additional CRA policy mandates living wages for employees at hotels built on CRA land. As of 2011, there were 144 CRA projects completed or in process that had a living wage component (Spivack 2011). These involved over $8 billion in private investment and $400 million in CRA investment and covered office space, commercial, industrial, and hotel space, and nonprofit developments and affordable housing. Altogether they covered approximately 48,700 construction jobs and 23,000 permanent jobs, or 339 construction jobs and 160 permanent jobs per project. The average per project cost was about $56 million in private funding and $2.8 million in agency public money.

According to a recent report from Good Jobs First, cities and states currently spend about $70 billion per year on economic development (Mattera et al. 2011).[13] They conducted a study of 238 state programs and found that only 135 had job creation standards, and only 98 of those had a wage standard. The wage levels varied widely, from just above the federal minimum wage up to over $40 an hour, with a median wage requirement of $11.82 per hour.

The remaining 140 programs had no wage requirement. These programs cost states $8 billion a year in direct costs. If the CRA projects in Los Angeles can be taken as an average, $8 billion in public money, at $2.8 million per project, translates to approximately 2,857 development projects per year. Again, using CRA numbers, this could create approximately 457,000 permanent jobs per project nationally. However, not all of these are low-wage jobs. If we assume the national average of 25.5 percent low-wage employment, a living wage requirement could affect 116,535 workers.

Another possibility for reaching large numbers of retail workers is via shopping malls. One of the largest mall developers in the country is General Growth Properties (GGP). Another Good Jobs First study examined the subsidies given to fifty General Growth Properties projects that received over $200 million in subsidies and $9 million in tax savings (Mattera, Lack, and Walter 2007).[14] Malls employ an average of 177 to 3,449 employees (REMI Consulting 2006). Using an average of 1,391, we can estimate that the fifty GGP malls employ a total of 69,550 people.[15] There are certainly higher-wage employees at malls, but the percentage of poverty-level jobs in these workplaces is probably much higher than 25.5 percent. However, these figures relate to malls that are already in existence, while ordinances covering economic development apply to new projects. Thus, to cover employees working in existing malls, living wage activists would most likely need to pass legislation that applies to a geographic zone—a measure covering a tourist district or shopping center zone, for instance, but also perhaps a citywide measure.

Airports and Stadiums

The Federal Aviation Administration (FAA) reports that there are almost twenty thousand airports in the country, but many of these are small and private. About 30 percent are public entities—and all of the public passenger airports in the country are run by public entities. Most are run through the city or county, and some through a public airport authority. In a few places, an airport is run through the state, such as in Maryland.

A living wage campaign can be directed at the airport through a city or county ordinance campaign to require all firms receiving contracts for work at the airport to comply with the ordinance.[16] The North American Industry Classification System (NAICS) code for airport operations (48811) provides data on establishments that operate airports or support airport operations, though it does not include food services and janitorial contractors. This makes it difficult to get comprehensive data on the number of people employed in airports, particularly the number of low-wage workers. Also, as some airports have moved from a "master concessionaire" model to a "developer" model for food and retail, there are more subtenants and more discrepancies over employment numbers.[17]

Formal employment in NAICS 48811 has been declining rapidly as airports subcontract work and replace jobs with technology (such as electronic check-in), but airports remain a large source of employment. Large airports can be the largest employer in the state, as with the Hartsfield-Jackson Airport in Atlanta, where over 58,000 people work for the airlines, ground crew, security, TSA, and concessionaires.[18] The San Francisco International Airport has 30,000 employees, and the living wage policy affected about 10,000 of them (Reich et al. 2005).

A study by Airports Council International (2006) found that 2,042,000 people work in airports in North America. Data are not available for the U.S. share, but if we estimate that 85 percent of these workers are employed in U.S. airports, and that, based on the San Francisco case, one-third of those are low-wage, then we get approximately 573,000 low-wage workers. Unions have already organized some of these workers, who work in everything from food service to retail concessions, janitorial, security guards, airport parking, parking garage, rental car agencies, and other passenger services. UNITE HERE represents 30,000 workers at sixty-eight airports. According to an Airport Group report, unionized concession workers at the Cleveland airport earned $9.96 per hour in 2007, while nonunion employees at the same airport earned $8.50 an hour. (All the unionized workers also received health and retirement benefits, compared to fewer than half of the non-unionized workers.)[19] Other unions also represent airport workers, including the United Food and Commercial Workers Union (UFCW), the International Brotherhood of Teamsters (IBT), and the Service Employees International Union (SEIU). We do not have good density numbers, but if we assume 12 percent density based on the density for food preparation workers, it means that approximately 68,000 of the 573,000 low-wage workers are unionized. This leaves a potential 505,000 airport workers who are low-wage, are not represented by a union, and could be covered by a living wage ordinance. In July 2012, the city council of Syracuse, New York, extended its municipal living wage ordinance to cover the city's airport, which is expected to affect about fifty food service workers (Abbott 2012).

Some living wage ordinances also cover sports stadiums, such as the living wage policy that was won in 2007 covering Camden Yards in Baltimore. The stadium is owned and run by the state (through the Maryland Stadium Authority), and the living wage campaign was targeted at this state authority. The majority of the ninety-two professional sports stadiums in the country were built with at least some public money (Good Jobs First 2010).

In addition to campaigns targeting the authority, a living wage could be won through a community benefits agreement (CBA) that covers a specific project. The CBA that covers the San Diego baseball stadium mandates a living wage for all service contract employees in the ballpark. Activists could run a CBA campaign with a living wage component approved before or during the building or expansion of a stadium.

A drawback to a stadium-based campaign is the limited number of workers affected. According to economists John Seigfried and Andrew Zimbalist (2000), the average sports team employs 70 to 130 people in the front office, and 1,000 to 1,500 people are hired on game days to work in security, concessions, ticket sales, and cleaning.[20] If we assume those same 1,000 to 1,500 workers are employed per stadium, we get between 92,000 and 138,000 workers in stadiums, primarily in low-wage, temporary jobs. The ninetieth-percentile worker in food preparation earns $11.19 per hour, so it is likely that a large proportion of stadium workers would be affected. Taking the midpoint, we get a total of 115,000 workers. However, these workers would not experience a large jump in income, owing to limited work hours.

Geographic-Based Ordinances

Another option is to promote more living wage ordinances or policies that apply to a specific geography. Of course, the most comprehensive of these are the citywide ordinances, but the opportunity to pass these is restricted by law in some cases, and also by aggressive employer countercampaigns. Smaller zones within a city might be more feasible. However, a zone is not necessarily easier to win just because it is smaller. The Santa Monica City Council passed a living wage that would have applied to large hotels, restaurants, and retail establishments in the Third Street Promenade area, but employers organized a ballot initiative to repeal the law and spent large sums of money and employed dirty tricks to defeat it (Luce 2004).

Still, living wage activists might consider attempting the strategy in other places. Most large cities have tourist zones that have benefited from large economic development subsidies. These might include tax-incremental financing, business improvement districts, industrial development agency loans, and other policies that provide subsidized land purchases, below-market-rate loans, tax abatements, tax credits, and subsidized job training, as well as public-sector investment in the infrastructure necessary for promoting tourism and retail (parking garages, landscaping, well-paved roads and sidewalks, traffic lights, and adequate streetlamps). As the Good Jobs First study shows, some of the state subsidy programs do include wage requirements, as do a few of the geographic or "zone" programs (Mattera et al. 2011). For example, the Pine Trees Development Zones in Maine require employers to pay wages that are "at least equal to the per-capita income of a county where the project is located." Currently, this translates into an hourly wage of $14.04 to $21.71 per hour. Businesses locating in an Iowa enterprise zone must pay 90 percent of the average county or regional wage, whichever is lower, but not below $7.50 per hour. Currently this results in hourly wages of $10.29 to $16.44. Many other states have zone programs that do not include a wage mandate, so this might be an obvious place to start attaching living wage requirements.

Another geographic-based strategy is to pass ordinances that cover land at or near ports and airports. In Los Angeles, the city living wage ordinance initially covered the publicly owned airport directly, but in 2007 the city council passed an extension to the ordinance so that it now covers hotels in the "airport corridor." The council argued that the hotels benefit from their proximity to a public facility, as well as from public investment in the roads in the area. The extension to the ordinance covers approximately a dozen hotels. This campaign was difficult to win and faced legal challenges, so while it could be a model to cover hotels in every city, anyone undertaking such a campaign should expect a hard fight.

Unfortunately, it is difficult to estimate the number of workers covered by geographic zone ordinances. We can get some estimates of existing proposals or policies. For example, Robert Pollin and Mark Brenner (2000) predicted that 2,477 workers would be directly affected by the Santa Monica living wage ordinance. The State of Iowa (Gordon 2008) reports that 9,000 jobs were created through the enterprise zone program across the state through 2007, although this does not tell us what kinds of jobs these were.[21] Yet to get a comprehensive estimate of potential workers covered by geographic zone ordinances, we would need to estimate employment in all enterprise zone programs, all tourist districts, all airport corridors, and so on, which is beyond the scope of this chapter.

HOURS WORKED

A second way in which the living wage movement might expand to more effectively bring low-wage workers out of poverty is to address the issue of hours of work. A major challenge for low-wage workers is that in addition to earning low hourly wages, many fall even further behind financially because they are not given as many hours to work as they would like. "Involuntary part-time" workers make up one of the largest components of "labor underutilization" today, and their numbers are on the rise (Bureau of Labor Statistics 2013).

The problem is endemic in retail, where employers are increasingly using "just-in-time" scheduling practices to fine-tune employment based on customer flow and decrease their payroll costs. Some retailers classify workers as "part-time" even if they regularly work full-time hours because this allows them to avoid paying some of the benefits that are restricted to full-time employees. This "flexibility" so desired by managers comes at a big cost for workers, whose paychecks are unpredictable from week to week and whose work schedules can vary day by day, making it especially difficult to coordinate child care or elder care, school, or another job.

Much of labor economics predicts that a rise in wages will result in a drop in the demand for hours, similar to the finding that higher wages leads to fewer jobs. Daniel Hamermesh (1996) finds that a 1 percent decline in total labor costs is associated with a 0.3 percent increase in the demand by employers for hours worked. Yet other researchers have found some evidence that this prediction might not always hold true. Susan Lambert, Anna Haley-Lock, and Julia Henly (2012) argue that low-wage employers tend to treat workers as a variable cost, but when forced to increase wages they may begin to treat them more like fixed costs and increase their demand for hours.

Our research on the Boston living wage found this same phenomenon: employers that were mandated to comply with the city living wage ordinance appeared to convert part-time jobs into full-time ones (Brenner and Luce 2005). In the firms we surveyed, the living wage ordinance prompted a shift away from part-time jobs. Total employment went up by 22 percent, on average, and the number of part-time jobs fell by 11 percent.

The Los Angeles study found that while the majority of firms did not cut employment or hours, employers did cut back on overtime hours compared to firms that were not covered by the living wage (Fairris et al. 2005). The San Francisco airport study did not find evidence that hours were cut or increased with the implementation of the living wage program (Reich, Hall, and Jacobs 2003).

Lambert, Haley-Lock, and Henly (2012) argue that employers might increase hours when they are required to provide benefits to all employees, such as health insurance. Many firms limit benefit packages to a small number of full-time workers and fill in employment gaps with low-wage, nonbenefited, part-time workers. In addition, some government programs incentivize this practice. For example, employees must work at least 1,250 hours in twelve months to be eligible for family medical leave, and the majority of states have rules that exclude many part-time workers from unemployment insurance (National Employment Law Project 2004).

Policies that mandate benefits for all employees might push employers away from this strategy.

This might also happen with minimum hours-per-shift, or pay-per-day policies. Haley-Lock (2011) studied restaurant chains in the United States and Canada and found that U.S. managers tended to send workers home early if business was slow. In the same chain in British Columbia, Canada, managers never did this. Provincial law requires them to pay a minimum of four hours for any shift scheduled up to four hours, and a minimum of eight hours for shifts scheduled for up to eight hours. The "minimum daily wage" leads to employers increasing their demand for hours per employee.[22]

THE LIVING WAGE AS A STEPPING-STONE

The estimates presented here are crude, and further research is needed to refine the numbers and assess potential obstacles to these campaigns. Table 8.2 summarizes the estimates. Excluding the impact of geographic zones, the campaigns listed here have the potential to affect over 2 million low-wage workers. However, several of these estimates are not realistic because they would require a state-level campaign, which would more likely be cast as a statewide minimum wage campaign than as an industry-specific living wage campaign. At the same time, home health care and domestic workers organizations have conducted—and are working on—statewide, industry-specific campaigns and policy, and so perhaps the strategy to include a living wage is possible.

Table 8.2 estimates only the direct impact of living wages. In reality, more workers would benefit from indirect increases (ripple effects). In addition, the table does not include the future jobs created—those expected to be added to the economy in the next ten years. Still, the numbers are far from reaching all of the 37 million workers estimated to earn poverty-level wages.

In the end, living wage campaigns may work best as a tool for improving wages indirectly and as a way to build movements for broader policy changes. In particular, the living wage movement may be responsible for ensuring raises to statewide and federal minimum wages, which is where the greatest coverage lies. Ideally, we would have a way to test the counterfactual case: specifically, would Congress have raised the minimum wage in 1996 and 2007, and would over thirty states have raised statewide wages, without the living wage movement? We cannot know the answer, but the evidence suggests that these phenomena are related. For example, some of the organizations and staff most heavily involved in living wage campaigns, such as ACORN and the Brennan Center for Justice, were key

Table 8.2   Estimated Impact of New Living Wage Campaigns

Target	Estimated Workers Affected	Type of Campaign
Home health care	619,284	Statewide
Maids and housekeeping	611,151	Statewide
Airports	505,000	City or county
CRA-type economic development policy	116,535	State programs
Stadiums	115,000	County or state sports authority
Total	2,040,746	

Source: Author's calculations based on Bureau of Labor Statistics (2013).

players in the 2006 state minimum wage ballot initiatives. Those efforts had a direct impact on several million workers at the time of the increases, and the effects continue in the states that now use indexing. For example, the Economic Policy Institute estimated that just over 1 million workers benefited from indexed wage increases in eight states on January 1, 2012 (Cooper 2012). According to Jen Kern, former director of the ACORN National Living Wage Resource Center, the experience gained and lessons learned from working on local campaigns helped advocates pass stronger minimum wage laws, such as ones that include indexing for inflation (Jen Kern, personal correspondence with the author, May 13, 2013).

CONCLUSION

Living wage campaigns have been one of the most successful pro-worker policy efforts of the last fifteen years. Popular support has been consistently high, and most major cities now have ordinances. However, living wage ordinances cover only a small proportion of low-wage workers. Wage levels have been significantly improved, but not necessarily high enough to raise workers out of poverty. And while the wage increases are substantial, on average they are lower than the median wage increase that low-wage workers experience from unionization (37 percent).

Raising the federal and state minimum wages, and indexing them, would be a more effective way to cover a large number of low-wage workers. Senate bill S.460 (Fair Minimum Wage Act of 2013) would affect over 30 million low-wage workers. Programs like universal health care and universal child care, as well as expanded affordable housing, would reduce expenses for low-wage workers and therefore lower the hourly wage needed for a living wage. Living wage activists have pursued living wage campaigns not because they are necessarily the most effective way to address the needs of low-income workers, but because they are more politically feasible, and because of other potential benefits as well, such as building new coalitions, developing or strengthening alliances, and supporting unionization efforts. Therefore, living wage ordinances should not necessarily be evaluated by the same criteria we might bring to evaluating other low-wage worker policy.

Other research assesses the impact of living wage campaigns on these other outcomes (coalition building, support for unionization). Here we have just tried to focus on the possibility of expanding living wage campaigns to cover a greater share of low-wage workers through campaigns that might be more feasible and might have some of the side benefits. The results suggest that certain avenues are more fruitful than others. Big-box ordinances would address some of the largest and most powerful low-wage employers, but if they cover only stores larger than 90,000 square feet and apply only to new development, their impact might not be great. And because ordinances affecting home health workers must be won primarily at the state level, these relatively difficult fights might just as likely be statewide minimum wage campaigns.

The more promising avenues for campaigns that would affect large numbers of low-wage workers yet remain local are ordinances that cover airports and ordinances or policies that apply to economic development projects, like the CRA policy in Los Angeles.

In addition, living wage activists should support campaigns that extend benefits to all workers, regardless of hours worked, and possibly "minimum shift hours" policies, in order to encourage the shift away from part-time work to more full-time jobs. In addition to a higher hourly wage, a reduction in involuntary part-time work would greatly assist workers living below the poverty line.

Still, our estimates suggest that living wage policies are not likely to reach the majority of the 37 million low-wage workers. The expansion proposed here would involve numerous difficult campaigns, each probably taking years and many resources and staff hours. The process of building a campaign may be useful in itself, however, and for that reason living wage campaigns can be valuable in ways that other policies may not be. But to truly make a dent in addressing low-wage work in the United States, much more dramatic efforts are necessary. The living wage movement may not be the most effective way to increase wages for large numbers of low-wage workers in the short run, but it may be one of the few ways to build the political power needed for greater change in the long run.

NOTES

1. The author thanks Arin Dube, Jen Kern, and Heidi Shierholz, plus anonymous reviewers, for comments on this chapter

2. See Julia Rosen, "Working Californian's L.A. Living Wage Poll," Calitics, January 29, 2007; and David Seifman, "74 Percent Support Increase in Living Wage. Poll," *New York Post,* December 14, 2011.

3. These laws have exemptions. For example, the Santa Fe law exempts firms with fewer than twenty-five employees and employees of the school district. The San Francisco law exempts workers who are not covered by the state minimum wage, such as workers classified as independent contractors.

4. They may bid by total hours of work instead of full-time equivalents (FTEs). Even if they bid by number of FTEs, there is no monitoring to verify the actual number of workers who do the job in the end.

5. For example, when my colleague and I submitted a Freedom of Information Act (FOIA) request to see the contracts held by the city of Boston, we were initially told that we would have to pay $18,000 for photocopying and staff time.

6. In fact, the lack of transparency around contracting practices and subsidy money is a strong motivation for living wage activism. Policymakers have been advocating greater reliance on the private sector for many years, on the premise that this automatically leads to cost savings and more effective service provision and development. Yet research shows that these promises often do not hold up (Chang 2008; Luce 2004; Sclar 2001). There is fraud and waste in the contracting and subsidy process, and some contractors have extracted excess profits by paying very low wages and providing no benefits. Living wage campaigns challenge the logic of privatization and reliance on the private sector.

7. In a few cities, employers challenged the scope of the law, arguing that their employees should not be covered since they worked on other contracts as well as on contracts with the city. For example, the industrial laundry company Cintas argued that it should be exempt from the L.A. living wage ordinance because its employees worked fewer than twenty hours a month on laundering city uniforms (covered under the city living wage ordinance), and because they launder city uniforms with other items, it was not possible for them to distinguish which employees washed the city uniforms. An appellate court ruled in favor of the workers. Cintas agreed to pay $6.5 million to settle the suit, giving over five hundred workers over $3.3 million in back wages and interest (McDonell 2009).

8. Three cities in Wisconsin passed citywide wage ordinances, but state law has since repealed these.

9. Data are from *State of Working America* (Mishel et al. 2013), using total non-farm employment. "Poverty level" is defined as the hourly wage needed to bring a full-time worker to the federal poverty line for a family of four.

10. See Wicks-Lim and Thompson (2010) for estimates of how high a minimum wage could go before there might be some job loss.
11. For more on using living wage campaigns to assist unionization, see Luce (2004).
12. This was Daley's only veto in nineteen years as mayor of Chicago.
13. There is no consistent data source for this information, but one estimate, by Timothy Bartik (2002), is that states and local governments spend $20 billion to $30 billion a year on economic development programs, and the federal government $6 billion per year.
14. GGP owns over two hundred malls and probably received much more than this in public subsidies, but the report focuses on only fifty of its malls.
15. I use data for "Regional Shopping Malls" for years 6 to 10. REMI provides estimates for malls in different types of settings (city, suburban, and metropolitan statistical area).
16. These might be tied to worker retention ordinances (WROs) that apply when the airport switches contractors. The WRO mandates that the new contractor must retain the existing employees and can fire them only for just cause. For example, the WRO at the Los Angeles airport mandates that a new contractor retain the workforce for ninety days. The initial campaign was launched after one thousand unionized food service workers on an airport contract were faced with losing their jobs when the airport awarded the contract to a non-union firm.
17. See, for example, Airport Group, UNITE HERE, "Five Things to Know About Developers: How BAA and Other Developers Shortchange Workers and Airports," available at: http://www.airportgroup.info/documents/Airport%20 Development%207-08.pdf (accessed September 2013).
18. Hartsfield-Jackson International Airport, "ATL Fact Sheet," available at: http://www.atlanta-airport.com/Airport/ATL/ATL_FactSheet.aspx (accessed September 2013).
19. Airport Group, UNITE HERE, "Five Things to Know About Developers."
20. The average shift for a football game is four hours, and with only ten home games a year, a football team generates only twenty to thirty full-time-equivalent jobs outside of the front office. However, the living wage applies to all employees, not just FTEs.
21. However, Colin Gordon (2008) finds that almost 30 percent of the jobs created were paying wages below the mandate, because they were probably set just above the mandate when created and then were not subject to annual cost-of-living increases.
22. The law requires a minimum of three hours' pay for shifts initially scheduled. Some U.S. states have a similar law. For example, New York State Protection of Employees (Part-time Work) Act of 2001 requires employers to pay workers for a minimum of four hours per shift, even if the employee is sent home early.

REFERENCES

Abbott, Ellen. 2012. "Syracuse Adds More Workers to Living Wage Law." WRVO Public Media, August 1. Available at: http://www.wrvo.fm/post/syracuse-adds-more-workers-living-wage-law (accessed September 2013).

Airports Council International. 2006. "Airports Stimulate Employment and Economic Growth." Geneva, Switzerland: ACI (April 11).

Allegretto, Sylvia A., Arindrajit Dube, and Michael Reich. 2011. "Do Minimum Wages Really Reduce Teen Employment? Accounting for Heterogeneity and Selectivity in State Panel Data." *Industrial Relations* 50(2): 205–40.

Bartik, Timothy J. 2002. "Evaluating the Impacts of Local Economic Development Policies on Local Economic Outcomes: What Has Been Done and What Is Doable?" Working Paper 03-89. Kalamazoo, Mich.: W. E. Upjohn Institute for Employment.

Brenner, Mark D., and Stephanie Luce. 2005. "Living Wage Laws in Practice: The Boston, New Haven, and Hartford Experiences." Amherst: University of Massachusetts, Political Economy Research Institute.

Bureau of Labor Statistics. 2012. *Occupational Outlook Handbook*. Washington: U.S. Department of Labor.

———. 2013. "Employment Situation Summary." Washington: U.S. Department of Labor.

Card, David, and Alan B. Krueger. 2000. "Minimum Wages and Employment: A Case Study of the Fast-Food Industry in New Jersey and Pennsylvania: Reply." *American Economic Review* 90(5): 1397–1420.

Chang, Ha-joon. 2008. *Bad Samaritans: The Myth of Free Trade and the Secret History of Capitalism*. London: Bloomsbury Press.

Cooper, David. 2012. "A Rising Tide for Increasing Minimum Wage Rates." Washington, D.C.: Economic Policy Institute, Working Economics blog (April 13). Available at: http://www.epi.org/blog/proposals-increasing-minimum-wage/ (accessed September 2013).

Cooper, David, and Doug Hall. 2013. "Raising the Federal Minimum Wage to $10.10 Would Give Working Families, and the Overall Economy, a Much-Needed Boost." Washington, D.C.: Economic Policy Institute (March 13). Available at: http://www.epi.org/publication/bp357-federal-minimum-wage-increase/ (accessed September 2013).

Dube, Arindrajit, T. William Lester, and Michael Reich. 2010. "Minimum Wage Effects Across State Borders: Estimates Using Contiguous Counties." *Review of Economics and Statistics* 92(4): 945–64.

Economic Policy Institute. 2006. "Hundreds of Economists Say: Raise the Minimum Wage." Washington, D.C.: Economic Policy Institute. Available at: http://www.epi.org/page/-/pdf/epi_minimum_wage_2006.pdf (accessed September 2013).

Fairris, David, David Runsten, Carolina Briones, and Jessica Goodheart. 2005. *The Los Angeles Living Wage Ordinance: Effects on Workers and Employers*. Los Angeles: Los Angeles Alliance for a New Economy.

Fox, Liana. 2006. "Minimum Wage Trends: Understanding Past and Contemporary Research." Washington, D.C.: Economic Policy Institute.

Good Jobs First. 2010. "Case Study of Professional Sports." Available at: http://www.goodjobsfirst.org/corporate-subsidy-watch/professional-sports (accessed August 9, 2012).

Gordon, Colin. 2008. "EZ Money: Assessing Iowa's Enterprise Zone Program." Iowa City: Iowa Fiscal Partnership.

Haley-Lock, Anna. 2011. "Place-Bound Jobs at the Intersection of Policy and Management: Employer Practices in Seattle, Chicago, and Vancouver Restaurant Chains." *American Behavioral Scientist* 55(7): 823–42.

Hamermesh, Daniel. 1996. *Labor Demand.* Princeton, N.J.: Princeton University Press.

Hirsch, Barry T., and David A. Macpherson. 2010. "Union Membership, Coverage, Density, and Employment by Occupation, 2012." Available at: www.unionstats.com (accessed September 2013).

Jacobs, Ken, Dave Graham-Squire, and Stephanie Luce. 2011. "How a Higher Wage Standard Would Impact Walmart Workers and Shoppers." Research Brief. Berkeley: University of California, Center for Labor Research and Education.

Kellerman, Josh, and Stephanie Luce. 2011. "The Walmartization of New York City." New York: ALIGN: The Alliance for a Greater New York. Available at: http://www.alignny.org/wp-content/uploads/2011/09/The-Walmartization-of-NYC-Sep-2011.pdf (accessed September 2013).

Lambert, Susan J., Anna Haley-Lock, and Julia R. Henly. 2012. "Schedule Flexibility in Hourly Jobs: Unanticipated Consequences and Promising Directions." *Community, Work, and Family* 15(3): 293–315.

Luce, Stephanie. 2004. *Fighting for a Living Wage.* Ithaca, N.Y.: Cornell University Press.

Mattera, Phillip, Thomas Cafcas, Leigh McIlvaine, Andrew Seifter, and Kasia Tarczynska. 2011. "Money for Something: Job Creation and Job Quality Standards in State Economic Development Subsidy Programs." Washington, D.C.: Good Jobs First.

Mattera, Philip, Allison Lack, and Karla Walter. 2007. "Growing at Whose Expense? How Tax Avoidance by Shopping Mall Developer General Growth Inc. Harms Communities and Burdens Other Tax Payers." Washington, D.C.: Good Jobs First.

McDonell, Patrick J. 2009. "Industrial Laundry Firm Settles 'Living Wage' Lawsuit." *Los Angeles Times,* December 18.

Mishel, Lawrence, Josh Bivens, Elise Gould, and Heidi Shierholz. 2013. *State of Working America,* 12th ed. Washington, D.C.: Economic Policy Institute.

National Employment Law Project. 2004. "Part-time Workers and Unemployment Insurance." March. Available at: http://www.nelp.org/page/-/UI/parttimeui0304.pdf (accessed September 2013).

Neumark, David, J. M. Ian Salas, and William Wascher. 2013. "Revisiting the Minimum Wage Debate: Throwing Out the Baby with the Bathwater?" Discussion Paper 7166. Bonn, Germany: Institute for the Study of Labor (IZA).

Neumark, David, and William Wascher. 2006. "Minimum Wage and Employment: A Review of Evidence from the New Minimum Wage Research." Working Paper 12663. Cambridge, Mass.: National Bureau of Economic Research.

Pollin, Robert. 2005. "The Albuquerque Living Wage Proposal: Rough Estimates of How Workers and Businesses Will Be Affected by the Measure." Working Paper 103. Amherst: University of Massachusetts, Political Economy Research Institute (September).

Pollin, Robert, and Mark D. Brenner. 2000. "Economic Analysis of the Santa Monica Living Wage Proposal." Amherst: University of Massachusetts, Political Economy Research Institute.

Pollin, Robert, Mark D. Brenner, Jeannette Wicks-Lim, and Stephanie Luce. 2008. A Measure of Fairness. Ithaca, N.Y.: Cornell University Press.

Reich, Michael, Peter Hall, and Ken Jacobs. 2003. "Living Wages and Economic Performance: The San Francisco Airport Model." Berkeley: University of California, Institute of Industrial Relations.

———. 2005. "Living Wage Policies at the San Francisco Airport: Impacts on Workers and Businesses." Industrial Relations 44(1): 106–38.

Reich, Michael, and Amy Latinen. 2003. "Raising Low Pay in a High-Income City: The Economics of a San Francisco Minimum Wage." Working Paper 99. Berkeley: University of California, Institute of Industrial Relations.

REMI Consulting, Inc. 2006. "Economic Impact of Shopping Center Developments: Final Report." Amherst, Mass.: Regional Economic Models, Inc.

Schmitt, John. 2013. "Studying the Studies on the Minimum Wage." Washington, D.C.: Center for Economic and Policy Research (February 26). Available at: http://www.cepr.net/index.php/blogs/cepr-blog/studying-the-studies-on-the-minimum-wage (accessed September 2013).

Schmitt, John, Margy Waller, Shawn Fremstad, and Ben Zipperer. 2007. "Unions and Upward Mobility for Low-Wage Workers." Washington, D.C.: Center for Economic and Policy Research.

Sclar, Eliot. 2001. You Don't Always Get What You Pay For: The Economics of Privatization. New York: Century Foundation.

Seigfried, John, and Andrew Zimbalist. 2000. "The Economics of Sports Facilities and Their Communities." Journal of Economic Perspectives 14(3): 95–114.

Spivack, Donald R. (retired Deputy Chief of Operations and Policy, Community Redevelopment Agency of Los Angeles). 2011. Testimony on INT. 251-A (The Fair Wages for New Yorkers Act) before the New York City Council Committee on Contracts. May 12.

Wicks-Lim, Jeannette, and Jeff Thompson. 2010. "Combining Minimum Wage and Earned Income Tax Credit Policies to Guarantee a Decent Living Standard to All U.S. Workers." Amherst: University of Massachusetts, Political Economy Research Institute.

Part IV | Social Insurance Programs and Low-Wage Work

Chapter 9 | Improving Low-Income Workers' Access to Unemployment Insurance

Jeffrey B. Wenger

UNEMPLOYMENT INSURANCE (UI) was passed into law in 1935 as part of the Social Security Act. The system was designed to serve two purposes: provide income to eligible workers during periods of involuntary job loss, and stabilize demand in local economies with high unemployment rates. The program provides benefits to workers who have a strong workforce attachment and who lose their jobs through no fault of their own. While the UI program in the United States aims to achieve these goals, it was designed to allow the methods by which the individual states pursue them to vary. Instead of operating as one national system, the UI program in the United States comprises fifty-one separate systems.[1]

Each of the separate systems is operated by the state in partnership with the federal government, and each state develops UI policies that establish the conditions for eligibility, benefit amounts, and tax schedules. However, the federal government ensures that state policies comply with federal statutes. On occasion, the federal government utilizes financial incentives and penalties to encourage states to adopt its preferred policies. To fund the UI program, the federal government collects tax revenue, while states collect the taxes that pay for UI benefits to individuals. Employers pay a lower tax rate if their former employees do not collect UI benefits, so employers have an incentive to minimize the number of unemployed workers receiving UI benefits.

Figure 9.1 illustrates the percentage of the U.S. labor force who were unemployed and the percentage of the labor force who received UI benefits during the last three decades. The insured unemployment rate is simply the percentage of the U.S. labor force receiving regular weekly

247

Figure 9.1 U.S. Total and Insured Unemployment, 1980 to 2011

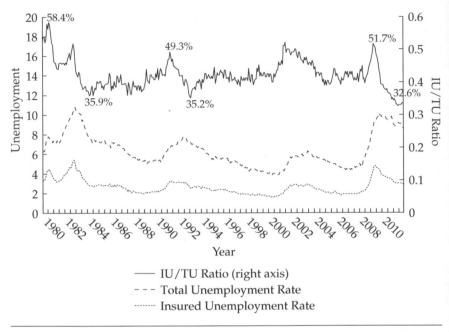

Source: Author's compilation based on U.S. Department of Labor, Employment and Training Administration (various years) and Center for Economic and Policy Research (2012).

benefits, and this rate is always less than the total unemployment rate. Between 1980 and approximately 2008, the gap between the two rates declined, meaning that a growing proportion of the unemployed had been receiving UI benefits; this modest increase followed two decades (1960 to 1980) of declines in the UI recipiency rate. As can be seen in the figure, during recessions the gap between the total unemployment (TU) rate and the insured unemployment rate increases. Surprisingly, the current recession has generated the largest decline in the IU/TU ratio since the 1980s, despite policies extending benefits for up to ninety-nine weeks. In 2011 the ratio reached a minimum at 32.6, indicating that fewer than one-third of the unemployed were receiving UI benefits.

In the 1920s and 1930s, when the UI system was designed and implemented, men represented a significant majority of the labor force; they were typically the "breadwinners" for their families and were the primary focus of the UI program. Many men worked in manufacturing and in unionized shops. During this early period, the percentage of the unemployed who received UI benefits often exceeded 60 percent. This high rate was due in part to UI's eligibility criteria being designed to benefit full-time workers with incomes large enough to support a family; as such, the eligibility rules explicitly made low-income and part-time workers ineligible for benefits.[2] This led to a system that often failed to cover earnings losses by women, workers in the service sector, or those without union representation. State eligibility rules failed to consider the social and economic issues that affect low-income workers' employment patterns (Lovell and Hill 2001; Um'rani and Lovell 2000). This was particularly true in the service sector, where workers experienced higher turnover and informal employment arrangements. From its inception, the design of the UI system created inequities between "core" workers (such as unionized manufacturing workers) seeking access to benefits and those on the "periphery."

Prior to the onset of the Great Recession in 2007, part-time workers were still largely ineligible for UI benefits because many states had interpreted "seeking employment" to mean searching for full-time employment (Wenger, McHugh, and Segal 2002). This stipulation is applied to workers who have historically worked part-time as well as individuals whose obligations, such as child care, prohibit them from working full-time. This criterion disproportionately hinders UI eligibility for women, since one-fourth of all unemployed women are seeking part-time jobs (U.S. Department of Labor 2000). To aid these part-time job-seekers, the American Recovery and Reinvestment Act (ARRA) of 2009 sought to expand UI eligibility among part-time workers. However, an analysis of national data indicates that this policy change is likely to have little effect (Shaefer 2010).

Overall, research also shows that the UI system tends to deny benefits to many workers while many others fail to file for benefits (Lovell and Hill 2001; National Employment Law Project 2001a, 2001b; Um'rani and Lovell 2000). The cumulative effects are evidenced in the consistently lower filing rates and take-up rates for women, part-time workers, service-sector workers, and those without union representation.[3] In general, it appears that the kinds of factors that limit eligibility (earnings requirements, intermittent employment, rules for part-time employment, and other disqualifications) have a sizable impact on UI take-up rates. However, there are other state-specific effects that reduce UI take-up but are more difficult to ascribe to UI policy attributes.

Nevertheless, UI remains an important program, owing largely to a lack of other resources for the working poor and the generally meager benefits from other poverty assistance programs. In this chapter, I discuss the structure of UI policy, focusing on the determinants of eligibility, financing, and benefit generosity and the disproportionate impact of these determinants on the working poor. I also discuss the UI program's implementation issues, which have received minimal attention in the literature. The effect of bureaucratic errors should not be underestimated—as many as 10 percent of UI claims are wrongfully denied owing to administrative error. After investigating the long-term trends in UI recipiency and discussing state-level effects and policy changes to determine the factors that lead to low UI recipiency rates, I conclude with policy recommendations and implications.

RISK-POOLING AND FAMILY RISK CAPACITY

Many people believe UI is the primary safety net for workers who have lost their job through no fault of their own, but this view cannot be consistently applied to the entire U.S. workforce. Because of the often burdensome requirements to qualify for UI, the primary safety net for low-wage workers who lose their jobs is family. Workers' families allow for pooled risk, helping cushion the effects of bad economic, social, and health-related outcomes. Recognizing the role of the family is not to harken back to a day when Ozzie and Harriett ruled the airwaves or to romanticize an age when women were economically trapped in marriages. My purpose in mentioning family here is to recognize that modern family structures and the lack of extensive family networks make the operation of the social insurance system more necessary, and the lack of access to UI potentially more problematic.

Although the Great Depression is often credited as the driving force behind the adoption of the Social Security Act, what is often omitted from this history is that work was already under way to set up the system. By the turn of the nineteenth century, economists had already recognized the severity of the poverty problem and how close to poverty many in the newly industrialized society were living. What made the phenomenon of poverty increasingly salient was its concentration in cities. Prior to mass industrialization, rural life afforded people access to food during economic downturns, whereas urban life offered no such relief. More importantly, moving from farm to factory often meant leaving extended family networks of support.

> Urbanization disrupted vital family support networks. The extended family had long served as a critical risk management device in rural communities. When one family member fell sick or was otherwise incapacitated for a lengthy period, others often lent a hand to support him and his dependents. (Moss 2002, 154–55)

The consequence of mass urbanization was to leave industrial workers entirely dependent on their wages. With the disruption of family networks, spells of unemployment—even relatively short spells—could lead to a downward spiral of increasingly desperate poverty. The risk of poverty, even absent an economic depression, made providing unemployment insurance a necessity.

The necessity comes about because the economic risks faced by most families are greater than a single family can self-insure against. Families remain an extremely important buffer against economic hardship, but a buffer that is insufficient given modern exigencies. However, when families have a very limited capacity to help (their insurance capacity is limited), one spell of unemployment or illness may result in economic catastrophe for the extended family. Indeed, even when families have the capacity to help, there is no guarantee that help will be forthcoming, and given the low levels of savings and the skewed distribution of wealth, most families have only a limited capacity to help during economic crisis.

Most analysts who evaluate the risk-pooling effects of family have focused on families' positive benefits. For insurance to be fully effective, however, risks have to be independent. This is clearly not the case with families—illnesses are often contagious, industrial disruption may be regional or industry specific, and many workers within the family are often employed in the same industry. The lack of independent risk makes families less than the ideal social unit for self-insuring. This is especially true when the size of the economic misfortune is larger than a single family's capacity to carry itself through the hardship. It is often said that UI was designed to provide temporary income to people during periods of involuntary unemployment. But it is equally true that UI was designed because families lacked the capacity to bear the economic risks of industrial production. Since the benefits of insurance are coupled with the costs of providing aid, it is not clear that families can shoulder the burden. Instead of being able to provide benefits to family members who are unemployed, a family may be unable to pay such benefits, and one person's misfortune may then compromise the financial security of the entire family.

Similarly, workers with limited resources may have significant demands placed on them by elderly parents or children and may become involuntarily unemployed through their own illness or because of their caretaking responsibilities. In most cases, "involuntariness" is understood to mean that the unemployment spell was not the worker's fault, and many states have provisions for leaving work because of illness and caregiving tasks. However, most states fail to apprise workers of these policies, and their utilization is uncommon. In other states, laws and regulations make it more difficult to leave employment for good cause related to illness or caregiving.

In the sections that follow, I discuss the policies that create barriers for low-income workers to be eligible for UI. Unlike previous analysis, I also examine the role of policy implementation and the role of the UI bureaucracy (to the extent possible) in making UI less available to low-income workers.

POLICY ISSUES

To be eligible for UI benefits in a given state, a worker must satisfy three requirements: meet or exceed the minimum earnings threshold; have a qualifying reason for job separation; and be actively and continuously searching for employment. The earnings threshold is set by each state and helps determine the extent of labor force attachment, while separation requirements determine who was responsible for separation from the job in question. In cases where the worker was responsible for the job separation because he or she quit or was terminated for misconduct, benefit payments are denied. When the employer lays off workers due to slack demand, the unemployed person is most likely to meet the separation requirements. The final test of eligibility is whether the worker is able to work and continuously available for work. An unemployed person is eligible for UI benefits when all three conditions are met.

For many low-income workers who leave their jobs, the reasons for job separation are complex. Many low-income workers quit employment because of work conditions, personal illness, child care necessities, or transportation issues. In most states, leaving employment as a result of illness or to provide care or meet other family obligations is considered "good cause," and the UI policies in place allow workers to be eligible for UI benefits. In other states, the requirements for establishing good cause for illness or family obligations fall heavily on the employee. In these states, a physician must advise leaving work for a worker to be eligible for UI benefits due to illness, or the worker must negotiate with the employer for reasonable accommodations. Both of these added requirements make it more unlikely that workers will receive UI benefits, and if they are eligible, it is unclear whether they will satisfy the "able and available" requirements.

The second issue related to illness and family obligations is that these factors tend to reduce wages and cause employment to be sporadic. Even prior to welfare reform, most women who received welfare worked while receiving benefits, and most welfare exits occurred as a result of transitioning to work (Harris 1993). However, work histories were often interrupted, and job tenures were short (Edin and Lein 1997). As a consequence, workers earned less and thus found it more difficult to qualify for UI benefits. With the current weak labor market and stagnant or declining wages, many workers find it increasingly difficult to qualify for UI. Even in the robust labor market of the late 1990s, many workers left welfare and failed to earn enough money to qualify for UI benefits (Boushey and Wenger 2006).

A third issue facing the unemployed is the financing of the UI system. Many state trust funds are depleted, requiring them to borrow heavily from the federal government. The UI system has a negative net balance, with total borrowing by the end of the third quarter of 2011 in excess of $38 billion while trust fund balances equaled only $12.7 billion. In the late 1970s and early 1980s, such trust fund insolvency led to considerable reductions in benefit generosity and eligibility. Similarly, between 2004 and 2009, twenty-five states made significant increases in the earnings requirement necessary to qualify for UI benefits. Along these lines, Daniel Smith and Jeffrey Wenger (2013) find that trust fund balances play an important role in altering benefit generosity: when UI trust funds are exhausted, the amount of available benefits falls, and the effect can be large and last for a number of years. Also, given that the fiscal situation of the UI trust funds is not likely to improve in the near future, legislatures will be faced with the dilemma of raising taxes, cutting benefits, or reducing the number of eligible beneficiaries. This will clearly have a disproportionate impact on lower-income workers should they become unemployed.

IMPLEMENTATION ISSUES

Among the lesser-studied and more poorly understood aspects of the UI system are the differences between state UI recipiency rates. The recipiency rate, which is simply the ratio of the number of unemployed individuals receiving regular UI benefits to the number of unemployed individuals, varies widely across states. Six states have recipiency rates that exceed 40 percent of the total unemployed population, while five other states have rates below 20 percent. Although some of this difference is due to industrial composition that differs by region and to varying policies that determine eligibility, these two aspects cannot fully explain the wide range of recipiency rates across the United States.

Perhaps more disconcerting is the gap between total unemployment in the United States and the percentage of unemployed receiving benefits. When the unemployment rate peaked at 10.8 percent in November 1982, the percentage of the labor force receiving UI benefits was 5.4 percent—a ratio of 0.50. In the current economic downturn, national unemployment peaked at 10.1 percent in October 2009 while the percentage of unemployed workers receiving benefits was 4.4 percent—a ratio of 0.44.[4] A one-percentage-point decline in the percentage of workers receiving UI benefits translates to nearly 1 million fewer workers receiving UI benefits.

Finally, what is particularly interesting about the decline in benefit payments relative to unemployment is that the gap between unemployment rates and the percentage of the unemployed receiving benefits has narrowed during the thirty years preceding the current economic crisis; it is only during the most recent recession that the gap has increased. While policy changes probably explain some of this (in particular increases in earnings requirements), those changes are insufficient to fully explain the differences in UI recipiency across states.

It would seem plausible that the administration of the UI program would make a difference in the proportion of the unemployed population eligible for benefits. Research on bureaucratic discretion has produced several different views of how bureaucrats use their discretion and its ultimate impact on outcomes for clients. One view holds that bureaucrats use their discretion to "stretch the law" to respond to the needs of their clients (Keiser 1999; Keiser et al. 2002; Maynard-Moody and Musheno 2003). Under this view, minority and female bureaucrats use their discretion to reduce the disparate treatment that minority and female clients have historically received from an agency and to improve outcomes for these clients. This allows bureaucrats to pursue more equitable outcomes for their clients. In her work on social security disability benefits, Lael Keiser (1999) finds support for this view. She concludes that street-level bureaucrats who administer disability programs rely on professional norms and consider the client's level of need when making decisions. Similarly, Steven Maynard-Moody and Michael Musheno (2003) examine the stories of 150 street-level bureaucrats and offer evidence that they act as agents of the clients (or citizens). According to Maynard-Moody and Musheno, these "citizen agents" assess the needs and worthiness of individual clients in determining eligibility and do not rely exclusively on the rules and hierarchies of the organization.

The bureaucrats working in public agencies are often the first, and sometimes the only, contact that the public has with the bureaucracy. Because this contact is most often with street-level bureaucrats who exercise discretion, their attitudes, values, and predispositions are important factors in determining whether clients are provided aid or are further disadvantaged (Lipsky 1980). In some contexts, the race and sex of the bureaucrat and the culture of the bureaucracy may determine, at least in part, how willing a public agent is to advocate on behalf of a client.

When the bureaucrat and the client share an attribute (such as race), the bureaucrat may be more willing to stretch the rules to overcome past discriminatory factors. In the administration of UI benefits, the majority of bureaucrats are male, and they may be less willing (or able) to sympathize with the combination of difficulties arising from child care and family responsibilities combined with unemployment. Jeffrey Wenger and Vicky Wilkins (2009) have tested this claim by examining the recent introduction of telephone claims in state unemployment insurance offices. Using state-level panel data from 1992 to 2005, they estimate the effect of filing a claim via telephone rather than in person. They contend that if street-level bureaucrats in this agency use their discretion to disentitle and punish clients they deem "undeserving" of policy benefits, then the introduction of automation could increase UI payments for clients. Indeed, they found that automated telephone claims filing increased the number of women receiving UI benefits while having no effect on the number of men. They posit that this finding is due in part to the elimination of the biases that women previously faced when they entered a UI office.

Altering the amount of discretion that bureaucrats are able to exercise or the number of errors made by frontline workers can have tremendous effects on the UI system and UI recipients. Besides its possible effect on eliminating biases against women clients, the automation of the claims process has curtailed discretion in UI systems in other ways as well. In an increasingly automated environment, bureaucrats have little control over the input of data by claimants and management has increased opportunities for monitoring. Also, given the possibility that clients will deal with multiple bureaucrats, coworkers can now identify agents whose denial rates are higher or lower than the norm. In these ways, automation of the UI system has been not entirely detrimental to the unemployed.

The public administration literature has also begun paying attention to bureaucratic error as a critical performance measure. Unlike most programs, the UI program has systematically collected performance data and independently audited those data to determine error responsibility (employer, employee, or agency). In a recent analysis of these data, Sangyub Ryu, Jeffrey Wenger, and Vicky Wilkins (2012) examine the probability that a bureaucrat will make an error and theorize about the reasons for bureaucratic errors. They find that the previous UI office error rate is a good predictor of current error rates, demonstrating that poor performers remain poor performers. This finding is somewhat disheartening for UI claimants, in that low performance is systematic and often leads to their being wrongfully denied benefits. Additionally, local offices with high error rates account for a disproportionate percentage of the errors, indicating a need to examine agency management.

Second, errors are more commonly made on cases involving white UI claimants and claimants with a college education. In the cases studied by Ryu, Wenger, and Wilkins, white claimants and college-educated claimants were more likely to be wrongfully denied benefits. The authors indicate that bureaucrats may work from "rules of thumb," or preconceived ideas, about whose application needs additional scrutiny. When claims conform to the expectations of bureaucrats (when the situation is "normal"), the bureaucrat can safely rely on shortcuts and easily adjudicate the claim. This kind of assessment is often optimal: bureaucrats must process many claims, and paying strict attention to details cannot be sustained over the course of months and years. In cases that are outside the norm, the bureaucrat is less likely to rely on rules of thumb and will more heavily scrutinize the claim; the extra scrutiny, in turn, lowers the likelihood that the claim will be wrongfully denied. The bureaucrat may provide additional scrutiny to a claim by an African American, thereby reducing the likelihood of making a wrongful denial; this is the same as making more errors for white claimants by providing less scrutiny to those claims. Finally, we find that claimants who have higher self-valuation are less likely to experience agency errors. Taken together, these results point to the presence of systematic agency errors in UI programs. Public managers and the unemployed would be better served if training efforts and performance targets were developed with these systematic error effects in mind.

STATE-TO-STATE DIFFERENCES AND THE CHANGING NATURE OF UNEMPLOYMENT INSURANCE

Trends in UI Recipiency Before and After Welfare Reform

Figure 9.2 presents a picture of state-level recipiency rates for UI benefits. In this figure, we examine state-to-state differences in UI recipiency. The recipiency rate is the percentage of unemployed receiving UI benefits relative to total unemployment. For reference, the U.S. average recipiency rate (not shown) in 2011 was 28 percent. We should note that no state has a recipiency rate higher than 53 percent (Alaska) and that the remainder of the states have recipiency rates below 50 percent. This is a surprising development considering that the national average was 51 percent in April 2009. Even with this low national average, many states have rates significantly below the U.S. average, owing, in part, to the level of discretion that each state exercises in setting UI policy, as well as industrial composition and unionization rates. For example, Arkansas is the only Southern state that has a recipiency rate above 30 percent; Florida and Texas more accurately reflect the regional norm with recipiency rates of

Figure 9.2 UI Recipiency Rates (by Region), 2011

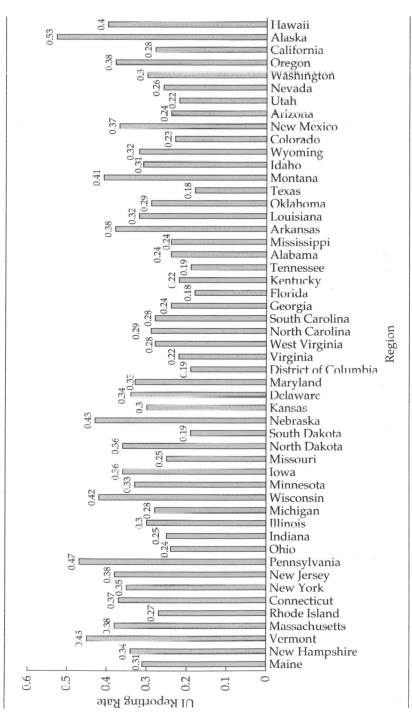

Source: Author's compilation based on U.S. Department of Labor, Employment and Training Administration (various years).

18 percent. Clearly when fewer than one in five unemployed workers is receiving UI, the program is failing to provide temporary income or maintain consumer demand.

Contrasts between adjacent states can be stark as well. In Ohio, for example, only 24 percent of the unemployed are receiving regular state benefits, while 47 percent of the unemployed in neighboring Pennsylvania receive regular state benefits. Meanwhile, in the Southwest, New Mexico's UI recipiency rate (37 percent) dwarfs Arizona's (24 percent).

Our examination of the trends in UI recipiency concludes with a look at the percentage of first payments as a fraction of initial claims, using a standard regression framework. For the period prior to welfare reform (1976 to 1995) and the period after welfare reform (1996 to 2011), using monthly data from each state, we estimate the following equation:

$$\left(\frac{First\ Payments}{Initial\ Claims}\right)_{i,t} = \alpha + \beta_1 Trend + \beta_2 Unemployment\ Rate_{i,t} + \sigma_i + \mu_{i,t} \quad (9.1)$$

We also include in each specification a state fixed-effect and month indicator variable to adjust for seasonality. In the first model, we find that, over time, states increased the proportion of first payments made relative to the number of initial claims. For each year that passed before welfare reform, we see an increase in the first payment rate of 0.116 percent. In the years after welfare reform, we find that the trend reverses sign, lowering the first payment rate by 0.047 percent each year. However, this change in the trend is probably not the effect of welfare reform, but rather an effect of the current recession, which has caused states to tighten their fiscal belts. When we estimate equation 9.1 from 1976 to 2005, the trend variable is still positive and statistically significant. It is only when we estimate the effect from 2005 to 2011 that the coefficient on the trend variable turns negative and becomes statistically significant. It appears that the trend has been for states to make fewer first payments relative to initial claims as a result of the weak recovery and recession. One interpretation is that over time workers have learned not to apply for UI benefits if they are unlikely to receive them, and this would make each applicant more likely to receive benefits but would also lower overall recipiency rates, since fewer people are applying and thus "self-selecting" out of participation.

A second set of evidence gathered from these results is the state-level effects. In each model, we include a state-specific dummy variable that controls for time-invariant effects. Although many state-level parameters are changing (such as benefit generosity, earnings requirements, and labor force demographics), the state indicators tell us about the potential unique effect of each state owing to the other unobserved (and time-invariant factors). It is interesting to note that in no case are we able to reject the null hypothesis that the state-level fixed effects are jointly zero. This provides at least tangential evidence that state-specific attributes such as implementation, culture, and the financial soundness of the UI program can determine policy outcomes in a fundamental way. In general we find that Northeastern states have higher recipiency rates and more generous benefits, while states in the South fare considerably worse on both measures.

Multiple researchers have investigated the reasons behind the long-term decline in UI recipiency, which peaked at 49.2 percent in 1975.[5] Daniel McMurrer and Amy Chasinov (1995) investigated the reasons for the long-term decline and concluded that the characteristics of the U.S. labor force have changed in ways that systematically reduce recipiency. Migration from the Midwest to the Southeast and Mountain regions of the country, where UI recipiency rates are lower than the national average, lowered overall recipiency; this finding is similar to the findings of Rebecca Blank and David Card (1991). A second reason for the overall decline was employment reductions in industries with traditionally higher UI recipiency rates (construction, manufacturing, mining) as well as declines in private-sector unionization rates. McMurrer and Chasinov also determined that the shift in demographics to a younger, more mobile, and more female workforce led to lower UI recipiency rates.

Monetary Eligibility

Did differences among states make a difference in UI uptake? When we examined whether states with illness and caregiving "good cause" exemptions are more likely to pay benefits to workers, we found that these states paid a small proportion of first payments as a fraction of initial claims. This result held for the whole sample (1990 to 2010) and for the 2005 to 2010 subsample. The difference between take-up rates in states with hard-to-satisfy good cause exemptions compared to states with more liberal good cause exemptions was statistically significant at better than the 1 percent level.

Table 9.1 provides summary information about the earnings requirements for UI eligibility in each state for the 2010 calendar year. As discussed earlier, UI earnings requirements differ dramatically across the states. Although some states have week- or hours-based requirements, states typically require earnings in multiple quarters. The base year constitutes the four quarters of earnings that determine eligibility, with one of the four quarters in the base period marked as the "high quarter" (that is, the quarter during which the worker earned the most money during the base period). Some states require relatively large earnings within the high quarter in order to achieve eligibility; these high-quarter requirements are often more difficult

Table 9.1   State-Level Earnings Requirements
and Median Wages, 2010

State	High Quarter (HQ)	Base Period (BP)	Median Hourly Wage (Women, High School or Less)	Hours Required to Qualify for Benefits	
				HQ	BP
Alabama	>$1,157	>$2,314 (in two HQs)	$10.00	115.70	231.4
Alaska		$2,500	$12.35		202.4
Arizona	$1,500	$2,250	$11.00	136.4	204.5
Arkansas		$2,187	$10.00	—	218.7
California	$900	$1,125	$10.75	83.7	104.7
Colorado	$1,084 (in two HQs)	$2,500	$11.00	98.5	227.3
Connecticut		$600	$12.60	—	47.6
Delaware		$720	$12.57	—	57.3
District of Columbia	$1,300	$1,950	$12.15	107.0	160.5
Florida	$2,267	$3,400	$11.08	204.6	306.9
Georgia	$567	$1,134 (in two HQs)	$10.25	55.3	110.6
Hawaii		$130	$12.00	—	10.8
Idaho	$1,872	$2,340	$10.00	187.2	234.0
Illinois		$1,600	$10.70	—	149.5
Indiana	$2,800	$4,200	$10.25	273.2	409.8
Iowa	$1,290	$1,940	$10.89	118.5	178.1
Kansas	$2,542	$3,240	$10.25	248.0	316.1
Kentucky	$1,963	$2,944	$10.00	196.3	294.4
Louisiana	$800	$1,200	$9.80	81.6	122.4
Maine	$1,383 (in two HQs)	$4,148	$10.90	127.2	380.6
Maryland	>$576	$900	$12.00	48.0	75.0
Massachusetts		$3,500	$12.00	—	291.7
Michigan	$2,871	$4,307	$11.00	261.0	391.5
Minnesota	$1,000	$1,250	$11.50	87.0	108.7
Mississippi	$780	$1,200	$10.00	78.0	120.0
Missouri	$1,500	$2,250	$11.00	136.4	204.5

(Table continues on p. 261.)

Table 9.1   (Continued)

State	High Quarter (HQ)	Base Period (BP)	Median Hourly Wage (Women, High School or Less)	Hours Required to Qualify for Benefits	
				HQ	BP
Montana	$1,521	$2,305	$10.30	147.7	223.8
Nebraska	$800	>$2,807	$10.90	73.4	257.5
Nevada	$400	$600	$12.00	33.3	50.0
New Hampshire	$1,400	$2,800	$12.00	116.7	233.3
New Jersey		$2,900	$12.00	—	241.7
New Mexico	$1,750	$1,751	$10.25	170.7	170.8
New York	$1,600	$2,400	$11.50	139.1	208.7
North Carolina	$1,118	$4,558	$10.50	106.5	434.1
North Dakota	$1,864	$2,795	$10.65	175.0	262.4
Ohio		$4,300	$11.13	—	386.3
Oklahoma	$375	$1,500	$10.25	36.6	146.3
Oregon	$667	$1,000	$10.00	66.7	100.0
Pennsylvania	$800	$1,320	$11.50	69.6	114.8
Rhode Island	$1,480	$2,960	$11.00	134.5	269.1
South Carolina	$1,092	$4,455	$10.25	106.5	434.6
South Dakota	$728	$1,288	$10.52	69.2	122.4
Tennessee	>$780	>$1,560	$10.20	76.5	152.9
Texas	$1,488	$2,220	$10.00	148.8	222.0
Utah	$2,066	$3,100	$10.68	193.4	290.3
Vermont	$2,203	$3,085	$11.50	191.6	268.3
Virginia		$2,700 (in two HQs)	$10.15	—	266.0
Washington	600 hours		$11.12		—
West Virginia		$2,200	$10.02	—	219.6
Wisconsin	$1,350	$1,890	$11.00	122.7	171.8
Wyoming	$2,215	$3,100	$10.00	221.5	310.0

Source: Author's compilation based on Center for Economic and Policy Research (2012) and U.S. Department of Labor, Employment and Training Administration (various years).
Note: Median wages are for all women, with high school diploma or less education. The author thanks John Schmitt for making and updating the CEPR ORG files.

to satisfy for low-income workers than base period earnings requirements. High-quarter earnings requirements range from a high of $2,800 in Indiana to a low of $375 in Oklahoma.

Monetary requirements provide only part of the information necessary to assess how difficult it will be for low-income workers to qualify for UI benefits. To make an accurate assessment we must compare monetary requirements to labor market earnings information. Table 9.1 shows the median hourly wage for women in each state, calculated by using the Current Population Survey (Outgoing Rotation Groups); that median hourly wage is used to determine the number of hours that a woman would have to work in order to satisfy the high-quarter and base period earnings requirements. In general, the states with the highest earnings requirements also require the most hours of work in order to qualify. In Indiana (the state with the highest quarterly earnings requirement), a woman earning the median wage ($10.25 per hour) would have to work 273 hours in a quarter to qualify for benefits. If she earned wages at the twenty-fifth percentile ($9.00 per hour), she would have to work 311 hours in the quarter. In both of these cases, low-income women would have to work more hours for the quarter than a typical part-time schedule allows. Kansas and Michigan would also require that women earning at the twenty-fifth percentile work, on average, more than twenty hours per week (for at least a quarter) in order to qualify for benefits.

Although we have highlighted those states where earnings requirements may be difficult to achieve, fourteen states have earnings requirements necessitating fewer than one hundred hours of work at the median wage in order to meet the state's high-quarter threshold. In general, the main issue is not workers failing to meet the earnings requirements for monetary eligibility. Anu Rangarajan and her colleagues (2001), in their analysis of welfare-leavers (post–welfare reform), find that most workers achieve monetary eligibility. Their study focused exclusively on New Jersey, a state with relatively low earnings requirements ($2,900 in the base period). But New Jersey also required that a worker have wages in at least twenty weeks to be eligible. Of those who left welfare for employment (that is, they had employment earnings in the three months after leaving welfare), 60 percent attained UI monetary eligibility. The largest percentage of welfare-leavers to attain monetary eligibility occurred five quarters after welfare exit; in no other quarter did eligibility exceed 60 percent. Utilizing national data and the UI eligibility thresholds in all fifty states, Boushey and Wenger (2006) found that, despite a strong labor market in the late 1990s relative to the early 1990s, former welfare recipients were less likely to meet the earnings requirements for UI eligibility, owing largely to an increase in the share of welfare-leavers with little or no earnings. Selection effects (positive selection into leaving welfare prior to reform) played a significant role in Boushey

Table 9.2   States That Raised the Base Period Earnings Requirements
Faster Than the Median Wage, 1990 to 2010

1990 to 1995	1995 to 2000	2005 to 2010
Delaware	Alabama	Alaska
	Colorado	Arkansas
	Florida	District of Columbia
		Idaho
		Indiana
Iowa		Iowa
Kansas		Kansas
Maine		Maine
Massachusetts	Massachusetts	Massachusetts
	Michigan	Michigan
	Nebraska	Nebraska
Montana		New Jersey
New Mexico	New Mexico	New Mexico
	New York	
North Carolina		North Carolina
Ohio		Ohio
Texas		Rhode Island
Utah	Utah	Utah
Vermont		Vermont
		Virginia
		Wisconsin
Wyoming		Wyoming

Source: Author's analysis of U.S. Department of Labor, Employment and Training Administration (various years).

and Wenger's conclusion that welfare-leavers in the post-welfare reform era were qualifying for benefits, because many leavers, by dint of not having wages, were not included in the post-reform analyses.

We should exercise caution in inferring too much from any of these studies for today's labor market. These analyses of welfare-leavers were conducted at a time of historically low unemployment and significant wage gains for the lowest quartile of the earnings distribution. Additionally, this was a time when UI monetary eligibility requirements were relatively low and had not been increased in the recent past. Table 9.2 provides information on the increase in monetary requirements over three periods; only states that raised their monetary eligibility requirements are listed. Immediately prior to welfare reform (1990 to 1995), only thirteen states had raised their earnings requirements at all. Consequently, as wages increased the proportion of workers eligible to receive UI benefits in the event of becoming unemployed also rose. Similarly, only nine states raised their earnings requirements immediately following welfare reform (1995 to 2000). The last period (2005 to 2010) paints quite a different picture—twenty-one states raised their earnings requirement during this five-year span. Given the relatively weak labor market and slow wage growth from 2005 to 2010, these increases were significant. In fact, all of the increases were larger than the median wage growth in the respective state over the same period.[6]

As an example, Massachusetts raised its earnings requirements at a faster rate than the rate of growth in the median wage during all three time periods—from $1,200 to $2,000 between 1990 and 1995, from $2,000 to $2,700 between 1995 and 2000, and from $3,000 to $3,500 between 2005 and 2010. The cumulative increase, when compared with the rate of growth for the average wage of women workers, paints an even bleaker picture. While the earnings requirement nearly tripled ($3,500/$1,200 = 2.92), the median wage of women in Massachusetts increased by less than double (from $9.20 to $17.50; $17.50/$9.20 = 1.90). During the same time period, the median wage of women across the United States also increased at a rate well below that of the earnings requirement in Massachusetts (from $7.50 to $14.50; $14.50/$7.50 = 1.93). Massachusetts is not alone, however, in raising the earnings requirement at a rate greater than wage growth: Utah and New Mexico have also engaged in the practice, despite state politics that are considerably different. The determinants of earnings requirements certainly warrant additional research since research on these factors is virtually nonexistent.

Further increases in earnings requirements are likely to come. As a way to directly cut costs, states can reduce the total number of weeks that individuals are eligible to receive UI, reduce benefit amounts, reduce access to the program, or enact a combination of these approaches. Given the poor fiscal health of the UI trusts, states are likely to reduce access to their UI programs by continuing to raise earnings requirements for eligibility. It is likely that it was more difficult to make changes in 2012 since it was an election year, but steps to reduce access are likely to be taken in 2013. Additionally, raising the earnings requirements directly affects the lowest-wage workers who are the most vulnerable, but as a "technical" issue, it captures scant media or public attention.

Nonmonetary Eligibility and Nonfilers

Although much attention has been focused on monetary eligibility for UI, this is not the most significant barrier to UI receipt for low-income workers. The biggest barriers to receiving UI benefits are nonmonetary in nature, such as shifts in population and industry, failure to apply for UI benefits, failure to meet nonmonetary eligibility requirements, and inability to retain a qualifying job. Despite the quantity and magnitude of these barriers, they may be the most difficult to overcome in an effort to increase UI recipiency. Luke Shaefer (2010) finds that a large majority of disadvantaged workers in the United States meet UI earning requirements. However, low-income workers face barriers to accessing UI benefits because they assume that they are ineligible or they fail to meet nonmonetary eligibility requirements (for example, having voluntarily quit or having been terminated for cause). These finding are consistent with survey data on why unemployed workers do not receive UI benefits (Vroman 1991; Wandner and Stettner 2000).

Unfortunately, there is limited evidence about the specific reasons why large populations of workers fail to apply for UI benefits when they are eligible. More direct and microlevel evidence about nonfiling comes from Wayne Vroman (1991), who evaluated the responses to the first Current Population Survey supplementary questionnaire on UI nonfiling. The survey was administered to approximately three thousand households where at least one worker was unemployed and inquired as to whether the unemployed person in the household applied for and received UI benefits. If the unemployed person had not received benefits, follow-up questions explored why that person had not applied for, received, or otherwise believed himself or herself to be eligible for benefits. Vroman found that there were three factors that led to the decline of the percentage of the unemployed receiving benefits: the change in the regional composition of unemployment (movement from Rust Belt states to Sun Belt states); a change in the industrial composition of unemployment; and a decline in union membership.

Wandner and Stettner (2000) conducted a follow-up analysis using data collected in 1993 that included 4,500 respondents. The data included more detailed information about job prospects, such as whether the worker was expecting a recall, whether the worker had a job in hand, or whether the worker was confident about finding a job quickly. Wandner and Stettner (2000, 6) found that "between 55 and 65 percent (depending on the business cycle) of experienced unemployed workers do not file for benefits." Even among job-losers (those most likely to be eligible for benefits), 40 percent of nonfilers chose not to apply for reasons unrelated to their perceived ineligibility.

Analysts have long recognized the importance of nonmonetary barriers to UI. Christopher O'Leary and Stephen Wandner (1997) point to important policy changes in the UI system that have made it much more difficult for certain groups of workers to receive UI benefits, in particular those who left work voluntarily, were discharged for misconduct, or refused suitable work. In 1952 only twelve states disqualified a claimant for the duration of the unemployment spell if the claimant had left employment voluntarily; by 1990 all fifty states had such a policy. Kelleen Kaye (1997, 2001), Rangarajan, Corson, and Wood (2001), and Shaefer (2010) all note that nonmonetary eligibility presents significant barriers for low-income workers to qualify for benefits. For example, Rangarajan and her colleagues (2001) find that among welfare recipients earning enough to achieve eligibility, 50 percent were ineligible for UI because they had voluntarily left their job. In general, only 30 percent of welfare recipients achieved both monetary and nonmonetary eligibility; the largest share (45 percent) earned enough, but their reasons for job separation were likely to have made them ineligible for benefits; 25 percent of welfare-leavers (who had left for employment) did not achieve monetary eligibility.

Luke Shaefer (2010) arrives at a similar set of conclusions using nationally representative data from the Survey of Income and Program Participation (SIPP). Shaefer finds evidence that most workers surveyed had attained monetary eligibility and finds no evidence that restricting UI benefits to full-time workers significantly reduced UI receipt among part-time workers. Perhaps most importantly, he questions whether reforming UI eligibility policies related to part-time work or the alternate base period will significantly reduce disparities between higher- and lower-paid workers. Similar to other findings, Shaefer reports that only half of the workers who are disadvantaged and eligible for benefits actually receive them. This may be largely due to the lack of understanding about the program or the administrative burden of applying for benefits.

Job Retention Programs

Research has consistently found that earnings among the poor are not the most important barrier to achieving UI eligibility. Instead, the reasons for job separation are the single most important factor in disqualifying workers from eligibility. Rangarajan and her colleagues (2001) find that for former welfare recipients who had experienced a job separation, 44 percent had quit their job, 16 percent were fired, and 40 percent were laid off (all self-reported numbers). Of those who quit, more than half (52 percent) quit for job-related reasons. As discussed earlier, health and child care reasons were also important factors: fully 25 percent of those who quit work did so for these reasons. If the definitions of leaving for good cause were systematically expanded and consistently applied by state agencies, many workers might be in a better position to attain eligibility.

However, there are still more than 50 percent of job-quitters who leave work for job-related reasons. Recent research has focused attention on job retention for lower-wage workers; in general, the results have not been encouraging. From 2003 to 2006, a series of experimental studies were conducted in seven regions of the United Kingdom. In the Employment Retention and Advancement Program, workers were provided with advisory and financial incentives to help sustain their employment and promote their job advancement. A rigorous evaluation of the experimental evidence found short-term earnings gains for two of the single-parent treatment groups, generally in the form of a larger proportion of the treatment group working more hours. By year three there were no differences between control and experimental groups on most measures. However, the long-term unemployed treatment group, consisting mostly of men, experienced significant, substantial, and sustained increases in earnings (see Hendra et al. 2011).

Another set of studies in the United States used random assignment design to test the effectiveness of programs designed to help "at-risk" workers stay employed and advance in their jobs. Of the twelve sites evaluated by MDRC, only three had positive impacts. Although this evaluation demonstrates that policy interventions aimed at employee retention can work, it also points to the difficulty of developing, implementing, and maintaining these programs, since 75 percent of them showed no significant improvements. Even among the programs that were successful, differences between experimental and control groups tended to fade over time. Finally, rates of job loss among the at-risk population were high, and staffing the program with qualified candidates was difficult. This second issue was critical, since the actions of the staff were often instrumental in influencing work outcomes for program participants.

Overall, the experimental evidence on job retention is somewhat discouraging. In their review of the policy evaluation literature, Harry Holzer and Karin Martinson (2005, 21) find that "relatively few programs improve retention and advancement with certainty. Many promising efforts have not yet been rigorously evaluated; others have, but their success rate is mixed, and our ability to replicate successes and implement them on a large scale remains uncertain." They also describe some policies that might be helpful in mending the safety net for low-income workers. In general, financial incentives and supports tend to be more successful than programs without these features. Policies that promote full-time work and longer spells of employment are more likely to enable workers to qualify for benefits if they should be laid off. Despite these attempts to ensure qualification for benefits, however, "voluntary" turnover among the low-paid remains high.

CONCLUSION AND POLICY RECOMMENDATIONS

Many analysts of the unemployment system of the United States, arguing that the system is in need of major reform, point to the changes in the demographics of the U.S. labor force, industrial composition, level of trade unionism, and interstate mobility. However, few analysts have commented on the fact that the UI systems of the states have changed a great deal since the program was initiated. Some programmatic changes have tended to reduce access to benefits, while others have expanded access or reduced the cost of applying for, and receiving, benefits. Often left unstudied is the administrative culture of UI programs. In states with low union density and weak worker representation, UI programs may be subject to administrative capture by business interests, which generally seek to make benefits less available and less generous while reducing their tax burden. Companies such as Talx now provide business services to handle UI claims and contest experience-rating assessments, further tilting the balance toward business interests. Most of the resistance by business interests to expanding the UI system is due to the experience rating of UI taxation and the fact that businesses perceive that they "pay" UI taxes, despite the well-known findings that most UI taxes are paid by workers via lower wages.

Given the lack of access and the administrative difficulties discussed in this chapter, there are significant policy changes that could alter the long-run effectiveness of the UI program. I highlight four changes that would be easy (although perhaps politically difficult) to implement. I focus primarily on funding, since that issue is likely to be addressed regardless of administration or political party. Additionally, there is some research linking funding with program generosity (Smith and Wenger 2013). Funding may also lead to reductions in access to the program.

Generate policies that require states to have adequate UI trust fund reserves. In the absence of adequate reserves, states reduce access to the program by raising earnings requirements and making programs less generous by lowering benefit amounts or weeks of benefits available to unemployed workers, or both.

To build adequate trust fund reserves the federal government should *raise the wage base used to assess UI taxes to equal the social security wage base and index it to wage growth.* This change will make the program considerably more progressive and less tax-distortionary (that is, it will broaden the base and lower the tax).

Reduce employers' tax burden by shifting the bulk of UI taxes onto workers. Only the firm-specific turnover proportion of UI taxes should be assessed to the firm. The worker should pay the base tax rate associated with the industry. Changes to this type of financing will result in an experience-rated system, but one that changes the employee's expectations about benefits and changes the political economy of UI legislation and representation on UI boards. The added advantage of this change is that when the UI trust funds are solvent and legislatures provide a UI tax holiday, workers will see their wages increase in the short term.

The U.S. Department of Labor should analyze—and independent researchers should evaluate—states with low levels of UI recipiency. Do states with low levels of UI recipiency have disparate benefit eligibility for low-income workers? If so, can advocates pressure those states to raise recipiency rates? As discussed at length here, monetary eligibility is not the most significant barrier for most workers. Advocates should focus more attention on getting states to adopt and enforce "good cause" leaving. The penalties for voluntary leaving, discharge for misconduct, and refusal of suitable work have all increased since the 1950s. Instead of disqualifying workers for the duration of the unemployment spell, we could work to make benefits available after a suitable waiting period.

Overall, there are simple and significant changes to UI policy that would make benefits more readily available to low-income workers. Since benefits are unlikely to replace more than 50 percent of lost wages, low-income workers may not receive much in the way of benefits from the UI program. However, in difficult labor markets with limited job openings and high unemployment, a small benefit from the UI system may make a substantial difference in the lives and livelihoods of families.

NOTES

1. With programs in the U.S. Virgin Islands, Puerto Rico, and Washington, D.C., there are actually fifty-three "state" programs. We analyze the performance of all the states and Washington, D.C., in this chapter.
2. In this context, I am using "low-income" to denote both workers who had insufficient earnings to qualify for unemployment benefits and those who worked in historically low-wage industries, such as agriculture and domestic service, who were excluded from UI coverage.
3. In general, filing has become less common among the unemployed, as discussed by Stephen Wandner and Andrew Stettner (2000). Many of the unemployed fail to file for unemployment benefits because they do not believe that they are eligible or that they worked or earned enough to receive benefits. Additionally,

some stated that they voluntarily left their previous employment or that they expect to have a new job soon. However, we do not know if this effect differs by gender, since Wandner and Stettner (2000) do not provide a separate analysis for men and women.

4. Note that in the current recession the peak in the insured unemployment rate (the percentage of unemployed receiving benefits) occurred in June 2009 at 4.8 percent, when the unemployment rate was 9.5 percent.

5. This was the annual average in 1975. The rates shown in figure 9.1 are based on monthly data.

6. All comparisons use nominal median wage growth in the state and nominal increases in UI base period earnings requirements.

REFERENCES

Blank, Rebecca M., and David E. Card. 1991. "Recent Trends in Insured and Uninsured Unemployment: Is There an Explanation?" *Quarterly Journal of Economics* 106(4): 1157–89.

Boushey, Heather, and Jeffrey B. Wenger. 2006. "Unemployment Insurance Eligibility Before and After Welfare Reform." *Journal of Poverty* 10(3): 1–23.

Center for Economic and Policy Research. 2012. *CPS-ORG Uniform Extracts*, Version 1.7. Washington, D.C.: Center for Economic and Policy Research.

Edin, Kathryn, and Laura Lein. 1997. *Making Ends Meet: How Single Mothers Survive Welfare and Low-Wage Work*. New York: Russell Sage Foundation.

Harris, Kathleen Mullan. 1993. "Work and Welfare Among Single Mothers in Poverty." *American Journal of Sociology* 99(2): 317–52.

Hendra, Richard, James A. Riccio, Richard Dorsett, David H. Greenberg, Genevieve Knight, Joan Phillips, . . . and Jared Smith. 2011. *Breaking the Low-Pay, No-Pay Cycle: Final Evidence from the U.K. Employment Retention and Advancement (ERA) Demonstration*, vol. 765. London: Department for Work and Pensions.

Holzer, Harry, and Karin Martinson. 2005. "Can We Improve Job Retention and Advancement Among Low-Income Working Parents?" Washington, D.C.: Urban Institute.

Kaye, Kelleen. 1997. "Unemployment Insurance as a Potential Safety Net for Former Welfare Recipients." Paper presented to the conference of the National Association of Welfare Research and Statistics, Atlanta, Ga. (July 27–30).

———. 2001. "Re-examining the Potential Role of Unemployment Insurance as a Safety Net for Workers at Risk of Public Assistance Receipt." Paper presented to the National Research Conference on Workforce Security Issues, Washington, D.C. (June 26–27).

Keiser, Lael R. 1999. "State Bureaucratic Discretion and the Administration of Social Welfare Programs: The Case of Social Security Disability." *Journal of Public Administration Research and Theory* 9(1): 87–106.

Keiser, Lael R., Vicky M. Wilkins, Kenneth J. Meier, and Catherine A. Holland. 2002. "Lipstick and Logarithms: Gender, Institutional Context, and Representative Bureaucracy." *American Political Science Review* 96(3): 553–64.

Lipsky, Michael. 1980. *Street-Level Bureaucracy: The Critical Role of Street-Level Bureaucrats*. New York: Russell Sage Foundation.

Lovell, Vicky, and Catherine Hill. 2001. "Today's Women Workers: Shut Out of Yesterday's Unemployment Insurance System." Washington, D.C.: Institute for Women's Policy Research.

Maynard-Moody, Steven W., and Michael C. Musheno. 2003. *Cops, Teachers, Counselors: Stories from the Front Lines of Public Service*. Ann Arbor: University of Michigan Press.

McMurrer, Daniel P., and Amy B. Chasanov. 1995. "Trends in Unemployment Insurance Benefits." *Monthly Labor Review* 118(September): 30.

Moss, David A. 2002. *When All Else Fails: Government as the Ultimate Risk Manager*. Cambridge, Mass.: Harvard University Press.

National Employment Law Project. 2001a. "Part-time Workers and Unemployment Insurance: Expanding UI for Low-Wage and Part-time Workers." New York: NELP.

———. 2001b. "Expanding Unemployment Insurance for Low-Wage Workers: State Legislative Highlights (1996–2001)." New York: NELP.

O'Leary, Christopher J., and Stephen Wandner. 1997. "Summing Up, Achievements, Problems, and Prospects." In *Unemployment Insurance in the United States: Analysis of Policy Issues*. Kalamazoo, Mich.: W. E. Upjohn Institute for Employment Research.

Rangarajan, Anu, Walter Corson, and Robert G. Wood. 2001. "Is the Unemployment Insurance System a Safety Net for Welfare Recipients Who Exit Welfare for Work?" Princeton, N.J.: Mathematica Policy Research.

Ryu, Sangyub, Jeffrey B. Wenger, and Vicky M. Wilkins. 2012. "When Claimant Characteristics and Prior Performance Predict Bureaucratic Error." *American Review of Public Administration* 42(6): 695–714.

Shaefer, H. Luke. 2010. "Identifying Key Barriers to Unemployment Insurance for Disadvantaged Workers in the United States." *Journal of Social Policy* 39(3): 439–60.

Smith, Daniel L., and Jeffrey B. Wenger. 2013. "State Unemployment Insurance Trust Solvency and Benefit Generosity." *Journal of Policy Analysis and Management* 32(3): 536–53.

Um'rani, Annisah, and Vicky Lovell. 2000. "Unemployment Insurance and Welfare Reform: Fair Access to Economic Supports for Low-Income Working Women." Washington, D.C.: Institute for Women's Policy Research.

U.S. Department of Labor, Employment and Training Administration. Various years. "Comparison of State Unemployment Insurance Laws from 1990 to 2010." Washington: U.S. Department of Labor, Employment, and Training Administration.

Vroman, Wayne 1991. "The Decline in Unemployment Insurance Claims Activity in the 1980s." Unemployment Insurance Occasional Paper 91-2. Washington: U.S. Department of Labor, Employment and Training Administration.

Wandner, Stephen, and Andrew Stettner. 2000. "Why Are Many Jobless Workers Not Applying for Benefits?" *Monthly Labor Review* (June): 21–32.

Wenger, Jeffrey B., Rick McHugh, and Nancy Segal. 2002. "Part-time Work, Inadequate Unemployment Benefits." *Indicators: The Journal of Social Health* 1(4): 99–111.

Wenger, Jeffrey B., and Vicky M. Wilkins. 2009. "At the Discretion of Rogue Agents: How Automation Improves Women's Outcomes in Unemployment Insurance." *Journal of Public Administration Research and Theory* 19(2): 313–33.

Chapter 10 | Can the Affordable Care Act Reverse Three Decades of Declining Health Insurance Coverage for Low-Wage Workers?

John Schmitt

ABOUT HALF OF all U.S. residents without health insurance are workers (Rho and Schmitt 2010a). Indeed, non-elderly workers are less likely to have health insurance than many groups generally viewed as more economically vulnerable. According to the most recent census data, for example, only 2 percent of adults age sixty-five and older and about 10 percent of children under the age of eighteen lacked health insurance coverage in 2010. By contrast, about 20 percent of workers age eighteen to sixty-four—and 15 percent of full-time workers in that age range—had no health insurance in the same year (U.S. Census Bureau 2011, 26–27, table 8).

Yet, we know surprisingly little about workers and their health insurance or how their coverage has changed over the last three decades.[1] In recent years, the annual reports on health insurance coverage produced by the Census Bureau have included a brief mention of the share of workers with health insurance, but these same published data give no breakdowns by workers' earnings, gender, race, or education level, and no breakdowns by the source of coverage (their own employer, a spouse's employer, Medicaid, Medicare, directly purchased private insurance, or other sources).[2] Moreover, consistent, publicly available data for workers' coverage start only in the late 1990s, long after the decline in overall health insurance rates was well under way.[3]

The most important attempt to fill this data gap has been the regular estimates produced by the Economic Policy Institute (EPI) for its biennial publication *The State of Working America*.[4] The EPI figures, however, focus exclusively on own-employer-provided coverage for private-sector workers. These data provide important information about compensation, employer costs, and job quality, but do not tell us about the strategies used by workers—especially low-wage workers, who are least likely to have employer-provided insurance—to secure coverage through other means.[5]

All estimates of health insurance coverage must contend with several important changes over time in the Current Population Survey (CPS), the large, nationally representative survey that is the source of official coverage numbers.[6] During the last three decades, the Census Bureau has made improvements to the survey methodology, most of which have increased the ability of the survey to identify health insurance coverage. The improvements are welcome, but can make it much more difficult to track trends. If the Census Bureau were to travel back in time to 1980, the first year the CPS asked respondents about their health insurance, and field the same survey it uses today, it would almost certainly find a higher health insurance coverage rate in that year than what was actually found using the earlier version of the survey. As a result, comparing current coverage estimates with older estimates without adjusting for the methodological changes systematically understates the long decline in health coverage. The Census Bureau typically sidesteps this methodological challenge by reporting coverage rates only over the recent period (since 1999), when the survey design has been stable. The EPI takes a more conservative route and reports the changes as they appear in each year's survey, which has the effect of underestimating the decline in coverage over time.[7]

In this chapter, I seek to paint a more complete picture of trends in health insurance coverage for workers, especially low-wage workers. To do so, I first calculate low-wage workers' coverage rates from all sources of health insurance, including their own employers, other family members' employers, directly purchased policies, Medicaid, and other public sources, with separate breakdowns for the most important of these categories. I then adjust these data to reflect changes in the survey methodology over time.

To give some idea of the likely future path of coverage rates for low-wage workers, I also summarize outside projections of the impact on coverage rates of the Affordable Care Act (ACA) of 2010. Given the strong similarities between the ACA and health insurance reforms passed in Massachusetts in 2006, I also review the experience of workers in that state.

Based on public and private forecasts of the impact of the ACA—and on the concrete experience of Massachusetts—I conclude that the full implementation of recent health care reforms would substantially increase health insurance coverage for low-wage workers. The main mechanisms for raising low-wage workers' coverage under the ACA would be expanded eligibility for Medicaid for low-wage workers in families below 133 percent of the federal poverty line and federal subsidies for the purchase of private insurance for low-wage workers in families between 100 and 400 percent of the poverty line.[7] If, however, full implementation of the ACA is blocked by federal or state executive or legislative action before 2014, every indication is that low-wage workers will continue to lose access to health insurance.

DATA AND METHODS

The source of all estimates of health insurance coverage presented here is the Current Population Survey, the nationally representative survey of 50,000 to 60,000 households conducted monthly by the Census Bureau. Since 1980, the March version of the CPS has asked respondents detailed questions about their health insurance coverage during the preceding calendar year. These responses serve as the basis for the official annual estimates for health insurance coverage in the United States.

Over the past thirty years, the March CPS has undergone several important methodological changes that have had an impact on the survey's estimates of health insurance coverage rates. Most of these changes had the effect of raising the reported coverage rate for health insurance, with the result that comparisons of recent coverage rates with those of three decades ago systematically understate the decline in health insurance coverage that actually took place over the period. Hye Jin Rho and I (Rho and Schmitt 2010b) have provided a detailed summary of these changes and proposed a methodology for adjusting results from the raw CPS data to make earlier survey data more directly comparable with the current survey methodology. All estimates here use this recommended adjustment.

The main focus in this chapter is on low-wage workers, defined for simplicity as those in the bottom quintile of the hourly earnings distribution in each year of the survey.[9] For purposes of comparison, all figures also report results for the second quintile of wage earners (the quintile immediately above the bottom quintile), as well as for the top quintile. Following Elise Gould (2009), the analysis is limited to "attached workers," defined as those who worked at least twenty-six weeks in the year and usually worked at least twenty hours per week. Since the interest here is in low-wage employees, the data exclude self-employed workers.

All reported data refer to workers between the ages of eighteen and sixty-four. Younger workers may be covered under parental plans or through government programs aimed at children (most notably the Children's Health

Figure 10.1   Health Insurance Among Workers Age Eighteen to Sixty-Four, Own-Employer, by Wage Quintile, 1979 to 2010

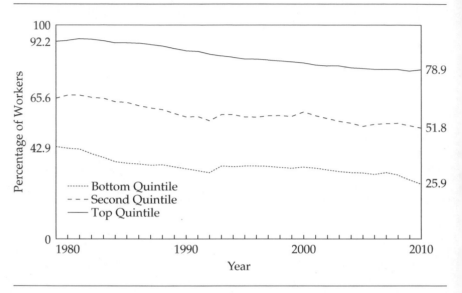

Source: Author's analysis of March Current Population Survey (Center for Economic and Policy Research 2013).

Insurance Program, or CHIP). Almost all workers (and all U.S. residents) age sixty-five and older are covered by Medicare, the universal, single-payer health insurance program for the elderly established in 1965.

COVERAGE LEVELS AND TRENDS, 1979 TO 2010

As figure 10.1 shows, in 2010 only about one-fourth (25.9 percent) of low-wage workers had health insurance through their own employer, down from 42.9 percent in 1979 (see also table 10A.1 in the appendix).[10] The 2010 rates for low-wage workers were well below even those in the next quintile up, where just over half (51.8 percent) of workers had coverage through their own employer (see also table 10A.2). In the same year, 78.9 percent of workers in the top quintile had health insurance through their employer (see table 10A.5).

The last three decades have seen substantial erosion in employer-provided coverage across workers at all pay levels. Low-wage workers saw the biggest decline in own-employer coverage—17.0 percentage points

Figure 10.2   Health Insurance Among Workers Age Eighteen
to Sixty-Four, Other Family Member's Employer,
by Wage Quintile, 1979 to 2010

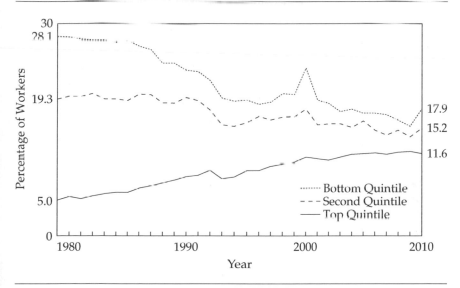

Source: Author's analysis of March Current Population Survey (Center for Economic and
Policy Research 2013).

between 1979 and 2010. But coverage losses were almost as large for
workers in the second quintile (down 13.8 percentage points) and the top
quintile (down 13.3 percentage points).

A rise in families with second earners, particularly women in married-
couple families, could arguably have reduced the need for own-employer
coverage, because second earners may be able to obtain coverage through
their spouse (or, in some cases, through another family member). Figure 10.2
shows that for low-wage workers, coverage through a spouse's (or another
family member's) employer has not made up for the decline in own-
employer insurance. In fact, for low-wage workers, coverage through a
spouse or other family member actually fell ten percentage points between
1979 and 2010. Workers in the second quintile saw a similar, but smaller,
decline. Coverage through another family member's employer, however,
did increase for workers in the top quintile (and, to a smaller degree, for
workers in the fourth quintile [not shown]).[11]

Nor have low-wage workers been able to make up for the decline in
employer-provided coverage through other forms of private insurance—

Figure 10.3   Health Insurance Among Workers Age Eighteen
to Sixty-Four, Other Private Insurance,
by Wage Quintile, 1979 to 2010

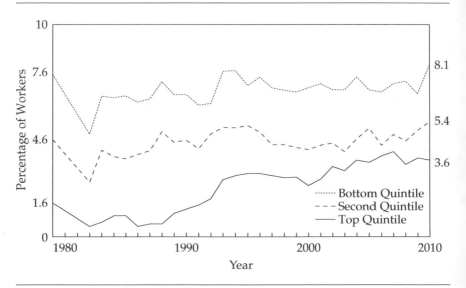

Source: Author's analysis of March Current Population Survey (Center for Economic and Policy Research 2013).

most importantly, individual policies purchased directly from insurers. As figure 10.3 shows, in 2010 only about one in twelve low-wage workers (8.1 percent) had directly purchased or other private coverage, a rate that had increased only slightly in the preceding thirty years. An even smaller share of higher-wage workers had directly purchased insurance or other private coverage: about 5 percent of second-quintile workers and about 4 percent of those in the top quintile. (The low reliance of workers in the top quintile on non-employer-based private insurance suggests that these policies are probably not as good as employer-provided coverage.)

The only area where low-wage workers have seen any improvement over the last three decades is in coverage through public insurance programs, particularly Medicaid. As figure 10.4 demonstrates, in 2010 about one of every eight low-wage workers (12.8 percent) had some form of public health insurance, up from about one in twelve in 1979 (8.8 percent). And as figure 10.5 illustrates, the vast majority of low-wage workers receiving public health insurance in 2010 were covered by Medicaid. (Higher-wage workers with public insurance were much less likely to be

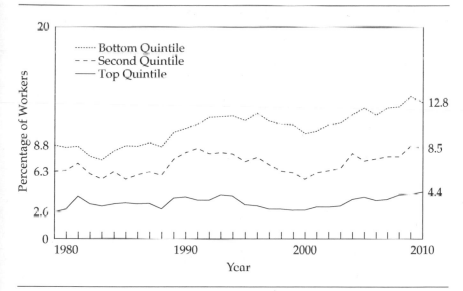

Figure 10.4 Health Insurance Among Workers Age Eighteen
to Sixty-Four, All Public Sources, by Wage Quintile,
1979 to 2010

Source: Author's analysis of March Current Population Survey (Center for Economic and Policy Research 2013).

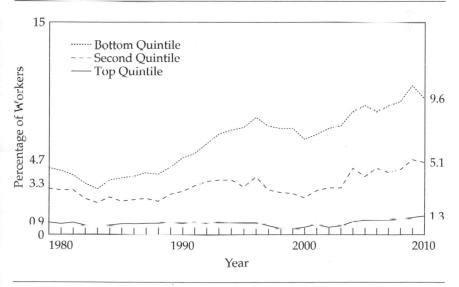

Figure 10.5 Health Insurance Among Workers Age Eighteen
to Sixty-Four, Medicaid, by Wage Quintile,
1979 to 2010

Source: Author's analysis of March Current Population Survey (Center for Economic and Policy Research 2013).

Figure 10.6   No Health Insurance Among Workers Age Eighteen to
Sixty-Four, from Any Source, by Wage Quintile,
1979 to 2010

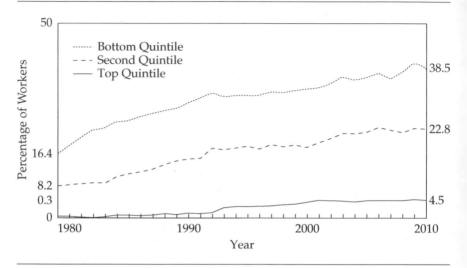

Source: Author's analysis of March Current Population Survey (Center for Economic and Policy Research 2013).

on Medicaid and more likely to have coverage through other government programs, including those covering military veterans.) Currently, almost one of every ten low-wage workers (9.6 percent) is covered by Medicaid, more than double the rate in 1979 (4.7 percent).

After counting coverage from all possible private and public sources, almost four in ten low-wage workers (38.5 percent) have no health insurance coverage whatsoever (see figure 10.6). This is more than double the noncoverage rate in 1979 (16.4 percent). By contrast, fewer than 5 percent of high-wage workers have no form of coverage (though that figure is up somewhat from the essentially universal coverage that prevailed for high-wage workers in 1979).

Sample-size limitations make it difficult to obtain corresponding estimates of coverage rates for low-wage workers by race and ethnicity. Data for all workers, however, indicate that coverage problems are particularly severe for Latinos. As figure 10.7 indicates, almost 40 percent of *all* Latino workers (that is, not just low-wage Latino workers) have no health insurance of any form. Assuming that access to health insurance for low-wage Latinos is below the average for all Latinos, a very high share of low-wage

Figure 10.7   No Health Insurance from Any Source, by Race-Ethnicity, 1979 to 2010

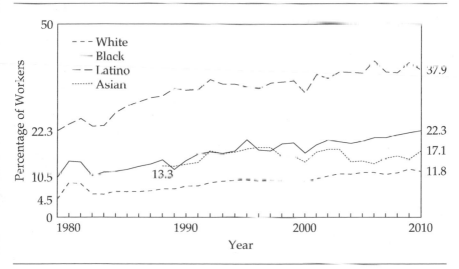

Source: Author's analysis of March Current Population Survey (Center for Economic and Policy Research 2013).

Latinos workers are likely to be without any coverage. African American workers (about 22 percent) and Asian workers (about 17 percent) are also much more likely than whites (about 12 percent) to be without coverage. In all cases, the noncoverage rates are probably much higher for low-wage workers within each racial and ethnic group.

FUTURE TRENDS

The decline in coverage rates has its roots in two long-standing economic processes. The first is the rising cost of health care, which has squeezed workers' wages and made it less economical for firms to offer health insurance, especially to low-wage workers. In the absence of reforms to the existing health care system, these costs—and implicitly the pressure on workers' after-health-insurance compensation—are projected to continue rising indefinitely.[12]

The other force behind falling coverage rates, especially for low-wage workers, is the decline over the last three decades in the bargaining power of most workers. Beginning in the late 1970s, a set of structural changes in the economy significantly reduced the bargaining power of workers, especially those at the middle and bottom of the wage distribution. These structural changes included: a steep decline in unionization; an erosion in the inflation-adjusted value of the minimum wage; the deregulation of many historically high-wage industries (trucking, airlines, telecommunications, and others); the privatization of many state and local government functions (from school cafeteria workers to public-assistance administrators); the opening up of the U.S. economy to much higher volumes of foreign trade; a sharp rise in the share of immigrant workers, who often lack basic legal rights and operate in an economy that provides few labor protections regardless of citizenship; and a macroeconomic policy environment that has typically maintained the unemployment rate well above levels consistent with full employment. All of these changes have acted to reduce the bargaining power of workers, especially those at the middle and bottom of the wage distribution. As a result, low- and middle-wage workers have seen their relative (and even absolute) wages fall and the availability and quality of health insurance and retirement plans decline.[13]

Despite the Great Recession and the ensuing national debate on economic inequality, there are few signs—at least at the time of this writing—that any of these structural factors undermining workers' bargaining power are likely to change anytime soon. The passage of the Affordable Care Act in 2010, however, holds out the prospect that low-wage workers could see a significant expansion in their health insurance coverage rates—and at least some possibility that the rate of growth of health care costs could be reduced relative to the long-term trend.

THE AFFORDABLE CARE ACT OF 2010

The ACA sets in motion a large and complicated restructuring of the nation's health care system, with a particular emphasis on the public and private health insurance sectors. A full analysis of the ACA—particularly the measures designed to address long-term cost concerns—is beyond the scope of this chapter, which focuses instead on those elements of the ACA that are most likely to affect coverage rates of low-wage workers.

The centerpiece of the ACA is a requirement that most U.S. citizens and legal residents enroll in some form of private or public health insurance.[14] When fully phased in, the act will require that those without coverage pay a tax penalty of between $695 and 2.5 percent of taxable income (and indexed, subsequently, to inflation).[15]

Arguably, the path to coverage preferred by the ACA's sponsors is through existing employer-provided private insurance. To this end, the ACA establishes a "pay-or-play" system for employers with fifty or more full-time employees. Employers above this size threshold that do not offer coverage or that have employees who rely on government tax credits to fulfill their personal requirement to maintain coverage will pay a tax penalty.[16] Smaller employers will not face tax penalties, but many will be eligible to receive tax credits for providing coverage and will be permitted to buy insurance through newly created, state-level health insurance exchanges.

However, expansions of coverage through the existing Medicaid program and through new health insurance exchanges for individual and family coverage are likely to provide the biggest boost in coverage to low-wage workers. Low-wage workers who have family incomes above 100 percent of the poverty line and whose employers either do not provide insurance or provide insurance that is deemed too expensive by ACA criteria will be eligible to receive a federal subsidy to buy private insurance through a health exchange, as long as their family income is less than 400 percent of the poverty line.

Two kinds of uncertainty hang over any analysis of the likely impact of the ACA on low-wage workers. The first uncertainty is the exact nature of the final form of the law and related regulations. On the judicial front, the ACA has survived several court challenges centered on the constitutionality of the individual mandate.[17] On the legislative front, however, Republicans in the House and Senate have vowed to repeal all or part of the ACA. At the state level, several Republican governors and Republican-controlled state legislatures have announced their intention to block or slow the implementation of key aspects of the ACA, especially those related to the expansion of Medicaid, which is particularly important for low-wage workers.[18]

The second element of uncertainty is related to the inherent difficulties in predicting individual and institutional responses to large and complex changes in existing systems, an issue compounded by the fact that many particulars of the law—especially those involving the workings of the separate state-level insurance exchanges and the states' decisions about full implementation of the ACA's proposed Medicaid expansion—are still evolving.[19] The following analysis assumes that the ACA will be implemented as passed, and it relies on the educated guesses made by health care experts concerning the final features and behavioral responses to the system put in place from 2014 forward.

With these caveats in mind, the Congressional Budget Office (2011, 17) projects that under the ACA, "the share of legal non-elderly residents with insurance coverage in 2021 will be about 95 percent, compared with a projected share of about 82 percent in the absence of that legislation (and an estimated 83 percent currently)." Meanwhile, CBO continues, "about 23 million non-elderly residents will remain uninsured; about one-third of that group will be unauthorized immigrants, who are not eligible to participate in Medicaid or the insurance exchanges; another quarter will be eligible for Medicaid but are not expected to enroll; and the remaining fraction will include individuals who are ineligible for subsidies, are exempt from the mandate to obtain insurance, choose to not comply with the mandate (and take the risk of paying a penalty), or have some combination of those characteristics."

Other researchers generally agree with the CBO that the ACA will result in a substantial increase in coverage rates.[20] Disagreements arise, however, around the likely mix of coverage. The CBO, like most analysts, believes that the large majority of the increase in coverage will flow from increases in directly purchased insurance (which is particularly relevant for workers in families between 100 and 400 percent of the poverty line) and Medicaid (particularly relevant for workers in families with incomes below 133 percent of the poverty line), with only a small net decline in employer-provided coverage.[21] The net drop in employer-based coverage, the CBO believes, will reflect declines in employer offers of coverage. Those declines will be made up disproportionately of "smaller employers and employers with predominantly lower-wage workers—people who will be eligible for Medicaid or subsidies through the exchanges," and will largely offset increases in coverage through other employers responding to the "combined impact of the insurance mandate, the penalties for employers, and the tax credits for small employers" (Congressional Budget Office 2011, 19–20). Other analysts believe that the high costs of providing health insurance to low-wage workers will lead many employers to reduce their provision of coverage, pushing many workers currently covered by employer plans onto Medicaid and the new state-level health exchanges.[22]

For present purposes, however, the exact mix of the coverage is less relevant than the net increase in total coverage for low-wage workers, which by almost all accounts is likely to be substantial. Unfortunately, neither the CBO nor other sources have produced coverage projections for workers specifically, let alone for low-wage workers. The CBO estimate of a 95 percent coverage rate for the non-elderly population in 2016, however, can—with a few assumptions about the distribution of this coverage—give some general guidance about the likely improvement in health insurance access for low-wage workers.

To produce a rough estimate of the share of low-wage workers who will remain without coverage after the implementation of the ACA, let's start with the CBO's projection that by 2016 the noncoverage rate for the non-elderly population of the United States will be 5 percent. The CBO does not provide a separate breakdown for children (ages zero to seventeen) and adults (ages eighteen to sixty-four), but we can assume that improvements in coverage will maintain the same (roughly) two-to-one ratio for the noncoverage rates of adults to children. Given the relative size of the child and adult populations in 2010, a 5 percent overall noncoverage rate and the two-to-one ratio imply that the noncoverage rate for all adults will be about 5.8 percent after the ACA (and 2.9 percent for children). For simplicity, if we assume that all adults—both workers and nonworkers—have the same coverage rate, then under the CBO's projections, workers as a group will have a 5.8 percent non-coverage rate after the ACA.[23] By comparison, in 2010 the actual noncoverage rate for all workers was about 17.7 percent. The CBO gives no guidance about how the coverage improvements for workers will be divided across the wage distribution. If, at the extreme, we assume that all of the uncovered workers are low-wage workers by our definition—that is, that all 5.8 percent of the workers remaining without coverage are in the bottom quintile—then the noncoverage rate for low-wage workers will be about 29.0 percent.[24] This would be a reduction of one-fourth in the share of low-wage workers without coverage relative to the actual noncoverage rate for low-wage workers in 2010 (38.5 percent). A less extreme assumption about the distribution of noncoverage rates by wage level after the ACA produces larger gains for low-wage workers. For example, if instead we assume that the top 80 percent of workers have a frictional 3 percent noncoverage rate, then an overall noncoverage rate for workers of 5.8 percent implies a 17.0 percent noncoverage rate for low-wage workers—well short of universal coverage, but a noncoverage rate that is less than half of the current rate.

MASSACHUSETTS

The recent experience of Massachusetts provides an important bench-mark for the likely impact of the ACA.[25] The 2006 Massachusetts reforms included many key elements that would be written into the ACA, including an individual mandate, a (weak) penalty for employers that fail to provide coverage, expanded eligibility for Medicaid, and government subsidies to purchase private insurance for individuals in families with incomes up to 300 percent of the federal poverty line.[26] Early results suggest that this com-bination of policies has substantially increased health insurance coverage in the state. Sharon Long, Lokendra Phadera, and Victoria Lynch (2010), for example, find that after the implementation of the reforms, the share of the state's population between the ages of nineteen and sixty-four without coverage was less than 6 percent, compared to a 15 percent rate for the rest of the nation. Massachusetts had higher coverage rates than the rest of the country even before the 2006 reforms. But as suggested by Sharon Long, Alshadye Yemane, and Karen Stockley's (2010) comparison of changes in coverage rates in Massachusetts before and after the 2008 implementation of the reforms with the change over the same period in coverage rates in New York State—which also had relatively high coverage rates but was not implementing any reforms—the reforms did substantially increase coverage rates for non-elderly adults. Aakanksha Pande and her colleagues

(2011) reached similar conclusions when they compared adults in Massachusetts with a control group in Connecticut, New Hampshire, Rhode Island, and Vermont.

Unfortunately, evaluations of the Massachusetts experience have paid little attention to the specific outcomes for workers. The sharp declines in noncoverage rates for all working-age adults, as well as survey evidence that non-elderly workers in Massachusetts have very low noncoverage rates (3 percent in 2008, compared to about 17 percent nationally in the same year),[27] suggest that the various reforms have greatly reduced non-insurance rates for workers, even for those earning low wages.[28]

The experience of Massachusetts, therefore, offers support for the various model-based projections that the ACA will substantially increase coverage rates for non-elderly adults, including non-elderly workers. To put the Massachusetts results into perspective, if we assume that the United States in 2010 had the same 3.0 percent noncoverage rate for workers that Massachusetts achieved in 2008, and even if we assume that all of the workers without coverage were in the bottom quintile of the wage distribution, only 15 percent of low-wage workers nationally would have been without coverage in 2010. As figure 10.6 shows, the actual share of low-wage workers in 2010 was 38.5 percent, more than twice as high. If, instead, we assume that workers at all wage levels experience at least some frictional level of noncoverage, then the Massachusetts results would imply even better outcomes for low-wage workers.

CONCLUSION

Overall, health insurance coverage for low-wage workers has been falling steadily over the last three decades. The drop in employer-provided health insurance coverage is the single most important explanation for this trend. A rise in the share of low-wage workers receiving Medicaid was able to counteract only a small portion of the falloff in coverage for low-wage workers. However, based on reasonable projections of the impact of the ACA, as well as on the experience of Massachusetts with state-level reforms similar in spirit to the ACA, recent reforms to the health insurance system stand a reasonable chance of reversing this long-standing trend.

Low-wage workers are likely to be among the biggest beneficiaries of the ACA, particularly those provisions that seek to increase employer-sponsored insurance, expand access to Medicaid, and subsidize the purchase of private insurance. The coverage gap between low-wage workers and the rest of the workforce will almost certainly fall sharply after 2014.

The ACA does not provide the universal coverage that many health care reformers were seeking before the bill's passage, but the ACA may also act, in the words of economist Heather Boushey (2012), as a "beachhead" for universal coverage down the line. If, however, full implementation of the ACA is blocked or delayed, every indication is that coverage rates will continue their three-decades-long decline.

Table 10A.1   Adjusted Health Insurance Coverage of Low-Wage Workers, Age Eighteen to Sixty-Four, 1979 to 2010

Year	Health Insurance (Total)	Private Health Insurance				Public Health Insurance		
		Total	Employment-Based		Other Private	Total	Medicaid	Other Public
			Total	Own				
1979	83.6%	78.7%	71.1%	42.9%	7.6%	8.8%	4.7%	4.0%
1980	n.a.	n.a.	70.4	42.3	n.a.	8.6	4.5	4.0
1981	n.a.	n.a.	69.7	41.9	n.a.	8.7	4.2	4.4
1982	77.3	72.4	67.6	39.9	4.8	7.8	3.6	4.1
1983	77.1	72.5	65.9	38.2	6.6	7.4	3.2	4.1
1984	75.2	69.8	63.3	36.0	6.5	8.3	3.8	4.4
1985	75.1	69.6	63.0	35.4	6.6	8.8	4.0	4.7
1986	74.0	68.3	62.0	35.2	6.3	8.7	4.1	4.5
1987	73.1	67.0	60.6	34.3	6.5	9.0	4.4	4.6
1988	72.4	66.3	59.1	34.7	7.3	8.6	4.3	4.3
1989	72.0	64.7	58.1	33.7	6.7	10.0	4.8	5.2
1990	70.5	62.8	56.2	32.8	6.7	10.4	5.5	4.9
1991	69.3	61.2	55.1	31.9	6.2	10.8	5.8	5.0
1992	67.9	59.1	52.9	30.9	6.3	11.4	6.5	4.9

Year								
1993	69.0	61.0	53.3	33.8	7.8	11.5	7.1	4.4
1994	68.5	60.5	52.7	33.8	7.8	11.6	7.4	4.2
1995	68.5	60.2	53.1	34.0	7.1	11.1	7.6	3.5
1996	68.7	60.0	52.5	34.0	7.5	11.9	8.3	3.6
1997	67.7	59.7	52.7	33.9	7.0	11.1	7.7	3.4
1998	67.8	60.1	53.2	33.2	6.9	10.8	7.5	3.3
1999	67.3	59.6	52.8	32.9	6.8	10.7	7.5	3.2
2000	67.0	64.2	57.2	33.5	7.0	9.9	6.7	3.2
2001	66.6	59.3	52.1	33.0	7.2	10.1	7.1	3.0
2002	65.5	57.9	51.0	32.3	6.9	10.7	7.5	3.2
2003	63.8	55.8	48.9	31.4	6.9	10.9	7.7	3.2
2004	64.7	56.3	48.8	30.9	7.5	11.7	8.7	3.0
2005	64.0	55.0	48.1	30.8	6.9	12.3	9.1	3.2
2006	62.9	54.2	47.4	30.1	6.8	11.6	8.7	2.9
2007	64.3	55.2	48.0	30.9	7.2	12.3	9.1	3.2
2008	62.6	53.4	46.1	29.8	7.3	12.4	9.4	3.0
2009	60.1	49.7	43.0	27.5	6.7	13.4	10.5	2.9
2010	61.5	51.9	43.8	25.9	8.1	12.8	9.6	3.2
1979 to 2010	-22.1	-26.8	-27.3	-17.0	0.5	4.1	4.9	-0.8

Source: Author's analysis of Center for Economic Policy Research extract of March Current Population Survey (2013).

Notes: Low-wage workers are defined as those in the bottom fifth of the wage distribution. "Other private" includes directly purchased insurance; "other public" includes Medicare, Veterans Administration, and other public sources. Raw CPS data are adjusted for survey changes using the procedure described in Rho and Schmitt (2010b).

Table 10A.2 Adjusted Health Insurance Coverage of Second-Quintile Workers, Age Eighteen to Sixty-Four, 1979 to 2010

Year	Health Insurance (Total)	Private Health Insurance				Public Health Insurance		
		Total	Employment-Based		Other Private	Total	Medicaid	Other Public
			Total	Own				
1979	91.8%	89.5%	84.9%	65.6%	4.6%	6.3%	3.3%	3.1%
1980	n.a.	n.a.	86.7	67.0	n.a.	6.4	3.2	3.3
1981	n.a.	n.a.	86.7	67.0	n.a.	7.1	3.2	4.0
1982	91.0	88.7	86.1	66.0	2.6	6.1	2.6	3.6
1983	91.1	89.0	84.9	65.6	4.1	5.6	2.3	3.4
1984	89.4	87.1	83.3	64.0	3.8	6.3	2.7	3.7
1985	88.7	86.4	82.7	63.6	3.7	5.6	2.4	3.3
1986	88.2	86.0	82.1	62.1	3.9	6.0	2.5	3.6
1987	87.5	85.1	81.0	61.2	4.0	6.3	2.6	3.7
1988	86.3	84.1	79.1	60.4	4.9	6.0	2.4	3.6
1989	85.4	81.7	77.2	58.6	4.4	7.5	2.9	4.6
1990	84.9	81.0	76.4	56.9	4.5	8.1	3.1	5.0
1991	84.7	80.4	76.2	57.2	4.1	8.5	3.5	5.0
1992	82.1	77.8	72.9	55.2	4.8	8.0	3.8	4.2
1993	82.5	78.9	73.7	58.1	5.1	8.1	3.9	4.2

1994	82.1	78.5	73.4	57.9	5.1	8.0	3.9	4.1
1995	81.6	78.1	72.9	56.9	5.2	7.3	3.4	3.9
1996	82.3	78.6	73.7	56.8	4.9	7.7	4.1	3.6
1997	81.2	78.0	73.7	57.3	4.3	7.0	3.2	3.8
1998	81.7	78.6	74.3	57.5	4.3	6.4	3.0	3.4
1999	81.3	78.2	74.0	57.2	4.2	6.2	2.9	3.3
2000	81.9	81.2	77.1	59.2	4.1	5.5	2.6	3.0
2001	80.7	77.5	73.2	57.5	4.3	6.2	3.1	3.1
2002	79.6	76.4	72.0	56.2	4.4	6.4	3.3	3.1
2003	78.3	74.7	70.7	54.9	4.0	6.6	3.3	3.3
2004	78.4	73.9	69.3	54.0	4.6	8.0	4.7	3.3
2005	78.0	73.8	58.7	52.5	5.1	7.3	4.1	3.2
2006	76.8	72.7	58.4	53.5	4.3	7.5	4.7	2.8
2007	77.5	72.8	68.0	53.8	4.8	7.7	4.4	3.3
2008	78.1	73.5	69.0	54.1	4.5	7.7	4.6	3.1
2009	77.0	71.8	66.8	52.8	5.0	8.7	5.3	3.4
2010	77.2	72.4	67.0	51.8	5.4	8.5	5.1	3.4
1979 to 2010	−14.6	−17.1	−17.9	−13.8	0.8	2.2	1.9	0.3

Source: Author's analysis of Center for Economic Policy Research extract of March Current Population Survey (2013).

Notes: "Other private" includes directly purchased insurance; "other public" includes Medicare, Veterans Administration, and other public sources. Raw CPS data are adjusted for survey changes using the procedure described in Rho and Schmitt (2010b).

Table 10A.3 Adjusted Health Insurance Coverage of Middle-Quintile Workers, Age Eighteen to Sixty-Four, 1979 to 2010

Year	Health Insurance (Total)	Private Health Insurance				Public Health Insurance		
		Total	Employment-Based		Other Private	Total	Medicaid	Other Public
			Total	Own				
1979	94.5%	93.1%	89.6%	75.9%	3.4%	5.8%	1.8%	4.1%
1980	n.a.	n.a.	90.2	75.7	n.a.	5.6	1.7	4.0
1981	n.a.	n.a.	89.7	75.4	n.a.	6.5	1.4	5.2
1982	93.8	92.7	90.0	75.7	2.6	5.5	1.3	4.3
1983	93.8	92.6	89.4	75.3	3.1	5.2	1.1	4.2
1984	93.4	92.2	88.8	74.7	3.3	5.3	1.2	4.2
1985	93.4	92.1	88.9	74.4	3.1	5.5	1.3	4.3
1986	93.6	92.1	89.1	74.2	2.9	5.4	1.3	4.2
1987	93.5	91.7	88.7	73.7	3.0	5.6	1.3	4.2
1988	93.2	91.2	88.0	74.0	3.2	5.7	1.4	4.2
1989	93.3	90.5	87.4	72.6	3.1	6.7	1.4	5.2
1990	93.0	90.3	87.0	72.1	3.3	6.2	1.5	4.6
1991	92.7	89.5	86.4	71.3	3.1	6.7	1.7	4.9
1992	91.8	88.9	85.8	69.8	3.1	6.3	1.6	4.6
1993	91.0	88.5	84.4	70.7	4.1	6.2	1.8	4.3

Year							
1994	90.7	88.3	84.1	70.5	4.1	5.9	1.8	4.1
1995	90.1	87.9	83.2	69.4	4.6	5.5	1.7	3.8
1996	90.2	88.0	83.3	68.8	4.6	5.7	1.7	4.0
1997	90.5	88.5	84.8	69.6	3.6	4.7	1.4	3.3
1998	90.2	88.3	84.7	70.7	3.6	4.6	1.3	3.3
1999	89.9	88.1	84.6	70.5	3.5	4.5	1.3	3.2
2000	89.5	89.0	86.1	71.1	2.9	4.2	1.3	2.9
2001	89.8	87.9	84.4	70.8	3.5	4.3	1.4	2.9
2002	88.9	86.8	83.3	68.7	3.5	4.7	1.6	3.1
2003	88.4	86.6	82.9	69.0	3.7	4.8	1.7	3.1
2004	88.2	86.0	82.5	69.2	3.5	5.7	2.5	3.2
2005	88.4	86.0	82.3	68.6	3.7	5.7	2.4	3.3
2006	87.7	85.4	81.8	68.0	3.6	5.4	2.4	3.0
2007	88.0	85.6	81.7	67.9	3.9	6.0	2.6	3.4
2008	87.5	84.7	81.1	67.4	3.6	6.1	2.7	3.4
2009	87.2	84.0	80.2	66.8	3.8	6.9	3.3	3.6
2010	86.8	83.6	79.6	66.0	4.0	6.4	2.9	3.5
1979 to 2010	−7.7	−9.5	−10.0	−9.9	0.6	0.6	1.1	−0.5

Source: Author's analysis of Center for Economic Policy Research extract of March Current Population Survey (2013).

Notes: "Other private" includes directly purchased insurance; "other public" includes Medicare, Veterans Administration, and other public sources. Raw CPS data are adjusted for survey changes using the procedure described in Rho and Schmitt (2010b).

Table 10A.4 Adjusted Health Insurance Coverage of Fourth-Quintile Workers, Age Eighteen to Sixty-Four, 1979 to 2010

| Year | Health Insurance (Total) | Private Health Insurance | | | | Public Health Insurance | | |
| | | Total | Employment-Based | | Other Private | Total | Medicaid | Other Public |
			Total	Own				
1979	97.8%	96.6%	95.5%	87.3%	1.2%	4.8%	1.5%	3.3%
1980	n.a.	n.a.	96.8	88.5	n.a.	4.7	1.3	3.4
1981	n.a.	n.a.	97.1	89.2	n.a.	4.9	1.1	3.8
1982	98.3	97.1	96.6	88.2	0.6	4.9	0.9	4.0
1983	98.2	97.2	96.6	87.6	0.7	4.4	0.8	3.6
1984	97.7	96.6	95.4	86.1	1.3	4.5	0.8	3.7
1985	98.0	96.9	96.1	86.8	0.9	4.6	0.9	3.7
1986	98.3	97.3	96.3	86.5	1.1	4.6	0.8	3.8
1987	98.2	97.2	96.0	85.9	1.2	4.7	0.8	3.9
1988	97.6	96.5	95.2	84.8	1.3	5.0	0.8	4.2
1989	98.1	96.2	94.3	84.0	1.9	5.3	0.8	4.5
1990	97.5	95.8	93.9	83.3	1.9	5.5	0.8	4.7
1991	97.6	95.9	94.5	83.1	1.4	5.6	0.8	4.8
1992	97.0	95.1	93.2	81.5	1.9	5.5	0.9	4.6
1993	96.3	94.6	92.2	81.7	2.4	5.5	1.0	4.5

1994	96.0	94.3	91.9	81.3	2.4	5.4	1.0	4.4
1995	95.4	93.6	91.2	80.1	2.4	5.1	1.2	3.9
1996	96.2	94.6	92.1	80.2	2.5	4.6	1.1	3.5
1997	95.7	94.3	91.6	79.7	2.7	4.2	0.8	3.4
1998	95.2	93.8	91.4	79.9	2.4	4.2	0.8	3.4
1999	94.9	93.6	91.1	79.3	2.5	4.0	0.8	3.2
2000	94.1	93.3	91.0	79.0	2.3	3.5	0.7	2.8
2001	94.1	93.0	90.5	78.5	2.5	3.5	0.9	2.6
2002	93.6	92.2	89.7	77.2	2.5	4.2	0.8	3.4
2003	93.5	92.2	89.2	76.3	3.0	3.9	1.0	2.9
2004	93.5	92.0	88.9	75.8	3.1	4.8	1.3	3.5
2005	92.9	91.3	88.1	75.1	3.2	4.7	1.4	3.3
2006	92.1	90.5	87.2	74.4	3.3	4.5	1.5	3.0
2007	93.2	91.7	88.5	75.9	3.2	4.5	1.3	3.2
2008	93.1	91.3	88.3	75.4	3.0	4.6	1.3	3.3
2009	92.1	90.2	86.9	74.9	3.3	5.2	1.7	3.5
2010	92.6	90.6	87.1	74.6	3.5	5.2	1.9	3.3
1979 to 2010	−5.2	−6.0	−8.3	−12.7	2.3	0.4	0.4	0.0

Source: Author's analysis of Center for Economic Policy Research extract of March Current Population Survey (2013).
Notes: "Other private" includes directly purchased insurance; "other public" includes Medicare, Veterans Administration, and other public sources. Raw CPS data are adjusted for survey changes using the procedure described in Rho and Schmitt (2010b).

Table 10A.5   Adjusted Health Insurance Coverage of Top-Quintile Workers, Age Eighteen to Sixty-Four, 1979 to 2010

| Year | Health Insurance (Total) | Private Health Insurance | | | | Public Health Insurance | | |
| | | Total | Employment-Based | | Other Private | Total | Medicaid | Other Public |
			Total	Own				
1979	99.7%	98.8%	97.2%	92.2%	1.6%	2.6%	0.9%	1.7%
1980	n.a.	n.a.	98.1	92.6	n.a.	2.8	0.8	2.0
1981	n.a.	n.a.	98.6	93.4	n.a.	4.0	0.9	3.1
1982	100.2	99.3	98.8	93.2	0.5	3.3	0.7	2.6
1983	99.8	99.1	98.4	92.5	0.7	3.1	0.6	2.5
1984	99.4	98.6	97.6	91.5	1.0	3.3	0.7	2.6
1985	99.4	98.6	97.6	91.5	1.0	3.4	0.8	2.6
1986	99.5	98.5	98.0	91.3	0.5	3.3	0.8	2.5
1987	99.4	98.3	97.7	90.7	0.6	3.3	0.8	2.5
1988	99.0	98.0	97.4	90.0	0.6	2.8	0.8	2.0
1989	99.3	97.7	96.6	88.8	1.1	3.8	0.9	2.9
1990	98.9	97.4	96.1	87.8	1.3	3.9	0.8	3.1
1991	99.0	97.5	96.0	87.5	1.5	3.6	0.9	2.7
1992	98.8	97.2	95.4	86.2	1.8	3.6	0.8	2.8
1993	97.5	96.1	93.4	85.4	2.7	4.1	0.9	3.2

1994	97.2	95.9	93.0	84.8	2.9	4.0	0.8	3.2
1995	97.2	96.1	93.1	84.0	3.0	3.2	0.8	2.4
1996	97.1	96.0	93.0	83.9	3.0	3.1	0.8	2.3
1997	97.0	96.1	93.2	83.5	2.9	2.8	0.6	2.2
1998	96.7	95.9	93.1	83.1	2.8	2.8	0.4	2.4
1999	96.5	95.8	93.0	82.6	2.8	2.7	0.4	2.3
2000	96.0	95.6	93.2	82.1	2.4	2.7	0.5	2.2
2001	95.5	94.7	92.0	81.1	2.7	3.0	0.7	2.3
2002	95.6	94.7	91.4	80.7	3.3	3.0	0.5	2.5
2003	95.7	94.9	91.8	80.7	3.1	3.1	0.6	2.5
2004	95.9	94.9	91.3	79.8	3.6	3.7	0.9	2.8
2005	95.6	94.6	91.1	79.5	3.5	3.9	1.0	2.9
2006	95.6	94.6	90.8	79.1	3.8	3.6	1.0	2.6
2007	95.6	94.6	90.6	79.1	4.0	3.7	1.0	2.7
2008	95.6	94.3	90.9	79.1	3.4	4.1	1.1	3.0
2009	95.3	93.9	90.2	78.3	3.7	4.2	1.2	3.0
2010	95.5	94.1	90.5	78.9	3.6	4.4	1.3	3.1
1979 to 2010	-4.2	-4.7	-6.7	-13.3	2.0	1.8	0.5	1.4

Source: Author's analysis of Center for Economic Policy Research extract of March Current Population Survey (2013).

Notes: "Other private" includes directly purchased insurance; "other public" includes Medicare, Veterans Administration, and other public sources. Raw CPS data are adjusted for survey changes using the procedure described in Rho and Schmitt (2010b). The adjustment procedure yields a coverage rate above 100.0 percent in 1982.

NOTES

1. For a brief introduction to the origins and development of the employer-provided health insurance system in the United States, see Blumenthal (2006).
2. See, for example, U.S. Census Bureau (2011, 27, table 8). The census, instead, devotes extensive analysis to health insurance coverage by age (particularly for the population zero to seventeen and eighteen to sixty-four) and other demographic characteristics.
3. See U.S. Census Bureau, "Health Insurance Historical Tables—HIB Series," available at: http://www.census.gov/hhes/www/hlthins/data/historical/HIB_tables.html (accessed May 2013).
4. *The State of Working America* has been published biennially for two decades. The most recent data are available at: http://www.stateofworkingamerica.org/ (accessed May 2013).
5. Paul Fronstin (2000, 2009) tracks the health insurance coverage of workers and examines workers' coverage through all possible sources, not just employer-provided insurance. Lisa Clemans-Cope and Bowen Garrett (2006) analyze coverage rates for adults, workers, and children through employers and other sources. This chapter differs from this earlier research in two key ways. First, I divide workers into wage quintiles and focus on low-wage workers; Fronstin and Clemans-Cope and Garrett analyze all workers as a group. Second, I produce consistent estimates from 1979 through 2010; Fronstin (2000) covers the period 1987 through 1998, and the period 1994 through 2008 (Fronstin 2009); and Clemans-Cope and Garrett cover 2001 through 2005.
6. See Rho and Schmitt (2010b) for a review of changes in the CPS methodology related to health insurance coverage.
7. I use the same approach (Schmitt 2008). Using unadjusted CPS data, Hye Jin Rho and I (Rho and Schmitt 2010b) find a 7.5-percentage-point decline between 1979 and 2008 in overall coverage rates for workers age eighteen to sixty-four (see our table 10A.2); after adjusting for survey changes, we estimate that the decline was 10.2 percentage points—about 36 percent higher than the unadjusted estimate.
8. U.S. House of Representatives, Office of the Legislative Counsel, "Compilation of Patient Protection and Affordable Care Act," as amended through May 1, 2010, 111th Cong., 2nd session, p. 113, available at: http://housedocs.house.gov/energycommerce/ppacacon.pdf (accessed May 2013). In practice, the ACA allows states to disregard up to 5 percent of family income, potentially raising the effective threshold to 138 percent of the poverty line (Kaiser Family Foundation 2012a).
9. Hourly wages are calculated in the standard way by dividing each worker's annual earnings from work by the product of the worker's total number of weeks worked in the year and his or her usual hours per week. The upper

limit for hourly wages received by workers in the bottom wage quintile in 2010 was $10.10; the upper limit for the second wage quintile in the same year was $14.96; and workers in the top quintile made at least $30.77 per hour (all in 2010 dollars).

10.   A worker is covered if the employer offers a plan and the employee participates in that plan. Low-income workers are both less likely to be in a job that offers health insurance and less likely to accept coverage when it is available (Clemans-Cope et al. 2007, 1).

11.   For details on coverage for workers in the fourth quintile, see table 10A.4. Coverage through a spouse's or other family member's employer was basically unchanged for workers in the middle quintile (see table 10A.3).

12.   On the long-standing rise in health care costs, see, for example, Congressional Budget Office (1991), Goodell and Ginsburg (2008), and the Center for Economic and Policy Research's "Health Care Budget Deficit Calculator," available at: http://www.cepr.net/calculators/hc/hc-calculator.html (accessed May 2013).

13.   For a longer discussion of these structural shifts, see, among others, Baker (2007), Bivens (2011), Mishel, Bernstein, and Shierholz (2009), and Schmitt (2009). For a discussion of the importance of full employment, see Bernstein and Baker (2003).

14.   The Kaiser Family Foundation (2011) provides an excellent summary of the main provisions of the legislation.

15.   As the Kaiser Family Foundation (2011, 1) notes: "Exemptions will be granted for financial hardship, religious objections, American Indians, those without coverage for less than three months, undocumented immigrants, incarcerated individuals, those for whom the lowest cost plan option exceeds 8% of an individual's income, and those with incomes below the tax filing threshold (in 2009 the threshold for taxpayers under age 65 was $9,350 for singles and $18,700 for couples)." See also Blue Cross/Blue Shield of Rhode Island, "Federal Healthcare Reform," available at: https://www.bcbsri.com/BCBSRIWeb/pdf/Individual_Mandate_Fact_Sheet.pdf, p. 2 (accessed May 2013); and U.S. House of Representatives, Office of the Legislative Counsel, "Compilation of Patient Protection and Affordable Care Act."

16.   The tax penalty will apply (but differently) in both the case where the employer does not provide coverage and the case where the employer provides coverage but the employee does not accept it.

17.   See, for example, "Justices to Hear Health Care Case as Race Heats Up," *New York Times*, November 15, 2011.

18.   For a summary of state-level actions to challenge the ACA, see Cauci (2013).

19.   As passed, the ACA made all legal residents under the age of sixty-five eligible for Medicaid if their family income is less than 133 percent of the federal poverty line. The Supreme Court's June 2012 ruling on the constitutionality of the ACA, however, allowed states to opt out of this requirement. States may decline

to expand Medicaid coverage, but in doing so they stand to lose some federal support for their Medicaid program. In the discussion of future projections, I assume that states will (eventually) agree to the proposed ACA Medicaid expansion, on the assumption that cash-scrapped states will not long leave free money on the table (federal funds cover up to 90 percent of states' added costs). This assumption is consistent with state behavior after the initial creation of Medicaid and Medicare in 1965. For a discussion of the Supreme Court's decision and the implications for implementation of the ACA's proposed Medicaid expansion, see Kaiser Family Foundation (2012a, 2012b).

20. The CBO cites studies by the Centers for Medicare and Medicaid Services (Foster 2010), the Urban Institute (Buettgens, Garret, and Holahan 2010), the Lewin Group (2010), and RAND (Eibner, Hussey, and Girosi 2010).

21. The CBO estimates that by 2019 the ACA will have reduced offers of employer-provided health insurance about 4 percent relative to what the figure would have been in the absence of the legislation.

22. See, for example, Holtz-Eakin and Smith (2010) and Pizer, Frakt, and Iezzoni (2011). A more recent CBO analysis has also suggested that a higher number of workers will lose employer-provided health insurance; see also Congressional Budget Office, staff of the Joint Committee on Taxation, "CBO's February 2013 Estimate of the Effects of the Affordable Care Act on Health Insurance Coverage," available at: http://www.cbo.gov/sites/default/files/cbofiles/attachments/43900_ACAInsuranceCoverageEffects.pdf (accessed May 2013).

23. In fact, non-elderly workers in 2010 had a slightly lower noncoverage rate (19.5 percent) than nonworking adults (21.8 percent). If we were to adjust for this difference, the results for workers under the ACA would be somewhat better than appears under the assumption of a uniform rate for non-elderly adults.

24. Imagine that there are exactly one hundred workers divided into five groups by wage level, each with twenty workers. If six of the total are without insurance (rounding up from 5.8 percent), and if they are all in the bottom group, then six of twenty members of that group, or 30 percent, are without coverage.

25. In 1974 Hawaii passed a law requiring employers to provide health insurance coverage to all full-time employees. Legal challenges delayed implementation until the mid-1980s, but the law has been in place and enforced since then. The lack of an individual mandate in Hawaii significantly reduces the usefulness of the Hawaiian experience for projecting the likely effects of the ACA. For a recent and comprehensive review of the Hawaiian experience, see Buchmueller, DiNardo, and Valetta (2011).

26. For a brief overview of the Massachusetts reforms, see Dorn, Hill, and Hogan (2009) and Gruber (2008).

27. The Massachusetts figure is from Long, Cook, and Stockley (2009, 11); the national figure is from Rho and Schmitt (2010b, table 4).

28. Long, Phadera, and Lynch (2010) also note that those non-elderly adults who remain uncovered are less likely to be employed than those with coverage — though this does not rule out that low-wage workers are even less likely than the non-employed to have coverage.

REFERENCES

Baker, Dean. 2007. *The United States Since 1980.* Cambridge: Cambridge University Press.

Bernstein, Jared, and Dean Baker. 2003. *The Benefits of Full Employment: When Markets Work for People.* Washington, D.C.: Economic Policy Institute.

Bivens, Josh. 2011. *Failure by Design: The Story Behind America's Broken Economy.* Washington, D.C.: Economic Policy Institute.

Blumenthal, David. 2006. "Employer-Sponsored Health Insurance in the United States—Origins and Implications." *New England Journal of Medicine* 355(1): 82–88.

Boushey, Heather. 2012. Remarks at the conference "What Works for Workers? Public Policies and Innovative Strategies for Low-Wage Workers." Washington, D.C.: Georgetown University (February).

Buchmueller, Thomas C., John DiNardo, and Robert G. Valetta. 2011. "The Effect of an Employer Health Insurance Mandate on Health Insurance Coverage and the Demand for Labor: Evidence from Hawaii." *American Economic Journal: Economic Policy* 3(4): 25–51.

Buettgens, Matthew, Bowen Garrett, and John Holahan. 2010. "America Under the Affordable Care Act," Washington, D.C.: Urban Institute (December). Available at: http://www.urban.org/uploadedpdf/412267-america-under-aca.pdf (accessed May 2013).

Cauci, Richard. 2013. "State Legislation and Actions Challenging Certain Health Reforms." Denver: National Conference of State Legislatures (July). Available at: http://www.ncsl.org/issues-research/health/state-laws-and-actions-challenging-ppaca.aspx (accessed May 2013).

Center for Economic and Policy Research. 2013. *Extract of the March Supplement of the Current Population Survey, 1980–2012.* Available at: http://ceprdata.org/cps-uniform-data-extracts/march-cps-supplement/ (accessed May 2013).

Clemans-Cope, Lisa, and Bowen Garrett. 2006. "Changes in Employer-Sponsored Health Insurance Sponsorship, Eligibility, and Participation: 2001 to 2005." Menlo Park, Calif.: Henry J. Kaiser Family Foundation (December 31). Available at: http://www.kff.org/uninsured/upload/7599.pdf (accessed May 2013).

Clemans-Cope, Lisa, Genevieve M. Kenney, Matthew Pantell, and Cynthia D. Perry. 2007. "Access to Employer-Sponsored Health Insurance Among Low-Income Families: Who Has Access and Who Doesn't?" Washington, D.C.: Urban Insti-

tute. Available at: http://www.urban.org/UploadedPDF/411533_fringe_benefits.
pdf (accessed May 2013).

Congressional Budget Office. 1991. "Rising Health Care Costs: Causes, Implications, and Strategies." Washington: CBO (April 1). Available at: http://www.cbo.gov/ftpdocs/76xx/doc7665/91-CBO-001.pdf (accessed May 2013).

———. 2011. "CBO's Analysis of the Major Health Care Legislation Enacted in March 2010." Testimony of Douglas M. Elmendorf before the Subcommittee on Health of the House Committee on Energy and Commerce, March 30. http://www.cbo.gov/ftpdocs/121xx/doc12119/03-30-healthcarelegislation.pdf (accessed May 2013).

Dorn, Stan, Ian Hill, and Sara Hogan. 2009. "The Secrets of Massachusetts' Success: Why 97 Percent of State Residents Have Health Coverage." Washington, D.C.: Urban Institute (November). Available at: http://www.urban.org/Uploaded PDF/411987_massachusetts_success.pdf (accessed May 2013).

Eibner, Christine, Peter S. Hussey, and Federico Girosi. 2010. "The Effects of the Affordable Care Act on Workers' Health Insurance Coverage." *New England Journal of Medicine* 363(15): 1393–95.

Foster, Richard S. 2010. "Estimated Financial Effects of the 'Patient Protection and Affordable Care Act,' as Amended" (memo). Washington: U.S. Department of Health and Human Services, Centers for Medicare and Medicaid Services (April 22). Available at: http://www.cms.gov/ActuarialStudies/Downloads/PPACA_2010-04-22.pdf (accessed May 2013).

Fronstin, Paul. 2000. "The Working Uninsured: Who They Are, How They Have Changed, and the Consequences of Being Uninsured." Issue Brief 224. Washington, D.C.: Employee Benefit Research Institute (August). Available at: http://www.ebri.org/pdf/briefspdf/0800ib.pdf (accessed May 2013).

———. 2009. "Sources of Health Insurance and Characteristics of the Uninsured: Analysis of the March 2009 Current Population Survey." Issue Brief 334. Washington, D.C.: Employee Benefit Research Institute (September). Available at: http://www.ebri.org/publications/ib/index.cfm?fa=ibDisp&content_id=4366 (accessed May 2013).

Goodell, Sarah, and Paul D. Ginsburg. 2008. "High and Rising Health Care Costs: Demystifying U.S. Health Care Spending." Research Synthesis Project Report 16. Princeton, N.J.: Robert Wood Johnson Foundation (October). Available at: http://www.rwjf.org/files/research/101508.policysynthesis.costdrivers.rpt.pdf (accessed May 2013).

Gould, Elise. 2009. "Employer-Sponsored Health Insurance Erosion Continues." Briefing Paper 2473. Washington, D.C.: Economic Policy Institute (October 27). Available at: http://www.epi.org/publication/bp247/ (accessed May 2013).

Gruber, Jonathan. 2008. "Massachusetts Health Care Reform: The View from One Year Out." *Risk Management and Insurance Review* 11(1): 51–63.

Holtz-Eakin, Douglas, and Cameron Smith. 2010. "Labor Markets and Health Care Reform: New Results." Washington, D.C.: American Action Forum (May 27). Available at: http://americanactionforum.org/sites/default/files/OHC_LabMktsHCR.pdf (accessed May 2013).

Kaiser Family Foundation. 2011. "Summary of New Health Reform Law." Menlo Park, Calif.: Henry J. Kaiser Family Foundation (April 25). Available at: http://www.kff.org/healthreform/upload/8061.pdf (accessed May 2013).

———. 2012a. "A Guide to the Supreme Court's Decision on the ACA's Medicaid Expansion." Menlo Park, Calif.: Henry J. Kaiser Family Foundation (June 29). Available at: http://www.kff.org/healthreform/8332.cfm (accessed May 2013).

———. 2012b. "Implementing the ACA's Medicaid-Related Health Reform Provisions After the Supreme Court's Decision." Menlo Park, Calif.: Henry J. Kaiser Family Foundation (August 1). Available at: http://www.kff.org/healthreform/8347.cfm (accessed May 2013).

Lewin Group. 2010. "Patient Protection and Affordable Care Act (PPACA): Long-Term Costs for Governments, Employers, Families, and Providers." Staff Working Paper 11. Falls Church, Va.: Lewin Group (June). Available at: http://www.lewin.com/publications/publication/409/ (accessed May 2013).

Long, Sharon K., Allison Cook, and Karen Stockley. 2009. "Health Insurance Coverage in Massachusetts: Estimates from the 2008 Massachusetts Health Insurance Survey." Boston: Massachusetts Division of Health Care Finance and Policy (March). Available at: http://www.urban.org/UploadedPDF/411815_Massachusetts_Insurance.pdf (accessed May 2013).

Long, Sharon, Lokendra Phadera, and Victoria Lynch. 2010. "Massachusetts Health Reform in 2008: Who Are the Remaining Uninsured Adults?" Washington, D.C.: Robert Wood Johnson Foundation (August). Available at: http://www.shadac.org/files/shadac/publications/MassReform2008UninsuredBrief.pdf (accessed May 2013).

Long, Sharon K., Alshadye Yemane, and Karen Stockley. 2010. "Disentangling the Effects of Health Reform in Massachusetts: How Important Are the Special Provisions for Young Adults?" American Economic Review: Papers and Proceedings 100(2): 297–302.

Mishel, Lawrence, Jared Bernstein, and Heidi Shierholz. 2009. The State of Working America, 2008–2009. Ithaca, N.Y.: Cornell University Press.

Pande, Aakanksha H., Dennis Ross-Degnan, Alan M. Zaslavsky, and Joshua A. Salomon. 2011. "Effects of Healthcare Reforms on Coverage, Access, and Disparities: Quasi-Experimental Analysis of Evidence from Massachusetts." American Journal of Preventive Medicine 41(1): 1–8.

Pizer, Steven D., Austin B. Frakt, and Lisa I. Iezzoni. 2011. "The Effect of Health Reform on Public and Private Insurance in the Long Run." Unpublished paper.

Boston: Boston University (March 9). Available at: http://papers.ssrn.com/sol3/papers.cfm?abstract_id=1782210 (accessed May 2013).

Rho, Hye Jin, and John Schmitt. 2010a. "Who Are the 46.3 Million Uninsured?" Center for Economic and Policy Research (April 5). Available at: http://www.cepr.net/index.php/graphic-economics/who-are-the-463-million-uninsured/ (accessed January 16, 2012).

———. 2010b. "Health-Insurance Coverage Rates for U.S. Workers, 1979–2008." Washington, D.C.: Center for Economic and Policy Research (March). Available at: http://www.cepr.net/documents/publications/hc-coverage-2010-03.pdf (accessed May 2013).

Schmitt, John. 2008. "The Decline of Good Jobs." *Challenge* 51(1): 5–25.

———. 2009. "Inequality as Policy: The United States Since 1979." Washington, D.C.: Center for Economic and Policy Research (October). Available at: http://www.cepr.net/documents/publications/inequality-policy-2009-10.pdf (accessed May 2013).

U.S. Census Bureau. 2011. "Income, Poverty, and Health Insurance Coverage in the United States, 2010." *Current Population Reports.* Washington: U.S. Department of Commerce, U.S. Census Bureau (September). Available at: http://www.census.gov/prod/2011pubs/p60-239.pdf (accessed May 2013).

Chapter 11 | Low-Wage Workers and Paid Family Leave: The California Experience

Ruth Milkman and Eileen Appelbaum

As FAMILY AND work patterns have shifted over recent decades, the demand for time off from work to address family needs has grown rapidly.[1] "Work-family balance" has become an urgent but elusive priority for millions of Americans, driven by high labor force participation rates among mothers as well as the caregiving needs of an aging population. Women—and increasingly men as well—often find themselves caught between the competing pressures of paid work and family responsibilities, especially when they become parents or when serious illness strikes a family member. Affluent families can often fill the gap with paid caregiving services, but their low-income counterparts can rarely afford to do so.

The United States is notoriously lacking in public policies that support workers who need time off to attend to family needs. Across the industrialized world, long-standing government-sponsored programs provide mothers—and, in many countries, fathers as well—with wage replacement and job security for extended periods immediately before and after the birth of a new child. Paid sick leave and vacation policies are universal in most industrialized nations, and some governments make provision for elder care as well (see Gornick and Meyers 2003).

By contrast, the only major federal legislation to address these issues in the United States was the 1993 Family and Medical Leave Act (FMLA), which guarantees up to twelve weeks of job-protected leave, with continuing fringe benefits, for both men and women who need time off from work to attend to their own medical conditions or for family care. However, FMLA's coverage is limited to only about half of the nation's workers, and

305

to less than one-fifth of all new mothers (Ruhm 1997; Waldfogel 2001).[2] And because the leaves that FMLA provides are unpaid, even those workers who are covered often cannot afford to take advantage of it.

In the absence of government provision for wage replacement during family leave, U.S. workers typically rely on a patchwork of employer-provided benefits to make ends meet, such as paid sick leave, vacation, disability insurance, and/or parental and family leave. However, such employer-provided benefits are by no means universally available. Managers and professionals, as well as public-sector workers and others covered by collective bargaining agreements, often have access to benefits that provide some form of wage replacement during a family leave. But vast sectors of the U.S. workforce have little or no access to paid sick days or paid vacation, and paid parental or family leave is even rarer. The situation is particularly acute for low-wage workers as well as for the growing number of "precarious workers"—independent contractors, freelancers, and others who lack any stable connection to an employer.

Against this background, California's passage of the nation's first comprehensive paid family leave (PFL) program on September 23, 2002, was a historic breakthrough. Only two other states (New Jersey in 2009 and Rhode Island in 2013) have established such programs.[3] Both programs were enacted into law as a result of sustained campaigns led by broad coalitions of paid leave advocates, including women's organizations, advocates for children, senior citizens' groups, medical practitioners, and critically, organized labor, which supplied much of the necessary lobbying expertise and political clout. Although the business lobby opposed these programs (in both states) and succeeded in scaling them back to some extent, the advocates of paid leave prevailed, in part owing to the broad public support for the issue.

California's PFL benefits became available on July 1, 2004. Unlike the FMLA, California's PFL program covers the entire private sector, regardless of employer size. Self-employed workers are not automatically covered, but can opt into the program; unionized public-sector workers can also opt in through the collective bargaining process. Workers need not have been with their current employer for any specific period of time to be eligible for PFL; they need only to have earned $300 or more in a job covered by state disability insurance (SDI) during any quarter in the "base period," which is five to seventeen months before they file a PFL claim. With this very minimal earnings requirement, most part-time workers are covered by the program. In short, with its near-universal coverage, the California PFL program presented a pathbreaking opportunity to address the issue of inequality in access to paid leave.

The program offers partial wage replacement for covered workers who go on leave to bond with a new biological, adopted, or foster child; this benefit is available to fathers as well as mothers during the first year after a child is born or placed with the family. The program also offers wage replacement during leaves to care for certain seriously ill family members (a parent, child, spouse, or registered domestic partner). For both bonding and caring leaves, covered workers can receive up to six weeks of wage replacement at 55 percent of their usual weekly earnings, up to a maximum benefit of $987 per week in 2011. (The maximum is indexed in relation to the state's average weekly wage.) The six weeks of leave can be continuous or intermittent.

The PFL program is funded by an employee-paid payroll tax, with benefit levels indexed to inflation. It builds on California's long-standing state disability insurance system, which has provided income support for medical and pregnancy-related leaves for many years. PFL is available to biological mothers for six weeks *in addition to* the SDI benefits they may receive during pregnancy leave.[4] Unlike SDI payments, however, PFL benefits have been deemed taxable income by the U.S. Internal Revenue Service.

The PFL program is structured as an insurance benefit, like SDI. There are no direct costs to employers: the wage replacement benefit is funded entirely by an employee payroll tax. (Currently a 1.0 percent tax on the first $95,585 in earnings finances both SDI and PFL.) All California private-sector wage and salary workers, except for the self-employed (unless they opt in), pay this modest tax. Workers can claim PFL benefits after a one-week waiting period by submitting appropriate documentation, including certification from a health care provider, to the state's Employment Development Department. Employers may require workers to take up to two weeks of earned (unused) vacation before collecting PFL benefits; in such cases, this vacation period runs concurrently with the one-week waiting period required under the PFL program.

The PFL program does not provide job protection, although in many cases leave-takers have such protection under the FMLA or the California Family Rights Act (CFRA), a state law that took effect in 1992, a year before the federal FMLA became law, but which has broadly similar provisions. For those who are covered by these laws, the PFL leave and the FMLA/CFRA leave must be taken concurrently.

In operation for nearly eight years now, the California program has a track record of sufficient length to permit a serious evaluation of how well it is working and the extent to which its potential to improve the access of low-wage workers to paid leave has been realized. How well has the program served the growing numbers of low-wage workers, many of them female, who have limited access to employer-sponsored fringe benefits providing paid time off? How widespread are awareness and usage of the program? What has been the experience of workers who have used the program, and how has it affected their families? These are among the questions we address in this chapter.

To explore these issues we have conducted a series of surveys of California employers and workers since 2004. Here we focus primarily on a screening survey, with telephone interviews in both English and Spanish, conducted between December 2009 and February 2010. It included five hundred employed respondents who had experienced an event in the preceding four years (becoming a parent or having a close family member become seriously ill) that could have triggered a paid family leave.[5] Although the screening survey did not attempt to capture a representative sample but rather screened for individuals who were eligible for PFL, the 2009–2010 survey sample proved demographically diverse in regard to age, gender, race and ethnicity, and immigrant status, like the California population. It includes workers across the economic spectrum, with varied levels of education and income. One of the most useful features of the sample, and one that we exploit extensively here, involves the contrast between respondents with what we call "high-quality jobs," defined as those that pay more than $20 an hour *and* include employer-paid health insurance, and those who have "low-quality jobs" that fail to meet this standard. In our sample of 500 workers, 30 percent (149 respondents) held high-quality jobs and 70 percent (351 respondents) held low-quality jobs—roughly similar to the proportions in other studies of California workers that differentiate between good and bad jobs.[6] Comparing and contrasting their experiences with family leave offers insight into the on-the-ground effect of the California PFL program and allows us to assess its effectiveness as a social leveler in particular.

We also briefly discuss the findings of a more recent national survey regarding the FMLA that was conducted for the U.S. Department of Labor in 2012 and focused on the situation of low-income and non-college-educated workers. These additional data are especially valuable for the broader perspective they provide on our analysis of California, situating it in the context of the United States as a whole.

PAID FAMILY LEAVE AND THE PROBLEM OF INEQUALITY

Inequalities between "haves" and "have-nots" in the United States have grown steadily in recent decades, along with rapid expansion in the ranks of low-wage workers whose jobs not only provide minimal pay but also have few or no benefits; such workers often lack employer-provided health insurance coverage, for example. At the other end of the spectrum, professional and managerial workers not only are paid relatively well but also typically have access to an array of employer-provided benefits.

This growing polarization among workers is also manifested in the availability of employer-provided wage replacement during parental and other family-related leaves. As many commentators have pointed out (see, for example, Heymann 2000; Williams and Boushey 2010), benefits that can be used to support family leaves—from paid sick leaves and paid vacations to short-term disability benefits and explicitly defined paid parental leave benefits—are offered disproportionately to well-paid workers like managers and professionals, while low-wage workers frequently are offered few or no such benefits. Ironically, although women typically continue to have far greater family caregiving responsibilities than men do, employers tend to provide male employees with more extensive wage replacement for family-related absences or leaves from work than female employees receive—not because they are men but because they are concentrated in the better jobs. More generally, because many employers are especially interested in retaining their most highly trained workers and are aware that providing income support during leaves from work increases retention, they are disproportionately inclined to offer professional and managerial workers wage replacement during family-related leaves. In contrast, employers tend to view low-wage workers as dispensable and are less concerned about reducing their high turnover rates.

The resulting disparities in access to the range of employer-provided benefits that can be used during family leaves are now well documented. For example, a 2011 report from the U.S. Census Bureau (Laughlin 2011) covering the 2006 to 2008 period found that, among women who worked during the pregnancy preceding the birth of their first child, the percentage of those with a bachelor's degree who received some type of wage replacement during their maternity leave (66.3 percent) was more than double that of high school graduates (31.6 percent) and more than triple that of those with less than a high school education (18.5 percent). Similarly, the National Compensation Survey of Employee Benefits (2011) conducted by the U.S. Bureau of Labor Statistics found that in 2010 the top 25 percent of private-sector wage-earners had access to paid family leave at *four times* the rate of the bottom 25 percent.[7]

Our 2009–2010 screening survey of California workers who experienced life events that might qualify them for the state's PFL program offers further confirmation of the inequality in employer-provided benefits. Whereas 93.5 percent of respondents who had high-quality jobs (with pay over $20 per hour and employer-provided health insurance) also had access to employer-provided paid sick days and/or paid vacation, only 62.1 percent of those with low-quality jobs had such access, a statistically significant difference ($p < 0.001$, using a two-sample independent Z-test).[8]

The U.S. Department of Labor's 2012 survey on family and medical leave shows that workers who lack access to paid leave often are unable to afford to go on leave even when they have a need to do so. Among respondents who reported that they needed family or medical leave but did not take it, by far the most common reason reported—by 42.7 percent—was that they "couldn't afford to take an unpaid leave." For non-college-educated respondents, this figure rose to 53.8 percent, compared to 36.6 percent for those with at least some college education. Similarly, for those whose household incomes were below $40,000, 50.6 percent reported that they did not take a needed leave because they could not afford to do so, compared to 38.9 percent of those with household incomes between $40,000 and $74,999 and 32.6 percent of those with household incomes of $75,000 or more.[9]

California's PFL program, with its nearly universal scope, was designed in part to address these unmet needs. The state's professionals, managers, and others whose employers already provide them with paid time off can now draw on PFL as well as the benefits they had before. For this group, indeed, access to wage replacement historically has been as good as or better than what the new state program offers. By contrast, low-wage workers who previously had limited or no access to wage replacement during leaves stood to gain far more from the PFL program, which promised to narrow or even close the gap in access to paid leave between the "haves" and "have-nots."

As we show later, those low-wage workers who take advantage of PFL do benefit greatly from the new program, both economically and in terms of its impact on their health and well-being, as well as that of their family members. The program remains largely ineffective, however, in reducing inequality. One reason for this is that many Californians remain unaware of the program's existence. Although Californians, like most Americans, strongly support the concept of paid family leave (see Milkman and Appelbaum 2004), public awareness in California of the PFL program remains limited nearly eight years after it began operations. Moreover, those Californians who need the program most—low-wage workers and other disadvantaged groups—are the least likely to be aware of it.

Another factor limiting the effectiveness of PFL as a social leveler is that it often operates as a subsidy to those employers that have historically provided benefits of their own for workers who go on family leaves. Most of those employers now coordinate their benefits with the state PFL program, which gives them an incentive to encourage their employees to access the state program. In contrast, low-wage workers with no employer-provided benefits receive no such encouragement. As a result, the preexisting inequality in access to wage replacement is reproduced in a new form rather than eliminated.

Inequality in Awareness of PFL

Over the past decade, we have conducted a series of surveys to assess the extent of public awareness of the program in California. The first of these surveys was fielded in late 2003, a year after the PFL legislation was passed (but prior to the program's implementation). At that time, we found that only 22.0 percent of California adult respondents were aware of PFL (for details see Milkman and Appelbaum 2004). Awareness rose somewhat after benefits became available: our mid-2005 follow-up survey of California adults found that 29.5 percent of respondents were aware of the program a year after its initial implementation, and about the same proportion (28.1 percent) were aware of it in mid-2007, when we conducted another awareness survey. In all three of these surveys, we found that low-income respondents, those with less education, young workers, Latinos, and immigrants had substantially lower levels of awareness of PFL than the state's adult population as a whole.

In 2011, this time in association with the California Field Poll, we once again assessed Californians' awareness of the state's PFL program. The Field Poll included 1,001 registered voters and was conducted September 1–12, 2011. Well under half (42.7 percent) of the Field Poll respondents had "seen, read [about], or heard [of]" the PFL program. As in the previous surveys, awareness varied by ethnicity, gender, and age, as figure 11.1 shows, and once again awareness of PFL was substantially lower among economically disadvantaged groups such as those with lower household incomes, those with limited education, and renters.

The Field Poll methodology differed somewhat from that of our earlier surveys, but a systematic comparison to the results of our initial 2003 survey shows that awareness has increased by about 50 percent over the past eight years, as shown in table 11.1. Here the comparison is limited to respondents who voted in the last general election (the 2008 election for the 2011 poll, and the 2000 election for the 2003 survey), so the data do not correspond to those shown in figure 11.1.

Although fewer than half of these voters (44.9 percent) were aware of PFL in 2011, this is a dramatic and significant increase over 2003, when the figure was only 29.7 percent. Awareness grew even more among female voters, from 25.9 to 51.2 percent. For men, however, there was very little change. Awareness nearly doubled among Latinos and Asians who voted in the 2008 election. (It is important to note, however, that immigrant non-citizens are not part of this group.)

Awareness of FMLA is far higher than awareness of PFL, but the patterns of inequality are similar. Overall, 64.2 percent of respondents in the 2012 U.S. Department of Labor survey were aware of FMLA's existence, and awareness was higher among women—71.1 percent, compared to 57.5 percent for men. As with PFL, the sharpest disparities in awareness were by education and income: 82.9 percent of college graduates were aware of FMLA, compared to only 44.2 percent of those with no college

Figure 11.1 Awareness of Paid Family Leave Among Registered Voters in California, by Selected Respondent Characteristics, September 2011

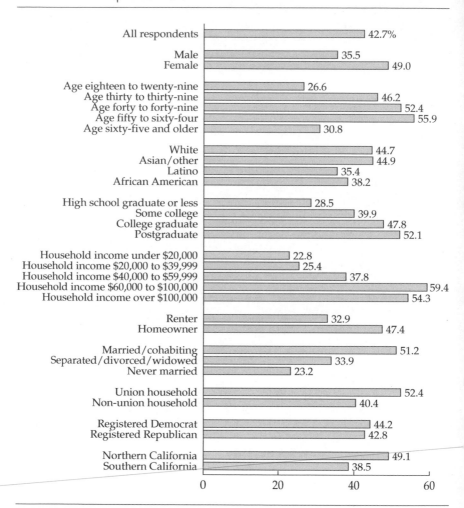

Source: Authors' analysis of 2011 Field Poll data (N = 1,000).

Notes: The categories Asian/others, whites, and African Americans do not include Latinos. For these race-ethnicity groups, using whites as the reference group, the only statistically significant difference is for Latinos ($p < 0.05$). The gender differences shown are statistically significant ($p < 0.001$). Using age forty to forty-nine as the reference group, the only statistically significant differences are for ages eighteen to twenty and sixty-five and older (for both $p < 0.001$). For household income, the differences between the top two and bottom two categories and the reference group (the middle category, $40,000 to $59,999) are statistically significant ($p < 0.05$). For education, with college graduates as the reference group, the only statistically significant difference is for the high school graduates, which includes respondents with less than high school education ($p < 0.001$). The difference between renters and homeowners is also statistically significant ($p < 0.001$).

Table 11.1   Paid Family Leave Awareness Among Respondents Who
Voted in the Previous General Election, 2003 and 2011

Percentage Aware of Paid Family Leave	2003	2011
All respondents	29.7	44.9***
Women	25.9	51.2***
Men	34.3	37.7
Latinos	22.0	40.8***
Blacks	35.3	38.0
Whites	30.9	45.7***
Asians/other	24.9	49.3***

Source: Authors' analysis of 2011 Field Poll data (N = 1,000).
***p < 0.001

education. Among respondents with household incomes over $75,000, 71.0 percent knew about FMLA, compared to only 47.7 percent among those with household incomes below $40,000. Race disparities were also present: 72.2 percent of white respondents were aware of FMLA, compared to 53.8 percent of blacks and 40.7 percent of Hispanics.[10]

Our 2003 and 2011 PFL surveys did not probe in any detail the extent to which respondents were familiar with the details of the PFL program, nor how they learned about it. However, we were able to include questions about those topics in the 2009–2010 screening survey. Not surprisingly, because all five hundred screening survey respondents were employed and all had experienced a life event that the PFL program was designed to cover (a new child or a seriously ill family member), their awareness of PFL was greater than in the representative surveys, with nearly half (48.6 percent) indicating that they were aware of PFL's existence.

Among PFL-aware respondents to the screening survey, knowledge of the details of the program followed a similar pattern of inequality to that of the overall awareness data, as table 11.2 shows. Respondents with high-quality jobs consistently knew more about the details of the PFL program than those with low-quality jobs; although these differences are more modest than those in overall awareness, all but one of them is statistically significant.

The screening survey also explored how PFL-aware respondents had learned about the program. As figure 11.2 shows, the most common source of information was employers: 63.4 percent of respondents employed in the private or nonprofit sector indicated that they had learned about the program from their employer—twice the proportion for any other information source except family or friends. Of particular interest for

Table 11.2   Knowledge of Paid Family Leave Program Details Among
Respondents Aware of PFL, by Job Quality, 2009 to 2010

Specific Information About Paid Family Leave	All Respondents	Respondents with High-Quality Jobs	Respondents with Low-Quality Jobs
Can be used for bonding with a newborn	86.4%	92.3%	82.9%*
Can be used for bonding with an adopted or foster child	68.5	75.9	63.6*
Available to both fathers and mothers	78.2	88.1	72.2***
Can be used to care for a seriously ill family member	64.2	68.2	62.0

Source: Authors' 2009–2010 screening survey (N = 246).
*p < 0.05; ***p < 0.001

Figure 11.2   How Respondents Learned About Paid Family Leave,
2009 to 2010

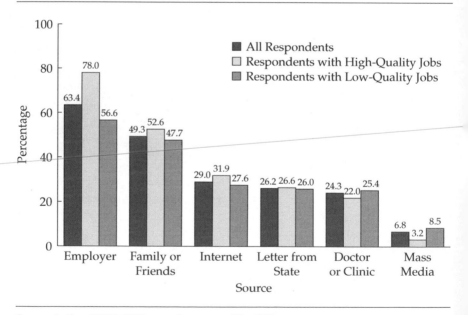

Source: Authors' 2009–2010 screening survey (N = 178).
Note: Includes only respondents who were aware of paid family leave and who were employed in the private or nonprofit sector; total adds to more than 100 percent because respondents could cite more than one information source.
***p < 0.001

our purposes here, 78.0 percent of respondents in high-quality jobs had learned about PFL from their employers, compared to only 56.6 percent of those in low-quality jobs, a statistically significant difference.

This disparity reflects the reality, as noted earlier, that employers that provide paid time off to their workers have an economic incentive to inform those employees about the existence of PFL: if such workers draw benefits from the state PFL program in lieu of some part of what the employer would otherwise provide, the employer enjoys a cost savings. Since employers are more likely to provide wage replacement to higher-paid workers, it follows that those workers are more likely to receive information about PFL from their employers. As one manager we interviewed just before PFL benefits became available predicted, "Paid family leave in California was intended to help people who don't have any pay during maternity leave or other family leaves. But in fact the main beneficiaries will be higher-paid workers who already have paid sick leave and vacation and who will use the state program to top off their current benefits."

Indeed, among PFL-aware respondents to our 2009–2010 screening survey, half (49.8 percent) of those with high-quality jobs who were eligible for the program had used PFL, but only 36.6 percent of those in low-quality jobs had done so, a statistically significant difference ($p < 0.05$).[11] Similarly, an analysis of PFL claims data by the California Senate Office of Research (Sherriff 2007) found that low-wage workers were underrepresented among PFL claimants.

Why PFL-Aware Workers Did Not Take Up the Program Benefits

Limited awareness has obviously contributed to what has thus far been a lower-than-expected take-up rate for California's PFL program. Our screening survey suggests some other factors that also help explain the low take-up. Among respondents to that survey who were aware of PFL, some were ineligible because they worked in the public sector, others were eligible but believed that they were not, and still another group received full wage replacement from their employer and thus had no reason to draw on PFL benefits.

But even after eliminating all these groups from consideration, about one-fifth of the total screening survey sample (those who were aware of PFL, worked in the private or nonprofit sector, believed they were eligible for the program, and did not receive full wage replacement from employer-provided sources while on leave) still did not use the PFL program for a covered life event. When asked why they did not apply for PFL when they needed to go on a family leave, these respondents cited a variety of concerns, summarized in figure 11.3.

Figure 11.3   Reasons Cited by Selected Respondents Who Were
Aware of Paid Family Leave and Who Did Not Apply for
Paid Family Leave, 2009 to 2010

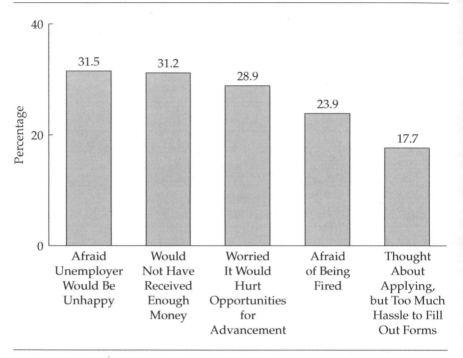

Source: Authors' 2009–2010 screening survey (N = 89).
Note: Total adds to more than 100 percent because respondents could cite more than one reason.

Caution should be used in interpreting these data, as the sample is limited and unrepresentative. Nevertheless, it is striking that many of the reasons cited involve concerns that taking advantage of PFL would have negative consequences for them at work: that their employer would be unhappy, that using PFL might hurt their chances for advancement, or, at the extreme, that they might actually be fired for doing so. In all, 36.9 percent of the subset of respondents who were asked why they did not apply for PFL cited at least one such concern.

This highlights one key limitation of the PFL program, namely, that it does not include job protection—an unfortunate result of the fact that PFL was established through an amendment to California's preexisting SDI program, which does not explicitly offer job protection to workers on disability leaves. At the time PFL was won, advocates feared that including a job protection provision in the program legislation would provoke insurmountable opposition from employers. Some PFL-covered workers do have job protection under other statutes, such as the federal FMLA. But for the rest, taking a PFL leave could mean that they would not have a job to return to, or that they would suffer other negative consequences. Fear of these outcomes appears to be another important reason—apart from lack of awareness of the PFL program—for the low take-up rate.

Finally, almost one-third of the PFL-aware respondents who were asked why they did not use the program pointed to the limited wage replacement it provides. Indeed, the PFL program provides only 55 percent of workers' usual pay, which for many workers—especially those in low-wage jobs—may make it unaffordable.

THE IMPACT OF PFL ON LOW-WAGE WORKERS AND THEIR FAMILIES

For those workers who did use PFL, however, our data show that the program made a highly positive contribution to their well-being and that of their families. Respondents to the 2009–2010 screening survey who utilized the PFL program when they took a leave from work to bond with a new child or to care for a seriously ill family member reported far better economic, social, and health-related outcomes than those who did not use the program. PFL users had significantly higher levels of wage replacement, were able to take longer leaves, and were more satisfied with the length of their leaves. In addition, using PFL enhanced workers' ability to care for their children or ill family members and, for those in low-quality jobs, increased the likelihood of returning to work with the same employer.

As noted earlier, workers in low-quality jobs had the most to gain from the introduction of PFL but were less likely to be aware of its existence and (among those who were aware of it) less well informed about the details of the program than workers in high-quality jobs. But for the minority of workers in low-quality jobs who not only were aware of PFL but actually used it during their family leaves, outcomes were greatly improved over those for workers in low-quality jobs who did not use PFL.

Wage Replacement During Family Leave

Most importantly, use of PFL made a significant difference in the level of wage replacement. Over one-fourth (28.4 percent) of all workers who did not use the PFL program during their leave, as table 11.3 shows, received no wage replacement at all. In contrast, the vast majority (91.7 percent)

Table 11.3   Wage Replacement During Family Leave, by Paid Family Leave Use and Job Quality, 2009 to 2010

Proportion of Usual Pay Received During Leave	All	All Workers		High-Quality Jobs		Low-Quality Jobs	
		Used Paid Family Leave	Did Not Use Paid Family Leave	Used Paid Family Leave	Did Not Use Paid Family Leave	Used Paid Family Leave	Did Not Use Paid Family Leave
No pay	21.8%	0.0%	28.4%***	0.0%	11.0%*	0.0%	38.2%***
Less than half	11.5	8.3	12.5	0.0	12.4**	16.2	12.5
About half	20.1	40.2	14.1***	55.3	9.6***	25.9	16.7
More than half	20.0	43.1	13.1***	37.8	17.0	48.2	10.9***
Full pay	26.5	8.3	31.9***	6.9	50.0***	9.7	21.6
Total	100.0	100.0	100.0	100.0	100.0	100.0	100.0

Source: Authors' 2009–2010 screening survey (N = 204).
Note: Columns may not add to 100.0 percent due to rounding.
*$p < 0.05$; **$p < 0.01$; ***$p < 0.001$

Figure 11.4   Wage Replacement During Family Leave Among
Workers in Low-Quality Jobs, by Use of Paid Family
Leave, 2009 to 2010

Used Paid Family Leave   Did Not Use Paid Family Leave

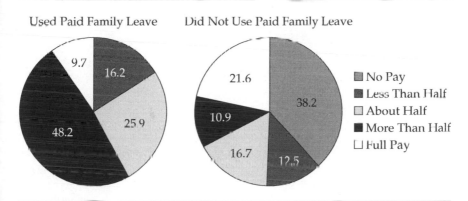

■ No Pay
■ Less Than Half
□ About Half
■ More Than Half
□ Full Pay

Source: Authors' 2009–2010 screening survey (N = 204).

of those who used PFL while on leave received at least half their usual
weekly pay, a much higher proportion than among those who did not use
PFL (59.1 percent) ($p < 0.001$).[12]

All workers who used the program benefited from PFL with regard to
wage replacement, whether they were in high-quality or low-quality jobs.
Among respondents with high-quality jobs, all of those (100.0 percent) who
used PFL drew at least half their usual pay while on leave, compared to
only 76.6 percent of those in high-quality jobs who did not use the program,
a statistically significant difference ($p < 0.001$). However, many workers in
high-quality jobs can draw on accumulated paid sick days, paid vacation,
or other paid leave benefits for wage replacement when they go on leave.
Indeed, in our sample, half (exactly 50.0 percent) of those in high-quality
jobs who did not use PFL nevertheless received full pay from such sources.
These employees, with access to generous employer-provided benefits,
may not need PFL. But for all other respondents employed in high-quality
jobs (that is, those who did not receive full pay), PFL sharply boosted the
level of wage replacement, as table 11.3 and figure 11.4 show.

Workers in low-quality jobs received even greater economic benefits
from PFL. Among respondents in this group who did not use PFL, 50.7 percent received either no wage replacement at all or less than half their usual
pay. In sharp contrast, among those in low-quality jobs who used PFL,
only 16.2 percent received less than half their income, a statistically significant difference ($p < 0.001$). All the other respondents in low-quality jobs

Table 11.4   Median Length of Family Leave (in Weeks), by Gender,
Leave Type, and Job Quality, 2009 to 2010

Type of Leave	All Respondents	High-Quality Jobs		Low-Quality Jobs	
		Male	Female	Male	Female
All					
Baby bonding leaves	9.5	3	14.5***	3	12***
Ill family member caring leaves	4	3	3.5	6	8
Used paid family leave					
Baby bonding leaves	12.5	4	18*	8	12
Ill family member caring leaves	7	3	5	6	11
Did not use paid family leave					
Baby bonding leaves	8	2	12***	3	12***
Ill family member caring leaves	4	3	3	4.5	8

Source: Authors' 2009–2010 screening survey (N = 98 for bonding leaves, 53 for caring leaves).
$*p < 0.05$; $***p < 0.001$, using the Mann-Whitney-Wilcoxon test

who used PFL (83.8 percent) received at least half of their usual income
while on leave, compared with only 49.2 percent of those who did not use
PFL; this also is a statistically significant difference ($p < 0.001$). For those
low-wage workers who actually use it, then, the PFL program is a critically
important source of income support when they go on leave from work to
attend to their families' needs.

Length of Leaves

Although PFL made a substantial difference in access to wage replacement during leave, especially for those in low-quality jobs, its effects on
the length of family leaves were more complex. As table 11.4 shows, the
median length of baby bonding leaves taken by all new parents in our sample was nine and a half weeks. Mothers took significantly longer bonding
leaves than fathers, regardless of job quality, and in most subgroups these
gender differences were statistically significant. (Those in low-quality jobs
who used PFL were the only exceptions.) However, for leaves to care for
an ill family member, there was no significant gender difference in median
leave length. Among mothers in low-quality jobs, the median length was

Figure 11.5   Workers Who Were "Very Satisfied" or "Somewhat
Satisfied" with Length of Family Leave, by Job Quality
and Use of Paid Family Leave, 2009

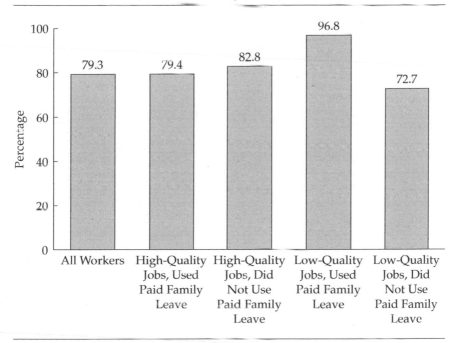

Source: Authors' 2009–2010 screening survey (N = 164).

the same whether or not they used PFL. Mothers in high-quality jobs took
longer bonding leaves, however, with a median length of eighteen weeks
for those who used PFL, compared to only twelve weeks for those who
did not take advantage of the program.

Most respondents (79.3 percent) reported being "very satisfied" or
"somewhat satisfied" with the length of their family leaves. Among
workers in high-quality jobs, many of whom had access to income from
employer benefits while on leave, satisfaction with the length of leave was
similar regardless of whether they used PFL or not; as figure 11.5 shows,
about four-fifths of these workers reported that they were very satisfied or
somewhat satisfied with the length of their leave.

For workers in low-quality jobs, however, the use of PFL made a striking difference in satisfaction with the length of leave. Among workers
in these jobs, nearly all (96.8 percent) of those who used PFL were very

Figure 11.6   Workers Who Returned to Former Employer After a Family
Leave, by Job Quality and Use of Paid Family Leave, 2009

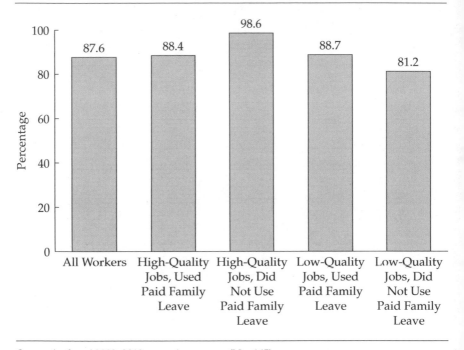

Source: Authors' 2009–2010 screening survey (N = 165).

satisfied or somewhat satisfied with the length of their leave, compared
with only 72.7 percent of those who did not use PFL, a statistically significant difference (*p* < 0.001).[13]

Turnover and Retention

More than 95 percent of screening survey respondents who took a family
leave returned to work at the end of their leave, and more than four-fifths
returned to the same employer they had worked for prior to the leave.
As figure 11.6 shows, the proportion of workers returning to the same
employer was highest among respondents in high-quality jobs who did
not use PFL. This probably reflects the more generous employer-provided
pay these workers received during leave—as noted earlier, nearly half the
workers in high-quality jobs who did not use PFL received full pay from
their employers.

Those workers in low-quality jobs who used the PFL program, however, were slightly more likely to return to the same employer after a family leave. Within this group, the retention rate was 88.7 percent for those who used the PFL program compared with 81.7 percent for those who did not. This difference is not statistically significant, but it suggests the possibility that California's PFL program provides an important benefit for employers, especially smaller employers that hope to retain workers who need to take a family leave but that are unable to afford high levels of wage replacement for them.

PFL's Effects on Caregivers and on Those Receiving Care

The screening survey data also offer insight into the impact of family leaves on outcomes for caregivers and care recipients. Relevant outcomes include the ability of respondents to care for their new children and for seriously ill family members, new mothers' ability to initiate and to sustain breastfeeding, parents' ability to make child care arrangements, and the effects on the ill family member's health. Table 11.5 summarizes our key findings regarding these outcomes.

About four-fifths (82.3 percent) of respondents who took leaves reported that the leave had a positive effect on their ability to care for their child or seriously ill family member. Among respondents in low-quality jobs, 87.0 percent of workers who used PFL reported that the leave positively affected their ability to care for the new child, compared with 72.2 percent of those who did not use PFL, a statistically significant difference.

Most new mothers in our sample (85.2 percent) reported that they had breastfed their new baby. Nearly all new mothers in low-quality jobs who used PFL (94.0 percent) had initiated breastfeeding, and the rate was nearly as high (89.1 percent) among those who did not use PFL. However, PFL use had no impact on the duration of breastfeeding for workers in low-quality jobs, whereas for those in high-quality jobs the duration of breastfeeding more than doubled (a statistically significant difference). Previous research suggests that longer leaves for new mothers are associated with longer duration of breastfeeding of the infant (Guendelman et al. 2009); our results confirm this, but also suggest that there may be important variation by social class (Blum 2000).

Leaves were also helpful in enabling parents of a new child to make child care arrangements. Among all parents, 62.5 percent reported that PFL had a positive effect on their ability to arrange child care. Among parents in low-quality jobs, 70.0 percent of PFL users reported a positive effect, compared to 58.3 percent who did not use PFL; however, this difference is not statistically significant.

Table 11.5 Family Leave Effects on Caregiving Ability and Health of Care Recipients, by Job Quality and Use of Paid Family Leave, 2009 to 2010

Effects of Leave	All Respondents	High-Quality Jobs		Low-Quality Jobs	
		Used Paid Family Leave	Did Not Use Paid Family Leave	Used Paid Family Leave	Did Not Use Paid Family Leave
Said that leave had positive effect on ability to care for new child or ill family member (N = 164)	82.3%	100.0%	91.8%*	87.0%	72.2%*
New mothers who initiated breastfeeding (N = 67)	91.3%	88.5%	89.7%	89.1%	94.0%
Median months of breastfeeding (N = 57)	6	11.5	4.5**	4.5	5
Said that leave had positive effect on ability to arrange child care (N = 92)	62.5%	56.7%	67.4%	70.0%	58.3%
Said that leave had positive effect on ill family member's health (N = 49)	86.5%	100.0%	100.0%	69.2%	79.9%

Source: Authors' 2009–2010 screening survey.
Note: For median months of breastfeeding, the Mann-Whitney-Wilcoxon test was used.
*p < 0.05; **p < 0.01

CONCLUSION

In some respects, California's PFL program provides a pathbreaking and positive example, one that might be replicated by policymakers in other states and nationally.[14] At the same time, however, the California case is a cautionary tale about the key obstacles such programs must overcome. These obstacles are different from those so often highlighted by the business organizations that routinely oppose efforts to create new programs to address work-family needs. Indeed, as we have documented elsewhere (Appelbaum and Milkman 2011), the alleged negative impacts of such programs on business are largely nonexistent. But the California PFL experience does expose other serious challenges that policymakers must address if they wish to provide access to paid leave to workers who have no other means of obtaining it.

On the one hand, our findings strongly suggest that public policy initiatives like PFL that support workers who need time off to care for their families can make a real and positive difference—even programs like California's PFL, which by international standards offers minimal benefits. As we have seen, PFL use is associated with better economic, social, and health outcomes for both workers and their families. Wage replacement levels were significantly higher for workers who used PFL than for those who did not, especially for workers in low-quality jobs. Among that group, the proportion receiving half or more of their usual weekly pay rose to 83.8 percent for those who used PFL, compared to just 19.2 percent for those who did not use the program. Moreover, workers in low-quality jobs who used PFL were more likely than those who did not to return to the same employer after a family leave, were more satisfied with the length of their leave, were better able to care for newborns and ill family members, and were better able to make child care arrangements.

As we have also shown, however, the problem of unequal access to paid time off remains a serious challenge in this case. Not only is general public awareness of the PFL program woefully limited, but those who stand to benefit most from it are the least likely to be aware of it. Low-wage workers, Latinos, blacks, and young workers—the very groups that have limited access to other sources of wage replacement during family leaves—have especially low levels of awareness of the program.

The main source of information about PFL—for those workers who are aware of it—is employers. Whereas employers who provide some form of paid leave themselves and are now coordinating the benefits they provide with the state program stand to gain if employees use PFL, those who provide no company-paid benefits have little incentive to inform employees of the state program. This employer behavior has combined with unequal awareness to re-create a new form of the previous inequality in access to wage replacement during leaves.

Among workers who were aware of PFL, some did not apply for the program when they needed a family leave because the level of wage replacement was too low. And many of them feared that taking PFL would lead to negative consequences on the job, perhaps even causing them to be fired. The lack of job protection in the PFL program is another key concern.

Thus, the promise of California's new program to extend access to paid leave to all the state's workers, including those who previously lacked access to wage replacement, has yet to be fulfilled, as awareness of the program remains unacceptably low among the groups who need it most. Until awareness of PFL spreads more widely, especially among low-wage workers and other disadvantaged groups, and until the issues of job protection and more extensive levels of wage replacement are addressed, the program will not achieve its intended effect of reducing the long-standing disparity between the workers, most of them well-paid managers and professionals, who have access to paid leave through employer-provided benefits and the less-privileged workers who lack such access.[15] Instead, this pattern of inequality has been reproduced in a new form. The challenge ahead is to ensure that PFL benefits are universally accessible in practice as well as in theory.

NOTES

1. The authors thank Laura Braslow and Sara Jane Glynn for assistance with the data analysis in this chapter. The chapter also draws on material from chapter 5 of Milkman and Appelbaum (2013), which offers a more comprehensive analysis of California's PFL program.

2. FMLA covers all public-sector workers and private-sector workers who work for organizations with fifty or more employees on the payroll at or within seventy-five miles of the worksite. In addition, to be eligible for FMLA leave, one must have been with the same employer for at least twelve months and have worked 1,250 hours or more in the year preceding the leave.

3. Washington State passed a paid family leave law in 2007, but to date no funding has been provided to implement it.

4. SDI benefits for pregnancy typically cover up to four weeks before delivery and an additional six to eight weeks afterward, at the doctor's discretion. For biological mothers, the PFL benefit supplements the pregnancy disability benefits previously available under SDI. Although it does not increase the amount of job-protected leave available to women who have given birth, it provides six *additional* weeks of partial wage replacement.

5. Fifty of the five hundred respondents lived in households whose only telephone was a cellular one; on average, they were younger and had lower incomes than the rest of the sample. All results are weighted to adjust for the number of telephones per household, which affects the probability of selection in random digit dialing.

6. See, for example, Neil Fligstein and Ofer Sharone's (2002, 91–92) analysis of the California workforce in 2001–2002, which found two worlds of work: one at the top, "with lots of pressures but many rewards . . . in income . . . job satisfaction, paid benefits and more security on the job," that comprised 34 percent of the workforce; and another where 66 percent of respondents worked at jobs that were "more onerous . . . with fewer paid benefits and . . . more insecurity." By the time we conducted our 2009–2010 survey, almost a decade later than Fligstein and Sharone's and immediately following the Great Recession, the proportion of desirable jobs was presumably lower.

7. These data are for paid family leave as such—in contrast to the Census Bureau report (Laughlin 2011)—and do *not* include paid sick leave and vacation benefits, which are often used as wage replacement during family leaves. The National Compensation Survey found sharp disparities in access to paid sick leave and paid vacation benefits between high earners and low earners as well.

8. All significance levels reported later in the chapter are based on Z-tests unless otherwise noted.

9. These differences by education and household income are statistically significant ($p < 0.05$). For this question in the 2012 survey, N = 410.

10. All these differences were statistically significant ($p < 0.001$). N = 2,824.

11. Eligible respondents are those employed in the private or nonprofit sectors (since most public-sector workers are not eligible for the state PFL program). Take-up rates did not vary much by race and ethnicity or between U.S.-born and immigrant workers.

12. The figure is 91.7 percent rather than 100 percent because some respondents took leaves longer than the six weeks for which they could receive wage replacement through the state PFL program.

13. The other differences in satisfaction levels (shown in figure 11.2) are not statistically significant.

14. This is much easier in the few states (Hawaii, New York, Rhode Island, and Puerto Rico) that already have temporary disability programs (as the New Jersey and Rhode Island cases exemplify) than elsewhere, because the necessary administrative machinery is already in place.

15. Specific recommendations for expanded outreach include requiring hospitals, clinics, and pediatricians' offices to inform new parents about PFL (see Milkman and Appelbaum 2013, 113)

REFERENCES

Appelbaum, Eileen, and Ruth Milkman. 2011. *Leaves That Pay: Employer and Worker Experiences with Paid Family Leave in California*. Washington, D.C.: Center for Economic and Policy Research (January). Available at: http://www.cepr.net/index.php/publications/reports/leaves-that-pay (accessed September 2013).

Blum, Linda M. 2000. *At the Breast: Ideologies of Breastfeeding and Motherhood in the Contemporary United States.* Boston: Beacon Press.

Fligstein, Neil, and Ofer Sharone. 2002. "Work in the Postindustrial Economy of California." In *The State of California Labor 2002.* Berkeley: University of California Press.

Gornick, Janet C., and Marcia K. Meyers. 2003. *Families That Work: Policies for Reconciling Parenthood and Employment.* New York: Russell Sage Foundation.

Guendelman, Sylvia, Jessica Lang Kosa, Michelle Pearl, Steve Graham, Julia Goodman, and Martin Kharrazi. 2009. "Juggling Work and Breastfeeding: Effects of Maternity Leave and Occupational Characteristics." *Pediatrics* 123(1): 38–46.

Heymann, Jody. 2000. *The Widening Gap: Why America's Working Families Are in Jeopardy—and What Can Be Done About It.* New York: Basic Books.

Laughlin, Lynda. 2011. "Maternity Leave and Employment Patterns of First-Time Mothers: 1961–2008." *Current Population Reports* P70-128. Washington: U.S. Census Bureau (October). Available at: http://www.census.gov/prod/2011pubs/p70-128.pdf (accessed September 2013).

Milkman, Ruth, and Eileen Appelbaum. 2004. "Paid Family Leave in California: New Research Findings." In *The State of California Labor 2004.* Berkeley: University of California Press.

——. 2013. *Unfinished Business: Paid Family Leave in California and the Future of U.S. Work-Family Policy.* Ithaca, N.Y.: Cornell University Press.

Ruhm, Christopher J. 1997. "Policy Watch: The Family and Medical Leave Act." *Journal of Economic Perspectives* 11: 175–86.

Sherriff, Rona Levine. 2007. *Balancing Work and Family.* Sacramento: California Senate Office of Research (February).

U.S. Bureau of Labor Statistics. 2011. "Employee Benefits in the United States—March 2011." Washington: U.S. Department of Labor, Bureau of Labor Statistics (July 26). Available at: http://www.bls.gov/ncs/ebs/sp/ebnr0017.pdf (accessed September 2013).

U.S. Department of Labor. 2012. *Family and Medical Leave Act in 2012: Final Report.* Available at: http://www.dol.gov/whd/fmla/survey/ (accessed September 2013).

Waldfogel, Jane. 2001. "Family and Medical Leave: Evidence from the 2000 Surveys." *Monthly Labor Review* 124(9): 17–23.

Williams, Joan C., and Heather Boushey. 2010. *The Three Faces of Work-Family Conflict: The Poor, the Professionals, and the Missing Middle.* San Francisco: University of California Hastings College of the Law, Center for American Progress and Work Life Law (January).

Index |